VINYL VENTURES

Popular Music History
Series Editor: Alyn Shipton, Royal Academy of Music, London.

This series publishes books that extend the field of popular music studies, examine the lives and careers of key musicians, interrogate histories of genres, focus on previously neglected forms, or engage in the formative history of popular music styles.

Published

An Unholy Row: Jazz in Britain and its Audience, 1945–1960
Dave Gelly

Being Prez: The Life and Music of Lester Young
Dave Gelly

Bill Russell and the New Orleans Jazz Revival
Ray Smith and Mike Pointon

Chasin' the Bird:
The Life and Legacy of Charlie Parker
Brian Priestley

Handful of Keys:
Conversations with Thirty Jazz Pianists
Alyn Shipton

Hear My Train A Comin':
The Songs of Jimi Hendrix
Kevin Le Gendre

Jazz Me Blues:
The Autobiography of Chris Barber
Chris Barber with Alyn Shipton

Jazz Visions: Lennie Tristano and His Legacy
Peter Ind

Keith Jarrett: A Biography
Wolfgang Sandner, translated by Chris Jarrett

Komeda: A Private Life in Jazz
Magdalena Grzebałkowska,
translated by Halina Boniszewska

Lee Morgan: His Life, Music and Culture
Tom Perchard

Lionel Richie: Hello
Sharon Davis

Mosaics: The Life and Works of Graham Collier
Duncan Heining

Mr P.C.: The Life and Music of Paul Chambers
Rob Palmer

Out of the Long Dark: The Life of Ian Carr
Alyn Shipton

Rufus Wainwright
Katherine Williams

Scouse Pop
Paul Skillen

Soul Unsung:
Reflections on the Band in Black Popular Music
Kevin Le Gendre

The Godfather of British Jazz:
The Life and Music of Stan Tracey
Clark Tracey

The History of European Jazz: The Music, Musicians and Audience in Context
Edited by Francesco Martinelli

The Last Miles:
The Music of Miles Davis, 1980–1991
George Cole

The Long Shadow of the Little Giant (second edition):
The Life, Work and Legacy of Tubby Hayes
Simon Spillett

The Ultimate Guide to Great Reggae: The Complete Story of Reggae Told through its Greatest Songs, Famous and Forgotten
Michael Garnice

This is Bop:
Jon Hendricks and the Art of Vocal Jazz
Peter Jones

This is Hip: The Life of Mark Murphy
Peter Jones

Trad Dads, Dirty Boppers and Free Fusioneers: A History of British Jazz, 1960–1975
Duncan Heining

Two Bold Singermen and the English Folk Revival: The Lives, Song Traditions and Legacies of Sam Larner and Harry Cox
Bruce Lindsay

Vinyl Ventures
My Fifty Years at Rounder Records

Bill Nowlin

SHEFFIELD UK   BRISTOL CT

Published by Equinox Publishing Ltd.

UK: Office 415, The Workstation, 15 Paternoster Row, Sheffield, South Yorkshire S1 2BX
USA: ISD, 70 Enterprise Drive, Bristol, CT 06010

www.equinoxpub.com

First published 2021
© Bill Nowlin 2021

All rights reserved. No part of this publication may be reproduced or transmitted in any form or by any means, electronic or mechanical, including photocopying, recording or any information storage or retrieval system, without prior permission in writing from the publishers.

British Library Cataloguing-in-Publication Data
A catalogue record for this book is available from the British Library.
ISBN-13   978 1 80050 006 8 (paperback)
          978 1 80050 007 5 (e-PDF)
          978 1 80050 035 8 (ePub)

Library of Congress Cataloging-in-Publication Data
Names: Nowlin, Bill, 1945- author.
Title: Vinyl ventures : my fifty years at Rounder Records / Bill Nowlin.
Description: Bristol : Equinox Publishing Ltd, 2021. | Series: Popular music history | Includes bibliographical references and index. | Summary: "Vinyl ventures: my fifty years at Rounder Records is less a standard history and more an idiosyncratic memoir written by one of the three Rounder founders. The book includes original photographs taken by the author or drawn from the Rounder archives"-- Provided by publisher.
Identifiers: LCCN 2020022505 (print) | LCCN 2020022506 (ebook) | ISBN 9781800500068 (paperback) | ISBN 9781800500075 (ebook)
Subjects: LCSH: Rounder Records (Firm)--History. | Sound recording industry--United States--History. | Nowlin, Bill, 1945- | Sound recording executives and producers--United States.
Classification: LCC ML3792.R68 N68 2020 (print) | LCC ML3792.R68 (ebook) | DDC 384--dc23
LC record available at https://lccn.loc.gov/2020022505
LC ebook record available at https://lccn.loc.gov/2020022506

Typeset by Witchwood Production House Ltd

To Ken and Marian, and John Virant, and all the many Rounders over the years; to all the musical artists with whom we were able to work; and to Yleana and Emmet.

Contents

Acknowledgments		ix
Preface		xi
The Record Business in the Late 1960s		1
1	The Backstory to Starting a Record Company	5
2	Rounder's First Two Records: October 1970	18
3	Building the Business: The Early 1970s	32
4	Helping Organize the Indie Side of the Record Business	63
5	The Concept of a Collective is Called into Question	79
6	The Second Half of the Seventies: George Thorogood and the Destroyers, and Wrestling with Change	88
7	Entering the 1980s: 50 States in 50 Dates – No Nights Off!	110
8	Starting Our Second Decade: A Maturing Company, and Some Real Growing Pains	125
9	The Middle 1980s	145
10	Alison Krauss: 1986 and for Decades to Come	156
11	1990: Rounder Turns Twenty	165
12	1995: A Quarter of a Century In, and Still Scuffling	197
13	John Virant: "The Fourth Rounder"	210
14	2000: Rounder Turns Thirty as We Enter a New Century	236
15	Selling the Company: The Next Iteration – The Concord Connection (2010)	255
16	Rounder's Sense of Mission	274
	Afterword	280
	Endnotes	298
	Index of names	306
	Index of albums	315

Acknowledgments

Quite a number of people have helped in reconstructing memories of years gone by. This book has been in the works for maybe fifteen years or more, and some of those are unfortunately no longer with us. They played their part in filling out the story, though, and for that I am grateful. There follows a list that I maintained over time, but I am sure there are some people I have missed, and to them I apologize. A far longer list that would run on for pages would thank all those who helped make Rounder such a rewarding life's work. Those below are the ones who directly helped me, in one way or another, in writing this book.

Thanks to: Ray Alden, Mary Katherine Aldin, Rob Allingham, Glen Barros, Fred Bartenstein, Loy Beaver, Barrie Bergman, Bill Blough, Scott Billington, Bing Broderick, Hal Brody, Duncan Browne, Peggy Bulger, Jennifer Cutting, Dwight Diller, Carl Fleischhauer, Dave Freeman, Mitch Greenhill, Ivor Haarburger, Jeff Harris, Steve Harris, Dianne Heeley, Bill Hicks, Joe Hickerson, Ann Hoog, Bruce Iglauer, Ken Irwin, Regina Jaskow, Adam Jones, Louis E. Jones/Wayne State University, Mike Kappus, Gerry Katz, Paul Knutson, Bill Kornrich, Steve Leeds, Marian Leighton Levy, Liza Levy, Yleana Martinez, John McCutcheon, Joe McEwen, Sharon McGraw, Mike Melford, Mary Meyer, Matt Miller, George Mitchell, Pat Monteith, Mark Moss, Steve Netsky, Jim Netter, Ted Olson, Alexandra Owens, Clay Pasternack, Brad Paul, Bert Pijpers, Barry Poss, Steven Price, Millie Rahn, Fred Robbins, Gene Rosenthal, Neil Rossi, Elizabeth Rush, Sheri Sands, Michael Scully, Sandra Shifrin, Betsy Siggins, Alyn Shipton, Stephanie Smith, Leland Stein, Chris Strachwitz, John Strohm, Nancy Talbott, Mike Toney, John Virant, Stephen Wade, Wayne State University, Mary Weber, Pete Wernick, Katie Willard, Marty Willard, Chris Wilson, Dan Wilson, Mark Wilson, and Robin Wise.

Special thanks for a careful reading of the manuscript to Ken and Marian, Alyn Shipton, Dean Bargh, and Yleana Martinez.

All royalties from the sale of this book are being donated to the Highlander Research and Education Center in New Market, Tennessee. Highlander has been a movement school since 1932 in the U.S. South and Appalachia, supporting leaders and group to fight for racial, environmental, and economic justice alongside the ongoing essential fight for true democracy. Highlander's work continues today with visions for a more equitable, peaceful future for all (www.highlandercenter.org).

Preface

This is the story of a "hobby that got out of control," a fledgling record company more or less conceived while the Sixties were still in flower, which began on just over $1,000 and over its first few decades produced over 3,000 record albums of American roots music and its contemporary offshoots. Rounder artists would go on to win fifty-six Grammy Awards in the company's first forty-nine years, and document a swath of music that in many cases might otherwise never have been presented to a broader public. It is arguably a quintessentially American success story.

This book focuses on the early years – up to and just through when Rounder evolved into its second stage, with a generational change that has kept the label healthy and flourishing when so many other cultural enterprises from the era have folded or gone dark. It is the story of three people with no background in business who took an idea and, through hard work and passion, built up something of some lasting cultural significance.

This book is not intended to be a standard history. One could reasonably call it a history of Rounder's early years, but it does not purport to be *the* history of Rounder Records. For much of the book, I have written in the first person, so it reads more naturally. If one of the other founders – Ken Irwin or Marian Leighton Levy – had been the principal author, no doubt there would be different nuances and emphases in the telling of the Rounder story. And there are so many more people other than the three Rounder founders who could have written their own books about the company. Consider this more of an idiosyncratic memoir. Vinyl to cassettes and 8-tracks, to compact discs and digital sound.

Bill Nowlin
January 2021

Listen to the Rounder artists

Readers of the ebook editions of this title will find numerous links attached to artists' names and releases (those in blue text). These take you to a relevant Spotify page where you can listen to material by the artist in question. Where possible, you will be directed to the Rounder releases being discussed. Disclaimer: we have no control over Spotify's licenses and therefore cannot guarantee what material each link will yield as time passes; this may also vary according to territory. All links were verified at time of going to press.

The Record Business in the Late 1960s

Rounder was by no means the first of the raft of independent labels that sprang up in the 1970s, but we were among the first. In one sense, we were perhaps in the forefront of a second generation of independent labels.

There were indies that preceded us – both in "our area" and in other areas. There were "roots-oriented" labels which directly inspired us: Folkways, Arhoolie, County, Delmark, and a few others. There were independent labels in other fields of music: Blue Note in jazz, for instance. By the middle 1970s, there were scores of small labels. Yet, when we launched our first albums in October 1970, there were relatively few. They tended to be devoted to a particular kind of music, the music that was the love of the original founder. Most of these record labels were born out of one person's passion.

Rounder differed from some of the other indies in that there were three of us, from the start, and our collective musical tastes prompted us over our first five or six years to focus less on one specific genre.

Recorded popular music wasn't really all that old. It had just begun to grow in the middle to late 1920s, and to expand into regional genres like "hillbilly" or "race" recordings, catering to niche audiences. The record business quickly suffered a setback due to the onset of the Depression, followed by the Second World War, during which the shellac from which records were made was strictly rationed. It wasn't until the post-war period that conditions permitted a revival of the record business.

There had been independent labels in the 1920s, such as Gennett Records out of Richmond, Indiana. Founded in 1939, Blue Note began to grow after the war. Folkways was founded in 1948. There were a number of regional labels that began to record bluegrass – Rich-R-Tone began in Johnson City, Tennessee, in 1946 – and a number of small local labels began to issue occasional records as we entered the 1950s. By the mid to late 1950s, there were enough American homes with record players to mean that retail stores often had record departments, sometimes in music stores.[1]

There had been record stores – stores that focused on selling recorded music – but, as the 1960s got under way, they became relatively common. If you said you were going to a record store, most everyone knew what you meant. Fifty years later, record stores had become an endangered species.

But record retail was expanding in the 1960s, as the "baby boom" generation entered its early teenage years. This was a generation that had grown up in relative peace and prosperity; they had not experienced two world wars and the Depression. The three Rounder founders were born in the years 1944–1948. Though from different backgrounds, we were, like others of our generation, afforded the ability to be curious, look around us, and seek out other experiences. That partly involved being open to different cultural influences – music among them.

In 1956 Elvis Presley first broke on the scene. A lot of other music was starting breaking out at the same time: Chuck Berry, Little Richard, and others. It's worth keeping in mind that, when Rounder launched in 1970, it was barely more than a dozen years after rock'n'roll had transformed the music scene. Let's call it fourteen years from Elvis's 45 rpm record of 'Hound Dog' to Rounder's first record, on 33 rpm vinyl. So, from Elvis to George Pegram (for that was the record) was a relatively short space of time. And yet, even then, explorations of other musics were already well under way. Back in 1952, experimental film-maker and 78 collector Harry Smith had overseen the six-album *Anthology of American Folk Music*, a compendium of eighty-four tracks released on Folkways Records that showcased the regional country, blues, and folk recordings of the late 1920s and early 1930s.

In the later 1950s, a number of things came together and set the stage for some of the recorded music that preceded Rounder by a decade. By then, two New York City-based independent labels were well established, with both Vanguard and Elektra Records having begun in the same year: 1950. *Sing Out!* magazine was also launched in that year. There was already an audience for "folk music." The Weavers, for instance, had a hit with 'Goodnight Irene' and enjoyed some significant popularity as the 1940s became the 1950s. The song went to #1 in 1950.

In 1952, Elektra released its first couple of folk music albums, on 10" LP: one by Jean Ritchie and one by Frank Warner. By the middle 1960s, they had released albums by Sonny Terry, Theodore Bikel, Josh White, Cynthia Gooding, and Ed McCurdy. Vanguard was very active with record releases as well.

In 1957, Izzy Young opened the Folklore Center in New York. In the same city, Mike Seeger, John Cohen, and Tom Paley founded the New Lost City Ramblers in 1958, and Mike and John began extended forays into recording folk musicians. John and Alan Lomax had preceded them, with Alan still active in recording at the time. Also in 1958, in October, the Kingston Trio released their first album on Capitol. Spurred by their song 'Tom Dooley,' the album went to #1 on the charts. And, in Chicago, Bob Koester operated

Delmark Records, which he had started in St. Louis. Bob recorded a lot of jazz, but we followed his blues recordings.

Sometime in the late 1950s, guitarist John Fahey launched his own label, Takoma.

In July 1959, the first Newport Folk Festival was staged.

Joan Baez released her first album in 1960, on Vanguard.

In 1960, Chris Strachwitz founded the Arhoolie label.

Bob Dylan's first album debuted in 1962. And Dave Freeman started County Records in 1963–64.

There was a "folk revival" going on at the time, led by a lot of people a half-generation ahead of us. It was a golden age of sorts for people who enjoyed folk music. In the middle 1960s, though, came the British Invasion: the Beatles in early 1964, the Rolling Stones just a few months later. The mania that followed swept folk music off the charts and resulted in companies like Elektra and Vanguard cutting back on their folk albums. Around the same time, Folkways entered into arrangements with Verve and then with Scholastic, which more or less threw it off its game. For more than five years, Folkways wasn't putting out records the way they had.

Ken Irwin and I were the two oldest of the three Rounders, Ken about nine months older than me. We had started college in 1962, and we'd become regular attendees at Cambridge and Boston folk music events – mostly coffeehouses like Harvard Square's Club 47. We had started to build our record collections, too, but during our later college years the record companies

The three Rounder founders, c. 1975: (left to right) the author, Marian Leighton Levy, and Ken Irwin

began to put out fewer of the kinds of records we wanted. I was a huge Rolling Stones fan myself, but I also wanted to buy records by some of the acts that the Stones themselves had drawn on. We hadn't turned our backs on the folk performers we'd come to love. We just couldn't get records by them the way we could just a year or two earlier. They weren't being made.

I'm not trying to write a history of recorded music here, or offer a full description of the state of folk music in the late Sixties heading into 1970. I'm just trying to quickly set the stage for the story that follows. As this bare-bones recitation may indicate, there was an active music scene with a significant audience for what we could broadly call folk music. There was something of a pause, though, as new folk recordings largely dried up for about five years. When we began Rounder in October 1970, we were able to become a part of, and ride, a second wave of sorts. We often felt like we had come along at the right time.

When we began, this was definitely not something we intended would become a business. We did create a record company but we only expected to put out maybe two or three records a year, when we came across a project that interested us. We had already embarked on other careers we expected to pursue. But not only was starting Rounder fun, it also became fulfilling. And we got a great deal of positive feedback from folks telling us they loved our records and asking us what albums we were going to do next. That propelled us along a path that unfolded over the months and took us in directions we never would have anticipated.

There was no way to know that, within our first five years, we would have released close to 100 albums, set up a distribution company – even started a trade organization – and hired a couple of employees. Or that we'd hit 1,000 albums, and then 2,000, and then 3,000. And find it a calling.

1 The Backstory to Starting a Record Company

Ken and Bill go to college

In 1962, I found myself in college. Tufts College in Medford, only seven miles from home in Lexington, Massachusetts, where I had grown up with my sisters Joyce and Lisa. The powers-that-were assigned me a room-mate from outside New York City named Ken Irwin. We didn't really like each other at first. It took a few weeks, even a month or two. What brought us closer together was breakfast cereal from the cafeteria. Every morning for weeks, I took an extra single-serving box of Rice Krispies back to the dorm. At least a couple of months into our freshman year, I rigged up a booby trap so that, when Ken came into the room, dozens of these little boxes crashed down on him. I was hiding in the closet to enjoy the reaction, started laughing, and so did he – as he trapped me in the closet. There came a time much later that year, when we emptied out a hundred or more of the boxes into a large suitcase and hitch-hiked with it to New York, where around 2 am we dumped all the Rice Krispies onto the doorstep of some dentist's home in the Scarsdale area, pushed the doorbell a few times, and ran.

There was another time that we collected 242 copies of the South Suburban telephone directory (which had been delivered to all Tufts students who had phones, but which no one wanted) and wedged them all into an old-fashioned phone booth, completely filling it. It was just fun wondering what sort of puzzled reaction that prank received – from people wanting to use the phone and then the phone company itself, in due course. Rarely did a month go by at Tufts without us pulling one kind of prank or another – we even made *Newsweek* at one point for starting an intercollegiate sport of competitive speed toilet paper unrolling. We called it the American Tissue Games Association, figuring that the word "toilet" in the title was perhaps too unseemly. It was the same issue that first featured the Beatles on the cover; the British quartet edged us to an inside page. Ken was "Good Time

Charlie," I was "Bronco Bill," and co-conspirator Don Wilcock was "Don the Indomitable."

Ken was born in New York City in 1944, moving to Westchester County north of the city before he turned five. Both of his parents were writers. They had each written a couple of books before Ken was born. Ted Irwin wrote some books on medical matters, travel, and a couple of novels, *Strange Passage* and *Collusion: The True Story of a Divorce Detective.* Rita Irwin had co-authored *Practical Birth Control: A Guide to Medically Approved Methods for the Married.* When she had Ken's older brother Jed, and then Ken, she become a full-time mother and homemaker. Ted Irwin was a freelance writer, at one point President of the Society of Magazine Writers. Ken's mother was active in the peace movement. His brother had once taken him to a protest in New York City and he had seen Pete Seeger at a concert at nearby Scarsdale High School, but Ken himself was not so political until after college.

I tried to learn piano. Ken learned some concertina. Neither really took. I wanted to play baseball. He wanted to play basketball. Unlike me, Ken really got into dancing. A Rounder press kit from around 2001 called Ken "a complete stranger to vacations" but also offered the recollection that in high school he'd been voted Best Dancer, Friendliest, Wittiest, and (this might come as a surprise to many) was just one removed from being named Best Dressed. He went to dancing school, too, but also taught himself by watching Dick Clark's *American Bandstand* and practicing dancing holding onto a doorknob on a swinging door. I could never dance like Ken.

Ken had some records that he brought from home, and I had a few, too. I didn't approve of his Pete Seeger records, because some of the songs were too radical for me politically. I'd rebelled against my parents' lukewarm Republicanism by becoming a Goldwater conservative and joining Young Americans for Freedom. In 1962, I worked during the summer between high school and college in the campaign of Laurence Curtis, running against Ted Kennedy for the U.S. Senate. I even had my own desk and a lunchtime expense account – and I was only seventeen. I still have a 45 rpm record from that time – an early (and rare) example of Republican pop music called 'The Man Who Can is Curtis!' I wasn't doing anything substantive in the campaign, nothing that dramatic, mostly just intern type of work, but I went in often when I wasn't working on the Battle Green in Lexington. Pete Seeger records made me uncomfortable with their politics, but as Ken played them I got to know the tunes and I came to like them in spite of myself.

There was one record in particular that both Ken and I really latched onto: the first album by a New York City group, the Greenbriar Boys, on Vanguard. Apolitical. It was straight bluegrass, though done by city dwellers. I didn't really appreciate that distinction at the time. To me, it was cornball, but I really loved it. There were echoes there, I realize now, going back to Rusty Draper (my first record), and to Hank Williams, and some of Elvis's country recordings. At the time, it was just a lot of fun. I liked their singing. I liked their playing. The whole package. Ken and I learned the words to some of the songs, and we'd sing them on buses on our way back from Harvard Square or wherever else we'd gone roaming. Our favorite was 'We Need a Whole Lot More of Jesus (and a Lot Less Rock and Roll),' which we sometimes played on kazoo as well.

Then we heard that the Greenbriar Boys were coming to do a concert in downtown Boston. Ken had learned about becoming a "campus representative," so we contacted the company producing the show, Folklore Productions, and the promoter Manny Greenhill agreed to the deal that Ken proposed: we'd help promote the show by putting up handbills around the Tufts campus and he'd give us four complimentary tickets to the concert. What a deal!

The very first show we worked was for Odetta, who played Jordan Hall in Boston on Saturday evening, January 26, 1963. We even met her backstage and she signed one of the handbills for us with her trademark "Go well. Stay well." Two weeks later Folklore presented the Greenbriar Boys, Ramblin' Jack Elliott, and Eric Von Schmidt, with Tony Saletan as MC, at Jordan Hall on February 9. Thanks to Manny, we were able to see many more shows than we would have otherwise and we still owe him a debt of gratitude.

We did this work for the rest of our undergraduate years, into 1966, serving as campus representatives not only for Folklore Productions but also for the Charles Playhouse and frequently for the Theater Company of Boston. I can still remember seeing Dustin Hoffman and Paul Benedict perform on the small TCB stage, sometimes to as few as a dozen people. I really liked Benedict and Paul B. Price. There were rather few people there, and we were regulars. We probably could have gotten to know the actors very easily – but we were pretty shy and never once introduced ourselves. If we'd known about social networking then, maybe we'd be living in Bel Air or Beverly Hills today. I doubt we'd want to.

Then there was Club 47, in Harvard Square, Cambridge. We were regulars – typically, at least two to three nights a week. It only cost a dollar. For a good show, you'd often have to get in line two or even three hours in advance but there was good company, talking to others in line about the act that was going to perform. These were knowledgeable fans, and you could talk about records – you could say, "My favorite is the third track on side B" and they'd know what track you meant.

We were just fans of the music; we never really talked to the performers. We were in awe of them. We came to know many of them later, and found out they were mortals, too, but at the time they seemed so imbued with talent and, well, they were the stars. We were happy to be part of the audience. The idea of actually talking with them never really crossed our minds. There was also a cliquishness to the scene, and we were both too shy and not really interested to think about trying to break in.

We did go to some mainstream shows as well. Fellow Tufts student Don Wilcock subscribed to *Billboard* and read that the Rolling Stones were coming to Boston in June 1966. We immediately phoned the promoter, who said we were the first calls he'd taken and wondered how we'd learned about the show. We said that, if we were the first, we ought to be able to buy front-row seats. He agreed, and we were set. That was the night it poured rain at the Manning Bowl in Lynn, Massachusetts; and when 'Satisfaction' kicked in, a riot broke out with fans rushing the stage and overwhelming the police lines. I wound up lying across the top of the limousine in which Mick Jagger was seated, engulfed by the crowd, looking into the window from above and seeing some fear on his face. Only when tear gas was fired repeatedly did the crowds disperse. Ken, Don, and I also saw the Beatles at Suffolk Downs and James Brown at the Boston Arena.

Ken and I had started collecting records - not the old 78s, just 33⅓ LPs. When we saw that Sam Goody had a $2.49 sale on Folkways LPs, we would hitch-hike from Boston down to New York, stay at Ken's father's place there, and head into the city to buy $10.00 worth of new albums. Folkways albums were uneven in quality, but there were many real gems, and it was always a bonus to get the booklet included with each album. We do confess to a bit of a scam we pulled on two occasions: we wrote Folkways and told them when we bought the album, it came with the booklet but without the record. They mailed us a replacement record. Hopefully, we made it up to Folkways later on when we distributed their label and, years after that, helped them transition from LPs to CDs.

On one trip to Goody's, Ken was looking over two Earl Taylor albums, one on Capitol and one on United Artists, trying to decide which to buy, when he heard a deep voice behind him: "They're both good." Ken turned around and saw a big man in a dark suit looking down at him. They struck up a conversation during which Ken learned that the person he was speaking to, Loy Beaver, was a serious collector of old-time music and one of the main people Dave Freeman of County Records would go to for old 78s for his reissues. Loy invited Ken to come and visit him and hear some of his recordings the next time he was in the area. Loy Beaver worked at Gutterman's Funeral Home at 66th and Broadway in Manhattan, and frequented Sam Goody's and some of the other record stores that used to cluster around 49th Street. He was from Fannin County, Georgia, and more than three-quarters Cherokee. He spent most of a lifetime collecting music and had one of the largest collections of old-time country music 78s. He was very happy to see younger people getting interested in the music of the South. He had an apartment at Westchester Avenue and Bryant in the Bronx.

The next time we hitched to New York, I brought along an old, heavy Roberts reel-to-reel tape recorder. Looking back, it's hard to imagine cars stopping to pick up two college kids, with bags and this large machine, but in those days it was always a fairly easy hitch back and forth to New York.

At least twice, I hitched to New York and lugged that tape recorder onto the New York subway, got off at the Simpson Street stop, and walked to Loy Beaver's place where we spent many hours copying old 78s to 7 inch tape reels. These tapes provided many hours of listening pleasure in our dorm room. Loy Beaver passed away in 2011.

Once, after visiting New York friend Dorothy David, she dropped me off on a ramp to the parkway and I made the 225 miles to my own front door in Lexington in under two hours! The first car that came by picked me up and drove to a private airport a few miles away. The driver flew me up to Hanscom Field in Bedford and drove right by my house on his way to wherever he was going.

Speaking of dorm rooms, I was naive enough to believe that, if the other guys on the floor heard the music we loved, they'd come to love it, too. We became a little more evangelistic by our junior year. So we'd crank up the volume on the record player and the sound of the banjo would ring down the Miller Hall corridor. The reaction we received – almost uniformly – was the slamming of doors up and down the hall.

Ken and I both graduated in '66; I was the first in my family to graduate from college. Both of my parents had gone to Northeastern for a year in the early 1940s but the war intervened and neither completed their studies.

Club 47 and the coffeehouses

Some of the shows we went to remain memorable today. I've still got a banjo string that Dock Boggs broke at a show in the middle 1960s. I was in the front row at the Club 47. He said it was the first one he'd broken in thirty-five years. The old Club 47 on Mt. Auburn Street was so packed at times that it seemed like it might burst. (Ken remembers this happening twice when he was there, both times when Jackie Washington was performing – with the storefront window popping out and shattering on the sidewalk.) One night we went to see Koerner, Ray & Glover and were totally disappointed to hear they couldn't make it – but wound up enthralled with the debut of Jim Kweskin & the Jug Band. For the most part, though, our 47-going began in earnest after it moved to Palmer Street in 1963.

Speaking of Dock Boggs, nearly fifty years later I remain so grateful that we came along when we did, being in the right place at the right time. He'd recorded a dozen record sides in 1927–29 for OKeh Records, but with the onset of the Depression he then more or less disappeared for more than thirty years to work in the coal mines of southwestern Virginia. It was only in 1963 that Mike Seeger traveled to the area, located him, gave him encouragement, and brought him to the folk clubs and festivals. We were a half-generation behind the real pioneers of the folk revival like Mike and John Cohen, but the beneficiaries of their work in that we got to see artists who truly developed their own music and song first-hand, through direct transmission rather than mediating influences like radio or phonograph records – people like Dock Boggs and Roscoe Holcomb and many more. We were indeed very fortunate to be able to experience something that has effectively been unattainable anywhere in the modern world for the last thirty or forty years.

But there were things we did miss out on. Since we were far from fully tapped into the "inner circle" of the folks who ran the club – Betsy Siggins, Jim Rooney, and others – I know I missed out on some performers. There was often this night on the Club 47 program marked "Taj Mahal"; somehow no one ever mentioned him to us while standing in line, and I never read about him in *Broadside*. I remained oblivious, thinking it was a night for sitars or something, and missed many of what must have been magical musical evenings. I told Taj the story in 2018 at a post-Grammys party (he'd won one), but he wanted to enthuse instead about his own memories of Boston-area bluegrasser Joe Val.

We did get to see one of our favorite acts, the Holy Modal Rounders, at the original club. We were "educated" enough at this point to shout out from the audience when Peter Stampfel mentioned North Carolina banjo player/singer Charlie Poole (1892–1931). There was a marathon show put on down the street at the Folklore Center, a benefit show billed as a seventy-two-hour hootenanny. The duo of Stampfel and Steve Weber played all night one time, and won the "endurance prize." Ken stuck it out the whole way through.

One night at the Café Yana, practically next door to Boston baseball's Fenway Park, Bob Dylan was playing to maybe sixty people. He ran up against closing time and someone pulled down the shades to the street and we enjoyed the show for another hour past curfew. Maybe a year later, Peter, Paul & Mary did a show at Cousens Gym on the Tufts campus and mentioned this young singer who'd written a song called 'Blowin' in the Wind' – occasioning two whoops from students in the audience: that would be Ken and myself. One of the singers acknowledged us from the stage, saying something along the lines of "Good, someone here knows about Bob Dylan." We might not have hobnobbed with the performers but we didn't hesitate to shout out appreciation from time to time.

In 1966 we hitch-hiked to New York to see the Blue Sky Boys and others at Carnegie Hall. We were in the last row of the second balcony, but the minute they hit the stage – before they could even start their first number – we called out a request in unison: "'Are You from Dixie?'" Bill Bolick said, "We were *just* going to do that song!" The minute it was over, we called out another song, and he said the exact same thing. By the time we'd called either the third or fourth song in a row and earned the same response, that was enough. We didn't want to press our luck.

Dylan was booked at Tufts a year or so after the Peter, Paul & Mary show in the same Cousens Gym. By this time everyone knew about him and the place was packed. But the show was delayed and the audience getting restless.

Someone came on stage and said Dylan was running late but would be here soon. This happened a couple of more times over thirty to forty minutes, before the dissembling MC had to 'fess up: Dylan wasn't coming. There'd been a mix-up and his agent never told him of the show. At least that's the way we understood it.

There was another coffeehouse – the Unicorn. But Club 47 more than any other place forged our musical tastes. Ken says:

> It was an incredible club with a broad range of folk artists. From the folkier side of the world were people like Tom Rush, Jackie Washington, Joni Mitchell, Richard & Mimi Fariña, Joan Baez . . . The blues included the recently rediscovered legends up through Muddy Waters. Bluegrass was well represented from the locals like the Charles River Valley Boys, Lilly Brothers, Keith & Rooney, and Rooney, Val & Applin to national acts like the Kentucky Colonels and Bill Monroe. Doc Watson, Clarence Ashley, Roscoe Holcomb, and many others represented the old-time side. The music was so great and consistent that one could go there without knowing who was appearing and yet know that you would hear some great music.

The year we joined Club 47, membership cost 25¢. Admission was $1.00. Club historian Millie Rahn says the membership fee was to get around blue laws about "cabarets" – so the club formed as a nonprofit educational organization, and expanded to having chamber music, films, plays, and the like.

Ken has also told about our hearing the Union Grove Folkways album playing at Club 47 before a show. He recalls:

> On our next trip to the local record shop, Briggs & Briggs, we located the album and took it into the listening booth and listened to the whole album inside. You weren't supposed to stay in there more than a couple of minutes but we sat on the floor so the folks behind the counter didn't know there was anyone in there, and we listened to the whole thing – and read all the liner notes, too. We learned that the festival took place each Easter weekend down in North Carolina and we vowed then to try and get there that year. The following spring, Bill and I, by then experienced hitch-hikers, packed up, got our shirt cardboards and magic markers (or the equivalents) on which we could write our destinations, and headed for Union Grove.

The Union Grove Old-Time Fiddlers Convention was started in 1924 by H.P. Van Hoy, a musician and teacher at the Union Grove School, as an Easter weekend community event and a way of raising money for the Iredell County School. In 1961, Mike Seeger and John Cohen recorded the event and the album Ken and I heard was released on Folkways Records the following year: *The 37th Old-Time Fiddlers Convention at Union Grove, North Carolina* (yes, Folkways FA 2434). The convention maybe drew about 2,000 people in those days, almost all from the local area. To give an idea of the size of the production, the total receipts for the 1967 convention came to $6,496.56. The school netted $1,338.29.

On our first visit, there were maybe twenty people who seemed to be urbanites. People from the local area came during the day. Folks didn't camp out overnight. That first year at Union Grove, we had no place to stay, but there was this tractor trailer from Holly Farms that was filled with chicken for cooking and sale. The cab had been pulled away. We volunteered to sleep underneath the truck as "security" and our offer was accepted. I don't remember getting any free chicken, though.

How some aggressive bikers at the Fiddlers Convention helped start a record label

The real impetus for starting a label grew out of an experience Ken had with some bikers at a later Union Grove convention. Ken tells the story:

> The atmosphere had begun to change as it became a bigger and bigger event, even "a happening." My final year there was the first year the bikers arrived in numbers. I believe at the time the population of Union Grove during non-festival weekends was 125.
>
> Seeing and hearing the music live made lifelong converts of us. On one of our annual visits to Union Grove, I met a guy from South Carolina and we hung out together quite a bit at the festival. Nice guy. Skip ahead a year. I returned to Union Grove the following year, I ran into my friend from the year before along with a girl he was dating. (This would likely have been 1968 as I drove down with the Busted Toe Mud Thumpers from Ithaca, which included Walt Koken, soon to be a founding member of the Highwoods Stringband.)
>
> My South Carolina friend asked if I would be interested in doing some psilocybin with them, which I respectfully declined. I didn't see them for the rest of that day.
>
> That was the first year of the bikers. The festival was very weird with the usual country folks who had been coming to the festival for years, a growing number of college students from both North and South, and a large contingent of bikers. There were vans blaring rock music.
>
> The next morning, I got up early and went off to do some of my homework, reading about Maslow's hierarchy of values as

I was going to be behind in my work by the time I got back to school. While reading, my friend with his girlfriend stopped by and they looked incredibly stoned. Once again, they offered me some mushrooms and once again I declined. They were really enjoying their high until one of the bikers started hanging around them and started making passes at my friend's girlfriend. At one point, he even asked her to join him on his bike and go back to Florida with him. It was very strange. I saw this incredible tension in her face . . . it was like her face was being torn apart, like part of her wanted to go with him and part didn't.

After a while, my friend decided to bring his girlfriend back to their car and get away from the biker. The biker followed them and was telling them that she would never come down if they went inside and that they should walk it off. I tried tactfully to ask the biker to leave them alone, but he wouldn't listen. He kept on them and wouldn't leave the car. Finally, my friend decided to leave the festival and head back home. I said my goodbyes and watched them leave. As they left, the biker turned to me and asked me, "Why'd you get her stoned?" As I said that I didn't, a right cross or something like it hit my nose and face and blood starting pouring down my face, clothes, and Maslow.

Some locals helped find a policeman. I think they had two policemen at the festival at that point, and they asked me what happened and I told them. I even told them where the biker was. They asked me for his name and when I told them I didn't know it, they said they couldn't do anything. They were likely outnumbered by the bikers by about a hundred to two and they were obviously scared to death.

A couple of people drove me to Statesville, to the nearest hospital, with my nose facing in one direction and the rest of my body facing another and my nose still bleeding pretty heavily. Amazingly, I still had old Maslow with me. The doctor at the hospital looked at me with kind of sorry eyes and as he grabbed my nose, told me, "This might hurt some" and yanked my nose back to where it almost belonged. Did I ever have a bad headache for a while! They placed a metal plate over my nose and taped it into place and I spent the rest of the weekend looking like a character from some yet-to-be-made film.

The next year I returned to Union Grove and that was the year we met Neil [Rossi] and the Spark Gap Wonder Boys who had just won first prize in the old-time category at Union Grove. It was also the year my electric razor was stolen from our van and the last time I didn't have a beard.

Ken was asked to tell a little more about the later year when he first met Ken and Sheri Davidson, who had started their own independent Kanawha Records label in West Virginia.

> I don't remember much about the Davidsons' house, but I do remember that they took us out to visit Clark Kessinger and Billy Cox . . . he had left a tape recorder with Billy, so Billy could just record when he felt like it . . . He was living in a shack . . . wish I had had a camera . . .

It was quite by chance – hitch-hiking back to Boston after the Galax Fiddlers Convention, that Ken met the Davidsons and saw first-hand how someone of modest means could actually start their own label.

> It was getting late that night and they invited us to spend the night – and the next day they took us to meet Clark Kessinger and Billy Cox. Ken had founded Kanawha Records and had issued recordings by both Clark and Billy as well as a couple of other artists. Seeing what he had done, I came back to college and told Bill of my experiences and suggested that we start a record company. Fortunately, there was nobody around to tell us not to and we bungled our way through our first years until we learned something about the business.

Only on reading this book will the North Carolina bikers realize what forces they set in motion. (Of course, it's also possible that they have denied themselves that pleasure.)

Where did the name "Rounder" come from?

Marian was a few years younger than us. She was born in 1948, the oldest of the four children of Dorothy Parker Leighton and Alton "Brud" Leighton. She came from a very different background than Ken and me, both of us born in cities but raised in the suburbs. She grew up in Cherryfield, Maine, a town of fewer than 500 people at the time, in one of the most rural parts of Maine – the easternmost county in the United States, Washington County. Her high school class totaled twenty-three students. They lived in a house her father had built with his brothers when she was very young. Her parents mostly worked at seasonal jobs, and lived in large part off a subsistence garden and the game that her father had hunted.

He worked some in the lumber industry, but also worked as a guide for hunters and fishermen in spring and fall. The whole family pitched in to rake blueberries, a good way to earn a little more in the summer to buy clothes for school. Both parents instilled in her a love of reading.

She traveled through her reading, and she also knew her Bible well, serving at one point as president of the Baptist church's local Youth Fellowship. Like myself – though I had no religious bent – she became a dedicated conservative. She received a scholarship and enrolled at Boston's Northeastern University as a work/study student. She'd learned some critical thinking in high school and a number of things – such as stories in the *New York Times* about the killings of civil right workers in Mississippi, and a very influential March 1967 issue of *Ramparts* magazine – led her to begin to see the world in a different way.

She and Ken met in Portland, Maine, after her freshman year at Northeastern. She had a co-op job as an intern for the Portland Urban Redevelopment Authority, writing reports about projects under way around Portland. Ken was working as an intern, too, at the Spurwink School. She'd heard Hank Williams and some other classic country music while growing up in Maine, but Ken introduced her to a great deal of other music.

She transferred to Clark University in Worcester and got her degree in modern European history. Ken moved there, too. There was a good coffeehouse. Cambridge and Boston weren't that far away. Both Marian and Ken wrote record reviews for *Perspective*, an alternative newspaper in the Worcester area. The following year they moved to Ithaca where Ken pursued studies in early childhood education at Cornell. His interests had shifted, however, and he proposed a thesis on the role of women in early country music. That idea wasn't well received and he began to think of taking his life in a different direction.

Even in our earliest years, no one could remember quite how we first came up with the name "Rounder." We needed a name for our first two albums, so we started kicking ideas around. Somehow, at some point, the name "Rounder" emerged. Ken says,

> I remember going around the room and mentioning Radiators, Doorknobs ... Interestingly, there later was a group called the Radiators and a Nashville label called Doorknob.

Marian told me:

> I have a distinct memory that it occurred in Worcester, early in the morning, after the Holy Modal Rounders had played the Clark coffeehouse, and you dropped by our apartment on Woodland Street, maybe waking up Ken and me by knocking on the door, on your way back to Somerville ... and in whispered tones, as it was still early, and we had a room-mate or room-mates, you said you had come up with something that you thought would be good, and

there was never any further discussion about it, because we all liked it on the spot and from that time on.

As for myself, I have no memory of it at all.

However it arose, there was apparently no "eureka!" sounded, but it didn't take more than a few minutes for it to feel good to the three of us. We liked the fact that it could be taken on several different levels. A "rounder" is a term found in a lot of folk songs – like in 'Casey Jones': "Come all you rounders, if you want to hear / A story told about a brave engineer." A rounder is a drifter, a hobo, a bum. A dissolute person. A wastrel. There were the Holy Modal Rounders, who had intrigued us from the early 1960s, so the name reflected our love of their music. Another meaning of the word "rounder" is simply someone who made the rounds, be it an itinerant Methodist minister or a prostitute. Rounders is an English bat and ball game with a lot of similarity to baseball.[2] And, of course, records were round.

The "Rounder Man"

It was the romantic drifter image that appealed to us the most, and for the label on our very first records we adopted a barroom scene showing a young nineteenth-century dandy from out west with his foot on the rail and a drink hoisted in his right hand.

Years later, when the Grateful Dead launched their own label and named it Round Records, an eager attorney tried to talk us into suing them for the similarity in name and assured us we could make a lot of money in a settlement. We weren't even tempted. "We kind of like the Dead," we said, and besides, Rounder is *better* than Round. If they'd decided to name their label Roundest Records, we might have a problem. "Let them use it," we laughed.

2 Rounder's First Two Records: October 1970

Our first two records were numbered 1 and 2. Actually, we liked the four-number system employed by both Folkways and Arhoolie, so we started with Rounder 0001 and Rounder 0002. The first album was *George Pegram* and the second one – both released on the same day – was *Cluck Old Hen* by the Spark Gap Wonder Boys – more formally, it was *"Cluck Old Hen": Cluck six-ten, the Dow-Jones average is down again*), initiating a series of long album titles, the next-lengthiest being Rounder 2005, *Lake Michigan Ain't No River, Chicago Ain't No Hilly Town* by the Bob Riedy Chicago Blues Band.

One was more traditional (North Carolina banjoist Pegram) and the other more contemporary (Spark Gap). Fifteen years later, Ken told Boston weekly *The Tab*, "We've been described as doing roots music and contemporary offshoots of it. It wasn't planned that way, but it's turned out we've done both."

We've always dated the birth of Rounder to the day the first two pressings were completed and invoiced to us: October 22, 1970.

Invoice: an interesting word. In French, it's *facture*. In Spanish, it's *factura* or *cuenta*. I learned some of those words while building up our foreign distribution network, but in 1970 I really had no idea what an invoice was. Here we were, starting a record company, but it wasn't based on any Harvard Business School model. We had no business plan. We just had a little more than $1,000 (we now know it could have been called "startup capital" but as far as we were concerned it was just $1,000), which Ken had saved up.

It was enough to get our first two records out. At the time, I was living in a second-floor apartment at 727 Somerville Avenue in Somerville. The woman who lived on the first floor was elderly and, fortunately – given the loud music often emanating from the second floor – fairly deaf. Next door was a vacant lot where drivers would park trailer trucks from time to time. A truck might arrive in the middle of the day or night and be there for a few weeks.

It took a while to pull all the components of those albums together. Getting the music wasn't expensive. To acquire the rights to the George Pegram

Rounder 0001

Rounder 0002

GEORGE PEGRAM

George Pegram, formerly of Union Grove, and now living in Asheboro, N.C., sings and plays old-time banjo. He is accompanied here by Fred Cockerham on fiddle, Clyde Issacs on mandolin, and Jack Bryant on guitar.

For those who have seen George Pegram perform, no further introduction is necessary. For those not familiar with George, suffice it to say that he is one of the finest entertainers anywhere, as well as champion banjo picker in the old-time category at Union Grove in 1969. His dramatic singing style remains unique and pure to its tradition despite exposure to newer styles.

THE SPARK GAP WONDER BOYS

Cluck Old Hen, The Milwaukee Blues, Durham's Bull, Faded Coat of Blue, The Black Mountain Rag, The Dying Ranger, Baldheaded End of the Broom, Colored Aristocracy, Give Me Back My Five Dollars, Lee Highway Blues, The Auctioneer, Wish I Had Stayed in the Wagon Yard, The Good Physician, Dill Pickles Rag, God Made Woman After Man, Take a Drink on Me, Wreck of the Royal Palm, I Don't Love Nobody, Happy Trails to You. (19 songs).

This Boston based old-time band features Neal Rossi on fiddle, Dave Doubilet on banjo and George Nelson on guitar. In their first visit as a group to the Union Grove Old Time Fiddlers' Convention, The Spark Gap Wonder Boys won seven ribbons. On George's return from Viet Nam in 1970, they returned to Union Grove where they won first prize in the coveted Old-Time Band Competition. They love their music and their enthusiasm comes through on this record.

The first Rounder catalog

album set Ken back $110.00, paid to Charlie Faurot, who recorded the tapes, and which Ken had heard at the Davidsons'. So that was 0001 – total cost of the master tape: $125.00.

Who can know what George Pegram thought of a company in Massachusetts wanting to release an album of his music? He may have thought Rounder was the equal of RCA, for all we know. We did present him a contract that was all of about four brief paragraphs, all of which fit easily on one page of 8½ × 11½ paper.

Rounder 0002 cost a fraction of that. Through the good offices of the *Hillbilly at Harvard* radio show (which has been broadcasting over Harvard radio since 1948, billed as "Boston's original Saturday morning country-music jamboree"), we were able to record the Spark Gap Wonder Boys at the WHRB studios. For some reason we can't recall now, we recorded half the album at Harvard and half at MIT's radio station. The studios were free. Our only cost was the cost of the tape, and that was $3.50 per reel (we used two reels) of ¼ inch tape on 7 inch reels. Total cost to record the album? You don't have to be a graduate of either institution to do the math: that would be $7.00. The recording was done by Bruce Kinch, with the help of Durg Gessner and Brian Sinclair ("Ol' Sinc" from *Hillbilly at Harvard*). Even well into 2019, listening to the Hillbillies on Saturday mornings is a familiar ritual. These days, listeners at a distance can pick up the show "screaming on the Internet to the whole wide world on the World Wide Web," as Cousin Lynn Joiner puts it. There are few radio stations that can claim over a half-century of broadcast history and demonstrative ongoing influence.[3]

Next up was getting the physical records made. The components came from several places. We had masters made at Cook Laboratories in Stamford, Connecticut. The bill for 0001 came to $167.36, dated May 13, 1970 – it took us about five months to get everything together. We bought 1,057 black cardboard jackets to slip the records in, from County Box & Album of Mount Vernon, New York. They shipped them to Cook and charged us $105.70 on June 1.

We had to design both covers. I designed the original cover for George Pegram using Letraset type and a couple of photographs I'd taken of George at Union Grove at the 1967 Fiddlers Convention. For the Spark Gap Wonder Boys cover, we were presented with an offer we couldn't refuse. Banjo player David Doubilet was a photographer; he later became *National Geographic*'s principal underwater photographer, but for this album he set up a photo session by his friend Peter Simon (the back cover showed the group "outstanding in their field" – in other words, a photograph of them outside, standing in a field). The design was done by a friend of theirs from Boston University named Doug Parker. Doug worked for BU's graphic design department and he loved the idea of adding some record album covers to his portfolio. Doug offered us this deal: "I'll design the cover for free, but only on the condition that I can design ALL your covers, for free." He liked the idea of doing a whole series, and he wasn't looking to make money on the deal but rather to create a series of albums. How could we say no? Eventually, *he* learned to say no – it was probably those nineteen records we released in 1972 that forced the issue.

But we were off to a great start. Two album covers, with photos and design costing nothing at all. The covers were printed on paper by Pothier Brothers Printers of Medford, Massachusetts. I had come to know the printers when Don Wilcock, Barry Levy, and I started up *Eritas*, a humor magazine at the Tufts campus. That's "satire" spelled backwards, but it maybe sounded a little racier. We only launched it late in our senior year, and no one carried it forward after we left. Instead, the *National Lampoon* got all the attention – but ours was funnier than the *Harvard Lampoon*. Working on *Eritas* wasn't the first time I had been a "publisher." When I was twelve, my friend Stan Brown and I published a neighborhood newspaper. We lived on Maple Street in Lexington and Stan had a gelatin-based hectograph that transferred master stencils onto this purple gelatin which served as a printing plate. We ran off these two-page sheets and created the *Maple Street Mumbles*. I was the sports page editor; called "The Home Run," this page presented the statistics of the neighborhood kids and how they were doing in baseball games. I got really into doing this and going door to door trying to sell it for one or two cents. It was like selling lemonade. I also drew my own comic books, but those were one of a kind and not really for sale.

Pothier Brothers printed 300 copies of what they invoiced to us as "George Program" on a 20" × 12" sheet, which was shipped to Cook. The sheets were then pasted onto the black jackets to create a "Folkways-look" album jacket. The *Cluck Old Hen* sheet was 24" × 12" because the notes were longer and so took up the whole back of the jacket. Cost for the two sets of 600 sheets was $219.61, billed out on September 14, 1970. Pothier also printed four sets of 1,000 record labels for $143.17 – Side A and Side B of both albums.

The pressings were done by Sonic Recording Products, Inc. of Holbrook, New York – wherever that is. Cook and Sonic had both been recommended to me by Moe Asch of Folkways. The cost was 32¢ apiece (minimum 500 units), and there was a charge for $30.00 per side for "3 step mastering." The test pressings cost $10 apiece. The total mastering was $120.00 for the four sides. The first invoice to us was invoice #1369, dated October 22, 1970. We had 272 copies of 0001 made in mono, and 495 copies of 0002 made in stereo. We got hit up for an extra $80.00 for stereo remastering. They charged us $1.59 to return the tape to us, and shrinkwrapping had already come to the record business. That set us back 2¢ per disc. The total cost for everything was $372.37.

We had been anxious to receive the records in time to sell them at a Boston Area Friends of Bluegrass and Old-Time Country Music (BAF) concert on October 25, and Sonic shipped fifty ahead to us by air freight, the balance by truck. The method of shipping prompted our first business dispute. We hadn't asked them to be sent by air, and when we were charged the extra cost, I wrote back and complained. The president of Sonic, D. Dickerman replied, "I have received your letter, and want to offer my sincerest apologies. Your detailed letter hit me very hard, and all I can say is that I am extremely sorry to put you through so much nonsense aggravation . . . I agree that you should not be held responsible for the additional expense." He called his error "what must be the greatest goof of the year."

BAF had been founded in late 1969 by Nancy Talbott and Fred Bartenstein. "I was a freshman at Harvard," Fred recalled, "and Nancy was an administrative assistant at the Harvard Department of Social Relations in William James Hall. As a freshman, I was able to get use of the Freshman Union for our concerts. We had to go to Cambridge City Hall in Central Square to get a permit for 'Entertainment on the Lord's Day.'"[4] The first BAF concert, attended by the three future Rounder founders, was in December 1969 and featured the Lilly Brothers, Joe Val & the Old Time Bluegrass Singers, and the Spark Gap Wonder Boys.

The next BAF concert was one that we recorded live, hoping to produce an album. It was a great line-up: Red Allen, Frank Wakefield, Tex Logan, and Don Stover, with Bob Tidwell on bass. It could have been a very special album, had everything worked out as anticipated – but it didn't. Red was suffering badly from gout and, for whatever reasons, things just didn't click as well as we wanted. It was very disappointing, and there was no way to work with the tapes to try and justify an album. We didn't want to put out an album that would present them at less than their best, and these performances weren't even close enough to be debatable. We tried to record them outside of the concert setting both in Cambridge and in Ithaca but we never got anything that was good enough. We shelved the tapes, and they're still on the shelves.

Fits and starts trying to get going

That was actually the second time in 1970 that we had recorded what promised to be a very good live show, and both times the tapes were unusable – not auspicious for ambitions of starting a record company. The first was in February, when the Lilly Brothers and Don Stover were booked for a concert on the 14th at John Hancock Hall in downtown Boston. That was the record we wanted as our first. We'd been fans of the Lilly Brothers from the early 1960s: we got their Folkways album *The Lilly Bros. & Don Stover*, recorded by Mike Seeger in 1961, on one of our trips to Sam Goody's and played it dozens of times. And at least a dozen times, Ken and I had gone to see the Lillys and Don play at Boston's Hillbilly Ranch. Now that was something. The Hillbilly Ranch was in a grungy part of Boston's downtown area that catered to sailors in port and transplants (and transients) from the South who somehow found their way to this fairly seedy barroom. (John Hancock Hall was only maybe ten or eleven blocks away, but in a more upscale area.) The drinking age in Boston was twenty-one at the time. Ken and I were maybe eighteen the first time we went there. There was no one asking to see IDs, and as long as we stuck to nursing one ginger ale or 7 Up all evening, no one was concerned that we were underage and enjoying the music. The place was tricked out with a bandstand with wagon wheels, and wooden rails like you'd tie your horse to in front of a saloon. Instead of a cigarette girl, there was Hillbilly Tex – a rangy, grizzled guy who might have been missing a tooth or two – shambling around with a tray bearing cigarettes and the like. Our focus was on the music, and it was a treat.

We had that one Lillys album on Folkways. It wasn't until the late Sixties, that we realized that there had never been another Lilly Brothers album. And it wasn't just them. In the early Sixties "folk boom," it was exciting – a Golden Age for those of us who came to love this music with so many records coming out, and we started digging deeper trying to learn more about the roots of the music.

After we first heard Doc Watson, one of us bought a copy of an album on which he appeared, the Folkways various artists collection *Old Time Music at Clarence Ashley's*, and learned that Tom "Clarence" Ashley had originally recorded back in the 1930s as part of the Carolina Tar Heels. Then, we found out he was booked to come to Boston for a show arranged in cooperation with Friends of Old Time Music (FOTM) in New York. There were, after all, people in other parts of the country looking more deeply into folk music as well. We were excited at the opportunity to see one of the originals. I had an alphabet kit you could use to create your own rubber stamps, so I "set type" and made a stamp reading "CLARENCE ASHLEY IS COMING." I grabbed my ink pad, hand-printed a lot of little cards bearing these words, and we placed them in odd locations around the Tufts campus. We stamped "CLARENCE ASHLEY IS COMING" on flyers and papers all over campus. Within a week, half the student body probably knew that Clarence Ashley was coming – not that they knew who he was, when he would come, what he would do, and nor would they would care if they did know. It was like guerrilla art; for us, it was fun. Michael Scully noted that it reflected our "lunatic passion" at the time: the show was going to be full anyhow. It's not as though we were asked to publicize it, or that anyone presenting it ever knew we had.[5]

But then came the Beatles, and the Rolling Stones, and the whole British Invasion. Everyone quickly learned who *they* were. Bob Dylan went electric. It all happened over a couple of years, say 1964–66. By then, Elektra had an album by Love, and then a band called the Doors. Vanguard had Country Joe & the Fish. Both labels ran with it, following the popular trend and dropping almost all interest in folk music. (We later heard by word of mouth that, years after we began, Elektra's founder Jac Holzman was talking with a friend about Rounder and said, "Oh, that's what I wish we were still doing.")

We liked every one of these bands, but we still liked folk music, too. Even reliable Moe Asch at Folkways made a deal with Scholastic which took effect in the spring of 1966 – not to record psychedelic groups but to market his label. For the five years the Scholastic deal lasted, Folkways largely dried up as a source of new folk recordings. It was a really dry spell: we wanted to buy records of Ramblin' Jack Elliott, the Lilly Brothers, and all the rest – but they just weren't being made.

A number of companies used to enclose postcards in their albums to encourage correspondence. We duly mailed them back asking for records by the groups we wanted to hear. This gave us the idea to write letters, too. It was records by the Lillys we particular wanted them to make, or by the reunited Kentucky Colonels. Later we refined our approach and asked them what it would take for them to put out an album of the Lillys. I recall we got at least one letter back, which said they might be willing to put a record out if we made a tape and sent it to them.

We were a little startled: *we* would have to record it? Well, that would certainly be less risk for them. We'd be doing all the work, and then they could decide whether or not they wanted to release it. But the idea intrigued us. Then, when Ken got that ride from Ken and Sheri Davidson and found out about the George Pegram master, we began to think about it more. Meanwhile, we planned to do just what the company had suggested: record the Lilly Brothers and make a record. Ken, however, insists, "From the time I came back from meeting Ken Davidson, I don't remember ever thinking about sending tapes to any other company."

Our first thought was to maybe operate as a division of Kanawha Records, Ken Davidson's West Virginia label. Looking back on it, that seems like an absurd idea but we debated it for weeks: should we do that or start our own company? We'd never run any business. We didn't even aspire to running a business. In the end, we decided that if we were going to do all the work – making contact, arranging the recording, and so forth – we might as well put it out ourselves, too. It was a good call.[6]

So we talked to the Lillys about recording their show. They were fine with the idea. The concert date was set, February 14, but only a few weeks before, on January 17, Everett Lilly's son Jiles was killed, his car hit by a fire truck in Boston rushing on its way to what proved to be a false alarm. Everett and his family brought Jiles back to the family home to West Virginia to bury him, returning only to do the show they'd committed to in Boston. That they played the show at all was a tribute to the "show must go on" troupers the Lilly Brothers were. They were very obviously still weighed down with grief – and returning to where the accident had occurred probably made matters worse. The pall over the performance was palpable, so much so that it felt like Jiles's death had been the day before. There was no way we could consider releasing an album of such a sad show. After meeting their obligation by doing what became their farewell show, Everett decided to move back home to West Virginia for good.

In the end, therefore, our two attempts to record live shows both resulted in tapes we felt we couldn't use. Others might have thrown up their hands and quit. However, by the time of the October 1970 show, we did already have Rounder 0001 and 0002 in the bag.

So what was the total cost of making those first two albums? Add up all the figures presented above and it comes to $1,140.21. That's what we began with. That's all we began with. We never had startup money from a venture capitalist. It's actually a pretty good story of how, working with very little except a lot of passion and energy – and maybe being in the right place with the right idea at the right time – it's possible to build something from the bottom up. We had two records, and we were in business.

Learning we had to run a business

Not that it was ever really intended to be a business. It was just something we did. None of us had finished graduate school at the time. It wasn't clear what we'd end up doing in life. I had started working at Lowell Technological Institute (it later became the University of Lowell, and later part of the University of Massachusetts system), teaching political science. Marian took a position at a Greek Orthodox theological seminary. Ken taught the one semester at Lowell which encompassed taking his class to a Jethro Tull concert, landing him in a little hot water.

We sold some of these first two records at the October 25 concert. I took five copies of each to a store in the center of Harvard Square called Discount Records. I asked to speak to the manager and he came out from a back room. I told him we were a new record company in the area and these were our first two albums and we hoped they would put them in their store to see if they'd sell. He thought that sounded fine and said he'd take all ten. I wrote out a note on a 3" × 5" index card which declared he'd received five copies of 0001 and five copies of 0002 on such-and-such a date, and he signed that as a receipt. As I was leaving, he said, "You can just send us an invoice." I said I would – but I had no idea what he was talking about.

That's indicative of how schooled we were in business at the time. I knew I would send the store a bill, but didn't realize that the business term for the bill was an "invoice." It was about four years later that we realized it was probably time to think about paying taxes.

That Discount Records manager became a good friend over time. Jeep Holland was as obsessive a record collector as you could ever meet. He also reportedly had over 100,000 comic books crammed into his house. Jeep later donated his records to the ARChive of Contemporary Music in New York City.[7]

Our first purchase order

It took just a little longer to make a sale to the Harvard Coop, the largest retail store in Harvard Square at the time. But the head buyer, Linda Stellinger, signed purchase order #31-154704 for us on November 5, buying fifteen copies each of 0001 and 0002 for $2.75 apiece. We sold them on consignment, but it would prove to be another $82.50 for the Rounder coffers. The Coop reordered ten copies of each on December 8, and this time it was on net terms. By January 12, 1971, the Coop was also buying some Fortune, Paredon, Blue Flame, Muskadine, and Ahura Mazda records from us. Rounder's fledgling distribution effort was under way. Many a Saturday morning over the next ten years or so, Ken or I would visit the Coop and make sure any Rounder understock was brought up from beneath the store's sales bins so that customers would be sure to see our records. We always made sure that the Rounder (or Rounder-distributed) albums were the front records in the bins, too.

When we began, we had intended to be a nonprofit. We weren't in it for the money.

Getting a business off the ground

The records sold, amazingly. On December 11, we got another 126 pressings of George Pegram; it was our first reorder with the pressing plant. We had 600 more jacket flats printed in March 1971. Some forty years later, it's hard to recall how we could have sold that many records that quickly. There was hardly anyone outside of rural North Carolina who'd ever heard of George Pegram, though perhaps that was part of the appeal. And the Spark Gap Wonder Boys, who'd had their professional debut at the Polish-American Home in Boston, weren't drawing big crowds in Greater Boston. We can only recall one significant Spark Gap concert in town. But Jack's Record Cellar in San Francisco ordered twenty-five copies of each album to distribute on the West Coast – and then came back for more. Locally, we linked up with Dave Wilson of Riverboat Enterprises, a distributor operating out of a storefront on Columbia Street in East Cambridge which had newspapers taped over the window so passers-by wouldn't see the shelves of records inside. Dave was also the publisher of *Broadside*, Boston's first alternative weekly, which had good coverage of the folk scene.

Wherever we went, we carried a few records with us. When we would walk into a store in Washington DC, to give one example, we'd ask them about carrying our records, and the question would inevitably be, "Who's your distributor?" We were glad to get distribution through Riverboat as it allowed us to get our records into more stores in New England, but there were none other than small regional distributors at the time. Stores told us they couldn't buy records from people who just stopped by. They preferred to deal through a distributor, who could offer records from a number of labels and reduce the number of vendors for them. That made sense, so we talked to some of the other indie labels we were aware of – for instance, Dave Freeman of County Records. He agreed we could be a distributor, so the next time we were asked who our distributor was, we could answer, "We are!" – and hope to write up a small order. County Records offered our records through their mail order service, County Sales, which helped move a lot of records.

We were dealing with the smallest of the small labels, of course. And we mostly dealt with bluegrass and old-time country music, although – quirky as always – we carried Paredon Records, a far-left label run by Irwin Silber and Barbara Dane. It may have seemed odd to some stores that we were carrying the Michigan Bluegrass label on the one hand (and the even smaller Birch and Homestead labels), but also recordings of the Chinese communist opera *The East Is Red* and Paredon's *Vietnam: Songs of Liberation*. We really didn't care that much for the actual music on Paredon (that's an understatement), but they were a small indie, too, and needed better distribution.

It wasn't long before we started up our own newsletter, *à la* County Sales, to begin to communicate with folks we'd met on the road, people who had bought records from us at festivals we'd gone to over the summer of 1971.

The three Rounder founders selling out of the VW bus: (left to right) the author, Ken Irwin, Marian Leighton Levy

Whenever we'd set up shop – selling out of our VW bus – people marveled over the selection of obscure records we had, and asked where they could buy them. We said, of course, "From us!" If we could be a distributor, we could also be a mail-order company.

The first issue of *The Rounder Review* is dated October 1971. Basically, it was our first birthday. We mentioned that Birch Records had a new Mac & Bob reissue ($4.00) and that we'd turned up the last twenty-four copies of John Burke & the Yankee Carpetbaggers ($3.50 each). We reported on attending the Second Annual Pennsylvania Bluegrass Festival at Ontelaunee Park in New Tripoli from June 4–6. "Although one of the nicest parks in Pennsylvania, the facilities were poorly kept," we wrote, "the sound was basically good although it frequently distorted on the high parts. The turnout was small, attributable largely to a lack of publicity. Even within a few miles, most of the townspeople had no idea there was a bluegrass festival going on."

We also wrote about the appearance of Conway Twitty & the Twitty Birds, who appeared "much to the disgruntlement of most of the bluegrass crowd" and our concern that paying Twitty might well have cut into the ability to pay the bluegrass acts. The highlight was "an amazing set by the New Deal String Band, perhaps the funniest set ever performed by a bluegrass band." We didn't have a large mailing list, but it was large enough that we got a bulk mail permit from the post office in Somerville (# NM 54889).

Our next review was Bill Monroe's Fifth Annual Bluegrass Festival at Bean Blossom, Indiana, where you might have found us from June 15–20 that year. We raved about it, while noting, "Restroom facilities were passable, but need improvement." (We were being kind.)

Over the July 4 weekend, we commuted back and forth between Carlton Haney's festival in Berryville, Virginia and the Smithsonian Institution's Festival of American Folklife on the Mall in Washington. For reasons unclear at this remove, we didn't have much to say about Berryville, but were impressed by the Folklife Festival, which was featuring the state of Ohio. We saw Earl Taylor, Robert Junior Lockwood, U. Utah Phillips, Hazel Dickens, Sarah Ogan Gunning, Jim Garland, the Ardoin Family, and a combination of the New Lost City Ramblers and the Fat City String Band (later the Highwoods Stringband) – and "the great Professor Longhair."

Almost every night either at festivals or on the road, we slept in our Volkswagen van. For three people to do that for almost an entire summer required some contortions and a degree of orchestration. Since they were "an item" at the time, Ken and Marian slept on the floor of the van and I slept on the back seat, a couple of feet above them. We'd taken out the middle seat to help make room for all the cartons of records; at night, though, we'd have to take them all and pile them up on the front seats and in the back. There was just – barely – enough room. We would typically park in a church parking lot, someplace around the back, figuring the location was safer than the street or a commercial area. We brushed our teeth using the side mirror. We had the car rigged up for some privacy by stringing curtains on all sides of what was, effectively, the sleeping compartment. The curtains were homemade, from scraps of bright and multicolored swatches culled from fabric stores. We never really had any difficulty, though one night when we were parked on the street in New York City's Greenwich Village, I was startled by someone trying to break in while I was sleeping. I banged on the window from the inside a couple of times, then peeked out and saw the offender running away down the empty 4.00 am street.

Ken remembers something that – for whatever reason – neither Marian nor I do. He does tend to have a better memory for such things. He recalls a time when we needed to wash up, on our way to interview Whitey & Hogan for the Early Days of Bluegrass series, so we all put on our bathing suits and went to a self-service car wash; not only did we clean the cars but ourselves as well.

When in DC, we usually stayed with Frank Proschan, whose mother was always welcoming. There were others who welcomed us along the way. We received a great deal of positive feedback for the work we were doing; through the way people talked about it we came to believe ourselves that we were doing something special – not that we weren't somewhat predisposed to think so anyway. We were part of a generation that thought it could change the world for the better. Lofty ideals aside, we could see concrete results in the work we were doing – the records – and we knew that by recording people like Snuffy & Pappy and Clark Kessinger, and putting out the George Pegram album, we were filling a void. We were doing good, solid cultural work, helping preserve America's traditions. People wanted to help. Doug Parker, as I described, designed many early covers for us. Other people (Dick Spottswood comes to mind) contributed photographs, notes, suggestions, and offered us meals or places to stay. We could have gotten swollen heads: people were already talking about Rounder as "legendary." There wasn't a big disconnect, though, since we passionately believed in what we were doing and even felt it as a calling.

We weren't taking a penny, and didn't pay ourselves a salary at any time for the first four years. We were putting money in, rather than taking it out. Ken's and my jobs at Lowell and Marian's at the Greek Orthodox school gave us all more than we needed at the time, so we had extra to put into the company.

We conceived of ourselves as a nonprofit and took a couple of steps in that direction. For our artist contracts, we found an attorney and asked him to prepare a form contract. We wanted it simple and as short as possible, no more than a couple of pages, so that artists wouldn't be intimidated by reams of "whereas" and "the party of the first part." We found the right guy, and paid him with one copy each of our first two albums. The contract was one page long and served us for our first few years.

I applied to the Commonwealth of Massachusetts for recognition as a nonprofit, and we filed all the legal forms ourselves. It didn't take long before it was granted so we took the next step and applied for Federal nonprofit status. Here I made a mistake. I got a copy of the guidelines for applying for Federal tax-exempt status, and completed the forms. I didn't realize that we were supposed to copy verbatim some of the language from the guidelines into the form itself, the information explaining the not-for-profit purpose of the organization. I thought that copying the text would be frowned upon – a form of plagiarism – so I paraphrased. The application was rejected, and we were urged to resubmit. But we were so busy that I never got around to it. It was only a few years later that someone explained where I'd gone wrong.

Had Rounder become a nonprofit, we would have probably been constrained in more of our activities, and had more paperwork hoops to hop through, but we wouldn't have had to pay all the taxes we paid over the years and we wouldn't have suffered – in the way I felt we did at times – when competing against companies such as Smithsonian Folkways that enjoyed advantages we did not.

When we did incorporate, in May 1971, we found that the form required us to take titles to fill the three requisite corporate officer slots. We made Marian president because so few record companies had a woman as president. Ken, who might be the last person you'd want in charge of balancing the books, was made treasurer, just for fun. He was also the most "notoriously frugal" (the words are Scott Alarik's) one of the three. I became clerk of the corporation because I liked the notion of sitting in the back of the room with a green eyeshade on, being clerk-like while sorting everything out.

3 Building the Business: The Early 1970s

Building the business

We were on a mission. Two albums in October 1970, three more albums all released in the month of October 1971, and then suddenly nineteen (!) albums released from March through November 1972. There were so many ideas put before us, so many suggestions, and so much encouragement coming our way. We really were incredibly busy, starting up all these new albums, building our mail order, and developing our distribution. So we didn't file any tax returns for our first four years. Who had time for all that paperwork? Besides, in our hearts, we knew we were effectively nonprofit (as Massachusetts agreed); we knew we were putting money we earned into the company and never taking anything out. Our intentions were honorable and our hearts were pure.

We also saved money any way we could think of. This carried into every area of life and work, right down to wanting a listing in the phone book but not wanting to pay for a business line. That would have cost extra. We made up the name "Reco Rounder," and added "him" as another residential listing on my home phone, for something like an extra 35¢ a month. Naturally, this name showed up in the white pages and for directory assistance as Rounder, Reco.

We were relentless in our determination to save money any way we could. Around the time we started, underground newspapers were printing lists of phone company credit cards from major institutions. You'd just select one from a corporation involved in waging war on Vietnam, give the operator a card number, and your call was placed as long as the number was still valid. Most of those long-distance calls we made we never would have placed if we'd had to pay for them. One artist – who admits to using phony credit card numbers to call *us* – remembers to this day how we could sometimes get a message through even without using a fake credit card: "The new method would be when Ken would call person-to-person, and the operator would ask for Buzz Busby or somebody, and I would say he's not here, and I'd hear Ken blurt out, 'The records will be shipped in the morning' as he hung up."[8]

First we ran the company out of two successive Somerville apartments. There was 727 Somerville Avenue, and then one at 65 Park Street. The company kept growing, despite a few bumps in the road. Maintaining the trust of mail-order customers and providing a good service to our few distributors and retail accounts was important, but things happened. Ken remembers:

> Our first volunteer at Rounder when we lived and worked at Park Street had a dog who pissed on some of the orders causing the ink to run and we couldn't read the address on where to send the order and we had already cashed the check. They eventually wrote asking about their order and we tried to explain.

727 Somerville Avenue (Rounder operated out of the second floor)

By February 1972 we'd added the Folkways label to our distribution. Issue #2 of *The Rounder Review* announced the Folkways titles we had started carrying – a selection at first, from their huge catalog – and we added the Rimrock label as well (it was a budget line and they sold for just $2.00 each, retail) and Rural Rhythm and Jalyn. These were additions to our existing distribution/mail-order catalog which by the Spring/Summer 1972 edition embraced the following labels, several of which are likely not even remembered today: Adelphi, American Heritage, Arhoolie, Biograph, Blue Goose, Blues Classics, County, Delmark, Folk Legacy, Folkways, Historical, Jalyn, Jessup, King Blues,

BUILDING THE BUSINESS   **33**

King, Melodeon, Nashville, Old Timey, Origin Jazz Library, Pine Mountain, RBF, Rebel, Rimrock, Rural Rhythm, Spivey, Starday, Takoma, Testament, and Yazoo.

In a separate list, we included some smaller labels that were just beginning or were even smaller than the ones listed above; most of these only just had their first record out at that time: Ahura Mazda, Alligator, Arbor, Birch, Blue Flame, Davis Unlimited, F&W, Fortune, Herwin, Homestead, Irma, Kanawha, King Bluegrass, Lemco, Living Folk, Longhorn, Lucas & Harmon, Mamlish, Meadowlands, Melody, Muscadine, Pine Tree, Raccoon, Real, Southern Preservation, Riverboat, Swallow, Swallowtail, Symposium, Traditional, Vetco, Voyager, and Wango.

We also carried publications: *Old Time Music* from England, the *JEMF Quarterly* of the John Edwards Memorial Foundation, *Blues Unlimited*, *Bluegrass Unlimited*, *Muleskinner News,* and *Sing Out!*

The second issue of *Record Review* didn't cover any festivals, but it did contain eighteen album reviews. The fact that we were carrying so many labels with just one or two records to their name was indicative of two things: there were a *lot* of new labels springing up, and we were being true to our roots. After all, only eighteen months earlier, we ourselves only had two records. We were just a little bit ahead of the curve, in the right place at the right time. And, with there being three of us, perhaps we had an energy and dynamic that other labels – often sole proprietorships – couldn't match. Marian once told the *Providence Journal-Bulletin*, "A lot of indies are one-man operations, and that's very hard to sustain." She added, "With the three of us, no one person can get too carried away with one project."

Around this time, we bought a house. It didn't cost that much. And so we started working out of our basement at 186 Willow Avenue, a three-story house in a residential Somerville neighborhood. We had no permission to be running a business in this neighborhood, and did all we could to discourage frequent or large truck deliveries. We built our own racks: wooden shelves on cinder blocks that we'd "found" around town, and pretty much filled up the basement with them. For packing boxes there was a work table on one side of the basement, near the bulkhead door through which we brought shipments down into the underground. We picked up all our mail at the Union Square Post Office, rather than have it delivered to the house, and dropped off the outgoing boxes we'd packed up the day before. Our pressing plant, Wakefield, packed their records really well, with three boxes of twenty-five LPs apiece enclosed in a heavy cardboard outer box. A carton of seventy-five LPs weighed in at forty-four pounds. A lot has been written about "sweat equity" and a lot of actual sweat was expended in those days. We certainly had no air conditioning.

During the warmer months, we'd often drive to Logan Airport a little before midnight to take delivery of an "E-container" worth of records – shipping 3,000 pounds by air from Wakefield in Phoenix was typically more

Ken, Marian, and the author with their first five album covers on the 727 Somerville Avenue apartment wall. Photograph courtesy of Carl Fleischhauer.

economical than ground freight. But we'd have to unload the containers by hand at the cargo area of the airport (it was a perfect fit for the different old station wagons or VW buses that we had, one after another), and then drive them home.

Our "dining room table" was a large sheet of plywood which we had varnished and placed across some boxes of records. There weren't any chairs. We belonged to the local food coop and did a lot of shopping there, plus we kept an eye out for discarded furniture on the street. For a while, Priscilla Long ran a printing business – Red Sun Press – out of a side room just off the dining room, into which she'd somehow managed to fit a small offset press. We typically had three additional housemates at any given time.[9]

Around this time, Bruce Kaplan joined Rounder, which we announced in that same February 1972 issue of *The Rounder Review*, along with our hope: "Sure would be nice if he does move to Boston." The group grew to five with the addition of Skip Ferguson, who lived with us in Somerville.[10] The "Rounder Collective" never grew larger than five, although we often had people crash with us for a few days, or a week. Peter Stampfel was one such. So was some older homeless man who lived in our van parked out on the street in front of our first Somerville Avenue apartment, until a couple of months had passed and he was just getting to be too much. After all, we had to ask him to leave the van any time we wanted to go out to pick up records, or whatever. There were any number of characters we came across; there was, for instance, a guy from Lexington who I had known who kept coming by and claiming that he was the person who had invented whistling. Did we attract characters?

Adding Takoma Records was the single biggest step in building our distribution wing but it also added an early discordant note, because Takoma switched its distribution from Dave Wilson's Riverboat to us at Rounder, and Dave wasn't pleased.

This was alluded to earlier; I'll elaborate a bit. Takoma was a strong-selling indie label at the time, with both Leo Kottke and John Fahey on the roster. We met Fahey at a couple of shows. At the Second Fret in Philadelphia, the audience had to wait while he lit a cigarette on stage, then smoked the whole thing, then left to go to the bathroom before the show really got under way. At another place we saw him, someplace closer to Washington, he turned up fairly late for the show; apparently he'd gotten lost looking for turtles in the fields out back. Takoma was his label, and the people running it weren't that thrilled with Riverboat. They thought, perhaps justifiably, that Dave was too busy with *Broadside* and a new interest he'd developed in this thing that later became known as the personal computer. With these other involvements, they apparently thought he didn't have the necessary ambition to push the records. Charlie Mitchell, Takoma's manager, probably saw us as up-and-comers, and called one day to say he wanted us to rep Takoma. We can't do that, we said, because of our feelings for Riverboat. We wouldn't want it to look as though we'd approached them to take Takoma away from Dave.

"That's not an issue," Charlie said. "You haven't asked me. I'm not going to deal with Riverboat any longer. Do you want to represent Takoma or not?" Given the way he put it, we felt better about taking on the line.

We tried to do right. When we created that first one-page recording contract, we decided we'd pay higher royalties than the other labels. LPs at the time typically carried a $3.98 list price. We offered our own records by mail order for $3.50, with no extra charge for shipping. Our pricing was in line with the industry. Asking around, we learned that 25¢ per record sold was the going rate for artist royalties. We also knew that a lot of the older artists, bluesmen in particular, felt they'd been cheated on royalties. We determined to do two things: pay 50¢ an album – double the usual rate – and be scrupulous about paying royalties in full and on time. We also tried to do right another way. Our Spring 1972 mail-order catalog asked customers not to mail in the eight-page catalog to us as their order form: "In order to save paper and trees, we suggest you write down on another piece of paper the records you wish, holding on to this listing for future reference." We accepted checks or money order, but it was more than ten years before we took credit cards, and there was no such thing as PayPal then. For that matter, there was no such thing as the internet – except for an embryonic thing being built within the Department of Defense.

There were always some upfront costs in recording an album (even if the first one we ourselves recorded had only cost $7.00), but we didn't know that large labels recouped such expenses from royalties. Instinctively, though, we covered a few of those startup costs by creating a structure whereby we paid a half-royalty (25¢) for the first 500 units sold, and then 50¢ per unit thereafter. That saved us a full $125 on each album.

We also didn't ask for options. Each album was a "one-off" – non-exclusive. Major-label deals at the time often had multiple options, binding the artist to the label for as many as four to eight future albums. Rounder artists – for many years – were not bound to us, but free to record for another label. At one point, as Don Stover wrapped up his second album for us (Rounder 0039), he turned to me that last day in the studio and said, "So I am free to record for any other record company?" I said, yes, and he said good, and that he was going to leave the next day to record an album for the Old Homestead label. That was more amusing than anything, but labels understandably do like to protect their investment (however modest the investment may have been).

Most major-label contracts also provided for "cross-collateralizing" royalties due the artist. Say if an artist was due a thousand dollars from the sales of their first album, but the label had not yet recouped expenses from a second album, and was $2,000 short, the royalties due would be applied to the overall royalty account, and the statement would show $1,000 still due. For this reason, some artists never saw any royalties. We thought it was unfair: each album should be treated separately. So that's the way we

Cover of *Don Stover and the White Oak Mountain Boys* (Rounder 0039; July 1974)

structured things – until we didn't. In time, as we became more of a sizeable label ourselves, competing in the real-world marketplace, we adjusted our contracts and often asked for options. We also adopted some of the bigger labels' accounting methods. We never asked for more than three options, however, and there are several instances where we let an artist go if they had the opportunity to sign with a major label.

The Rounders on the radio

At some point while an undergraduate at Tufts, I read that the college had hosted the first radio station in the country to make regular broadcasts. The station of the Tufts Wireless Club first broadcast a three-hour concert on March 18, 1916 and had begun to broadcast more actively in 1919; and beginning in March 1920, the station with call letters 1XE began to broadcast classical music concerts every Sunday afternoon. When Ken and I were at Tufts, the college had no radio station. In the fall of 1969, I returned to Tufts as a graduate student and was among those who helped get the station that was to become WMFO on the air. For five years, between WTBS (the original MIT radio station, which later sold its call letters to Ted Turner and then became WMBR) and WMFO, I hosted the (largely) old-time music show called *Give the Fiddler a Dram* – although it was pretty eclectic, running from the Holy

Modal Rounders to the Last Poets. The station was set up so the DJ was also the engineer and ran the whole show from a small studio.

At WTBS, my weekly show started after the 9 pm news and ran until I decided to go home, at which point I simply turned off the transmitter and the station went off the air for the night. There was no show following mine. There was no fixed closing time, but few shows ran less than two hours. Around 1 am, I'd start asking for calls, advising the airwaves that if no one called in, maybe no one was out there listening, and I might as well pack it in. It was an odd sensation to wonder, at times, if there might indeed be no one at all listening to the station. It could have been like the proverbial tree falling in Bishop Berkeley's forest; was the station really broadcasting if no one was listening, or was it all an illusion?

Sometime around 1971 or 1972, the station decided to change from a freer-form station to one with a more structured format. On the last show of *Give the Fiddler a Dram*, I expressed dismay that WTBS had decided to "sound like every other station in town" and advised listeners that there were indeed plenty of other options. I started reading from the newspaper TV listings: "For instance, in this time slot next week, you could turn to Channel 7 and catch *The Carol Burnett Show*, followed by *Medical Center* – or tune in to Channel 4 and you can see *McCloud* and *McMillan & Wife*. Over on Channel 38, we have reruns of . . ." Station operatives on the other side of the glass were frantically making gestures to cut the transmission but the programmer/engineer held the power of the microphone and, short of powering down the transmitter, there was nothing they could do but sit through my five-minute rant.

Ken and Marian also did radio for a period of time on WVBR in Ithaca, the Cornell University station. It was a weekly show named *Salt Creek* on Sunday mornings from 6–11 am. Doug Meyer was the GM of the station and Ken and Marian frequently guested with Doug. Sometimes it was for a show they wanted to promote for Ithaca Area Friends. They brought up some of their records and also drew from the station library. Everyone's got their own tastes. Ken and Marian liked the play the harder-core bluegrass, like Red Allen or Joe Val. That was a little different from what Doug tended to play. Doug wasn't sure his audience would connect with the hardcore stuff, but a group like the Country Gentlemen or maybe Bill Harrell would work out fine.

Ithaca Area Friends of Bluegrass and Old-Time Country Music was something Ken and Marian had started and, as the name might suggest, it was modeled after Boston Area Friends of Bluegrass and Old-Time Country Music (a group we were active in, and which had been launched by Nancy Talbott). One morning, Ken had read in the *Cornell Sun* that the following day would be the final one to present applications for university funds for organizations.

I showed it to Marian and suggested we apply for funds to do some concerts along the lines of the BAF. We rushed to get the appropriate paperwork and information on how to fill them out. Marian wrote up most of the application and, after a day of scurrying around, we got our application in as the Ithaca Area Friends of Bluegrass and Old-Time Music. I think it was a few weeks later that we learned that we had been funded. We did a number of concerts that year and, at the end of the year, used the money which was left to buy some albums from Rounder which we donated to the Cornell Music Library which at the time I think only had one bluegrass album, the UA *Earl Taylor & His Stoney Mountain Boys*.

Acts that Ken remembers presenting include Joe Val, Larry Johnson, the Contraband Country Band (which evolved into Country Cooking), and a bluegrass supergroup that included Red Allen, Frank Wakefield, Don Stover, Tex Logan, and Bob Tidwell. It was through Ithaca Area Friends that they also met Ted Osborn, who served as recording engineer on several of the earliest Rounder albums.

After moving to Somerville, Ken and Marian also did a show for a while on WCAS in Cambridge.

Running a mail-order company out of a car

By 1972, we'd begun working with Mark Wilson, a Harvard graduate student. The summer before, in June and July 1971, we'd visited fiddler Blind Alfred Reed's house in Pipestem, West Virginia and taken some photographs. We met his son Arville, who accompanied his father on some of the 78s he cut for Victor in December 1927. Arville and his wife Etta welcomed us and introduced us to Arville's brother Collins and his wife Madline. We interviewed them all at length, and wrote up the Blind Alfred Reed story for the scholarly *John Edwards Memorial Foundation Quarterly* (Volume VII, Part 3, Autumn 1971). The Reeds even had original receipts from Victor dating back to the 1920s, showing how Alfred had been paid $50 per side for the recordings. We photocopied the receipts and included them and some family photographs in the booklet that we inserted into the first album in our "reissue" series. It was named after one of Blind Alfred Reed's most famous songs: *How Can a Poor Man Stand Such Times and Live?* (Rounder 1001, issued in July 1972).[11]

Dave Freeman of County Records let us use records from his collection for the reissue, and Frank Mare provided invaluable assistance. Mark Wilson helped in the final stages of putting the record together, and also helped with our Aunt Molly Jackson album, based on tapes from the Library of Congress. Mark then initiated an ongoing series of reissue albums on which he did most

Cover of *Library of Congress Recordings* by Aunt Molly Jackson (Rounder 1002; August 1972)

of the work: albums featuring Fiddlin' John Carson, Burnett & Rutherford, and Gid Tanner & His Skillet Lickers.

Mark was a graduate student in philosophy at Harvard, and played fiddle and banjo. We first met at the October 25, 1970 Boston Area Friends of Bluegrass and Old-Time Country Music show, where we had set up a table just outside the room: that was the first time and place we had our own brand-new records to sell. Mark, who was in his second year at Harvard, came by our table and started talking about records. He was surprised to see a George Pegram record on sale. He knew of a much older, obscure record featuring Pegram and Red Parham called *Pickin' and Blowin'* – one that he had been after for years. "There was a real vacuum in traditional music then, coming out of the post-Beatles musical shift," he wrote me in an email early in 2009. He went on:

> You said the records had been out for only a few days. I encouraged you to do more stuff like that, but the main solidifying event came when we got together a month or so later and swapped records. That was in your place on the Somerville line, where you mainly lived on popcorn over some nearly dead old lady. Soon thereafter we visited John Coffey and some of the 78 collectors you knew and began talking about doing reissues. There was a Clark Kessinger show later that year in which you guys were involved that was quite memorable. I think that's when I properly met Ken and Marian.

Mark also recalled our abortive attempt to bring George Pegram to Boston, too; I'd forgotten about it until Mark reminded me. "There was supposed to be a George Pegram show that you guys sponsored but he never showed up." Mark was going to put Pegram up at his apartment, had he arrived as intended. A concert at the Ithaca Area Friends of Bluegrass and Old-Time Country Music was planned, and then Pegram would travel to Boston. Ken and Marian sat waiting for him at the Syracuse airport. The flight arrived – quite late – but there was no banjo player from North Carolina aboard. They learned later on that, when George arrived at his first stop, to make the connection for Syracuse, there'd been no one to meet him and he didn't know what to do – so he turned around and flew back home.

That wasn't the only time a concert in Ithaca presented a problem. When Ithaca Area Friends put on the Red Allen/Frank Wakefield concert, Red stayed with Ken and Marian and smoked up a storm. And he said they'd promised him more money than they had – and there was no contract to prove the original offer. Red also ran up some big phone bills making calls on their phone without telling them. It was hard to learn that one of their idols had, as Marian put it, "very big feet of lots of clay."[12]

Mark Wilson edited some of our early albums and eventually learned how to record for himself, dissatisfied with some of the results we were obtaining from studios or other recorders (a relaxed atmosphere is critical to success with traditional performers). He became increasingly active and built up a very impressive body of traditional music recordings, many of which are available under the North American Traditions series on Rounder. Over the years, Mark has produced or been deeply involved in more than seventy-five albums for Rounder, and is the author of – among other works in his field of academic study – *Wandering Significance: An Essay on Conceptual Behavior* (Oxford University Press, 2006).[13] He was also instrumental in sustaining our fledgling mail-order operation the first summer or two that we traveled so extensively. He helped answer the age-old question: How do you run a mail-order company out of a car?

The mail came to our Somerville address, but the three of us were driving around North Carolina. People wanted this record or that, but we had them with us in the VW. Here's how it worked. Mark would open the mail and we'd phone in two or three times a week. He'd read us the name and address of each customer and tell us what records they'd ordered. We'd pull them from our stock in the van and pack them up to bring to the nearest post office. We needed mailing cartons to pack them in, so we'd drop by local radio stations and beg them for the boxes that they'd received from companies which had sent them promotional records. It was another way in which we recycled, and saved money in the process. The display cases we used when we set up shop at festivals were the seventy-five-LP boxes in which records had been shipped in. It would be a rare piece of paper that wasn't used on both sides before it got thrown away.

At festivals, sometimes we would take in a fair amount of money – $1,000 or more, all in cash. Credit cards weren't so common in those days, and we weren't set up to process them until years afterward. Selling records in public at festivals, we worried that we might be a good target for a robbery. Each night, and sometimes during the day if we had a good sales day, we would take the currency we had taken in and slip it into in socks and put them on the floor, usually covered with other clothing. We didn't really expect to have any trouble, but we thought that if somebody did try to break in, they wouldn't think of looking in what appeared to be dirty socks. On Monday, we would drive to the closest bank and have the cash transferred to a check which we would send up to Mark to deposit. We really enjoyed the banking experience and started to make a game out of it, stepping up to the teller's window and taking the bills out of our socks and sometimes out of a cap or our pockets. We were young and it just seemed like fun at the time.

Recording and recording

In the meantime, the trio started up work on a few more records. In the months of March through May of 1971, we recorded Joe Val & the New England Bluegrass Boys (Herb Applin, Bob French, and Bob Tidwell – who showed up without a bass for one session, forcing me to make a fast round-trip drive back to Cambridge so I could borrow one from Joe Diviney).[14]

Ted Osborn, Ken's and Marian's friend from Ithaca, came south in April at the time of the 1971 Union Grove convention and recorded Clark Kessinger with his guitarist Gene Meade in a motel room at the Vance Motor Inn, Statesville – described in the 1968 Union Grove program as "North Carolina's finest and most comfortable" inn. It wasn't. The Rounders – as our trio had already come to be known – conducted an extensive interview with Clark and presented the album in a gatefold jacket. Already, the Rounders had begun to show their dedication to setting the music in its context with the lengthy liner notes that covered all but a few square inches in small type on the back of the Spark Gap Wonder Boys album.

We had only a day to do the recording because Clark was competing at the festival. He took first place at Union Grove that year. We'd wanted to do some more recording, but Clark suffered a stroke in midsummer just before the planned second session. "It was one of the saddest things I've ever seen," Ken lamented. "His mind was there, and his right hand worked, but he couldn't hold down the strings with his left hand. It truly frustrated him." Our recordings were the last Clark Kessinger would ever make. We were well aware that, in some cases, we might be documenting music that otherwise would never be recorded. It gave us impetus, and also a sense of doing important work.

All three Rounder founders had academic backgrounds and we wanted to do far more than provide some entertaining music. We had two goals for our albums: to present it attractively, truly upholding the design and style in a way that treated the music with respect, and to offer informative (and sometimes exhaustive) liner notes. One advantage of the 12" LP format was that it provided a lot of room for notes. An early Rounder album was typically designed with densely packed annotation on the back; when we put out *419 W. Main* in 1972 by Red Cravens & the Bray Brothers (known to us as Rounder 0015), we had so many notes (written by John Hartford) that we used *both* the front and back of the album to carry them! We also began to include booklets inside the albums, *à la* Folkways, which allowed us to print the lyrics, include more photographs, and offer pages and pages of notes.

Front cover of *419 W. Main* by Red Cravens & the Bray Brothers (Rounder 0015; July 1972)

Those notes seemed to tick off at least one person, namely Milton G. Smith of Frewsburg, New York. On December 10, 1972, Mr. Smith wrote a letter to *Bluegrass Unlimited*. He said how much he liked the magazine, in particular the record reviews by "Mr. Sanders and Mr. Spottswood" (Walt Saunders and Dick Spottswood), adding that, since stores in his area did not stock bluegrass recordings, "I must rely on their judgement frequently before ordering from Mr. Freeman's County Sales." He added:

> As I play a recording I enjoy reading the liner notes. To quote Mr. Sanders and Mr. Spottswood the notes on Rounder 0015 were

said to be "absorbing." I sent the record and its "absorbing notes" back to County Sales. Why are these notes "absorbing"? I have a college degree in English, yet I found John Hartford's notes only an imitation of Bob Dylan's imitation of E. E. Cummings' style. "Cuteness" seemed, rather, to be the "order of the day"; there was no punctuation or capitalization, but there was plenty of profanity, which seems to hold esoteric delight for some today.

Most people who love old time and bluegrass music are church goers. The profusion of Gospel records in all fields of country music testifies for this fact. We have all heard profanity from time to time; some of us have used it on occasion. However, few people care to see it used in the wrong context, if it ever had a proper context.

I returned a fine album because its liner notes were offensive to me and my family. Please realize that the majority of your readers deserve to be considered when then taste of such publications is at all questionable.

There seems to be quite a few albums produced today with silly liner notes of pseudo "tramps" picture on the cover. Why?

Bluegrass Unlimited did not print the letter. The only reason we are able to quote from it today is that Mr. Smith sent a copy to us. He added a P.S. to us: "I feel your recordings are well worth their purchase price and it is a pity that I could not keep this one. Personally, I look for your company to become successful if you more carefully blend production enthusiasm with a thorough understanding of your clientele."

When I came across this letter in September 2018, reading it for just the second time in forty-six years, I was immediately prompted to pull out my LP and reread the liner notes. I read them twice, to see if I was missing something. John Hartford did write the notes, in something like a "stream of consciousness" style. Most of it was simply a transcription of a recording he had made of the band members talking about their music. Profanity? The word "bastard" showed up early on, in the fifth paragraph. Two paragraphs later, so did the word "dumbass." The second time I read it through, I noticed "we didn't give a damn" in the tenth paragraph. Near the end of the very lengthy notes, it said "by God" at one point, but not in any evidently profane fashion. Aha! Found something! Near the very end of the notes, I saw the "f-word" (and I don't mean "folk"). I had to hunt for it, but there it was.

Thirteen years later, the PTA and the RIAA (Recording Industry Association of America) combined to agree on a "parental advisory label" to be affixed to recordings that contained what could be described as "explicit lyrics." I'm not sure if it applied to liner notes with words such as these.

On three days in May 1971, Ted Osborn took two AKG mics and his Tandberg 6000X tape recorder and set them up in a quiet room at the student union building at Cornell, and recorded Country Cooking. This was a bluegrass group with as much innovation as you could hope for in a band. Just a listing of the musicians on that first album is like an all-star cast: the two banjos of Tony Trischka and Peter Wernick, with Russ Barenberg, Kenny Kosek, John Miller, and Harry "Tersh" Gilmore (who later changed his name to Lou Martin). Ken had first seen Tony when he was playing with Contraband Country Band, based out of Syracuse, and he was taken with the way the music crossed boundaries. Pete Wernick recalls phoning Ken from his office at Cornell and asking if he'd be interested in putting out a twin banjo record of him and Tony. "He readily said yes, as I expected, and it was so casual it felt like no big deal at the time. But I remember being very excited, thinking it would probably be a very good record and fun to do."[15]

Rounder was rarely in the middle in the early 1970s: we were either recording the more strictly traditional music or the more progressive – not the more middle-of-the-road sound like the Country Gentlemen with their mellower vocal styles. It was an uplifting moment for Country Cooking when they played the Delaware Valley Bluegrass Festival at Brandywine, Delaware and Bill Monroe came up to them and said, "Keep on playing them good notes."

There was one other very early Southern field trip – to Columbia, South Carolina, to record Snuffy Jenkins and Pappy Sherrill. Snuffy is widely credited as the predecessor of Earl Scruggs on the five-string banjo, and Pappy was an excellent fiddler. Once school was out in early June 1971, I drove west to Ithaca and picked up Ken and Marian, and we all drove south. About a half-hour out, Marian realized she had forgotten something. It's good we turned back, because there was a space heater that had been left on (in June?) and the apartment might have burned down. Snuffy and Pappy welcomed us warmly, as did Pat Ahrens, who not only had arranged for us to meet them but put us up at her house.

We had our first paid recording studio session at Music World Recording Studios of West Columbia, engineered by Joel Johnson. Snuffy and Pappy had been playing together for a third of a century, so they were real pros at recording quickly, and it just took parts of two days (June 12 and 13, 1971) to record enough for nearly two albums. Pat recalls, "Snuffy had his trusted 1934 Gibson Mastertone, Pappy his 1811 German fiddle, and Greasy Medlin his 1949 Gibson J-45 guitar." Twin brothers Dick and Buddy Harmon played rhythm guitar and bass. It was an inexpensive project – even with regard to the tape: Johnson used 7 inch reels of Irish Recording Tape, made in Opelika, Alabama rather than the more expensive Scotch brand manufactured by 3M. The resulting album was *33 Years of Pickin' and Pluckin'* (Rounder 0005, released October 1971). The album cover was a great photograph of the two of them playing in front of a massive mound of watermelons. Pat said the photo brought back memories for Pappy of playing the fiddle on the town square to draw customers for his dad to sell the watermelons they'd raised.

After the first session, we went back to Pat's house and she fixed up some dinner and homemade peach ice cream for everyone. Later in the year, on September 13, we came back to Columbia and recorded enough additional material – we wanted to get this good music down before it was too late! – toward a full second album, which was released in March 1976. Pat Ahrens recorded a few tracks to help flesh that one out. One of the tracks was an instrumental with no title, so Snuffy suggested "Home Made Ice Cream."

There was a delay in releasing Clark Kessinger's album because we were unsure whether we had enough usable music; but, because of his stroke, there was no chance of getting any more. In October 1971 – on the first anniversary of our first two releases – the catalog grew to five titles with the release of:

- Rounder 0003: *One Morning in May* by Joe Val & the New England Bluegrass Boys
- Rounder 0005: *33 Years of Pickin' and Pluckin'* by Snuffy Jenkins & Pappy Sherrill
- Rounder 0006: *Country Cooking*

Like *George Pegram*, Rounder 0006 was a self-titled album – and that caused some fun when the poster designer for a bluegrass festival hadn't realized that Country Cooking was the name of one of the groups and designed the poster naming "country cooking" as a major attraction, thinking perhaps of pies and homemade food. This fairly unknown group's name appeared in twice the type size of any other band on the bluegrass festival poster!

In March 1972, we released Rounder 0004: *Old Time Music with Fiddle & Guitar* by Clark Kessinger. A lot of things were happening by then.

We'd been keeping busy. We met Joe Wilson at a festival in Pennsylvania in the spring of 1971 and he told us about Clint Howard and Fred Price, who we knew of from the *Old Time Music at Clarence Ashley's* album on Folkways. (Yes, that Clarence Ashley, he of the CLARENCE ASHLEY IS COMING campaign.) Joe introduced us to Clint and Fred (and their sons Clarence Howard and Kenneth Price), and we visited them in Shouns, Tennessee in mid-August. Later, Joe booked them on a brief tour to play at Izzy Young's Folklore Center in New York, and in Cambridge, where they recorded *The Ballad of Finley Preston* (Rounder 0009). The album came out at the time of our second anniversary, in October 1972. Mark Wilson worked on the preparation of the eight-page booklet which told the story of Finley Preston, hanged on the gallows at Mountain City on November 7, 1905. Joe's design remains perhaps the only album cover that shows a man on the gallows, hood over his head, rope around his neck and the rope being tightened behind his back in preparation for the drop that would break his neck. Preston had killed Lillie Shaw two years earlier, having been paid $100 by a woman who was jealous. Four photographs from the hanging are reproduced in the booklet. Preston's last words were, "Well, folks, I'll meet you over on the other side."

Ted Osborn did the recording and Mark Wilson edited it – the first editing work he did for Rounder. In booking this brief tour, Joe Wilson was perhaps breaking some new ground in bringing traditional music to other communities, and taking the first steps in a career that saw him organize programming for over forty folk festivals. Within a few years, he became the longtime director of the National Council for the Traditional Arts (NCTA) and the National Folk Festival where he served from 1976 to 2004. Joe died in May 2015.[16]

Hangin' out at the Library of Congress

As a trio, we Rounder founders made our first pilgrimage to the Archive of Folk Song at the Library of Congress, on April 7, 1971 – that's the date we first signed in on the guest register that Joe Hickerson always asked visitors to sign. There we got to know Joe, and fiddler, folklorist and educator Alan Jabbour, also meeting folklorist Archie Green on one visit – author and photographer George Mitchell, too, learning about some field recordings of the blues that he'd made in Georgia around 1968. We also started writing to Alan Lomax about releasing albums of his tapes of Texas Gladden and Hobart Smith. The initial album drawn from George Mitchell's tapes was the first in our "blues" series, Rounder 2001: *George Henry Bussey/Jim Bunkley*, released in September 1972. Alan Lomax was busy doing so many things that it was thirty years before the Gladden and Smith albums were released in 2001. In January 1972, we had written to Earl Scruggs about releasing some early bluegrass recordings from masters he held. We're still hoping . . . Earl is gone now, but we'd still love to put together a release.

The first contact with the Archive of Folk Song dates back well before the company was started, a letter I wrote while a sophomore in college on February 17, 1964, asking about taping materials in the collection. I was back in touch again with a long letter on June 1, 1970 inquiring about researching "southern white protest music" at the Library. Rae Korson had retired by this point, and Alan Jabbour taken the position of "Head, Archive of Folk Song." After a couple of letters back and forth, honing in on the recordings of Aunt Molly Jackson, I visited the Archive for the first time on November 23, 1970. Next to my name, I wrote "Rounder Records" on the guest register page, indicating a desire to have the company become known. My letter of October 28 was signed over a custom-made rubber-stamped address:

Rounder Records
727 Somerville Ave.
Somerville, Mass. 02143

In a handwritten note sent to Joe Hickerson on the fourth of the days I spent at the Library, I added a postscript: "Please help spread the word about ROUNDER RECORDS that we might continue to survive." This for a company that was all of thirty-one days old. Continue to survive it has – perhaps in part due to Joe spreading the word.

Arnie Caplin of Biograph Records had visited the Archive three days before I had. Some people took the register a bit less seriously; "Adolf Hitler" signed in during my last day of that first visit, though I have no recollection of anyone goose-stepping around or giving Nazi salutes.

The Archive's register indicates frequent visits early on: all three Rounders dropped in on April 7, June 1, July 1, July 27, and Ken and me on August 28 in 1971. Visits by one, two, or all three Rounders in 1972 included June 5, July 3, July 6, August 1, August 4, and September 13. There were six visits again in 1973. This was indeed a frequent haunt.

Listed on the register pages at the time all three Rounders turned up in April 1971 were a number of people with whom we would work in the years to come: Gene Rosenthal of Adelphi Records, Ron Stanford, Chuck Perdue, and Rayna Green. In June, we met Archie Green and both Susan and Marc Pevar. Michael Cooney, Larry Hanks, Jon Wilcox, and Faith Petric were all there a couple of days before the July 1 visit. Duncan Emrich and Rich Nevins turned up, too.

The Library came to feel like home, and Washington was a very convenient stopping-off place for trips further south, or west into Tennessee. We had a number of homes away from home. Several times Ken and Marian slept on the floor of Ola Belle Reed's house in Rising Sun, Maryland. We never slept over in the Archive, but in Washington we variously stayed with Alan Jabbour, Ralph Rinzler, Dick Spottswood, and Frank Proschan. Over time, Ken developed a relationship with Hazel Dickens and would stay with Hazel on his numerous trips south.

We also helped bring a little to the Library as well. While on a field trip to fiddler J.P. Fraley's home with Gus Meade, Mark Wilson came across some home recordings of Ed Haley, a blind fiddler who spent his final years in Ashland, Kentucky. Haley had made his living as a musician, playing on street corners and at different events, but never recorded commercially. He'd died in 1951 but some home recordings had been made on a Wilcox-Gay disc-cutting machine and preserved by his son Lawrence. Mark was greatly impressed with Haley's virtuosity. A dialogue developed and Rounder helped bring Lawrence Haley to Washington where the home discs were transferred and added to the collection of the Archive of Folk Song. Mark produced an Ed Haley album for Rounder, titled *Parkersburg Landing* (Rounder 1010). Later, John Hartford took a special interest in Haley's story and wrote a biography about him, which also inspired the release of two double CDs of Ed Haley's music in 1997: *Forked Deer* (Rounder 1131/1132) and *Grey Eagle* (Rounder 1133/1134).

One of the more interesting documents the Library had published was the *Check-List of Recorded Songs in the English Language in the Archive of American Folk Song to July 1940*, which the Rounders and many others consulted to learn what was in the Archive. I also spent time going through the card catalog. While researching the recordings of Aunt Molly Jackson and others, I found a number of cards marked with a Δ symbol (a delta). I was told this was a mark placed on songs that had been excluded from the *Check-List*, typically because they were deemed either too salacious or too political. Now this was interesting! I worked with Deborah Deems and compiled a complete list of what were, in effect, songs "censored" by the Library of Congress. I thought about calling it *Dirty Songs from the Library of Congress*, but the title of the resulting June 13, 1977 publication was a bit less sensational: *Supplementary Listing of Recorded Songs in the English Language in the Library of Congress Archive of Folk Song Through Recording No. 4332 (October 1940)*.

Over the years, Rounder helped distribute the record albums released by the Archive itself, and we also licensed a number of albums from the Library's holdings, including multi-album sets by Woody Guthrie, Lead Belly, and Jelly Roll Morton. The Morton recordings took a long time to release. There were a lot of "delta" songs in Jelly Roll's body of work – in particular, his seven-part rendition of 'The Murder Ballad' in which he gave voice to violent misogyny. The lyrics are as vile as any, and the Archive worried what would happen if we released the complete Jelly Roll Morton recordings. Would some grandstanding congressman, promoting himself as the guardian of family values, seize on the release as objectionable and shut off funding for the Archive? It was many years before the Archive became the American Folklife Center and received permanent funding, rather than being subject to annual or biannual review. It was only in 1994 that Rounder released four compact discs embracing Jelly Roll's Library of Congress recordings. The release did result in one of the most hilarious letters we ever received.

How Jelly Roll Morton made Mrs. Cookie Cottrell a Methodist

Imagine our surprise when this letter dated October 25, 1995 arrived from Mrs. Cookie Cottrell of Hastings-on-Hudson, New York. I still don't know if it was real or a clever joke. Here's how the letter read:

> Dear Sirs,
>
> May I first warn you that this letter contains some extremely obscene words. I will replace the vowels with an asterisk – but please understand these are not my words – they're *yours*.
>
> I recently bought (from the Coop at Harvard Square) a copy of Jean Redpath singing the songs of Robert Burns on your label.

It was a brand new cassette – I broke the plastic seal myself. Apparently a mistake happened at your factory – when the tape is played instead of Jean Redpath's sweet voice you get the deep voice of some Blues singer, and the words he sings are very obscene. In other words the box and the cassette are both labled [sic] "The Songs of Robert Burns" but that is *not* what music is inside.

The awful thing is that this tape was used as part of the "Cultural Heritage Day" at our Episcopal church. You see, the children of each family were supposed to bring forward some baked goods to the front of the church as music from their culture was played – and then all the little children would line up at the front.

Well, my two little granddaughters, wearing kilts, proceeded down the aisle carrying trays of home baked Scottish shortbread cookies. The cassette that I bought was placed in the tape player, and as these girls proceeded to the front of the church instead of Robert Burns' 'There Grows a Bonnie Brier Bush,' this is what they, and the whole congregation, and God heard: "If I catch you f*cking that b*itch again I'll cut your f*cking throat, and drink your f*cking blood, if I catch . . ." etc.

The kid who was running the tape up in the balcony didn't have the brains to turn the thing off, and the door that led to the balcony was either stuck or bolted. It went on and on. I shouted up to them to turn it off, and finally they did.

I will enclose a copy of the cassette label and (at the risk of sending obscene materials through the mail) a recorded-copy of part of the offending song – but I will not return to you the original copy of the cassette, because nobody seems to believe or want to believe that this was not some kind of cruel joke on my part, and it's my only proof. I hope you will appreciate the full horror of this situation.

All I ask of you is would you please send me a copy of the *Songs of Robert Burns* (any volume) – which I paid for, but did not receive, and tell me if you know who the Blues singer is. And of course let me know if you have any ideas about what I should do or say if and when I decide to show my face again at the church.

Yours truly, Mrs. Cookie Cottrell.

The letter had some handwriting on it which looked very much like that of one of our employees, but I never directly raised the question with him. I did, in fact, write back a lengthy letter to Mrs. Cottrell (attempts to reach her again in 2009 were fruitless and the only Cookie Cottrell on the internet was not her).

I wrote back explaining our guess that somehow Philo 1093: *Songs of Robert Burns, Vol. 5* might have been confused by the tape manufacturer with Rounder 1093 which was a Jelly Roll Morton album that did contain lyrics of the sort quoted. "We have rather few albums with lyrics such as that," I explained. "Once heard, the lyrics remain rather unforgettable. I am sure you wish they were more forgettable."

I said that Morton was considered one of the great treasures of indigenous American culture and that we had released the album under the auspices of the Library of Congress of the United States. Further, it was always a good idea to pre-audition tapes – and this would be true even for Jean Redpath tapes. "Many of Burns' songs were of a bawdy nature, and Jean renders them with lusty performances," I said, pointing out that, had she purchased Philo 1114, the boys in the booth might have inadvertently played Jean's rendition of Burns' 'The Fornicator.' I added, "There are quite a few other Burns songs which might also lead to uneasiness in public settings, particularly in places of worship" and then offered to replace the cassette as well as suggesting she could show my letter to the congregation as evidence of what occurred.

Mrs. Cottrell replied with thanks for my "considerate letter" and said "this whole debacle has turned out to have a silver living." She said that she had learned that Episcopalians were snobs and she was welcomed across the street at the Methodist church.

Surprisingly, we never took any flak for the Jelly Roll Morton recordings. There was a moment, though, when Richard Harrington wrote a story with a BIG headline in the May 4, 1994 *Washington Post*. The headline, which may have caused a heartbeat or two to skip a beat inside the Beltway: "Dirty Doings at the Library of Congress." This was just what the Folklife Center people had feared, but we never heard a negative murmur, and they never told us of any feedback.

"You never know who you're gonna meet at the Library of Congress." The old saying held true for us in August when, as mentioned, we met Marc and Susan Pevar. It was just a chance meeting, but they both left for the Gambia that November and while there they studied with a master musician of the kora, Bai Konte. In early 2009, Marc recalled our first meeting:

> You were sitting at a wooden table, absorbed in listening to old records. Joe [Hickerson] arranged to ship me reels of tape, direct to Gambia via diplomatic pouch. After making a demo tape, I sent it to a friend, who made copies, sending one to Moe Asch of Folkways Records (who immediately wanted to release it).

After the Pevars returned from Africa in December 1972, Marc drove into New York to meet with Moe, who offered him a contract but only with a single-color cover. Marc was planning to bring Bai to the United States on tour, and wanted something more. He offered a recollection:

I felt that a full color cover was essential for marketing. Remembering you guys from the L of C, I contacted you and then drove to Boston to visit with you in at your first offices in a lovely old house, its walls filled with shelves overflowing with records. You agreed to a full-color cover, and that made the difference to me. I recall that you personally came up with the distinctive font for the album cover based on some text you located, and also that you had to use what was then a state-of-the-art notch filter to smooth out some of the amplitude in the bass for one selection.

We had no expertise in Gambian kora music. (In fact, we'd never heard of it before we met Marc.) The kora is a twenty-one-stringed harp; Marc wrote in the liner notes that Bai's solo performances established him as a virtuoso of this instrument, "ranking with Segovia, Clapton, and Shankar in his technical control and interpretive inventiveness." Marc was clearly sincere and he had slides that showed Bai and he talked a good, earnest game. In fact, the acclamation Bai Konte received showed that Marc was spot on. But we really had no way of knowing at first. Someone could have hoodwinked us into releasing something substandard, though perhaps some of that was paranoia reflecting one of our own mischievous thoughts. The releases of ethnic music on Folkways had always seemed uneven to us; in fact, some of them came across as musically dreadful. We figured Moe Asch similarly trusted in the good faith of the people who offered him recordings to release, but we couldn't help but muse about the idea of playing a trick on him by recording a number of us grunting and making percussive sounds, then writing some very scholarly-seeming notes about this remote tribe deep in the midst of South America or Africa – and seeing if he'd release it on Folkways. If it happened, we'd be distributing it. One other temptation: as often as not, customers we encountered in person at festivals called County Records "Country Records." So we naturally thought that it would be fun to print up a "counterfeit" Country Records release, looking in every way like a County LP except for it having an extra "r" in the logo. These were just musings; we were busy enough doing our own things. Looking back from nearly fifty years later, it's with a bit of wistful regret that we never did these couple of things.

As a matter of fact, as I learned years later, Moe Asch apparently did it himself once upon a time,. Richard Carlin mentions it in his book about Folkways.

> In early 1951, Asch was approached by Dr. Henry Tschopik, then assistant curator of anthropology at the American Museum of Natural History, to create an "audio backdrop" for an exhibit of artifact ... Asch lived in Brooklyn and had neither the time nor the budget to travel to the Amazon to record the real sounds.[17]

So he improvised, as Murray Schumach reported in the *New York Times*:

> The jungle rain [on the recording] came about in an interesting fashion, Originally, these jungle sounds were recorded by an expedition in Africa. However, the rain did not sound sufficiently realistic. So before the disk was put out by Folkways, some experiments were conducted to find more soothing rain. In charge of this project was Moe Asch . . . First he turned on the shower in his home and directed it against the curtain. Sounded too much like a machine gun engagement. He finally settled for the shower spray against towels. The drop of water from towel to rub was the finished product.[18]

So the sounds for the Amazonian exhibit was apparently comprised of recorded sounds from Africa and from Moe's bathroom in Brooklyn.

Back to Bai. The resulting album, *Alhaji Bai Konte* (Rounder 5001) was released in June 1973, the first album in what we styled our "international series." Bai toured the U.S. more than once and the record proved to be a good seller. Just six months later, we released an album that came from Mike Melford, *A Night in Jost Van Dyke* (Rounder 5002), a field recording from the Caribbean island not far from Tortola. Mike was a mandolin and guitar player, and a friend of Bruce Kaplan's who was listed as executive producer on the first Rounder albums by Tut Taylor, Norman Blake, and Brother Oswald.

Cover of *Alhaji Bai Konte* (Rounder 5001; June 1973)

He lives in Cambridge and works as an attorney, with a specialty in music law. It was Bruce who funded the records.

Years later (see below), Mason Daring and I visited Jost Van Dyke while doing some ambient environmental recordings on another island nearby which was devoid of human population. It was for a series on Daring Records billed as *In the Absence of Man*. Rounder's international series, over the years, grew to over 150 titles. It could have been much larger but, when the "world music" boom began, we kind of backed away and let others go to the forefront. That might have been a mistake from a business standpoint, but we had the sense that a lot of the world music enthusiasts, from England in particular, were able to invest far more time and work with more focus in that pursuit. Better that we concentrated on areas where we felt more confident.

In November 1971, a recording engineer forever known to history as "Snakeskin" recorded *Frank Wakefield* (Rounder 0007) (with Country Cooking as Frank's band). Nondie Leonard contributed vocals on three tracks. Those were the first tapes we recorded that used 10 inch reels, but it didn't keep us from recording many more albums on 7 inch reels. (Later, we worked with another producer – "Sundance" – on a number of Nashville recordings. These were years when the counterculture was very much active.)

That was the second attempt to cut with Frank. Before the first scheduled session, Ken and Marian had hitch-hiked to Saratoga Springs, where Frank was living. They all met at the Caffe Lena. Frank said he was leaving for a brief spell, and never came back. Neither Ken nor Marian had a car, and they didn't know exactly where Frank lived.

Even the second session with Frank wasn't that smooth. Pete Wernick remembers: "He was too drunk to practice the first night, and went out and got all messed up, and slept it off and we got the whole record recorded Saturday night and Sunday day, and he did perfectly. We were all so impressed." Rounder 0007 was released the following summer, in June 1972.

Over Thanksgiving weekend, Ted Osborn recorded the Ledford String Band in Bakersville, North Carolina. The band was Steve Ledford, Wayne Ledford, and James Gardner. Some details are lost to history: none of the Rounders can remember where we stayed while there. Marian thinks it was up the road apiece. Chances are it was indeed in the VW bus, parked far enough from Steve's house that we wouldn't cause him any embarrassment.

Other sessions occurred in November and December of 1971, though none of the Rounders was present. Bill Hicks, fiddler with an old-time music group from the Durham/Chapel Hill area, approached us about releasing an album of their music. The resulting Fuzzy Mountain String Band album featured a group of musicians who, like Country Cooking, would all go on to careers in music and folklore: Malcolm Owen and Vickie Owen, Blanton Owen, Eric Olson, Bobbie Thompson, and Bill Hicks. A second album was recorded in August 1972 at WDBS in Durham; Tom Carter and Sharon Poss (now Sandomirsky) had joined the band. Barry Poss, Sharon's husband, later

Cover of *The Fuzzy Mountain String Band* (Rounder 0010; May 1972)

went on to start the very successful Sugar Hill Records label: a label which in turn became part of the Rounder Group in the spring of 2015.

Expanding to include Bruce Kaplan

In August 1971, we'd set up our record stand in Virginia during the Old Fiddlers Convention at Galax, put on each year by the Galax Moose Lodge #733. We had our VW bus parked there and the cartons of records out on display along the side, doing business. An old friend of mine came by, Bruce Kaplan, whom I've already mentioned in passing. We had known each other at the University of Chicago where Bruce was one of the leaders of the Folklore Society which had put on a good number of concerts on campus and a folk festival during the winters. Now I was making folk music records and Bruce said he'd been thinking of starting up his own record company.

We started talking, and we asked Bruce who he was thinking of recording. He mentioned one artist, and we said, "Oh, we were thinking of recording him, too." He then mentioned E.C. Ball, and we replied that we'd been thinking of recording him as well. Bruce ran through about five names before it began to sound like we were just claiming to have been interested in everyone he brought up. To verify that we weren't just pulling his leg, or trying to discourage him from competing with us, I pulled out a Manila file

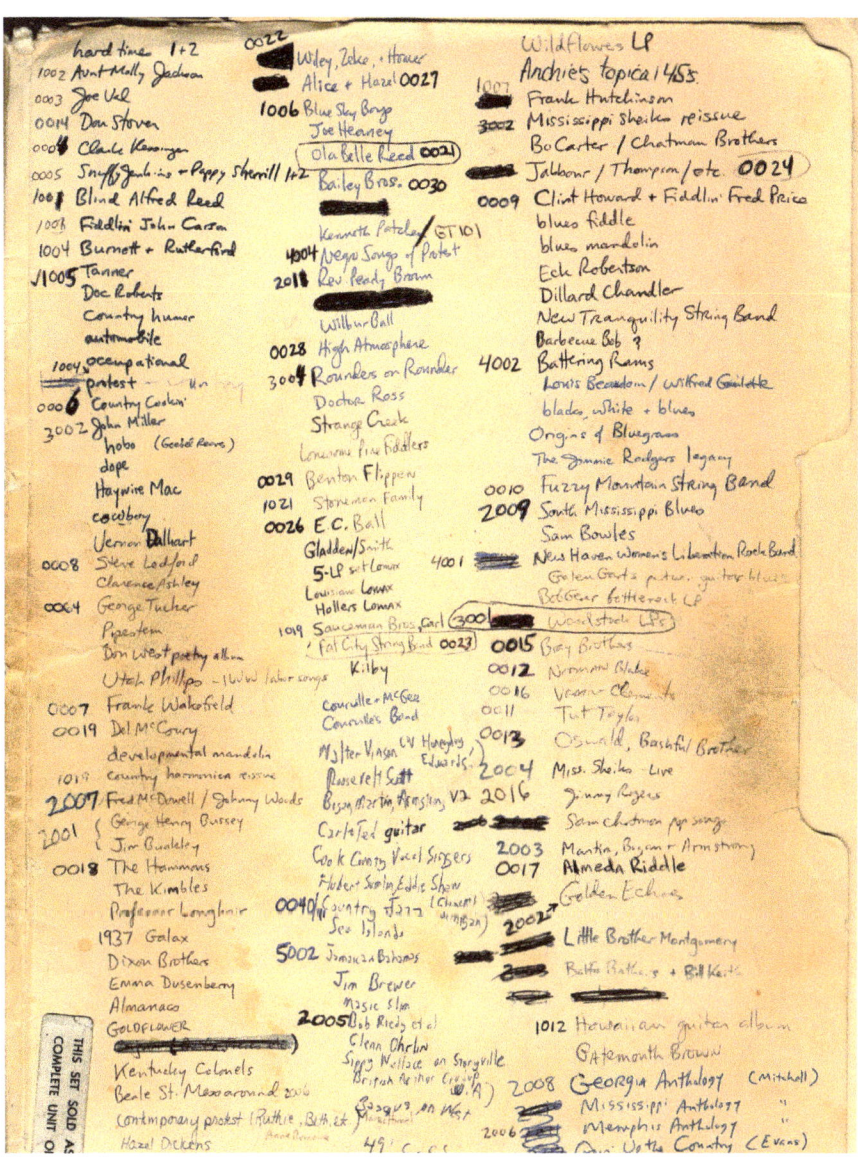

"Future Albums": the handwritten list

folder from inside the bus. It was marked "Future Albums" and right on the outside of the folder we had a list of sixty-seven ideas, which included every one that Bruce had named and many more that he would have gotten to had he kept on calling out names.

It only took a moment before we started talking about combining efforts and working as one company. Good, let's do it. And so we did it – again, without anything formal. Did we even shake hands on it? Nope. But it started happening.

Bruce was primed and ready to move. He funded one burst of recording during December 1971 and January 1972, arranging sessions that resulted in these releases in May and June 1972:

- Rounder 0011: *Friar Tut* by Tut Taylor
- Rounder 0012: *Home in Sulphur Springs* by Norman Blake
- Rounder 0013: *Brother Oswald*

John Hartford (left) and Norman Blake

Early in 1972, Bruce recorded *Heaven On My Mind* by the Golden Echoes (Rounder 2002), *The Barnyard Dance* by Martin, Bogan & Armstrong (Rounder 2003), *The New Mississippi Sheiks* (Rounder 2004), and the Bob Riedy album noted earlier for its lengthy title (Rounder 2005). And Bruce set things in motion to record Vassar Clements' *Crossing the Catskills* with David Bromberg and Mike Melford (Rounder 0016). It was Bruce's connection with John Hartford that resulted in the Bray Brothers album with the purportedly profane liner notes (Rounder 0015), as well as Hartford band members Clements, Taylor, and Blake.

Bruce brought a whole different approach to Rounder. His father Sam had been president and general manager of Zenith Radio Corporation, which also was a big television manufacturer in the late 1950s and 1960s.[19] Bruce may have inherited some entrepreneurial genes that the three of us were lacking at first. He took a different tack than ours. Where our goal was mostly just to release music that we liked, or were convinced was "important" in one way or another, Bruce paid more attention to the sales potential of the projects he undertook. We'd just put out a record and go on to the next. Yes, we sold at festivals and worked hard at that. We printed up our mail-order lists and worked with our distributors, and we shipped records to retail. We worked around the clock – but we didn't really take a strategic view of the records or think about them based on their sales potential.

Bruce looked around and saw a lot of great music begging to be recorded, just as we did, but he also thought about the fan base an artist or group might develop, he took into account whether the group was an active touring group (we were almost more inclined to record people who never performed in public, in order to document their creative work before it disappeared).

Bruce was putting his own money in, perhaps from another form of inheritance, and was considered a full 25% of the "collective" although there had never been any discussion of profit sharing or ultimate disposition of these "assets" we were creating. None of the four of us was drawing any salary at the time. We were putting money in, making the records, and simply not thinking about this as a business that might build in value. These were hippie days. The discussion about who contributed how much and how we might share any proceeds just never happened. We were thinking we had to get all this music down on tape, and we were enjoying the process. We were living in the moment, though producing an enduring legacy.

We were well aware that some of the music we were trying to preserve could indeed be lost forever. Ken recounts one illustrative experience:

> Among the labels that Rounder distributed in the 1970s was Melody, a subsidiary of Pine Tree Records out of Hamilton, Ohio. We picked up the label because of their bluegrass recordings which included several fine albums by Larry Sparks among others. Melody had several fine gospel recordings by a group called the Little Country

Trio which featured the very soulful and very traditional singing of Norma Jeffers. Jessie Hutson sang tenor and played guitar and occasionally mandolin, and Norma's husband, Loman, sang bass and played acoustic guitar. I loved their hard emotional singing as did Hazel Dickens. On a trip out that way, we decided to visit the Jeffers and had a lovely visit.

I had contacted the widow of Pine Tree/Melody's owner on hearing that he had passed away and told her that I planned to come out that way and would like to hear about the Little Country Trio's recordings. A couple of months later, I called her again when I got to Ohio. She remembered my call but told me that it had slipped her mind and she had brought the tapes to the dump just a few days before! After finding out where the dump was, Hazel and I drove out there hoping that it hadn't rained and that we might be able to find the tapes. We found the dump, but apparently they had turned the earth over. We didn't have a shovel and had to leave frustrated.

For Bruce it was hard to feel part of a living and working collective since he was in Chicago while the three of us were all living in the same place in Somerville. Indeed, Bruce's widow Sandra Shifrin said in late 2018, "He realized he hated sharing everything."[20] It's not that Bruce was conventional. Far from it. When they started seeing each other, Flying Fish was run out of a house on Halsted. "Bruce had the attic made into a bedroom, but you had to go up these pull-down stairs to get up there," explained Sandra. "He had windows put in, because he liked light and he liked to see the trees. I never lived at Fish, but I started staying overnight. The Fish staff knew, because Bruce had to use the one bathroom in the house that there was. When they started seeing contact lens solution and another toothbrush . . ." When they got married, rather than exchange rings, they came up with some poptops of the sort one finds on soft drink cans. And Bruce asked her, "Do you want to change your name?" "I said, 'What do you mean? I am Sandra Shifrin. I will always be Sandra Shifrin.' He said, 'That's not what I mean. We could both change our names. We both like chocolate. Do you want to be Chocolate? Any name you choose, I will go along with and change my name, too.'" After they got married, they found an apartment to rent, on the same block on West Schubert, so Bruce could walk to work and Sandra could be close to the El and continue her career as a social worker.

At this point we were still in the second-floor Somerville apartment in Park Street, often telephoning Bruce. But having a few conversations on the phone each week and living and working together were two different things. And this contrasted with Skip Ferguson, who pitched in, worked hard, and also lived at 65 Park Street. Four of us were a tight little community working day and night, and then there was Bruce, a thousand miles away, doing his own thing but no doubt feeling left out of so much of the dynamics. It was probably inevitable that Bruce eventually would feel it more natural to run his own company.

That day came. But, before it did, Rounder was beginning to blossom. Two releases in 1970, three releases in October 1971, and this is what happened in 1972:

March
- Rounder 0004: *Old Time Music with Fiddle & Guitar* by Clark Kessinger

May
- Rounder 0010: *The Fuzzy Mountain String Band*
- Rounder 0011: *Friar Tut* by Tut Taylor
- Rounder 3001: *Mud Acres: Music Among Friends*

June
- Rounder 0007: *Frank Wakefield*
- Rounder 0012: *Home in Sulphur Springs* by Norman Blake
- Rounder 0013: *Brother Oswald* by Bashful Brother Oswald
- Rounder 2003: *The Barnyard Dance* by Martin, Bogan & Armstrong
- Rounder 2004: *The New Mississippi Sheiks*

July
- Rounder 0015: *419 W. Main* – Red Cravens & the Bray Brothers
- Rounder 1001: *How Can a Poor Man Stand Such Times and Live?* by Blind Alfred Reed
- Rounder 2002: *Heaven On My Mind* by the Golden Echoes

August
- Rounder 0014: *Things in Life* by Don Stover
- Rounder 0017: *Ballads and Hymns from the Ozarks* by Almeda Riddle
- Rounder 1002: *Library of Congress Recordings* by Aunt Molly Jackson

September
- Rounder 2001: *George Henry Bussey/Jim Bunkley*

October
- Rounder 0009: *The Ballad of Finley Preston* by Clint Howard & Fred Price
- Rounder 2008: *Georgia Blues*

November
- Rounder 0008: *The Ledford String Band*

From two records, to three, to nineteen releases in our third year. The number increased to twenty-one in 1973, and tended to increase thereafter. By April 1974, we had earned our first story in the *Boston Globe*: "Rounder Records: Hitless Wonders of Rural Music."[21] We had fifty-one records at the time. We were distributing about a hundred small labels.

The pace picked up. In just one month, July 1974, we gave birth to eight albums – that's the way we thought about albums at the time: the offspring none of us had. Putting out that many records all at once wasn't too smart. There was no real plan: we just put them out as soon as we could get them ready. If we had stopped to think about it, we would have realized that there are only so many records that even the most passionate fan could afford to buy in a given month. Or that stores would want to take in. We could have spaced them out more intelligently; we put out no records in June and none at all in August, September, or October. But we wanted the records to sell on the road during festival time. That was an important source of income. Other than that, we weren't thinking in terms of strategic business planning.

The number of releases each year continued to increase. In 1983, Rounder released sixty albums: that was the first year we put out more than an album a week, on average. In 1988, it was eighty. It was only in the early 1990s – when the company was entering its twenties – that we started thinking about systematically scheduling releases, about what month to put out a given record, and not too many of the same kind in any given month. In later years, we were often accused of "flooding the market" but when we came across music we loved, what could we do? *Not* put out a record of it?

One approach we eventually took was to release records under other label names. It was still us, but if the record came out on Varrick Records (as the first Nighthawks record did in January 1983), maybe it didn't really look the same to some.

That year – 1983 – was the year we changed the address on the back of the records. It had been 186 Willow Avenue. We rented a warehouse with an office at two locations (96 Winchester Street, Medford, and 28 Thorndike Street, Cambridge) but never put either address on album jackets. We only changed addresses once we owned our next headquarters. In May 1983, we had some albums (for instance, 0168) come out with the 186 Willow address and some (for instance, 0171) come out with One Camp Street. That's the month the transition occurred. Fascinating esoterica. Hey – someone asked me while I was working on this book, so I put it in.

4 Helping Organize the Indie Side of the Record Business

Helping to fuel all this recording work was not just revenue from mail-order sales but also revenue from the sales of records from other labels to retail stores. The distribution business grew. Sometimes it generated more revenue than the label itself, while other times the label sales seemed to carry the distribution. As we added more labels, we became a small but reliable regional distributor. Because of our many forays into the southeast, we actually had accounts up and down the eastern part of the country. And sometimes retailers just found us and got in touch, maybe by word of mouth.

There were distributors in other parts of the country, and Riverboat was still around, too. We talked to a few of the other regional distributors starting very early on, and drove out to Chicago in early February 1972 for a meeting to discuss common concerns.

Representatives from six independent distributors met on February 3 at the Hotel Windermere on the South Side, more or less down the street from where I had gone to the University of Chicago. It was a full car heading west from Somerville with Ken, Marian, and me from Rounder joined by Steve Frappier and Ralph Dopmeyer of Cambridge's Riverboat Enterprises. The others attending were Gene Rosenthal from Adelphi (Washington DC area), Dennis Bursch from Aden (Minneapolis), Gary and Holly Seibert from Orwaka (Denver, but covering the northwest as well), and Ray Flerlage from Kinnara (Chicago).

Looking back on that time from fifty years after the fact, it's hard to believe we were so precocious so early in our history. We only had five records out on our own label, and no more than five or six very small labels that we were distributing – but here we were, with representatives of five other indie distributors, founding a trade organization: the National Association of Independent Record Distributors (NAIRD). The organization lasted until 1997, when it changed its name to the Association for Independent Music. It disbanded in 2004, and its place in the field has been taken by the still-active American Association of Independent Music (known as A2IM).

There was controversy right from the start, with two record labels seeking to join the discussions. Delmark's Bob Koester and Bruce Iglauer, who worked at Delmark at the time but was just beginning his own label, Alligator. Both were based in Chicago and they came by the hotel but were barred from entry to the meeting room. The idea was that the organization was for distributors and not for labels. Bruce and Bob argued that the three Rounders were from a label, and – whether they knew it or not – Ralph Dopmeyer had Titanic Records. We argued back that we were wearing our distributor hat, not our label hat. They were aggressive and tried to physically force their way into the room. That didn't work, but, in the end, the organization embraced both distributors and labels, and Bruce became one of the leading figures in NAIRD, which was still known by the abbreviation but it was now the National Association of Independent Record Distributors and Manufacturers. There was a follow-up meeting in September in Minneapolis, when it formally organized, and another meeting in Memphis in February 1973, which forty-two different companies attended.

At its peak, NAIRD represented several hundred labels and distributors and was a vital organization, with its own presence at international shows such as MIDEM (Marché International du Disque et de l'Édition Musicale – the "Cannes record festival"). All because the Rounders, Riverboat, and the four other similarly embryonic enterprises found the desire to meet and launch a trade organization. We all saw our work as separate from, and in some opposition to, the major record labels that dominated the day.

People from Rounder have been involved in the founding of other organizations over the years, from Folk Alliance to the Americana Music Association and IBMA, the International Bluegrass Music Association.

1972: our first national press and a *lot* more records

We got our first national press attention late in the year. An article by John Cohen appeared in the November/December 1972 issue of *Sing Out!* titled "Come All You Rounders, If You Want to Hear . . ." and it made much of the collective which had, we proclaimed, "No bosses, no division of labor really, everyone works on all aspects of work in order to prevent hierarchy or specialization." Further, we said we were trying to build in Rounder "a functioning example of the way work might be organized by the workers acting collectively in a post-capitalist society."

It also showed the only known photograph of the collective at its largest, showing the three Rounder founders with Bruce Kaplan looming large on the right and Skip Ferguson lying down across the bottom on the floor. John wished us well in the article, and expressed his hope that "they don't get bogged down in the pitfalls of the star system, the success syndrome, the competitive scene, the power scene, the anti-social scene, and other characteristics of business life in America which are too fierce to mention." Over the years, of course, we became acquainted with many of those scenes and we inevitably adapted to many of the realities of working in the world around us. Competition was there, whether we wanted it or not, and as we began to have a modicum of success it inevitably pressed in and asserted its claims. Perhaps we were young and a little naive, but the fervor with which we approached things gave us extra motivation and additional energy.

In the meantime, we were not just releasing albums in 1972 but cutting new ones as well, though some ideas from the "Future Albums" folder never made it: Doc Roberts, the Kimbles, Goldflower, French Carpenter, Joe Heaney, Wilbur Ball. We'd contemplated a few concept albums too: for example, an album on the theme of the automobile as reflected in the early country music recordings of the 1920s and 1930s. Of the first forty artists listed by name on the folder, however, we ultimately recorded albums by thirty of them; five of those missing ten were ideas for reissues in any case. So that wasn't bad: we recorded thirty of the thirty-five artists we'd set our sights on.

Other activity in 1972, included, in August, recording Del McCoury & the Dixie Pals at Dick Drevo's Urban Recordings in Bethesda. And, that same month, Drevo recorded Ted Lundy & the Southern Mountain Boys, with Bob Paisley. In September, Dick Drevo made field recordings of Wiley, Zeke & Homer on location at Black Mountain, North Carolina. Dick also recorded

Cover of *Hazel & Alice* (Rounder 0027; November 1973)

much of our first album by E.C. & Orna Ball at Grassy Creek, North Carolina on the same recording trip, with Bruce Kaplan also recording several of the numbers.

In October, said Drevo began work recording Hazel Dickens and Alice Gerrard for a record (*Hazel & Alice*, Rounder 0027) that has ever since its release been considered a pioneering work by women in bluegrass and old-time music. Lamar Grier, Tracy Schwarz, and Mike Seeger provided backup. The recording was completed in January 1973, and the record released in November.

Also that autumn, *Ola Belle Reed* was recorded by Gei Zantzinger in Devault, Pennsylvania. That became Rounder 0021.

Rounder's first forays into Louisiana

In late December 1972 and early January 1973, before teaching resumed, I drove down to Louisiana. We first met Ralph Rinzler, the head of the Smithsonian Festival of American Folklife, in the summer of '71, and Ralph played us some of the Cajun music tapes he'd made on field trips in the middle 1960s, recording under the auspices of the Newport Folk Foundation. The idea of releasing a couple of albums drawn from Ralph's field recordings was put forward and I spent two days in August 1972 visiting Ralph at his home on Naushon Island, off the coast of Massachusetts. The visit alone was another kind of field trip. The island is seven miles long, privately owned by the Forbes family of Massachusetts. Ralph's wife Kate was part of the Forbes family (as was John Forbes Kerry, later a United States Senator, candidate for President, and Secretary of State). When I arrived at the dock, it was just a moment later that a horse-drawn carriage arrived to pick me up, driven by Ralph. No motor vehicles were allowed on the island, he explained, and we went for a nice ride around the area before heading to the house, where we listened to all of Ralph's tapes and made selections, compiling a list of tracks and the musicians who recorded them.

Armed with his notes about all the music and performers, I arranged to visit Cajun country later that year and stayed at the home of Dewey Balfa and his family in Basile. I'd taken French in high school and college, and knew a little. That helped. But I was really surprised when I first arrived. I thought "STOP" signs would read "ARRÊTEZ" and thought I'd see French wording on storefronts – all over the place. I hadn't realized that it was a spoken and not a written language in Louisiana at the time. I was astonished, and a bit disheartened, to see Dewey and Hilda's daughters watching *Captain Kangaroo*, in English, on television. It was clear that the culture and even the language were threatened by the dominant culture pressing in. Dewey, a true and heartfelt keeper of the flame if there ever was one, was well aware that the culture of his childhood could be lost in the coming generation: there was almost no French-language broadcasting on TV, he informed me. It was a very enjoyable visit, and I was able to secure releases from all the musicians and photograph them for the booklet to go with the albums.[22]

It seemed to take forever for Ralph to write the liner notes for the two albums. Like Alan Lomax, he was incredibly busy doing truly important work. And it did take a few years. It was only with Rounder pushing to get the albums out in time for the 1976 Bicentennial – when the Festival of American Folklife was set up on the Mall all summer long – that Ralph was sufficiently prodded into producing the notes. The first album came out that July; the second volume followed in December.

(Let us note parenthetically that no record company would ever release an album in December these days: it just doesn't follow modern marketing logic about orchestrated timings of releases. But from 1975 through 1989, Rounder released one or more albums every December, with as many as seven in 1981 and five in 1984. We just put records out as quickly as we could. In the 1990s, when we began to schedule releases in a conscious, market-driven fashion, we tended to avoid the last quarter when so many of the majors were active with their releases. Our favored month was January: few majors were putting records out and radio was more open [and most colleges were back in session] and late August/early September, before the onslaught of major label releases and when colleges were starting up once more.)

The first Cajun music album that Rounder released preceded the Rinzler ones by two full years. It was one that Ken recorded with Dick Spottswood in October 1973, an album by D.L. Menard & the Louisiana Aces. Mine had been a research trip, but Ken's was our first recording visit to the area. Cajun music became a big deal, growing in popularity in the 1980s and booming in the wake of the 1987 movie *The Big Easy*. At the time Rounder began, the music was relatively unknown outside its home region, other than to those who saw a group like the Balfa Brothers play the Newport Folk Festival. In 1965 the generically billed "Cajun band" played the Thursday evening concert, along with Joan Baez, Reverend Gary Davis, Son House, the Lilly Brothers with Tex Logan, the New Lost City Ramblers, and others. The very first Cajun sound at Newport had come the year before when Dewey was asked to fill in – on guitar, not his customary fiddle – for someone who couldn't make it. By the early 1970s, there was interest shown from France in francophone cultures in Quebec and Louisiana, and French youths seeking alternatives to military service could perform cultural work in Louisiana. There had been field recordings done in Louisiana before: Alan Lomax recorded there in the 1930s and Harry Oster had recorded some in the late 1950s. It was Lomax who had urged the Newport Folk Foundation to underwrite Ralph Rinzler's trips in April 1964, April and October 1965, and May and October 1966.[23]

However, there was very little Cajun music out on record at the time. Floyd Soileau of Ville Platte's Swallow Records had put out a Balfas album, and Rounder helped distribute Swallow. Arhoolie had released some Cajun music, and zydeco. But there was very little available and some people in Louisiana weren't really sure what they thought about it – there were some who had a sense of embarrassment or shame at this old-fashioned music becoming known to the world at large. As the now-defunct Balfa Toujours website explained about Dewey's first foray at Newport: "This was to be the first time Cajun music was heard in such a context, and many were embarrassed at the thought of what they considered old 'chanky-chank' representing Louisiana at such a prestigious event." For a couple of generations, students in the public schools had been chastised – even punished with a ruler across the knuckles – for speaking French. It had been driven into the public consciousness that their culture was an inferior one, something to turn one's back on. This is a fairly universal phenomenon when a regional and perhaps more indigenous culture becomes surrounded by a faster-growing, more economically successful one. There were plenty of families along the border with Mexico who shunned the *conjunto* or *norteño* sound as similarly old-fashioned and beneath them in some regard. That the phenomenon might be universal didn't make it any less sad.[24]

The response at Newport stimulated Dewey to re-form a band he and his brothers had enjoyed, and he began to travel when bookings were offered. In 1974, there came a turning point when the first Tribute to Cajun Music (now the Festivals Acadiens) was presented in Lafayette, Louisiana. With its success, the validation of the music and Cajun culture from the outside world was brought back home and a sense of pride began to build. The Rounders take some satisfaction in having played a small role in this process.

In the 1970s, Rounder even promoted a few shows, which often involved taking over an evening at Club Passim. One such show featured the Balfa Brothers, and in the audience, on a first date, were two figures who were to become well known in Boston folk radio circles: Marcia Young, who hosted a Celtic music show for many years, and Dave Palmater. The music was great; they hit it off; and later they married. We also presented the Georgia Sea Island Singers with Bessie Jones, and we also had a night when we showed some John Cohen films.

Why had Ralph Rinzler chosen Rounder over, say, Folkways? Perhaps there was an element of changing generations about it. We were much more active and energetic than Moe Asch at this point. We were already involved in selling records at the Festival of American Folklife. We were a lot more visible; we weren't sitting in an office in New York, but were out at the Brandywine Festival and Wolf Trap, visiting the Library of Congress, and out doing our own field recordings. We were willing to travel to Naushon Island, which perhaps Moe would not have done. We pursued Ralph persistently. We had, in the approving words of Delmark's Bob Koester, transitioned from "hippie radicals to being young hustlers." Ralph was interested in popularizing folk music and stimulating an appreciation for folk culture. He'd been active with Newport and had managed Bill Monroe. Ralph was a representative of

A flyer for a 1973 Bessie Jones Concert, promoted by Rounder.
Courtesy of Mark Wilson

the "half-generation" who preceded us – people such as Alan Jabbour, Joe Hickerson, John Cohen, Mike Seeger, and so many others. In his 2018 book *Blue Grass Generation*, Neil Rosenberg offers some insight into that same generation which he himself is a part of.[25]

We really admired Moe Asch. He'd been in the business since the 1940s, a true pioneer; in a sense, his was the first independent label that endured. He'd pushed the boundaries of what could be released, in terms of genre, in terms of "political" albums, and he was not motivated by sales projections. And he'd helped us with advice on how to produce our first albums. He was a real character, too. While distributing Folkways, I'd talk with him on the phone, and he never said "goodbye." He just ended the conversation when he felt it was done. No niceties, no politesse. Click. There must have been a dozen times when I had to call him right back because I still had a question for him.

1973: a year of field trips

It was Dick Spottswood who inspired us to start a series of recordings documenting the early history of bluegrass, primarily focusing on the smaller independent labels that released 78 and 45 rpm records in the late 1940s and the 1950s. We applied for a grant, but didn't want to wait for it so plunged into researching the past of a number of largely unknown groups like Ronnie Knittel & the Holston Valley Boys and Buster Pack & His Lonesome Pine Boys. Among the people we interviewed in June alone were Connie Gately in Nashville and Wilma Lee & Stoney Cooper (at the Grand Ole Opry). In Kentucky, we visited the Caudill Family in Whitesburg, John Reedy in Corbin, Curley Parker in Flatwoods, and Cuddles Newsome in Pikeville. We talked with Dave Woolum in Trenton, Ohio, and Hobo Jack Adkins in Cincinnati. In early August, we very much enjoyed a lengthy visit and interview with Jim "Hobe" Stanton, who ran the small independent Rich-R-Tone record label out of Johnson City, Tennessee.

It took a lot of amateur detective work to track down these singers and musicians: we found as many as we could, and we were pretty successful. Relatively little was known about some of these artists – and nothing at all about others. Even with the advent of the internet, we still haven't learned a thing about the Hamm Brothers!

When we located one of the people we were seeking, we'd try to call ahead. Most were very open, though some a little bewildered to imagine there was any interest in the music they'd recorded twenty years earlier. The Church Brothers, from the North Wilkesboro area of North Carolina, had long since stopped playing and were amazed to find anyone showing any interest in them or their music – especially when it was three young people from New England. In their time, though, they had recorded enough good bluegrass that we could devote an entire volume of Rounder's Early Days of Bluegrass series to them.

The same was true with Connie & Babe & the Backwoods Boys; in their case, not only did we release a reissue but we recorded a brand-new album of them as well. Such was also the case with Danny and Charles Bailey – the Bailey Brothers. They were born in Happy Valley, Tennessee and the community name became the name of Rounder's first publishing company, Happy Valley Music BMI.

The grant was approved and we received $10,000 from the National Endowment for the Humanities, thanks to their Youthgrants program. That was a lot of money for us, but the Endowment got a lot of bang for their bucks: Rounder released a full ten LPs as our Early Days of Bluegrass series. Each album had extensive notes, photographs of most of the artists, and helped bring a lot of attention to the roots of the music. We'd venture a guess that the grant we received was one of the most productive ones the Endowment awarded.[26]

Dick Spottswood kept on coming up with ideas, most of them drawing on old 78s, and sometimes connecting us with others who specialized in other musics, such as Karl Signell. Nearly twenty years later, in May 1990, we released *Masters of Turkish Music* (Rounder 1051), which proved very popular in Turkey itself, enough so that we licensed it and a sequel that came out several years later. A review in France's *Trad* magazine of our *Rain Dropping off the Banana Tree* (Dick's 1996 anthology of Chinese classical recordings from 1902–30) talked about "cette étonnante et souvent déroutante musique classique chinoise." While Dick's anthology was winning praise in a third language, a British publication from Nottinghamshire, the *Retford Times*, commented, "The finished product isn't particularly easy on the ear but wonderfully evocative nonetheless." We could offer German-, Italian-, and Swedish-language reviews, too, but we will exercise some restraint.

Later in the year came my trip to Cajun country; it was the first time I'd experienced getting up at 6 am to go to a bar, much less being expected to crack a beer on arriving and watch Cajun music being played live over the radio in the early morning hours. The bar was Fred's Lounge in Mamou and the Saturday morning live show was broadcast by remote over KEUN in Eunice (as of 2019, KVPI carries the live show from Fred's).[27]

July saw Bruce Kaplan joining me to record an album of songs and games by Bessie Jones and a group that included seven children on several tracks, on the 30th & 31st at the Church of God in Christ on St. Simons Island, Georgia; some additional tracks for the album *So Glad I'm Here* were recorded at Doug Quimby's place in Brunswick.[28] Many of the songs came directly to Bessie through oral transmission from the children of slaves, her ancestors of a hundred years before.

Bruce and I continued our trip and recorded Reverend Pearly Brown in his home at Americus, Georgia. He was a blind street singer who played guitar and harmonica and was sometimes accompanied on vocals by his wife Christine. He wore a battered, hand-lettered sign around his neck which read "I AM A BLIND PREACHER. I WAS BORN BLIND. GOD LOVE A CHEERFUL GIVER," and also had his name, address, and telephone number. I didn't get much sleep between sessions. We stayed in their home that night and they gave up their bed for the two of us. It was set on plywood and a little rickety, threatening to tilt, and Bruce was big. He weighed maybe 75 pounds more than me, and the bed was uneven, so I was in constant fear of rolling onto him during the night. I slept with one arm tucked around and under the edge of the mattress to anchor me and keep me from tumbling onto Bruce. The album *It's a Mean Old World to Try to Live In* was released almost two years later in June 1975. Little did I know that the governor of Georgia at the time, Jimmy Carter (1971–75), knew Pearly Brown: Carter's home in Plains was only about ten miles from Americus. The year after the album came out, Carter was elected President of the United States. There was no known connection between the two events. I wish I'd had the foresight to have asked Jimmy Carter to write a blurb for the album cover.

Bruce made his way back to Chicago and I continued on to Pine Ridge, North Carolina where I recorded an album by the Smokey Valley Boys (Benton Flippen on fiddle) all by myself, an intimidating proposition under

Reverend Pearly Brown at home in Americus, Georgia

the best of circumstances. For reasons I don't recall over thirty years later, we only had the one evening to make the record. The five band members gathered around the mics and I set the tape recorder up in the living room, just as a thunderstorm rolled in. We'd be in the middle of a track and – *boom*! We tried to time the songs to start right after a peal of thunder, and had decent success. As the storm moved on, the gaps between thunderclaps grew longer. Even before it had truly stopped, we'd completed the album.

Ken traveled even further south later in the year, arriving in Montgomery, Alabama to record blues guitarist John Lee, who'd made some records for Federal back in 1951. At the time he was employed raking out sandtraps at a golf course. Ken and Dick Spottswood set up the equipment in a room at the Travelodge in Montgomery, but the timing wasn't right. Ken says, "We had to wait an extra day for John and we had to get him a guitar. He had plans to see a woman on our first day there and wouldn't postpone that for our recording. We ended up buying a guitar for him as it was cheaper than renting it for two days." Two days of taping, on October 2 and 3, and Rounder had another album. After *Down at the Depot* was released, however, there was a disappointing aftermath. Although these were his first recordings in over twenty years, John Lee had been a local figure in the late 1940s. "There wasn't a person in town who could run me off playing, black or white," he boasted, and Federal had printed up a small black-and-white card proclaiming him "King of the Guitar." So, believing himself to be a star, he refused to believe we hadn't sold more copies, and felt we'd cheated him out of royalties.

When a situation like this arose, since we didn't press our own records, we sent photocopies of the pressing invoices to the artist and told them they could verify the figures by contacting the pressing plant – we used Wakefield Manufacturing Inc., in Phoenix, Arizona, a plant noted for quality vinyl. Our royalties were based not on sales per se, but on pressings minus on-hand inventory, the difference being deemed sales. Thus, we were as transparent as could be if one verified the third-party pressing figures, then deducted out inventory. They needn't rely on our word for it.

Calculating royalties like this, based on movement rather than sales, led to a few wacky things. For instance, an asterisked notation on the inventory we did on February 5, 1976 in preparation for royalty calculations reads "see Marian's desk supports." The record in question was Rounder 0034, by Asa Martin & the Cumberland Rangers. The inventory had read 720 but had been changed to 1,020. The extra 300 copies were four of the heavy cardboard cartons each full of 75 LPs, which were being used to help prop up Marian's desk. We didn't actually have proper desks in those days, but worked on plywood sheets that we placed on top of LP boxes – just like the dining room table at 186 Willow Avenue.

Which reminds us of the Aunt Molly Jackson fiasco. This was early on. Her album was one of the first twenty records we released, coming out in August 1972. We sold through the first couple of thousand LPs and placed an order for another run of jackets. In the meantime, we needed some more albums and Ken called Wakefield and told them to just press up whatever quantity it took to fill all the remaining jackets they had on hand, figuring we could at least get in another fifty albums or so to tide us over. Fifty would actually have held us for quite a while at that point. They asked him to reconfirm that he was placing an order to fill all the jackets they had on hand. Yes, he said, with some exasperation. A week or so later, we received 1,817 Aunt Molly Jackson LPs. Ken hadn't realized that new jackets had been ordered, and the new order had just arrived. At the rate they'd been selling, we had enough Aunt Molly records to last us for the next twenty years. The boxes were lugged from place to place as we moved, and served as supports for our home dinner table at Willow Avenue, a number of employee desks at later warehouse locations, and more.

Over the years, only three or four artists actually bothered to "audit" the royalty statements. We were actually pleased when they did, because it provided the opportunity to show them how forthright we really were. In a way, it was kind of disappointing that more artists didn't come to inspect our calculations or ask to check the statements.

Ken and Dick Spottswood continued recording in Louisiana; they'd begun by recording Octa Clark on October 1, then traveled to Montgomery to record John Lee, but by October 10 were back in Cajun country recording Sady Courville and Dennis McGee, D.L. Menard & the Louisiana Aces, after which Ron Stanford and Ken joined forces to record the Lawtell Playboys on the 15th.

Recording the Aces was a real treat for Ken. There were "shirt off their back" people playing such infectious music. D.L. made chairs in a barn next to his home in Erath. For the actual taping in the Menard home, they set up with Ken and the Revox tape recorder in the bedroom and the whole band in the kitchen.

1974: Kaplan out, Kornrich in, Flying Fish launched, and Rounder keeps rolling

By the end of 1973, Bruce Kaplan had decided to launch his own label, Flying Fish Records. As mentioned earlier, a split might have seemed predestined, given that "the Rounders" were all living the music in a group setting day and night while Bruce was far away in Chicago.[29]

We don't have a lot of paperwork testifying to the "why" of Bruce's decision to split off. One undated letter from Bruce says, "I'm thinking of trying to do my own company. You see, I'm going to come into a lot of money soon. My father was a big capitalist and he died last year . . . I'm trying to evaluate the pros and cons of doing it myself . . . I really don't know enough about you or your ideas; you probably feel the same way I do."

In a letter of May 4 he suggested five different ways in which we might arrange the separation. Part of it went:

> Re-reading this, I'm afraid it might give the wrong impression. From the beginning, we have had serious misunderstanding through not being specific dating way back to when we first started; it wasn't made clear to me till very late in the game that you thought members of a non-profit collective shouldn't have a salary from it. On the other hand, I never made clear in advance that I thought they should. But this is an example, not an issue. I'm not trying to be cynical or nasty with my 5 proposals – I just think that maybe at last we should have an understanding which we all feel is clear and which we all understand to mean the same thing; then we could

forget all about this jive and get on to being friends and recording traditional music.

By the time of the November 1973 *Hazel & Alice* album release, we all knew what was coming and Bruce's name was no longer included in the list of the Rounders.

All things considered, the separation was effected relatively easily, since it was clear which artists Bruce had the initial or primary relationships with and which we did. Already in the works – already assigned Rounder numbers while in production – were five albums which soon appeared among Fish's first releases: a second album by Norman Blake, a second Martin, Bogan & Armstrong, the *Hillbilly Jazz* album featuring David Bromberg, Vassar Clements, and Doug Jernigan, a gospel album by the Zion Harmonizers of New Orleans, and an album by Jimmy Walker & Erwin Helfer. *Hillbilly Jazz* had originally been designated as Rounder 0040/41 and early copies of the Flying Fish release still show that number reflected on the disc, the identifying number that pressing plants inscribed on the metal parts from which records were pressed. We drew up and signed an agreement on March 3, 1974, whereby Rounder relinquished claim to most of the albums Bruce had in production, though there was a bit of dividing up, and Rounder kept the second Bashful Brother Oswald album which was in the works. Rounder was, from the start, the New England area distributor for Flying Fish. Our August 1974 new release sheet listed the first four Fish titles.

There were nine albums that Bruce had funded which had already been released on Rounder. Those were dealt with subsequently. Without either party feeling the need to talk with an attorney, we worked out an agreement near midyear re-characterizing the money he'd spent on the albums as a loan to Rounder and setting up a plan under which Rounder repaid Bruce by way of a "producer's royalty" of 95¢ per record sold for two years from initial release. Bruce paid royalties out of that amount. Additionally, Rounder paid Bruce a $1,000 lump sum and a monthly amount of $500 until the amount of money he'd put into Rounder was repaid. Bruce added a cover note to his copy of the agreement starting off, "I'm glad things seem to be working out in some sort of reasonable way. None of us are getting everything we might want, but I guess things are pretty fair." The final payment on the "loan" was in December 1975.

Around the time that Bruce was departing from the Rounder Collective, with Skip Ferguson leaving as well, another relationship was ending: the romantic one between Ken and Marian. Despite us all living in the same small apartment, I don't know what the issues between them were. Things happen. What I do know is that the breakup occurred while they were both sharing the same room at 65 Park Street, and neither of them moved out. Somehow they continued to share the same bed for weeks – even a few months – until we later bought the three-story house at 186 Willow Avenue. Then each of the three of us had our own rooms. With doors on them. It remains impressive to me that both Ken and Marian were so dedicated to Rounder that they made this all work out, sufficiently setting aside what could have been collective-shattering energies. No doubt each of us sublimated some self-centered impulses for the sake of the common goal of a successful cultural enterprise, but this was something else. Very impressive.

Flying Fish quickly began to give us some real competition in a way that most other labels had not – not because there was any animus on Bruce's part, but just because our tastes overlapped so much and he had a different approach to business. Bruce did tend to favor more contemporary offshoots at the time and Rounder was more inclined toward the more traditional (and less commercial). A story that Ken tells points up the problem that Bruce's more-defined business approach caused for Rounder:

> One of the most exciting new groups in the DC area was an all-woman *a capella* band called Sweet Honey In The Rock led by Bernice Reagon. They were of particular interest to us for two reasons: not only were they great singers with incredible harmonies and emotional lead singing, but they were also very political both as people and in their repertoire. I remember being very frustrated and disappointed when we learned that Sweet Honey had decided to sign with Flying Fish instead of Rounder. Not long afterwards, I was visiting our DC area distributor, Adelphi Distribution, and talking with Gene Rosenthal in his basement, from which he ran his label and distribution company. The subject of Sweet Honey's signing with Flying Fish came up and Gene told me that he had heard that they had chosen Fish over Rounder because they felt that Fish was more promotionally oriented than Rounder. That was an eye-opening conversation and I shared that with my partners. I think it had an impact on our becoming a more promotionally oriented label.

No question. That feedback definitely pushed Rounder across another threshold. No longer was it good enough to just release records and get on to the next one. We realized that, if we wanted to work with some of the artists who inspired us the most, we needed to try to sell the records, too! That might not seem like such a revelation today, but, as Ken says, it was an eye-opener for us at the time. Many of these artists had careers in music, and weren't only interested in having their music documented; they also wanted the records to make them money.

There were artists who were astonished we wanted to record them in the first place. When we asked them about recording, they thought perhaps we were scamming them, trying to sell them on the idea of paying Rounder to have some records made. When they learned that we were actually going to pay them royalties based on sales (no advances were given at any point in our first five years), some of them were flummoxed, but usually pleased. Still, there were some who preferred not to record at all. Ken tried for years to talk Cajun accordionist Walter Mouton into recording; it never happened.

Then again, some artists were quite ambitious. The more records Rounder could sell, the greater their royalties. The more the records got around, the more Rounder promoted them, and the more attention the artist would receive. This could lead to better bookings, and any number of other opportunities. We began to realize that we had a responsibility to these artists who had entrusted their music to us. Marian began to develop ways of reaching out to the media, becoming in effect our first publicist. She had more of a talent for it than either Ken or myself.

The first advance royalties we ever paid were on Norman Blake's *Whiskey Before Breakfast* album (which we fondly knew as 0063). The amount was $500. The record was released in February 1976, and it did very well right away, earning Norman an additional $5,292.25 in its first royalty period. It's a fact of life that most artists on most record labels never see any royalty checks; production costs are typically deducted from royalties as well as advances and they are rarely earned back. But not only did we keep our costs very low, we didn't even deduct them from royalties for the first several years. And with no (or minimal) advances to earn out, the Rounder artists accrued royalties if not immediately then without too much delay.

There were other conversations to be had that felt important to us, most of them nothing to do with sales or business. One was with labor folklorist Archie Green. He encouraged us early on to persevere and made us feel as though we truly had embarked on what could be a unique and even important venture. We were half in awe of Archie because of the work he had done on workers' traditions, some of it set down in his book *Only A Miner*, and on account of the zest with which he approached life.[30] He made a particular impression on us with one thing he said. As Ken put it, "Archie told us if we were going to create something by way of alternative culture, we had to do it at least as well, if not better, than anyone else." It was Archie who urged us to release the Aunt Molly Jackson album. It wasn't representative of Aunt Molly's broader repertoire; because of our interest, it was deliberately skewed toward her most "political" songs.

The faith that so many people showed in our potential at a very early stage, when we were really just feeling our way along, meant a great deal to us and also imbued us with a stronger sense of responsibility.

In July 1974, the album Ken and Dick Spottswood had recorded with D.L. Menard & the Louisiana Aces was released, just in time for the midsummer festival season.

As Bruce Kaplan was leaving Rounder, another B.K. – Bill Kornrich – was coming in. Bill and I had met in Crete and Istanbul in the summer of '67, and we had been roommates at the University of Chicago and on the Mall in

Washington at the time of the Poor People's Campaign. For the first year and a half of Rounder's existence, Bill K. had lived in southern New Hampshire but made frequent visits to Somerville. Then he traveled south and lived in Belize (still British Honduras at the time) from around March 1972 to the spring of 1974 when he moved back to his native West Hartford. As the summertime approached, I planned to take a half-year sabbatical from teaching and go to Europe to work on my dissertation about the political thought of Alexander Berkman, and get in some traveling. Bill K. remembers, "You were concerned that the business would fall apart if left to Ken and Marian. So, I moved up to 186 Willow. I think I arrived maybe a week before you left. When you returned, I guess we all decided that I would just stay and keep working. I stayed until the spring of 1976."

Some things take time to percolate. The dissertation I worked on in 1974 helped toward my getting a doctoral dissertation from Tufts in 1980, fourteen years after I graduated. The dissertation was published thirty-four years later, in 2014, thanks to British anarchist Stuart Christie, as *Alexander Berkman, Anarchist: Life, Work, Ideas.*[31]

As a young student in Russia, Berkman claimed to have heard the bomb explode that killed Tsar Alexander II in 1881. He emigrated to America and, inspired by the Haymarket Martyrs in Chicago (the original basis of May Day), he became active in Jewish anarchist circles, joining with Emma Goldman and a couple of others in a small commune in the Lower West Side of New York. When Henry Clay Frick of Carnegie Steel sent in armed Pinkertons who killed strikers at the Homestead plant, Berkman traveled to Pittsburgh and shot Frick in an assassination attempt of his own, hoping to inspire a workers' revolt. He spent fourteen years in prison, then rejoined Goldman and was active in the free speech movement, in setting up free schools, in the beginnings of the birth control movement, and in defending numerous activists charged by prosecutors. He and Goldman organized against conscription during the First World War and were deported to Russia, arriving shortly after the Revolution. There, as anarchists, they inevitably fell foul of the Communist Party authorities who were intent on consolidating political power. They had to leave Russia as well, and then – with the rise of Hitler – also had to leave Germany, finally seeking exile in France.

Several people had written about Emma Goldman but mine was the first study of Berkman. In the course of my research, I met (in Germany and in Mexico) a couple of his comrades from days long gone by. I corresponded with a few others, and did extensive research in archives in Amsterdam and Lausanne. Though Marian and I had both been conservatives when growing up, we were both entranced by the idealism and commitment to communal and non-hierarchical lifestyles of Berkman and Goldman. It helped infuse our own ideas of the Rounder Collective.

5 The Concept of a Collective is Called into Question

For us, the concept of the Rounder Collective was never perfect. One tenet had been that each member of the collective should be able to do anything – and it was always seen that the whole was greater than the sum of its parts. But I was worried about what might happen in my absence. Michael Scully, whose 2013 book *The Never-Ending Revival: Rounder Records and the Folk Alliance* was part of the Music in American Life series of the University of Illinois Press, kept notes from his interviews with the three Rounder founders. The notes give voice to this concern:

> Bill got disgusted that others couldn't be bothered with balancing the books. They showed remarkably little interest in balancing, making sure we had enough money coming in. Bill enjoyed doing it but thought it was proper for them to do it, too. "What if I got run over by a bus?" He also said there was an ideological aspect to sharing all knowledge. So people would come and go. Part of [the] reason [that other people left] was that they didn't have the shared experience.

Keeping the company books was a thankless task, not inherently interesting, but it had to be done. Fortunately, Bill Kornrich was up to the job – and more. He filled in while I was gone (from August 6, immediately after the National Folk Festival, through December 4) and pitched in 100%, establishing himself as a full member of the collective and doing all the work that needed to be done. The only real gap in record releases occurred during this period; there were no new releases from Rounder in August, September, or October – but the eight albums that had come out in July kept everyone plenty busy, and there were others in the works. The three Rounders back in Somerville – Ken, Marian, and Bill Kornrich – became entranced with the idea of moving the company to East Tennessee and operating out of the area where the Bailey Brothers lived, perhaps Happy Valley itself. Being told of this in correspondence while I was traveling, I freaked out. In no way did I want to make the move. Mark Wilson and I exchanged a number of letters on the subject, Mark in part because he and I were close but also because he was on the articles of incorporation that formally established the company.

Bookkeeping really wasn't all that interesting. It's no surprise that neither Ken nor Marian wanted to mess with it, even though the company books couldn't have been more basic. Both Bill K. and I seemed to have a degree of facility with it, and were willing to bite the bullet and stay up into the wee hours at the end of each month to make sure things balanced. That said, I came to more fully recognize that Ken and Marian had other strengths, in areas I wasn't as interested in, such as working in the studio and listening to take after take, whatever it took to get the music right. Ken had the patience for that. He became very good at finding songs to recommend to artists; we later learned that was called A&R work – artists and repertoire. He enjoyed working with artists in the studio, too, trying to get them to perform to the best of their potential.

I wasn't particularly interested in "networking" with people in radio and the media; Marian was much better at that. The ideological notion that each person should be equally capable of handling all aspects of the business fell by the wayside as people gravitated toward the areas they were better at. There was always a staggering amount of work to be done. No doubt those left behind while I was traveling across Europe and the Middle East often felt put upon while I was off having a great time, writing home these incredibly detailed letters documenting my travels.

Idealism was one thing, but it was becoming increasingly hard to find people who were willing to share our work ethic and food habits, or cared about old-time banjo music: every time you add a variable, it's more difficult to find someone who meets all the specs. The emerging division of labor and specialization contradicted at least one of the stated goals of the collective. It didn't feel like hypocrisy, though, but felt more like a natural evolution. It's probably not surprising that an enterprise operating in the context of its times inevitably takes on the characteristics of the dominant mode of doing business. It would be extraordinarily difficult to survive in a competitive environment doing otherwise. It never felt like a surrender of principles, though, but more of an adaptation to reality. After all, to restate a point: the Rounders always felt that the company itself was bigger than they were and that the whole was greater than the sum of its parts.

Going back a year or two, Mark Wilson's younger brother Danny had come to visit Mark in the Boston area sometime during his summer vacation in 1971 and we all met. He returned in the summer of 1973 and stayed for three years. "I enjoyed helping Mark with field recordings and occasional production work," Danny recalled in 2009. "I enjoyed traveling to summer folk festivals and the enthusiasts who corresponded thru the mail order."

Marian Leighton Levy

During this period, he began to take on running the mail-order side of things. Before my trip to Europe, Danny and I had traveled to visit Bill Kornrich in Belize over the 1973–74 Christmas and New Year's period. After returning, Danny got deeper and deeper into the mail order but never aspired to become a full part of the collective – neither had Mark, whose primary commitment was always the study of philosophy.

Danny had a facility for running a business and soon established a separate identity for the mail-order company, dubbing it Roundhouse Records and running it out of a separate location, an apartment he rented on Camp Street in North Cambridge. It was a load off the hands and minds of the Rounder founders and we were sufficiently content to see him run Roundhouse, though there a lack of clarity arose as to truly whose "company" the mail order had become. Rounder itself still didn't have any employees, and Danny paid himself a salary out of the proceeds. It was unfortunate that the arrangements weren't more clearly established at the time. We eventually renamed the mail order Roundup Records.

The month before my return, November 1974, saw the launch of another series, one that has been an important part of the life's work of Mark Wilson. In fact, all three releases in November were Mark Wilson productions – the only three albums that Rounder put out from July 1974 until the beginning of 1975. There was an album Mark recorded of Kentucky's Asa Martin & the Cumberland Rangers called *Dr. Ginger Blue*, a reissue album of white blues guitarist Frank Hutchison of West Virginia, and the first album of Cape Breton fiddler Joe Cormier. Joe lived and performed in the Boston area for many years, usually at the French Club in Waltham, but hailed from Chéticamp, Nova Scotia. The album was given the number 7001 and launched a series of albums from Canadian musicians, primarily fiddle players who appealed to Mark. There was an active and lively folk tradition still extant in Nova Scotia and Mark moved to document it in a series of albums that stretched over thirty years. I joined Mark on the first field trip to the island in 1976, and for a second one many years later in May 2002. Mark visited many times throughout and has produced more than two dozen albums from a variety of master fiddle players and musicians.

These recordings were not without their travails. I've repressed some of the memories, but Mark reminded me in 2018 of

> how much money you initially lost on these and the fights that you got into over high tariffs and non-payments for artist's copies. It all seemed like an unfortunate disaster at the time. In the fullness of time, it later turned out that those record issues played a significant role in boosting fiddle music as a tourist attraction on the island, helping plug a much-needed hole in a very depressed economy. One of the reasons that Natalie MacMaster and the Rankins recorded for you later on was precisely because of that initial impetus, although none of us realized this at the time.[32]

1975: filing taxes and hiring people

After about four years, we decided it was probably time that we file taxes. Someone recommended Eric Weinberger, who was an accountant for a number of peace and social justice organizations including the Mobe (the National Mobilization Committee to End the War in Vietnam). When he came to visit, he had a business card describing himself as "The Shaggy Accountant." It turns out Eric was quite an activist, and after his death in 2006 we learned about some of his work we'd not known about at the time. White civil rights advocate William Moore was murdered in Gadsden, Alabama in 1963 as he was making a personal "Freedom Walk" from Chattanooga to Mississippi to hand-carry a letter to the governor protesting the barring of James Meredith from the University of Mississippi. The very next week, ten more walkers followed in Moore's path. Each was badly beaten when they reached Alabama but none was killed; one of the ten was Eric. He never told us this. We only found out by reading posthumous tributes in December 2006.

By the time we met him, Eric was earning a subsistence doing accounting work, and he set up our books for us. At first, he was taken aback to learn we'd done nothing at all in the way of filing taxes – ever. "OK," he said. After at least metaphorically taking a deep breath, he asked me, "Where's your accounts receivable journal?"

"What's that?"

Eric explained that it was a list of who owed money to the company. "Oh, I get it. Here," I replied, handing over a notebook that had a list of everyone we'd sold records to, with the date and the amount owed, marked off if they'd paid us. "That's it," Eric said. "Now what about your cash receipts journal?"

"Uh, well . . ."

"It's a list of all the income you've received."

"We've got that!" I said. Another notebook came out.

After several similar exchanges, Eric marveled, saying, in effect, "This is impressive. You have a modern accounting system in place. You just don't know the terms for it."

"Well, it's just common sense," I said. "If we send someone some records, we have to keep track of how much we sent and when." True enough, Eric said, and he helped us give a little more structure to our system, filed four years of taxes (we hadn't owed anything, just as we'd thought, but at least we became "more legal"), and helped us with our books and taxes for many years. It wasn't long before we hired our first employee.

As an independent contractor, we found we couldn't always count on Eric being there. He would spend many of his weekends with the Clamshell Alliance protesting the building of the nuclear station in Seabrook, New Hampshire. He would frequently get arrested and fail to make it back to work on Monday.

A few years later, when Rounder started to get involved with computers (yes, it's true – we were way ahead of the curve in using IT in business), Eric became fascinated with the possibilities and would spend hour after hour experimenting and writing programs. He worked nights and days and exhausted himself. While we understood his excitement, he was getting behind in what he was supposed to be doing and even missed some deadlines. Eventually, we all saw that it wasn't working and Eric moved on. He had been such an important part of helping us get started and become more businesslike that we hated to see him go, but his work at Rounder was done and he had other work to do.

Hiring our first employee took some doing. There was an obstacle we had to overcome, and it wasn't just a matter of being cheap . . . or, let's say, thrifty. It was a matter of ideology. Marian and I had a good grounding in Marxist thought, and one of the bedrock principles was that hiring other people was by definition exploitation. It's true, of course, in its simplest form. It wouldn't be rational to hire someone at, say, $10,000 a year unless that person brought a value greater than that amount to the enterprise. The word "exploitation" sounds more pejorative than it needs to; in any event, we didn't want to be a party to hiring – and therefore – exploiting workers.

We had only just begun to pay ourselves after the first four years: $400 a month. Ken was shocked when he learned that the folks at Takoma were getting $10,000 a year and reckoned they would run the company into the ground with such astronomical salaries.

On the other hand, we were working ourselves to exhaustion. Strangely enough, the person who gave us "permission" to hire our first employee was Peter Stampfel of the Holy Modal Rounders. Peter stayed over at our place when he was up from New York to play at Somerville's Club Zircon. He was most impressed that we had recordings by (and even a poster on the wall of) Nolan Strong & the Diablos. He also noticed how hard we were working and asked us why we didn't just hire someone. We told him we didn't want to exploit anyone or be bosses. His reply? Pretty much, he said, "I wish you'd exploit *me*! I could use a good job. If I lived in Boston instead of New York, I'd beg you for a job like this. You'd be exploiting me by *not* hiring me, depriving me of the opportunity." We'd certainly never thought of it that way. Ken remembers Peter saying there were many people working in jobs like shoe salesman who would love to be working for a record company. He also told us that he wouldn't want to have to worry about the whole collective thing. He wouldn't want the doctrine, just the job.

Peter helped us get over the ideological hump. Soon afterwards, we hired our first two employees – two at once – Kathy Kete and Steve Harris. In no way were Steve and Kathy interested in becoming part of a living and working collective. There was never any thought of that. They just wanted a job, and enjoyed working with Rounder for a couple of years each. It's not that they applied. As Steve recalled late in 2015, they were both working at the Harvard Coop, which had the biggest record department around. Kathy was from New Jersey and, as it happened, knew Tex Logan's daughter Jody. Kathy was in customer service at the Coop; Steve had been in the record department, too, working with defectives at first before becoming a buyer in the folk music area (it was a big enough store, and there was enough interest in folk music at the time, to actually have a buyer specializing in it). Steve said that Kathy and he "shared an interest in folk music and bluegrass and eventually became romantically involved." He doesn't remember just how it came about but he says, "I think Ken walked into the Coop one day and offered Kathy a job at Rounder. Of course, I caught wind of it and stated that I was also interested. Needless to say the department manager Linda Stellinger was not so happy about it but c'est la vie." It's something none of us can quite pin down, but they both came to work at Rounder, if not on the same day then within a very short time of each other. When they broke up, Steve took a room in the Willow Avenue house, which he recalls set him back $60 a month. None of us can remember how much the pay was, but Steve says, "I was able to save up enough for a Martin HD-28 guitar which I still own today and cost me $860 dollars back in 1978." And he holds the kind of memories that warm the heart of a former employer, thinking back some forty years: "I appreciate the employment opportunity you provided. It was great working in the warehouse and being able to listen to all that great music. It was great meeting all those great musicians that would drop by: Hazel Dickens, John Hartford, Butch Robins, Snock, George Thorogood, Sam Bush, and John Cowan and others that I cannot remember."[33]

As to how the year unfolded with record releases, we'd been working hard throughout 1974 on the Early Days of Bluegrass series, and finally prepared the first couple of those albums for release in March 1975.

In an odd juxtaposition to this, February saw the release of *Alleged in Their Own Time* by the Unholy Modal Rounders, which emerged as the result of a suitably dissolute and chaotic recording session at Aengus Studios. It was the Rounders on Rounder, but what had we gotten ourselves into? The sessions included Steve Weber going missing while he was trying to score some marijuana and another artist shooting up (we were told) and pulling the bathroom sink out of the wall.

We released the first album of Mark O'Connor, already (at not quite thirteen years of age) a four-time National Junior Fiddle Champion. Mark was joined by Norman Blake and Charlie Collins on mandolin and guitar, respectively. Mark's mother Marty was active and appropriately aggressive on Mark's behalf – and look how it's all paid off for him. Roy Acuff had a few words about Mark before introducing him on the Opry in July 1974: "The word 'genius' is about the only way that I know that could fit a person twelve years old that can play a fiddle as this boy can play it." We released several

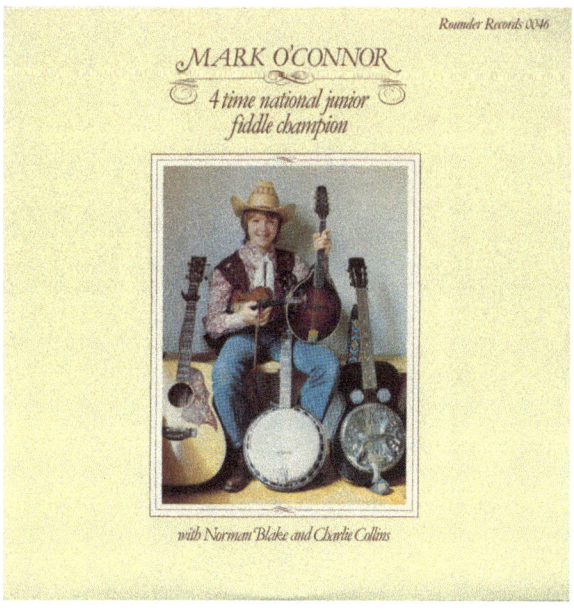

Cover of *4 Time National Junior Fiddle Champion* by Mark O'Connor (Rounder 0046; March 1975)

albums with Mark; much later, in 2016, after he had recorded numerous albums for other companies, the circle was closed when Rounder released a new album by Mark and the O'Connor Band.

In August, we released the classic album by J.D. Crowe & the New South (Rounder 0044), in which J.D. featured band members Tony Rice, Ricky Skaggs, Bobby Slone, and Jerry Douglas. This was the album that – more than any other – in Marian's words, "really put us on the map in the bluegrass world." The album had no title, and was soon widely known – unique among record albums in any genre so far as we know – by its selection number – 0044. Even forty years later, in 2015, when its anniversary was featured in a front-page tease by *Bluegrass Unlimited*, the headline on the magazine's cover simply read "Rounder 0044." The album expanded the envelope for bluegrass at the time, bringing in songs by contemporary writers such as Gordon Lightfoot. J.D. had a vision of a different approach to the music, and he and Tony pioneered and perfected the integration of songs such as Lightfoot's into bluegrass repertoire.[34] Had it been left to Rounder to do A&R, we might not have suggested such songs, but one of the principles Rounder typically held to was allowing the artists almost complete creative control.

From very early on, one of Ken's ambitions for Rounder was to see us produce one classic album. Who would have guessed in the early days that a Rounder album would win a Grammy for both Album of the Year and Record of the Year? In 2008, *Raising Sand* by Alison Krauss and Robert Plant did just that. But, looking back, there certainly have been several along the way that

Original cover of J.D Crowe & the New South, aka "Rounder 0044" (August 1975)

could claim the title of "classic"; and the 1975 J.D. Crowe & the New South album was unquestionably one of them. George Thorogood & the Destroyers cut a couple of classics, too. Needless to say, there were many dozens we loved then, and still love today, but they didn't all reach "classic" status with the general public. If you ask me what I think is the most underappreciated album Rounder ever released? I'd say Rounder 0031 by Buzz Busby & Leon Morris, released in July 1974 and still never put out on CD. Talk about hardcore bluegrass!

We were still more than a little unsure of ourselves and what we were doing – we weren't exactly music industry professionals. We were amateurs in the best sense of the word. It was probably just as well that we learned as we went along and hadn't gotten in over our heads. In the August/September 1996 issue of *Folk Roots* magazine, Marian said of the earliest days:

> One of the records we wanted to do was to try to get the Kentucky Colonels back together again. We didn't feel we had the wherewithal or prestige to speak to Clarence White. I was also very interested in a Don Reno guitar album, and similarly felt that approaching Don Reno was just way beyond. Of course, on the other hand, we approached J. Geils before their first release. I don't know what would have happened if they had said yes. We probably would have done a live record on a two-track.
>
> It took us about two years in starting to deal with folks like Norman Blake before we began to realize that you have a responsibility to the artist as well as trying to sell the greatest number of records by promoting them.[35]

At the time of Rounder's twenty-fifth anniversary, Marian told the *Providence Journal*:

> They always refer to us as "the tiny folk label in Cambridge." Well, I don't mind the tiny part, even though we're not that tiny anymore. But the mellow vibes thing that goes with it is a lot of malarkey. Ken has been known to throw a cassette case across the room at me. Creative conflict is the way to go.[36]

6 The Second Half of the Seventies: George Thorogood and the Destroyers, and Wrestling with Change

It was on a hot Friday night in July 1975 that a Head Start school bus driver named John Forward walked into a blues bar in Cambridge named Joe's Place. He was surprised to see a group he'd never heard of before – George Thorogood & the Delaware Destroyers –and became a convert on the spot. John was one of the biggest music fans we knew: an inveterate record collector and our single best individual customer. By this time we had a small warehouse at 96 Winchester Street in Medford and it was the first time we'd run the business out of anywhere but our own dwelling. John got paid on Fridays and would come over to see what new records had come in during the week. Since the Willow Avenue days, he had maintained a layaway box where he placed records he wanted but wasn't yet able to afford, and this was in a corner of the office. He'd consider what was new, look at what he'd set aside from before, and decide what to buy that week. Now he started talking up the Destroyers, telling us – over and over – that we had to see this band and make a record of them. But it was six months before we first saw them.

John kept trying to get us to go see George Thorogood & the Destroyers while they were in the area, but we never got around to it. Finally, after the band moved back home to Delaware, John took the extraordinary step of booking them to do a show less than a mile from our house, at the Logan Post VFW Hall on Broadway in Teele Square, Somerville. It was around January 1976. I went, out of a sense of obligation, but after hearing their first two numbers I was on the phone to Ken, urging him to come over. The band was a trio ("the original two-man quartet"): George, Jeff Simon on drums and Ron "Roadblock" Smith on second guitar. The music was high-energy and very well done. And, very importantly, we liked them as people.

We heard some demos that John got for us, on 7 inch reels. We liked what we heard there, too, but there was something that worried me. They sounded too much like the early Rolling Stones! We'd already seen the Stones several times in concert, and I had every one of their albums. But Stones clones on Rounder? It kicked off an internal debate: if we released an album of George Thorogood & the Destroyers on Rounder, would we lose our established following? We rationalized things to a degree because of how much George drew on blues tradition: John Lee Hooker, Muddy Waters, and the like. They came from a tradition themselves, we told ourselves, melding the "roots of rhythm and blues and the roots of rock." It helped a lot that Mark Wilson – the hardest-core traditionalist we knew – liked the Destroyers tapes, too.

That we liked the guys in the band mattered a lot. We'd come to the point of realizing that we'd rather work with people we enjoyed, and that a good working relationship was important to us. George had his own take on this: "If it isn't fun, it isn't worth doing."

Still, we hesitated – and John Forward decided to make a move. He set up a session at a recording studio in Jamaica Plain (Dimension Sound) and recorded the Destroyers, rushing from one song to another. He was aware that the clock was running and was anxious to get down every song the band knew, as quickly as he possibly could – pushing the band to start the next song the minute they completed one. John had it in mind to release the Destroyers on a label he was going to start up and name after his dog. Unfortunately, there were repercussions from this session that cropped up years later.

John invited us to the sessions and seeing the band working in the studio finally convinced us. Marian said:

> We fudged around for a year, deciding whether we really wanted to do that record or not. I will be the first to admit that I didn't think it was all that important. It was Ken and Bill who took George seriously. Categories really didn't matter to us that much; it was more a matter of "is this too commercial in terms of its potential to be on Rounder?" because we were very happy in thinking of ourselves as a specialty label. If it was too close to the mainstream or too commercial, then we thought it should be on a major label. George convinced us otherwise because he wanted to be on a label like Rounder or Arhoolie – even years later . . . we were the ones who convinced him to go for a major label rather than the other way around.[37]

We arranged a session that allowed the band a little more time to record, although it was still about as economic a session as one could hope for. John Nagy was the sound engineer, and he mixed the album as well. When we got the first test pressings, however, we weren't satisfied. It sounded too thin. Someone suggested that we bring in a bass player to add some extra depth and punch, so the band called on someone they knew from back home: Billy Blough. In effect, Billy's bass covered up a lot of Ron Smith's parts. On Record Store Day in 2015, Rounder re-released the album on vinyl and on CD with the original mixes.

Total costs of the sessions, even with the re-work: $2,646.56. But we weren't sure we'd ever get our $3,000 back – and we worried that we might suffer a backlash from disappointed fans who were used to more standard Rounder fare. We released the self-titled album *George Thorogood & the Destroyers* (or, as we came to fondly call it, 3013) in July 1977. Ken recalls taking a girlfriend to hear the band at the Cantab Lounge the night the record was released; there were five other people who came out.

The author with George Thorogood (Jeff Simon to the right)

So what else was Rounder doing that summer? The previous month – June 1977 – Rounder released:

- Rounder 0082: *Not A Word from Home* by Joe Val & the New England Bluegrass Boys (our third album by Joe Val)
- Rounder 0085: *Tony Rice* (his first solo album, which also featured J.D. Crowe, Jerry Douglas, David Grisman, Richard Greene, Todd Phillips, Tony's brother Larry, and Darol Anger
- Rounder 1023: *The Kickapoo Medicine Show* by Gid Tanner & His Skillet Lickers
- Rounder 2017: *Lonesome Road Blues* by Frank Hovington
- Rounder 3017: *Acoustic Guitar* by Eric Schoenberg

The Frank Hovington record particularly pleased George, because Hovington was a Delaware bluesman and all the Destroyers felt very good about being on a label that continued to work with the blues. The album was recorded at Frank's home in Felton, Delaware by Dick Spottswood and English folklorist Bruce Bastin.

We'd already released quite a few unconventional albums. The preceding year, in October 1976, we'd put out the first album of music from the People's Republic of China (familiarly known as Red China at the time); Moe Asch of Folkways had attempted to release one years earlier but was prevented from doing so by the Treasury Department of the United States under what – to our understanding – was an attempt to enforce provisions of the Trading with the Enemy Act. The music was traditional and instrumental music recorded by Guy and Candie Carawan in March 1976; it wasn't politicized in any way. We still worried, just a little. We didn't lose any sleep over it, though. The month before the release of the Chinese album, we'd released a double album called *Chile Vencerá!* It was an anthology of Chilean New Song recorded locally in Chile between 1962 and the violent overthrow of the Salvador Allende regime in September 1973.

It's safe to assume that the Destroyers weren't as entranced with those couple of albums as they were with Frank Hovington's and some of the other blues albums we'd released. They did share appreciation for some of the other musicians we'd recorded – Ola Belle Reed, for instance – who they'd seen in person and enjoyed. In 1976, Ken and Mark Wilson recorded another album, *Ola Belle Reed and Family*, which came out in September 1977.

We probably confused a few people who couldn't understand why we'd be releasing traditional music like *Early Shaker Spirituals* in May 1977, and also these more political albums. Back in January 1973 we had released *Mountain Moving Day* – one side of the album by the Chicago Women's Liberation Rock Band and the other by the New Haven Women's Liberation Rock Band. It was pretty cutting-edge at the time: *Ms.* magazine debuted in 1972, and that same month of January was the date of the *Roe vs. Wade* decision of the U.S. Supreme Court. That record, Rounder 4001, was widely considered the first music album from the women's liberation movement.

Another record that brought the two threads together (traditional music and the political) was November 1973's *Come All You Coal Miners,* an album of songs about the struggles and working conditions of coal miners, featuring Hazel Dickens, Sarah Gunning, Jim Garland, George Tucker, and Nimrod Workman. Much of the music was used in the soundtrack for Barbara Kopple's 1976 Academy Award-winning documentary film *Harlan County U.S.A.* The film investigated a 1973 strike against the Duke Power Company which began at the Brookside Mine in Harlan County, Kentucky. In 1974, Mark Wilson recorded a long session with Sarah and Jim Garland, some of which appeared as her full album, *The Silver Dagger*. Two years later, Mark traveled to Chattaroy, West Virginia, where he recorded the album *Mother*

Jones' Will, by eighty-three-year-old coal miner Nimrod Workman (still without a pension after forty-two years in the mines). In 2005, Rounder re-released *Mountain Moving Day* as *Papa, Don't Lay that Shit On Me*, and in 2006, released a CD of the coal-mining songs album under the title *Harlan County U.S.A.: Songs of the Coal Miner's Struggle*.

Cover of *Come All You Coal Miners* (Rounder 4005; November 1973)

A couple of the albums we'd gotten talked into because they were considered "important" were *The Battering Ram* (4002) and *Negro Songs of Protest* (4004), though we didn't really require much persuasion. A lot of very earnest people approached us with ideas and we could quite easily be convinced of a project's importance if the people doing the pitching were passionate enough. We weren't assessing albums on their commercial potential. The first album was one of Irish revolutionary songs sung by some young local Irish immigrants who sang at a Cambridge bar called the Plough and the Stars. They played an array of music, but we honed in on the rebel songs and I did a lot of research for the booklet, even contacting Greater Boston representatives of the IRA for a deeper perspective.

It was Archie Green who told us about the 1933–37 recordings of Lawrence Gellert, who had recorded more than 300 songs, including a number of what we could call protest songs, from amongst black folks living in western North Carolina, in South Carolina, and in Georgia. He'd released some of the songs himself several years earlier on his own Timely label, under the same title: *Negro Songs of Protest*. But of the 1,000 albums he'd made up, 960 remained unsold. He had the discs, in white paper sleeves, but he'd never even had jackets made up. Safe to say, he didn't have distribution! He faced another obstacle: When he first returned to New York, despite his leftist pedigree (one brother, Hugo, was involved with *Masses* magazine, and another, Ernst, was murdered while imprisoned as a conscientious objector during the First World War), there was suspicion up north that this wasn't genuine folk music and that Gellert had persuaded the singers to record these songs. After all, none of the trained folklorists – not even the Lomaxes – had been successful in finding such songs. To protect the anonymity of his "informants," Gellert refused to provide the sort of verifiable documentation that would enable scholars to check out their cynical suspicions.

At risk to himself, and the people he was recording, Gellert was able to gather numerous songs in which black folk of the South gave voice to the sort of songs no other collector was able to obtain. Many were somewhat veiled songs such as 'There Ain't No Heaven,' but a few were much more explicit, such as 'Negro Got No Justice.'

Gellert was a true eccentric, living in Greenwich Village in an apartment at 148 Sullivan Street which almost no one but him had ever visited. At one point, he'd received a Rockefeller grant to resume his work, but when John D. found out what he was recording, the grant was withdrawn. In a way, Marian and I were fortunate to get a glimpse of the life of this real character the time we visited him at home. His place was absolutely packed to the ceiling with books and magazines and it was difficult to edge in through pathways between the stacked-up materials. There were no tables or chairs, other than one seat he used for himself – a barber chair. No refrigerator. Just a lot of books and newspapers and other publications, many of which looked to have been there for a very long time.

Ultimately, we cleared a little space by striking a deal and taking the 960 pressings off his hands, but it hardly made a dent. We produced an eight-page booklet which, combined with our usual extensive album jacket notes, told the story of how he came to make these recordings in Tryon County, south of Asheville, and in the Greenville, South Carolina county jail. We ordered some self-adhesive labels of our own and carefully pressed them over the Timely labels on the LPs, leaving the spindle hole free. We used one of Hugo Gellert's drawings for the front cover of the album. And once we got the jackets and booklets, we hand-assembled the final albums. At last, Gellert's recordings were made available to the world at large. In 1982, a second volume drawn from his recordings was assembled by Bruce Conforth and released as *Cap'n You're So Mean* (Rounder 4013). In 2013, Bruce, by then in the American Music Department at the University of Michigan in Ann Arbor, saw his book published by Scarecrow: *African American Folksong and American Cultural Politics: The Lawrence Gellert Story*.

Despite all this emphasis on "political" music, the Rounder Collective had really become something of a fiction by this time. Only three members other than the three founders ever made it onto the back of an album cover as part of the collective: Bruce Kaplan, Skip Ferguson, and Bill Kornrich. Neither Mark nor Danny Wilson – though both were extremely important in building Rounder – ever aspired to become part of the group, maintaining their independence (and perhaps some sanity). Others came and pitched in, even if only for a couple of weeks, but none really considered staying. Perhaps there was already too much history among the three founders for a new arrival to feel fully comfortable; Bill Kornrich was the last of a breed, however: not only was he a tireless worker but he also had the advantage of having known all three Rounders from the days before the company began.

To persevere, you had to want to be in the record business for no real pay, and work sixteen hours a day. Both Ken and I were "slave drivers by example," working endless hours at speed and hoping that others would be stimulated to follow our example. It doesn't usually work that way with employees paid by the hour; although there were plenty who were very good workers, none was as possessed as we were. After all, it wasn't their company. Contagion didn't always take.

One employee who did put the "pedal to the metal" was Mike Annis, who worked at Rounder for years and wound up as warehouse manager. First to come, last to leave; and if you wanted to talk with him, sometimes you had to do so while he was on the move. Mike was later seriously injured in the Patriots Day Boston Marathon bombing on April 15, 2013.[38] Doctors saved his leg from amputation, and before too long he was back at work. When Rounder was sold and moved to Nashville, Mike made the move and brought his energy there as well. Sadly, Mike died in the autumn of 2016.

Bill K. was willing to put in long, hard hours moving records around, making freight runs to the post office or airport, and balancing the books. But he apparently wasn't that interested in production work. In early 2009, he wrote me, "So, at some point in spring 1976 I bought a Ford pickup truck and considered that to be equal to what Rounder owed me (I was also repaid my loan). Numerous distributors told me I was crazy and that I should ask for more, but I just wanted out and did not want to haggle." That's when Bill drove south, to British Honduras (Belize). He lived in such a remote area that only two or three cars a day would drive by on the unpaved road known as the Western Highway. On Christmas Eve, Danny imbibed enough alcohol that he lay down to go to sleep on the "highway" and we just left him there for a half an hour, knowing that no cars would be coming.

For his part, Danny recalls, with perhaps considerably more equanimity than he felt at the time:

> I enjoyed most the people I worked with because they were different and enterprising but I grew lonesome and homesick. When Mark was to take a job in San Diego, I sought a way to return to the Northwest. Frank Ferrel appeared, borrowed and wrecked

my Volkswagen, and became my friend. I set sail for Frank's Fiddle Shop in Seattle with some inventory provided by Rounder. Our enterprise blossomed, faded, and died.

The enterprise was Fiddler's Roundhouse, a shop in the Pike Place Public Market. When it failed, Mark came up in late August to help sell off the records and instruments and they were able to pay almost all their creditors. "I'm glad to be out of the retail business," Danny wrote us at the time. "It is exhausting and not worth the effort." His letter detailed some of the work undertaken to pay off this consignor or that creditor. He summed up: "I also want to make sure we're square. Whatever bumpy ground we've been over since 65 Park St., I think we exchanged pretty equivalent services. I certainly got a good view of the music business and business in general."

Danny became Dan Wilson, a professor of computer science at Southern Oregon University. Dan and Mark Wilson were both interviewed by Michael Scully in 2004 for his book *The Never-Ending Revival*, and neither saw it quite the way Bill Kornrich had. Scully wrote, "[Danny] Wilson remembers Kornrich with great affection, but recalls his departure as voluntary and devoid of any particular unpleasantness. Only Kornrich seems strongly affected by this now murky incident, which he characterizes as a betrayal of friendship."[39] Is it possible that sometimes one or more of the Rounder founders came across as a little too sanctimonious and that others cast something of a jaundiced eye at our expressed ideals? Yes, that is possible.

1977: the year the Destroyers started to break

Earlier in 1977, we announced an expansion of our overseas distribution with the addition of nine foreign distributors. None of them has been involved in distribution in the twenty-first century; as far as we know, most of them are long out of business. The companies were Plane Verlag (Germany), CRD (UK), Cézame (France), Evasion (Switzerland), Sinar (Norway), Hi Fi Home Produkties (Belgium and Hollard), CSA (Denmark), and Studer ReVox (Hong Kong). Our three pre-existing foreign distributors were Sonet in Sweden, Shinsei Service in Japan, and Almada in Canada.

In the U.S., distribution was an ever-evolving story, with a very active independent distribution scene. Some of the distributors who were present at the founding of NAIRD didn't even exist five years later. Here are some of the U.S. distributors with which we used to work at one time or another in our first decade or so. As far as we know, only the two with asterisks still existed by the second decade of the twenty-first century. With all the coming and going, we were truly fortunate to rarely get burned.

- Action
- Adelphi
- Aden
- All South
- Associated
- Austin Record Distributors
- Back Room (who later became Bayside)
- Big State
- California Record Distributors (CRDI)
- Dean Wallace
- DNA
- East Side
- Elderly Instruments*
- Gemini
- Horizon
- House
- Jack's Record Cellar
- Kinnara
- Ladyslipper
- MS
- Michael Ginsburg
- Mill City
- Music City
- Music Design
- Music for Little People
- Navarre
- North Country Music
- Northwest Territory
- Old Fogey
- Orwaka
- Pickwick
- Precision Sound
- Rabbit
- Record Depot*
- Record People
- REP

- Rhythm Research
- Richman Brothers
- Riverboat
- Schwartz Brothers
- Select-O-Hits
- Silo
- Supreme
- Tara
- Tone
- Western Merchandisers

We released *George Thorogood & the Destroyers* (Rounder 3013) in July 1977. That same month, we also put out:

- Rounder 0099: *Lady's Fancy* by guitarist Dan Crary, playing with Byron Berline and John Hickman
- Rounder 3016: *Safe Sweet Home* by John Miller, his second album (John was one of the members of Country Cooking)
- Rounder 3019: *Crown of Horn* by British guitarist Martin Carthy, which had come out on Topic Records in England in 1976, and from whom we licensed it
- Special Series 02: *Country Songs* by the Lilly Brothers, licensed to us by Prestige

In August, we released *Boone Creek* (a group comprised of Ricky Skaggs, Jerry Douglas, Terry Baucom, and Wes Golding, which we fondly called "0081") and a second album by Cape Breton fiddler Joe Cormier, *The Dances Down Home*, known to collectors as Rounder 7004.

In the months after the recording sessions, we paid two advances to the Destroyers, each of $1,000. And right after release of the album, before the first royalty statement was generated, the band asked us to pay $500 to John Forward, which we did. Another $1,200 was paid later in 1978. And a couple of years later we donated $1,000 to the Veterans of Foreign Wars in Newark, Delaware, George's hometown, to help finance construction of a baseball field. The Destroyers put up many times that amount.

We pressed 1,700 sales copies of *George Thorogood & the Destroyers*, and 300 promotional copies. And we waited to see what would happen. Not a lot, at first. It had come out midway through a year in which we'd released thirty-six albums. By the time it emerged into the world, Rounder had 144 albums in its own catalog and we were actively distributing well over a hundred other labels. It was a busy time, but this album kicked something off that carried the company to new heights. It took a little time to build, but by the time the first royalty statement was rendered, for sales from release through April 30, 1978, we'd sold 42,171 LPs and 3,889 cassettes and 8-tracks. The royalties paid went well into five figures. That year, 1978, was the first in which we recorded sales in excess of $1 million, having fallen $11,362 short of that total in fiscal 1977. In 1976, total sales had been $299,202.

It's interesting to note that, even in fiscal 1977, the year we nearly hit a million, our total expenditure for advertising was $4,517. Promotional expenses totaled $2,876. Wages and salaries (including to ourselves) came to $47,310. Business meals and entertainment were $206, which surely should have prompted an internal audit by company watchdogs – after all, that comes to nearly 57¢ a day across the whole company!

In all seriousness, it's always been the case that keeping a lid on expenses is key. Sales in 1979 surpassed $3 million in a period of very rapid growth in which advertising and promotion taken together leapt to $70,616, a tenfold increase from three years previously – but sales were ten times larger as well. We were keeping the percentages in line.

Ken tells how the first Destroyers album caught on:

> About the time the first album came out, the Destroyers were on their way out to the west coast to play a couple of dates for the California Homemakers Association, the first of which was a benefit for the association and the second would be for the band. The initial airplay came from Tony Berardini at KTIM, a 3,000-watt station in San Rafael, California where he was both the late-night jock and music director. He remembers getting the record in the mail and being blown away by it. He played it for the other jocks at the station and everyone loved its rawness and that it was just basic three-chord rock'n'roll. They started playing it right away and hit it hard. Being a small station and in the shadows of a number of major stations in the Bay Area, they were all in it for the music, one of the last vestiges of freeform radio. To them, the label didn't matter at all. It was all about the music.

The play over KTIM created an interest in the band which enabled them to stay, playing the west coast for close to a month. Ken adds:

> Where KTIM barely reached San Francisco on a clear day with the wind blowing in the right direction, the buzz was spread through Tony talking about the Destroyers in the tip sheets like *Album Network* and the *Bill Hard Report*. Tony remembers talking to Marian and setting up a station visit where the band played acoustic in their production studio for about an hour. George played acoustic and Jeff played bongo drums.
>
> On the way back, they had a gig in Colorado at the Little Bear. When the band arrived, they saw there was a line stretching around

the block, and felt they must have come to the wrong place. They weren't aware of the airplay which was taking place in the area.

Other early play came from WHFS in Bethesda, Maryland where brothers Damien and David Einstein played lots of roots music, even including Cajun artists like Ambrose Thibodeaux. The first time that George played the DC area was at the Bayou where they opened for the Nighthawks, the very popular local blues rock band which later signed with Mercury for a few minutes. I went down for the show. For the next several years, one of us frequently went on the road with the Destroyers.

The album broke in Boston when Tony Berardini phoned radio station WBCN, the leading freeform station there, and told them they had to start playing the record. We even licensed it to Eureka, a small company in Australia. And in early 1978, Bill made his first trip to the annual MIDEM convention in Cannes; MIDEM was in its twelfth year. Licenses were arranged with Sonet Records, with offices in London (Rod Buckle) and Stockholm (Dag Haeggqvist), and with Quality Records in Canada. By the time of the third statement, for the period ended April 30, 1979, we'd sold another 86,513 units. Sales were going up, not tailing off.

Semi-annual sales totals didn't dip below 10,000 until the statement of September 1988, a full ten years after initial release. We didn't have the album certified gold, though, until January 1992. (A look at Wikipedia in early 2019 informs me that the band has now sold over fifteen million copies of its various albums worldwide. Pretty good for "the original two-man quartet.")

A good part of the increase in sales in 1977 was due to word of mouth, to active touring by the Destroyers, and by assistance offered us – often free of charge, just for the love of the music, by people like Tony Berardini and publicist Steve Leeds of Atlantic Records. Shortly after the initial radio successes, we got a call from Steve, who had heard the record and wanted to help promote it. He did this of his own volition, while going around to stations on behalf of the Atlantic releases he was working. He had been hired to reach the younger radio people so he was the right person. He felt that letting DJs know about good music on his – or other – labels helped with his credibility and relationships with the stations.

While we were able to get quite a bit of airplay, we also ran into a number of obstacles. Many stations said they would play the album – when it came out on a major label. It didn't, and by the time the stations realized it wasn't going to, it was too late for them to get on it. Many other excuses were made not to play the record, many of which have been made indelible in "Steve Leeds Offers 48 Reasons Why Radio Won't Play Your Record" which appeared in Dave Marsh's *Rock Book of Lists*.

Meanwhile, the Rounders were working the phones out of Cambridge, primarily Ken and Marian doing the dialing. By this time, the company had a network of independent distributors around the country, most of whom had promotion people. *Thorogood* was the first record worked by Ted Higashioka at California Record Distributors, and he worked George with great energy. Other promotion people included Tony Dercole at Action, Noble Womble at Big State, Valerie Kargher at Richman Brothers, Roy Chiavori at MS, and Kevin Papuga at House Distributors in Kansas City.

It was, Ken told *Sing Out!* magazine:

> our biggest single learning experience ... a day-to-day process of each of us just jumping into things we had never done before: calling radio stations, writing promotional material. The George Thorogood experience dramatically changed Rounder. He was the first act that was really touring, getting airplay, that had distributors interested and calling us up. It forced us into the role of semi-manager, discussing career development, all kinds of things we had never done before.

1978: snowed in and breaking out

Right after MIDEM, a couple of major snowstorms hit Boston. The first struck on January 18 and that was bad enough, dropping eighteen inches of snow on the city. The weight of the snow collapsed the roof of the Civic Center in Hartford, Connecticut. It stayed cold and the snow didn't melt. Then, on February 6 and 7, came a true blizzard which doubled the previous amount, dumping thirty-six more inches of snow on Boston in thirty-six hours. The storm was so intense and the snowfall so heavy that plows could not keep up. Over 3,500 automobiles were abandoned on Route 128 and other Massachusetts roads. The state was placed under a state of emergency for six days.

The evening the second storm began, the Destroyers were playing at the Club Zircon in Somerville. It was kind of a belated Boston-area celebration of the release of their first album. Henry Horenstein's photos used on the cover had been taken at an early 1977 show at the Zircon. The snow was falling, but the show went on. There were maybe thirty people inside.

It wasn't a long walk back to the Willow Avenue house but the snow was coming down so fast that it was hard to see at times. The band made it back to the house, too, and we were all snowed in together for most of the week to come. When day broke the next morning, it was clear that we were going to be snowbound for some time. Private cars were banned from the streets so that emergency vehicles and key workers could try to get to work.

The six regular residents of the house were joined by the Destroyers, booking agent Elizabeth Rush who was hoping to sign the band, and a few other folks as well. Jeff Simon, Bill Blough, and I trekked down to Store 24, a convenience store about ten blocks away – and got there just in time. People

Bill Blough and the Destroyers outside 186 Willow Avenue in the Boston snow of 1977

were sweeping loaves of bread off the shelves and carting them to the register. We grabbed a box of large plastic bags and filled them up with spaghetti, bread, milk, and a couple of other staples. We got the last of the bread and the last of the milk, and felt lucky we'd acted as quickly as we had.

Meanwhile, there was a tug of war going on over the telephone which lasted a couple of days. Elizabeth was trying to sign up the Destroyers for management and booking, and had what could perhaps have been an advantage since we were all holed up together. But Mike Kappus of Rosebud was aggressively burning up the phone lines from San Francisco, leaning on George to sign with him. George didn't really want to have to make a decision, but he had to. In the end, Mike (who represented John Lee Hooker at the time) won out – in part. He became the group's booking agent, with no one getting the manager's gig. George never really wanted a professional manager. It might have done him good, but he resisted and always preferred to work with a friend like (at a later date) Irish Mike Donahue who was more or less willing to do his bidding. Rounder dealt with a lot of what a manager would have handled, but never in any formal sense and never seeking any compensation.

After about five days, the roads were clear enough for those trapped in the house to be on their way.

By this point, we were up to well over a dozen employees and, as mentioned, had moved operations out of Willow Avenue to a small one-story warehouse a few blocks away on the other side of Ball Square: 96 Winchester Street, Medford. We stayed there for a year or two until moving to the Lechmere area, to a one-block-long, narrow rented warehouse space at 28 Otis Street in Cambridge. The "underwear drawer" was now a thing of the past: in one of our attempts to appear more collectivist, we used to pool all our underwear into one common drawer. It was never anything but a gesture. It's not as though Ken or I wore Marian's underwear, or vice versa, or each other's.

In fact, Marian moved out after a while, simply to have more of a private life. She'd always been a self-described introvert, and as such it was not always easy dealing with people coming and going all the time, although she actually enjoyed the "after lights out" meetings on the third floor of Willow Avenue, which were reassuring reminders of the common interests we all shared. Each room had its own door, unlike the Somerville Avenue apartment, but they were typically left open and, even after everyone was in bed, someone would call out a question about some project, or a reminder of something we needed not to forget the next day. It never stopped. There was no respite. It was all Rounder, all the time. Ken and I were both, as Marian once put it, workaholics, maybe with something of a Puritan streak. There's a side to Ken, she said, who "doesn't feel like he should have nice things." On an early visit to Rounder, John Cohen had said to Marian, "You're the only one who'll be happy because you're not completely defined by work."[40]

She didn't want every aspect of her life to begin and end with Rounder; she really liked going to the movies, for example, and was finishing a master's in Modern European History. So she lived briefly in a place about a mile or so away, on Day Street. At one point, she moved to a house in Rangeley, Maine, stepping back from full participation in things Rounder. She later moved to a Garrison Avenue apartment near Teele Square, an apartment she shared with Jack Tottle (and his dog, Possum.) Béla Fleck lived across the hall on Garrison Avenue when he joined Tasty Licks, and was a roommate with a couple of Rounder employees. The *Tasty Licks* album came out in July 1978 (Rounder 0106), the month Béla turned twenty.

At the end of October 1978, we released the Destroyers sequel, *Move It On Over* (Rounder 3024), and it took off from the start. Our first pressing was at Wakefield for 45,140 LPs on October 26, with 11,582 tapes manufactured by GRT on November 2. This record cost us almost twice as much to produce in the studio: a whopping $5,024.57. We had to press more records within a week of the first pressing, and, by the time the royalty period ended on April 30, 1979, we were reporting first-period sales of 334,199. The record was certified gold – our first – on July 18, 1980. This was big business.

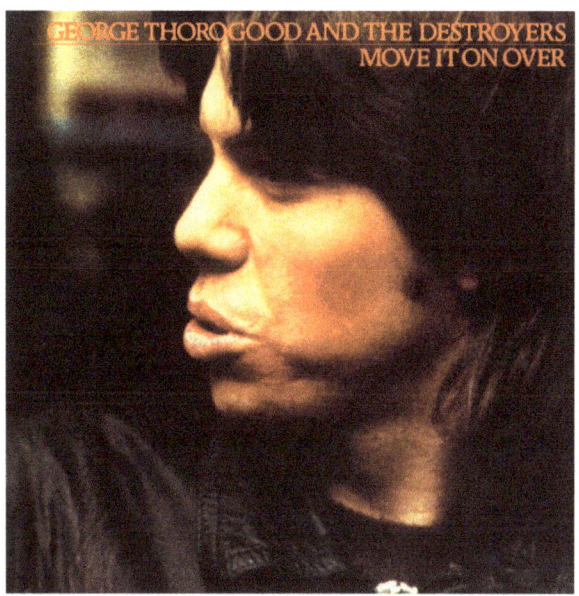

Cover of *Move It On Over* by George Thorogood & the Destroyers (Rounder 3024; October 1978)

Ken recalls the set-up for 3024:

> When the second album was scheduled to come out, we called Steve Leeds at Atlantic asking him if he knew anyone who might be good for us to hire to promote George's upcoming release. He told us that he didn't at the time, but would think about it. A few weeks later, Steve called us back and told us that he had given it some thought and felt he knew who would be good to work the next Thorogood album. Him. He had just recently left Atlantic and was working as an independent out of Tommy Mottola's office. We ended up working out things with Steve and, at his suggestion, also hired Augie Blume, an independent promotion person from the Bay Area.

Many of the radio stations that had passed on the first Destroyers album played this one. Steve Morse of the *Boston Globe* wrote an article on Steve and Augie, and it helped Steve secure some other clients.[41]

We also wanted to improve our distribution to take advantage of the increased exposure gained from the Destroyers' almost non-stop touring, the radio play, and press. We contacted some of the major one-stops and rack jobbers.[42] We developed a relationship with Lieberman Enterprises, where Dougie Ackerman took Thorogood on as a special project. When we went out to visit them as part of the Destroyers tour, they treated us and the band royally. As one of the two major rack jobbers in the country, they had a real impact on sales.

With both the first and second albums, our pressing plant, Wakefield Manufacturing, worked with us, giving us extended terms; and they even manufactured additional product themselves, over and above what we'd ordered, just to have it ready in case we needed it. They generally made us a top priority. Our good relationships with manufacturers continued through the years and was a major reason that we were able to meet the demand not only for Destroyers records but Alison Krauss as well some years later.

There was one concern, though. Our distributors were selling a lot of Destroyers albums, but it was looking as though they weren't selling as many of the rest of the catalog. I fired off a few letters near the end of January 1979 presenting comparative sales figures tailored to some distributors, noting that even though we had thirty-five new albums that had been issued in 1978, aggregate sales for these distributors hadn't really increased. Whereas Record People in New York was up 40%, even excluding Thorogood, and truly building on his success, CRDI in southern California, while doing an undeniably good job with George, was down in non-Destroyers sales. With regard to Jerry Richman, we found the same, informing him: "In the final three months of 1978 you did not act as a Rounder distributor but as a George Thorogood distributor. If we are to continue to work with you as a distributor there will have to be a reversal of the trend." Richman Brothers responded, and so did CRDI. But we were keeping our eyes on them.

We were incredibly fortunate that the sales of both albums were spread out over a reasonably long period. We had never applied for a credit line at any bank (and didn't for years afterward) but funded all ongoing operations from past sales. If we'd needed to place an initial order for 300,000 albums, we couldn't have done so. But revenue continued to come in from 3013 and, by the time we were ready to order the initial pressings of 3024, we'd been paid for the first year-plus of sales of the first album. Of course, there were other albums bringing in money, and we were as conservative as ever in what we spent money on. The distribution company and the mail order were ticking along.

Ken concludes:

> We had contact with major talent buyers, managers, groupies, publicists, and virtually every part of the industry. Each day was a challenge, each day was a learning experience. In a matter of few months, we learned more about the real world of the record business than we had in the previous eight years.

During this period, we were fielding phone calls from all over. Ken and Marian dealt with most of them, while I worked on the day-to-day. There were some strange moments, and George was even more uncomfortable than we were with some of the meetings we felt we needed to have. There were inquiries we diverted early on: people who'd call us from this company or that saying they wanted to buy Rounder – buy the whole company. We could usually tell right away that what they were really interested in was getting the rights to George Thorogood and neither knew nor cared what else we might have. We had a little fun at times:

— Hello, this is So-and-So from X Records. I love your label and I'd really like to talk with you about buying the company.

— Oh, really? That's great. We're really excited ourselves about the new album by Almeda Riddle. She's from Greers Ferry, Arkansas and just turned eighty this year. It's our second album with her, *More Ballads and Hymns from the Ozarks*. She's the best at old-time unaccompanied ballad singing.

We didn't even mention that Granny Riddle often didn't have enough cash on hand when she wanted to order more records from us, so she sent us homemade quilts instead.

Or we might question the caller more directly, with a little bit of exaggeration regarding the kind of music we produced. "Are you really familiar with Rounder? Do you know that we mostly release albums of banjo players in their seventies, recorded on the front porch of their homes in Kentucky?" Some of those calls ended pretty quickly. We really had no interest in selling the company, and so we enjoyed toying with the sharpies.

Some calls we took more seriously, however. Clive Davis, for example, renowned music executive, was a call we needed to take. Even though we were not official managers, we did in fact have George's interests to look after and we knew the Destroyers had a potential we might not be able to fully realize, given our lack of capital and lack of experience in the big business of the music industry. George was often less interested than we were in such meetings and felt uncomfortable in them. Davis and his personal assistant flew in for a quick meeting with us and we met at them at Logan Airport, where we ate, with George. I recall we were all fascinated by the executive's patent leather shoes and matching belt.

Not too many years later, Marian said, "There was no real danger of seduction by the commercial mainstream because none of us was all that interested. There's not anything self-righteous about it. That's just not who we are." Ken said almost the very same thing: "One of the pitfalls we avoided was the desire to become something other than what we are."

Newark, Delaware received their first-class baseball field courtesy of the Destroyers as a result of George not wanting to accept what he considered to be tainted money. The "tainted money" in question came from MCA Records. It turned out that an earlier friend of George's named Danny Lipman had recorded demos of George and his group at a Boston area studio named Music

Designers in 1973–75. After the Rounder albums became modest hits, he sold the demos to MCA, who then contacted George hoping for cooperation with cover photographs and the like. George was appalled. These were the early demos which had been sent round to any number of record companies, none of whom showed any interest, and most of whom were kicking themselves later. They were the same tapes we at Rounder had originally heard and found intriguing – but also lacking, which is why we were prompted to schedule new sessions. A legal stand-off ensued, including a memorable meeting in New York. With lawyers present, MCA acted like they were doing George a big favor – they were, after all, a Major Label! When a representative of MCA tried to show George some paperwork, George treated it as though it was contaminated with anthrax. He wouldn't even touch it with his hand and pushed it back across the table with a pencil.

George issued a personal statement on March 19:

> In the years that I have been a part of the wonderful world of entertainment, I have worked very hard to gain the respect of my audiences, peers, and professional cohorts. This effort seems about to be all in vain. A "professional outfit" which calls itself MCA has purchased material of Destroyers past, material looked on by me, my band, management, and friends as obsolete and inferior. I do not want this material released. MCA seems to be preparing (without my permission or even giving me the courtesy of consulting me), to release the material in album form. In my opinion this is a sign of disrespect towards me as a professional musician, but more importantly to me as a human being.

Attempts to work out an agreement went nowhere; MCA said they would permanently shelve the old tapes instead of releasing them but their "offer" said, "in such event, we would expect George to record for us two albums of newly-recorded material." In other words, if he would sign with them as a new artist, they would bury the old demos. MCA also threatened to sue Rounder for interfering with their business, alleging that we had requested that radio stations not play the record and that retail accounts not purchase it.

MCA proceeded to release the album, gratuitously and provocatively titling it *Better Than the Rest*. It wasn't. It didn't do well, relatively speaking, but still sold many tens of thousands of records – and the royalty income from those sales that came to the band was money they wouldn't touch. And that's how Newark got a new baseball field.

Building on the success of the Destroyers

Unsurprisingly, we were flooded with calls and demo tapes after the success of the Destroyers. Many of them confidently assured us that they were the "next George Thorogood." But that wasn't really what we were looking for.

One band that didn't take that tack was the Nighthawks – and yet they probably had the best claim of any to that mantle. They were a quite successful band, and very similar to the Destroyers in their musical approach. Jimmy Thackery played slide like George, yet they were different enough with Mark Wenner as their front man on mouth harp. The two bands respected each other, and it might have made a lot of sense to add the Nighthawks to our roster.

We held back, though, for a number of reasons – the main one being loyalty to George and the Destroyers. We were giving them our all, and it would inevitably have diluted our efforts if we started promoting a similar band. There were some good times, one of the best being one night in Washington's Georgetown neighborhood. The bands were playing across the street from each other, at the corner of 34th and M, with the Destroyers booked into the Cellar Door and the Nighthawks playing at Desperados. A plan was hatched. Late in the evening, both bands started playing a song that was a signature for both – 'Madison Blues' – and they both chose the key of E. Both slide guitarists – George and Jimmy – had very long cords attached to their guitars, and walked through their respective crowds toward the front door. Several of us went out into M Street and boldly stopped traffic, as the two principals met in mid-street, made sure they were synched up with each other, and then each unplugged their cords and exchanged them. George plugged in Jimmy's cord and Jimmy plugged in George's, neither missing a note, and each played their way into the opposite club – causing a simultaneous uproar as the two crowds realized what was happening. Years later, WTOP's website recalled the evening, also reporting that "What was the Cellar Door is now a cheesesteak restaurant. Desperados is now the Embassy of the Ukraine." Times change.

We didn't want to shift our musical direction too radically by chasing after similar bands to replicate the Destroyers' success. We had the opportunity to try the route Elektra had taken and capitalize on our success, but we took a more cautious approach instead. First of all, we liked doing what we had always been doing. We weren't chasing after money; we were doing what we loved to do. We didn't want to have to give that up. We also had an instinct that there was an element of luck involved, and that it might even be a serious mistake to try to duplicate the success we had had. We never believed it was Rounder that deserved all the credit; it was the unique appeal of George & the Destroyers that drove the excitement. By definition, something unique can't be cloned. And we wanted to be fair to the Destroyers by not chasing after other bands that might offer bigger possibilities. We had a shot at signing

Stevie Ray Vaughan, but by then some big-money figures were being bruited about and it seemed to be getting a little out of our league.

As I've already hinted, one of the things we were best at was keeping costs down. We didn't have a cleaning crew in to tidy things up nightly, or weekly ... or monthly. We took advantage of being the Little Record Company that Could, and continued to be prudent with regard to photography, graphic design, and recording studio costs.

We kept going with the Destroyers, although their third album was a disappointment in terms of sales. It was recorded out in the suburbs, at Blue Jay, a studio that was maybe "too nice" and lacked the grittiness of downtown Jamaica Plain's Dimension Sound. That may have hurt the sound of the record in some intangible fashion, though we thought the material and the performances as good as the first two albums.

At one point, the band wanted to escape from the sterile atmosphere of Blue Jay, so we all came back to Somerville's Davis Square (a very rundown area at the time) and into a dive named Johnny D's – which later became a superb local music venue. They were holding a "talent night." So the Destroyers, never letting on who they were, signed up for the competition as Sidewalk Frank & the Vandals. I even got up on stage (it was about six inches off the floor) for my one and only time as a "musician" and joined in with tambourine on 'Willie and the Hand Jive.' The band didn't win talent night. They didn't even place second. Winning was "Kevin from Somerville" who sang 'When Irish Eyes Are Smiling.' Sadly, Johnny D's is no more; after forty-seven years, it closed in March 2016.

Looking back on it, we could say that giving the third album the title *More* was perhaps not the best idea. And perhaps it was just a little too soon for another record. Our distributors ordered good quantities to start with, but rather than seeing sales build – as both 3013 and 3024 had – the new record (3045) meant just too many records in the marketplace. We wound up with 125,000 LP returns, enough to fill the entire garage at the Willow Avenue house, as well as some of the cellar. We never had to order that record again.

During this time we hired our first full-time employee to do publicity: Mary Weber. She had worked at WEA for a couple of years, but was laid off at the end of 1979. She gave us a call. She'd been planning to go back to law school in the fall of 1981, but became entranced with a rather special tour that the Destroyers planned (see the next section) and wanted to be around for it. Can you imagine? Deferring a year in law school to work on a rock'n'roll tour? She told us over thirty years later that she still has her backstage pass for one of the shows with the Rolling Stones framed and on the wall over her desk. "A lot of my time was spent doing things for George, since that was right around the time of the major label distribution change." Mary also remembers working a lot with the group Riders in the Sky. "I fondly remember taking them around to *Billboard/Cashbox/Record World* offices in NY, in a taxi with their instruments. Having Too Slim put the standup bass in a taxi wearing cowboy hats was something not even New Yorkers were used to seeing."[43]

Mary is regarded as one of those we were most sad to lose. Almost twenty years later, Ken said, "I remember asking her to add something to a package and was shocked to hear that it had already gone out. I was used to things not going out in a timely manner . . ."

7 Entering the 1980s: 50 States in 50 Dates – No Nights Off!

Even though the sales of *More* were a real letdown, the Destroyers were still as popular as ever on the road, and continued to draw large and devoted crowds (almost exclusively male). That latter part was a bit of a disappointment to the boys in the band, but you take what you can get. Somehow, early in 1981, George came up with an idea that captivated us all: it was billed as the 50/50 Tour. "50 States in 50 Dates – No Nights Off!!" The idea was to do a marathon of a tour hitting each one of the fifty states in the union, one night per state without taking a single night off. Audacious. And yet Mike Kappus of Rosebud pulled it off, in terms of booking, and the band was able to pull it off in terms of performance and endurance.

Here was the itinerary. The band flew to Honolulu to open the tour on October 23, flew to Alaska, then flew to Portland, Oregon where their roadie Dawes was waiting with their Checker cab and the rest of the tour was done by road.

Month	Date	Stop	Location	Venue
October	23	1	Honolulu, HI	The Wave
	24	2	Anchorage, AK	International Banquet House
	25	3	Portland, OR	Paramount Theatre
	26	4	Pullman, WA	Performing Arts Theatre at Washington State
	27	5	Boise, ID	SUB Building
	28	6	Salt Lake City, UT	New Faces Roadhouse
	29	7	Cheyenne, WY	Hitching Post
	30	8	Boulder, CO	Macky Auditorium, University of Colorado
	31	9	Rapid City, SD	The Barbarian
November	1	10	Billings, MT	Fox Theatre
	2	11	Mandan, ND	The Gaiety
	3	12	Moorhead, MN	Zodiac
	4	13	Omaha, NE	The Music Hall
	5	14	Ames, IA	C.Y. Stevens Auditorium

Month	Date	Stop	Location	Venue
	6	15	Lawrence, KS	Hoch Auditorium
	7	16	St. Louis, MO	Night Moves
	8	17	Lexington, KY	Student Center Grand Ballroom/Univ. of Ky.
	9	18	Indianapolis, IN	Vogue
	10	19	Madison, WI	Headliners
	11	20	Chicago, IL	Park West
	12	21	Ann Arbor, MI	Second Chance
	13	22	Columbus, OH	Agora
	14	23	Morgantown, WV	Mountainlair Ballroom/West Va. University
	15	24	Harrisburg, PA	Forum
	16	25	New York, NY	Savoy
	17	26	Boston, MA	Hotel Bradford
	18	27	Concord, NH	Capitol Theatre
	19	28	Brattleboro, VT	Flat Street
	20	29	Saco, ME	Longbranch
	21	30	Kingston, RI	Edwards Auditorium/Univ. of Rhode Island
	22	31	New Haven, CT	Toads
	23	32	Passaic, NJ	Capitol Theatre
	24	33	Newark, DE	Carpenter Hall/University of Delaware
	25	34	Catonsville, MD	Coast to Coast
	25	Capitol Stop	Washington, DC	Warner Theatre
	26	35	Richmond, VA	Much More
	27	36	Raleigh, NC	Music City
	28	37	Columbia, SC	Township Auditorium
	29	38	Atlanta, GA	Agora
	30	39	Tallahassee, FL	Ruby Diamond Auditorium
December	1	40	Mobile, AL	Saenger Theatre
	2	41	Oxford, MS	Abbey's Irish Rose
	3	42	Memphis, TN	The Music Hall
	4	43	Fayetteville, AR	Library
	5	44	New Orleans, LA	Superdome
	6	45	Oklahoma City, OK	Rainbows
	7	46	Amarillo, TX	The Jersey Lilly
	8	47	Albuquerque, NM	Popejoy Hall/University of New Mexico
	9	48	Flagstaff, AZ	Shakey Drakes
	10	49	Las Vegas, NV	Troubador
	11	50	Pasadena, CA	Perkins Palace

Plans were laid for the tour – and then the Rolling Stones called. They wanted the Destroyers to open their 1981 U.S. tour. It was a chance to play before three million people and get the sort of exposure the band had never had.

The Destroyers explained their dilemma: they wanted nothing more than to play the Stones tour, opening for the J. Geils Band and then the Stones. It would be a dream come true. But they had already booked this 50/50 concept tour, and they were afraid some other group would come along and steal the idea. As if.

Tour poster for George Thorogood & the Destroyers: "50 States in 50 Dates"

George Thorogood at the LA Coliseum

Amazingly, Bill Graham and the Stones accommodated them, letting them start the Stones tour and then close it, but interrupt it for fifty nights to carry out their commitment.

There were challenges playing in front of huge crowds. The Destroyers were used to playing in clubs and theaters. They didn't have the experience at projecting – both in amplification and stage performance – to crowds as large as the 100,000 at the Los Angeles Coliseum shows on October 9 and 11. Yet they pulled it off. There was Jack Nicholson, standing around bemused in his shades backstage. Ahmet Ertegun holding court at the performers' food tent. And 100,000 hyped-up fans out front. There was a fourth act on the Coliseum bill, the first opening act – this other guy named "Prince" who was booed off the stage. Bill Graham grabbed him as he was leaving the stage, physically spun him around and pointed him back at the crowd, and told him he had to finish the show or he'd never work in this town again (or words very much to that effect). Even with shoes and other objects being flung on stage, Prince worked through his set and then made room for the others. Both the

Destroyers and the Geils Band went over well, though there was work that had needed to be done quickly, both in terms of adjusting to a totally different audio environment and in terms of stagecraft.

One or the other of the Rounders went to most of the 50/50 dates. George had a thing going for a while where the band had to leave all of the accumulated food wrappers in the back seat of the Checker and smoke cigars with the windows rolled up; they were supposed to be like "animals" – it was kind of a wrestling posture, acting tough the way Vince McMahon would want them to. At some point, someone cracked and the band revolted. The cab also experienced frequent loss of license plates. Several times the Delaware plates were stolen off the Checker while the band was inside. They had some rabid fans.

Routing the tour presented some challenges

Mike Kappus recalls the preparation:

> Before the tour, George put himself on a training regimen to prepare for the rigors of a tour that would be tough for anyone, but especially for George who put on such an energetic and physical show and would never hold back a thing from one night's audience because of his surrounding schedule. In the meantime, I spent a good deal of time studying maps (in those days, long before the internet, these were paper maps I secured from AAA). I had to find performing spaces in all 50 states, and to minimize wear and tear on the band, I had to determine the shortest routing possible from gig to gig.
>
> In Wyoming, I had found a unique opportunity: to play in a prison basketball court for the inmates. I booked it, but as the date approached, the prison opened a second building for the inmates and feared repercussions if George played in one building and not the other – so they canceled the show. One mad scramble later, I booked the band in a little place called the Hitching Post.

One had to book by geography and not by size of venue. Mike continues:

> In more than one city, I had to make blind calls looking for any possible live entertainment venue I could find, using local phone books or calling directory assistance. At least once, I contacted a bowling alley so I could ask whether anyone in town ever presented music. In Mandan, I was referred to a club called the Playmore. I filled the owner in on what I was looking for: a Monday night show for George Thorogood & the Destroyers, and I explained the

concept as to why I was calling his club. He simply replied, "We don't do music on Monday nights and I never heard of George Thorogood." I let him know that, one way or another, we would make a deal that worked for him. In the end, I got a promoter from Wilmer, Minnesota to come in and promote the show – which then canceled because remodeling hadn't been completed in time in the first intended venue. It had to be moved to another club in town, the Gaiety.[44]

And so the band ended up playing in Mandan, North Dakota before 400 people. Even if the entire population of Mandan had turned out – little babies and all – the Coliseum's 100,000 crowd would have dwarfed them (Mandan showed 15,513 at the time of the 1980 census .. and that represented a growth spurt of 39.8% over 1970). This wasn't maximizing income; it was all in the service of the concept.

Two other similarly small venues were Zodiac, in Moorhead, Minnesota which also had a SRO capacity of 400 and the Hitching Post, in Cheyenne, with a 600 capacity. Those back-to-back nights in Mandan and Moorhead saw the band play to 800 people. The Stones had November 2 off, but on November 3 played to 18,210 people in Louisville, with a box office of $287,540, according to *Billboard*.

One club had stiffed Muddy Waters with bad checks two nights before the Destroyers show, so that date had to be switched on short notice. Another club (in Greensboro, North Carolina) went bankrupt between booking and the show date. Yet another one mistakenly booked two acts on the same night, and the Destroyers were the ones who got cut. Another scramble to find a suitable spot to set up and play. All this while the Stones were asking them to play consecutive nights at Madison Square Garden, and other promoters were fighting to secure bookings for other tours.

There was an eye-opener during the tour about the limitations of independent distribution. It revolved around the December 5 date when the Destroyers followed the Neville Brothers and opened for the Stones at the Superdome in New Orleans. This was not the Gaiety in Mandan. The Superdome seated an estimated 87,500; it was purportedly the largest indoor concert ever held anywhere. It was wonderful that the band was able to get its routing changed to link up for this one show (one of the fifty nights: the Louisiana entry), but the importance was perhaps lost on our lame distributor in New Orleans: All South. They ordered twenty-five copies of each LP. That's it. We tried to talk them up, but – nope – twenty-five copies. The Destroyers weren't as aware as we were of the disappointment, and the need we felt to prepare to move in another direction. If our distributors couldn't keep up with the growth of Destroyers, then we'd be holding the band back rather than helping them. Most of them did a good job, as did our licensees in Canada, Europe, and Australia, but it wasn't a perfect set-up.

The Destroyers with the Rolling Stones: (left to right) Ronnie Wood, George Thorogood, Bill Wyman, Bill Blough, Charlie Watts, Hank Carter, Jeff Simon, Ian Stewart

This was becoming big business of a sort, but 1981 was also the year in which we enjoyed releasing, in April, the first album of one of our all-time favorite bands, the Johnson Mountain Boys. It was Walt Saunders – a fireman in Falls Church, Virginia with a burning love of bluegrass – who had introduced us to the band. Walt had been involved in the founding of *Bluegrass Unlimited* and had written a glowing review of Rounder 0003 (Joe Val & the New England Bluegrass Boys) for *BU* back in 1971. He invited Ken and Hazel to dinner and played them some rough tapes. Walt's wife Ruby insisted they come check out the band at an afternoon show at a club in Maryland. Ken remembers women with rollers in their hair dancing to the music. Hardcore stuff. The band dressed in the old-fashioned style and didn't wait around for applause between numbers, rushing from one song to the next. Ken made sure they were booked into a hall in Massachusetts and within one minute both Marian and I were hooked, too.[45]

1982: collaborating with one of the majors

With both the 50/50 tour and the Stones tour behind them, the band was asked to open for the European portion of the Rolling Stones tour in the summer of 1982. And it was in 1981 that MTV was launched. It was evident to us that achievement of the band's possibilities was perhaps beyond our means without moving up to the next level. We loved the idea of making a music video but didn't feel we could afford the financial risk. We had a contract for another Destroyers record, but we didn't want to hold them back. There were similar occasions later when other artists, such as Iris DeMent or Tish Hinojosa, suddenly had opportunities open up for them. We never wanted to stand in the way of an artist's or group's success. We could imagine how they'd feel if they came to believe that entrusting their future to us with a two- or three-album deal prevented them from the best chance they might ever have in their career. (The grass often seems greener than it really is. Moving to a major label has not always helped an artist's career, but that would be something they would never have learned if they hadn't given it a try. Over the years, quite a few Rounder artists have left to go with a major label and come back later.)

In early 1982, it seemed like the time had come to see George signed to a major label. We decided we needed to talk to a music business lawyer about possibilities. We'd come to know Gerry Margolis from his role in representing the Destroyers against MCA over the *Better than the Rest* masters. Gerry had an idea, and it sounded to us like the best of both worlds. George was a quirky character, he knew, and distrusted the major labels. But he liked Rounder and felt a loyalty to us, and knew we could be good advocates and intermediaries for him in any dealings with a major. Gerry said it could be a mistake for George to "sign naked" to one of the majors, and that the best plan might be to form a joint venture and ask the majors to sign the venture not the band. That way, George would be protected to some degree, but the major would also benefit because they would get Rounder as part of the deal – not to own the company but to get Rounder's good offices and experience along with the talent of George and the Destroyers. So we went for it and formed the Rounder Destroyer Company. Because every major wanted to sign George, we could consider all the various labels that were out there and Gerry was able to set up interviews with a shortlist of our choice. We met with David Geffen, folks at Columbia, and with a new label starting up out of Capitol, EMI America. And that's where we signed, with Jim Mazza and EMI America on May 21, 1982. We had never intended to simply go to the highest bidder, and money truly wasn't a big part of it. The goal was to work out which situation we thought would be the best fit.

The band had already cut the *Bad to the Bone* album, but none of the companies were allowed to hear it until after we'd made our decision. Needless to say, once we had agreed on EMI America and the album came out, it was a hit. And the video got made, too, in an old boxing ring in New Jersey. It featured one of George's idols, Bo Diddley, and the legend of the poolrooms Willie Mosconi (with yours truly hovering in the background as an extra). As much as anything it was the video, played frequently on MTV, that made the album's title song one of the best-known songs the Destroyers ever cut. Both 'Bad to the Bone' and 'Who Do You Love?' have been used in literally dozens of commercials and movies over the years. Who could have predicted that 'Who Do You Love?' (the Bo Diddley number from the second

Destroyers album: Rounder 3013) would, over just a few years, earn us several hundred thousand dollars in advertising money from Samuel Adams beer?[46]

The deal was additionally intended to create a collaboration between Rounder and EMI America, and it led to the release of albums by two other groups that would likely have been out of Rounder's reach at the times: True Believers and the Neville Brothers. Unfortunately, nothing fully clicked with either. The Destroyers were clearly getting all the attention. Among the groups we specifically recommended to EMIA as part of the deal were: the BoDeans, Robert Cray, the Fabulous Thunderbirds, k.d. lang, and Nanci Griffith. Not a bad roster in itself. EMIA was slow to respond. We don't blame A&R man Neil Portnow (from 2002 to 2018 the longtime president of the Recording Academy – the Grammys). He had others he had to report to. And two years after we'd signed the deal, Jim Mazza was gone. Capitol Industries merged EMIA and Manhattan Records into one.

The whole experience was frustrating to us, because – other than k.d. lang and the BoDeans – these were acts with track records and acts we believed we were in a position to sign, with the additional funding from EMIA and the branch distribution network that a major label brought to the table. We also urged them to consider some acts we'd been working with and thought might be ready to move up the ladder, so to speak: Buckwheat Zydeco, Solomon Burke, and Marcia Ball. They didn't bite.

It was an unsatisfactory arrangement, and reinforced some inherent mistrust in dealing with major labels. Because of miscommunications, Rounder actually lost money on both the Nevilles and True Believers albums, even though none of the money at risk had ever been intended to be ours. Water under the bridge, now.

There were other opportunities that went by the board. We had been distributing Rhino Records since their inception, but Rhino had been looking for another sort of deal and signed with Capitol. They wanted to keep Rounder Distribution as well as going through Capitol, because they knew our more grassrootsy network would reach customers that the Capitol sales staff would not. Capitol's business affairs people proved too inflexible, less so than RCA which had worked out a supplemental distribution arrangement when it signed Windham Hill.

At Rounder's request, the collaboration agreement was dissolved save for the Destroyers. The *Billboard* headline read: "Rounder, EMI Sever Most Ties, Leave Options Open." Rounder made the move, but agreed that the Rounder Destroyer Company would continue to release recordings by GT & the Ds via EMI's branch distribution network. EMI had a right of first refusal on selected artists, but never expressed serious interest in other artists again.

It was ten years later – 1992 – before Rounder produced our own first music video: 'Every Time You Say Goodbye' by Alison Krauss.

The mid to late 1970s, in the rear-view mirror

Backing up to the mid to late 1970s, even while all the rockin' rhythm and blues was taking up a lot of our time, it wasn't as though Rounder had gone off the rails in pursuit of the big bucks. We were releasing plenty of the same sorts of albums as we'd always released, and working on many more. Thirty-two LPs were released in 1975 and the number stayed in the thirties until 1980, when it hit forty-five. It never dropped below forty again.

Early 1976 saw the release of Norman Blake's *Whiskey Before Breakfast* in February, noted above as the first album on which we ever paid an advance. That same month we put out a straight-ahead bluegrass album by Al Jones, Frank Necessary & the Spruce Mountain Boys, and an album called *Have Moicy!* which featured the Unholy Modal Rounders, Michael Hurley, and Jeffrey Frederick & the Clamtones. The Norman Blake album was one of our best sellers, and *Have Moicy!* sold well, too, also earning a number of plaudits – including being selected as the #1 album of the year by "the Dean of American Rock Critics" Robert Christgau in the *Village Voice*'s 1976 "Pazz & Jop" report.

March '76 saw second albums by Ted Lundy and Bob Paisley, by Snuffy Jenkins and Pappy Sherrill, and Tony Trischka. We also released an album by George Tucker of Beaver, Kentucky. Mark Wilson and I visited him, and Mark later edited tapes that had been made by Guy Carawan. George Tucker had been mining since the age of fourteen, but by the time we met he was retired, and a victim of black lung disease. He lived in a one-story house, *way* back up a holler. The house had window frames but no glass in the frames. Chickens kept walking in the door while we were talking, an occasional bird would flap through one of the window holes, and there were kids wandering around (George and his wife Della had nine children). This was real back-country Appalachia.

In May, we released an album recorded by Mark Wilson and named *Kitty Puss* which featured the remarkable fiddler Buddy Thomas, and we released an album of classic banjo by British banjoist William J. Ball, LRAM (that's Licentiate of the Royal Academy of Music, in case you are unfamiliar with the initials). His work with Buddy Thomas remains, over thirty years later, one of the highlights of Mark's recordings. The Emerson, Kentucky fiddler died in 1974 at age thirty-nine – just months after Mark and Gus Meade recorded him and got him to tell his life story.

In June we put out one of the more unusual albums – this really was quite a year for unusual or path-breaking recordings – one simply entitled *Hollerin'* (Rounder 0071). It was a "field recording" – of people from one North Carolina county (Sampson County) who, literally, hollered in their fields. A review in the *Tucson Citizen* explained it fairly succinctly: "If you think hollerin' is calling the pigs, it is. But it's also signaling distress, letting your neighbor know you're up and well, calling out when you're lost or just letting out the tune of your soul while you work." In the days before telephones, it was a form of communication from farm to farm in rural areas, and we recorded a number of practitioners of this folk art form hollering as best they could. One of them, Leonard Emmanuel, even appeared on national late-night TV, including *The Johnny Carson Show*, and was invited back. The record was produced in cooperation with the National Hollerin' Contest at Spivey's Corner, North Carolina. Mark Wilson, Bill Phillips, and I recorded ten practitioners of the art (including each of the seven previous champions, in one case "borrowing" current from an electrified farmyard fence in order to power the tape recorder). This was, literally, field recording. Mark remembered the reason why: "We recorded through the fence because the grandkids in the house were watching *American Bandstand* and wouldn't turn it off. The main trouble with the result (besides the buzz of the fence) was that flies kept hitting the microphone (*thonk!*). In those days you had to cut them out of the tape with a razor blade."[47] We did. The *Hollerin'* album sold fairly well, by our standards.

Mark O'Connor's second album, *Pickin' in the Wind*, came out in June, too. This one did more to establish him than his first, which we'd put out when Mark was just twelve (released back in March 1976). July saw the release of the first Cajun album from Ralph Rinzler's trip, and the second E.C. & Orna Ball album, *Fathers Have a Home Sweet Home*, with its gorgeous Blue Ridge scene gracing the front cover. An album of toasts that Bruce Jackson recorded, mostly in Texas Department of Corrections facilities, named *Get Your Ass in the Water and Swim Like Me*, offered an odd contrast. And the solo debuts of two progressive music artists – David Grisman and Bill Keith – both came out in July.[48]

All this while Ken was leading the summer-long effort to sell records from the Rounder stand at the Smithsonian Festival of American Folklife for seven days a week all twelve weeks of the summer, working on the Mall from June 16 through September 6, with Marian and I traveling back and forth to help out. This was really an astonishing effort – to get onto the Mall and open up shop, bringing out dozens of boxes of records to be on display for the thousands of customers who visited the festival all summer long, doing business while watching over them, then securing them all away every evening – maybe twelve hours later, for twelve full weeks. No days off. An array of volunteers helped, since there was a need for the occasional meal and bathroom break. Simply writing this down over forty years later, it's hard to imagine how much work we packed into one year, with quite a small staff.

There was an amusing time later in the year. A joint meeting of the Society for Ethnomusicology and the American Folklore Society was held at the Benjamin Franklin Hotel in Philadelphia from November 10–14, 1976. We thought, "What an opportunity to sell some records at a gathering of true folklorists" and we got permission to set up a record stand at the meeting. Mark Wilson organized a descriptive catalog of some of the most traditional

Ken Irwin at Willow Avenue

albums we had, from the various labels we were distributing – Folkways, Folk Lyric, Rounder, and more. We hauled a lot of records there, set up, and came back having sold almost nothing. These folklorists were asking us for records by Judy Collins and the like.

During that Smithsonian Festival in the summer, Scott Billington, who was to become Rounder's longest-serving employee, joined us, on June 16, 1976. As I've said, we had just two or three other employees there at the time – and that was it. As for us, we still didn't see it as "work" at the time; we were on a mission. It was just what we did.

Shortly before the Smithsonian festival began, at the end of the college year, Mark Wilson and I drove up to Cape Breton, Nova Scotia. It's hard to believe that some of the fiddlers there would, in days gone by, actually do a round trip to "the Boston states" over a long weekend to play a show, and then go back home. Mark Wilson says, "There's a French holiday akin to Halloween in Chéticamp and Edmond Boudreau told me of driving home one weekend, putting on a mask and saying 'boo' to the folks, and returning to Boston."[49] Even today, it's a long, long haul – around 750-plus miles and more than twelve hours of driving. Back in the 1940s and '50s, the only available roads made it a much longer haul. We recorded Theresa & Marie MacLellan playing a dance at Big Pond on Friday, June 11 and also cut albums with fiddler Carl MacKenzie and virtuoso Cape Breton pianist Doug MacPhee.[50] Over the course of time, Mark recorded more than twenty-five albums of Cape Breton music.

Later in the year, I took a trip to Sabbathday Lake, near Poland Spring, Maine, to visit the Shakers. Many people know of the Shakers as craftspeople, but not as much is known about the rest of their culture. Daniel Patterson of the University of North Carolina had recorded an album of music by the Shakers, and I wanted to visit. The Shakers remain known for the simplicity and elegance of the home furniture they designed, but Sister Mildred Barker, close to ninety years old, told me, "I don't want to be remembered as a chair." A later review in *NY Press* commented on her singing, "Her sharp and mannered vocals dig for every ounce of sacrament that the beautiful vocals allowed." This was the material for the record *Early Shaker Spirituals* of May 1977, coming out just two months before the first George Thorogood album. In June, we put out *Tony Rice* (0085), the first of many albums with this extremely influential bluegrass vocalist and guitarist.

I already mentioned the *Boone Creek* album of August 1977 and, earlier in the year, in April, we released our first licensed album. A Balxfa Brothers release, it was licensed from Cézame, based in Paris, France. It later turned out that Cézame stopped paying royalties to the Balfas. When Dewey Balfa told us about it, we interceded and got Cézame's permission to pay the artist's share directly to the Balfas and the remainder of the licensing royalties to the French company.

The year 1978 kicked off with nine albums in January alone, one of which was our first children's album, a three-LP box by Mike and Peggy Seeger, *American Folk Songs for Children*.

As a reminder that these were different times, in March we sent out a notice advising distributors that we were pleased to be doing such a great business in 8-track tapes as well as cassettes. We established a uniform list price ($7.98) for all three configurations. Our wholesale price was $3.30 per unit. Anyone still got a Rounder 8-track?

Were we rolling in dough? Ken was going through some old boxes in 2009 and came across his 1976 income tax return. His income for that year was $4,680. It jumped the following year to an astronomical $6,148.32.

And pretty much everything we had was going back into the company. We couldn't have imagined it any other way.

Once Scott Billington joined us, unlike the scores upon scores who have come and gone over the years, he stayed, and was still with Rounder in 2017, working for the Concord Music Group. Scott's work with Gatemouth Brown earned Rounder our first Grammy Award, in 1982. We've gone on since to average more than a Grammy a year, but Gate's was our first. Scott was a Renaissance guy who at one time or another was Rounder's head of sales, did some radio promotion, was head of the art department, head of A&R, and a record producer. In 2018, he went off payroll and became a consultant to Concord, but remained involved in producing albums for the company.

We first all met at a Boston Blues Society show at the Harvard Freshman Union.[51] Scott was one of the group running the BBS and Rounder had set up a record table in the hall outside the room where the concert was. This was in 1972 and Scott thinks it may have been a Little Brother Montgomery show. Scott was the manager of downtown Boston record store New England Music City. Always a prodigy, he'd been promoted to store manager at age nineteen or so. He had met Ken at the store when Ken came by to sell records, and Scott liked what Rounder represented.

Scott recalled in 2016:

> During that time, when I was managing the store, I also became editor of a monthly music magazine called *Poptop*. It was published by Barry Glovsky, who previously had a magazine called *Fusion*, a pioneering rock journalism magazine. People like Robert Christgau and Peter Guralnick wrote for *Fusion*, and *New York Times* music critic Jon Pareles wrote for *Poptop* – I may have been his first editor. I recruited specialists from different genres of music to write columns, including Ken and Marian, who wrote a bluegrass column. I got to know them that way, too. I would write an editorial every issue, about things like how records got to be cut out [remaindered] and how we were able to sell them for 99¢ or $1.99. I'd done a little bit of writing for it as well – an article on professional shoplifters.

This was before the days of compact discs; these were twelve-inch-square LPs. "Exactly. It was quite a feat to walk off with several LPs. I got an interview with one of these guys and talked with him for an afternoon about how he made his living stealing things."

But that wasn't all. There was something else that caused Scott to seek other employment. The magazine's lifeblood came from record company advertising. *Billboard, Record World,* and *Cashbox* all published weekly charts listing the bestsellers. Retailers wanted to stock what was selling; getting onto the chart, or moving up the chart, helped sell more records. There were no UPC codes with optical scanners; the charts were based on reporting from retailers. Scott wrote an editorial for *Poptop* about how the major labels tried to (as he put it, "sometimes more than gently") influence the reports that record store buyers would submit.

> That was quite an era in the record business when the money and the freebies were flowing. Columbia Records had a contest every week. They would call you every Monday with a list of three or four singles and four or five albums, and call you back on Thursday. If you could repeat to them that same list of records that they had read to you on Monday, you would get a prize that next week. The salesman would bring by a fifth of Jack Daniel's or something like that. I was not much of a drinker, so I had quite a collection of bottles of booze in the back of the store.

Scott was playing harmonica and singing in a band, Roseland, which was having some local success at the time. Greg Kinnamon, a promotion guy in the area, had the idea of starting an independent sales and promotion company that could represent different labels or distributors, and get the records into the stores and get them played on the radio.

> We came to the three Rounder founders with this idea that we would do sales and promotion. I think, at the same time, they were thinking of making their operation a little more professional and mainstream, to be able to do a better job for the artists that they had signed. Just getting the records better out there. So we went and had a meeting and we all decided that, yes, we would go forward with this idea.[52]

Well, there was far from enough business coming out of Rounder and the idea only lasted a few weeks, but Scott himself stayed with Rounder as a salesperson.

Scott had been subscribing to the British blues magazines since he was fifteen. Rounder had been issuing blues records, too.

> I had this idea that if I worked for Rounder, I could be closer to some of this music and maybe just be a fly on the wall for some of the recording sessions for this music that I loved so much. Little by little, the opportunity to do many more things than selling records materialized.
>
> I started out, as part of my sales job, preparing the new release flyers that would go out to the stores every month. Writing the blurbs – which I'm still doing right now. And doing some artwork. I'd always been artistically inclined as a kid, just drawing pictures and doing graphic kinds of things. I started looking over the shoulder of Susan Marsh, who was designing many of Rounder's album covers at the time. Partly, it was just to get my graphic skills together as they applied to the new release sheets and the sales flyers. I started thinking, "I bet I could design album covers, too."
>
> The first actual album production that I became involved with for Rounder was the Johnny Shines record Durg Gessner had recorded at our Boston Blues Society concerts. Peter Guralnick and I knew about these tapes and thought they would make a fantastic Johnny Shines record.

Hey Ba-Ba-Re-Bop (Rounder 2020) was issued in April 1979, and Scott designed the cover, too. Peter wrote the notes.

Not long afterward, Scott and I traveled to the Bahamas to record Joseph Spence; that was enjoyable. That record came out in April 1980.

8 Starting Our Second Decade: A Maturing Company, and Some Real Growing Pains

What was the reaction in other areas to all this hoopla around George Thorogood & the Destroyers? For one thing, it made Scott's job as a salary-plus-commission salesperson more viable. It was a windfall. But there were, as always, the unexpected oddities. Scott recalled one:

> This album by the Moms & Dads started to sell in Maine; it was on GNP/Crescendo, a label Rounder distributed. It was a band of four senior citizens playing accordion, clarinet, piano, and . . . I can't remember what the fourth instrument was . . . doing songs from the thirties and forties. They did a TV campaign and all of a sudden I was selling more Moms & Dads albums than George Thorogood. Five or six thousand a month. That was the biggest payday I had, on commission, at Rounder.

Otherwise, things maybe didn't change so much, other than the company kept growing and more people were needed.

Not every year saw major breakthroughs. In retrospect, 1979 looks like a "more of the same" year in terms of releases from Rounder, including second or third albums by quite a number of artists, with most of the other new albums fitting into pre-existing patterns. We released our first Dry Branch Fire Squad album, Jerry Douglas's first career solo album, our second by John Jackson, and our fourth by Joe Val. The *Togo* album (Rounder 5004) came out near the end of the year, as did a couple of reissues. The only releases that represented a departure from the norm were the two NRBQ (New Rhythm and Blues Quartet) albums *Kick Me Hard* and *All Hopped Up*. This was the classic Q, with Al Anderson on guitar and both Terry Adams and Donn Adams in the group. Over the years, we released twelve albums by NRBQ.

And even a couple by the Shaggs, an all-sister group from New Hampshire that the kinder reviewers (and Carla Bley) claimed had invented their own unique kind of music. Their album *Philosophy of the World* was unleashed on an unsuspecting world in April 1980. Some people got it, and some people didn't. Some people found it unlistenable, almost as though it was deliberately recorded to be sung off-key and to generally be off-kilter musically. We started hearing that record store clerks occasionally put the record on at closing time, to drive customers from the store. Those who "got it" raved about it. Frank Zappa called them "better than the Beatles" and in December 1999 Tom Cruise optioned *New Yorker* writer Susan Orlean's article about the group.[53]

What was the *Togo* album? I had heard a tape recorded by a woman named Lisa Leghorn. She was active for a while in the Cambridge women's movement (New Words Book Shop was one of our busiest accounts: we distributed Olivia Records, with Holly Near and others), and Lisa had lived in Togo for a while, with Victor Aladji, a Togolese poet and writer who lived in the capital, Lomé. He came from the town of Kpalimé, and a friend of mine, Dan Kahn, and I decided to strike out for a field recording trip to West Africa. We were there from July 6 to August 18, did a fair amount of recording, and then hitch-hiked north to Ouagadougou in what was then Upper Volta (now Burkina Faso), where Dan had a cousin working with a post-Peace Corps NGO. We then hitched back south through Ghana, and rejoined Victor before heading back home. Like everything we touched back then, the album did well enough. Three years later, Dan and I went to West Africa on another trip, too, to Nigeria, and then to Zambia in 1985 for a third recording venture tied into the struggle against apartheid in South Africa. More on that below.

Speaking of Olivia, that was pretty interesting. Several years earlier, a couple of people from Olivia had come to visit, asking us how we ran our record company. I can still remember sitting around our plywood dining room table at the Willow Avenue house. In NAIRD, it was quite common for all the members to happily share all kinds of details. We were all in it together, and we were the indie labels as distinct from the big corporate majors. Maybe we at Rounder were already something of a model.

The union

Something else happened in 1979. Rounder became unionized.

By springtime 1979, the distance and differences between the three Rounders and our employees had apparently grown – at least in the minds of some employees – to the extent that there was a campaign to unionize the "workforce" (all twenty-two of them). A sufficient number signed authorization cards indicating their desire to form a union. It came out of the blue. We were stunned. We didn't see ourselves as magnates, or even unreasonable employers. We were already offering things many unions wouldn't even *ask for* – not only the full array of holidays and vacation time, but we had also implemented (without it having been requested) twelve floating "sick/personal" days which allowed people to take off a day a month, no questions asked.

The creation of a union set up an adversarial relationship where none had existed before, or so it seemed. Perhaps we'd just been seeing things through rose-colored glasses. Inevitably, there are fundamental differences between employer and employee. But we'd never fired anyone, and never even faced a serious disciplinary problem of any sort.

What was the reason for the union? My take on it was that two factors contributed, both related to recent changes in the work and the workplace. The nature of the work had shifted dramatically, with the tremendous interest in George Thorogood & the Destroyers and the associated demands placed on the time of the three Rounders. Now, rather than us picking orders like everyone else, we were on the phone dealing with all these unfamiliar people. Or we were traveling – to this set of shows or to a meeting somewhere. It was exciting, and Ken and Marian handled the brunt of it. I was still teaching college, but even I was caught up in trying to hold things together and fielding calls when the other two were away.

Whether the employees were seeing dollar signs, we don't know. I never thought that was it. The best I could guess was – however patronizing this may come across – that they felt we had abandoned them in some sense. The notion of "the Rounder family" had been ruptured. We were off in the business world somewhere and had left them behind to the less glamorous work of packing boxes and shipping records. The language in the union's proposal certainly implied something along those lines: "We care about everyone at Rounder, as co-workers and friends. Unfortunately, possibly because of physical separations and external strains, the communication between the owners and workers has broken down considerably over the course of the past few months."

The campaign to collect signatures on the authorization cards began not long after we moved to our Otis Street warehouse. Before that, as you will recall, we'd been operating out of a small rented warehouse in Medford: an office area with a warehouse space directly behind it. We were all on top of each other all the time, and there was an intimacy to it that was lost with the move to East Cambridge. When the Medford toilet stopped working for a month or so in the winter, we all had to use the nearby gas station and, well, that was just the way it was.

The space on Otis Street was an elongated rectangle that was a full city block in length, but only perhaps fifty feet in width. It created a workspace where the front office was a considerable distance from the back shipping area and loading dock, with racks and racks of shelving in between. It created a physical division which perhaps emphasized other senses of division that

The warehouse at One Camp Street

were being felt by disaffected workers. And this was all while our attention was being demanded by George and the Destroyers. "They were increasingly spending their time on the phone, in meetings, traveling with artists," wrote Scott Alarik in *Sing Out!* "The workers felt estranged, and, worse, unmanaged. No one seemed to be around to make decisions necessary to the workplace." I'm not sure what those decisions were. But I take it on faith that there were some. It's not as though any of the three of us had any training in HR – or anything related to running a business.

One of the problems all three Rounders had is that none of us was a disciplinarian. None of us was a really good leader, in any way but leadership by example. We simply weren't good at managing people. That could arguably be a good thing but, in cases such as this, it was a weakness of our "management style." If we saw people standing around in the aisles whiling the time away talking to each other about something, we'd rarely ever say anything at all. Typically what we'd do is simply pick up the speed at which we were ourselves picking orders, and buzz past them hoping they'd notice that we were working at lightning speed while they were standing around doing nothing constructive. We behaved as though hard work was contagious and would somehow catch on, pushing them to work faster. It would have been much more straightforward to simply say what was on our mind. We could build up a degree of resentment for people who were goofing off too much of the time. One could say it was unrealistic of us to expect that anyone was ever going to work as hard as we did, since we were – after all – the owners and would stand to ultimately benefit.

As it happens, we've had a considerable number of employees who worked for ten, fifteen, twenty, or more years. But that only built over time. In 1980, no one had been there more than a few years.

One of them, of course, was Scott Billington, who'd begun in 1976. In early 2016, he was asked what he thought had prompted unionization.

> I had very ambiguous feelings about the union. I didn't vote. I just refused to participate in it. I didn't have much to do with it at all. [Scott, Laura Dickerson, and maybe one or two others were "grandfathered" in, and not forced to join the union.] Anyone can always get better compensation. I had always felt that I had done a pretty good job of negotiating compensation for what I did at Rounder, but also in negotiating opportunity. I look back at my long career with Rounder now and that's what I really appreciate – the opportunity to do so many things. Really, to learn on the job.
>
> When I started producing records, I had no real knowledge of how to do that. I had only enthusiasm, and a surety in what I wanted to hear. And when I started doing graphic design, I was really out on a limb. Again, I think I had the ability underneath it all, but I hadn't been to school. I actually did take some courses in graphic design at the Art Institute of Boston, once I started, and I kept studying music.
>
> To have those kinds of opportunities, and get paid for pursuing them, it just seemed like it always worked out.

But that was Scott. It is perhaps not unfair to suggest that he had the talent and the self-confidence to work out things for himself. Some others clearly had concerns of one sort or another, or maybe felt the need to combine with others to push for benefits or protections they thought they might not be able to secure on their own.

There were some odd notions. In October 1979, Steve Morse reported in the *Boston Globe* that some employees claimed the Rounder owners were "getting more into rock music" and "turning into hip capitalists." That characterization didn't feel like it fit at the time, nor does it decades later.

Some of the proponents of the union were a little heavy-handed at first, reaching out to some local organizations like the Cambridge Food Co-op and a left-wing bookstore, The Red Book. Someone from the Food Co-op wrote us and told us to "not interfere with what we feel is a basic right for workers under any condition – the right to unionize." To interfere would be illegal, a violation of federal law. We really didn't need one or more of our workers contacting a food cooperative to write us and tell us to obey federal law. This sort of thing made us wonder where some people's heads were at.

We did our homework, checking pay scales at our competition – both among other independent record labels and distributors, and in the Boston retail community we checked pay at places like the Harvard Coop. Among the distributors, we didn't just sample them. We checked in with every single distributor. Not one other record label or distributorship had a union, but the mutually supportive environment that NAIRD had fostered from the start helped make potential rivals willing to routinely share data of this type. We didn't think the wages we'd been paying were high at all, but we found that they were better than those being paid by every single one of the competing distributors. And not one of them offered twelve sick/personal days. The Harvard Coop was known for relying on rapid turnover among the student population to keep wage levels low.

Facts of this sort didn't seem to matter. After extensive discussion, an election was held on November 14, 1979. Of the twenty-two eligible voters, fourteen voted to unionize. The campaign had succeeded. For better or worse, Rounder now had a union. It was an unorthodox one, and some of the personalities among the workers at Rounder occasionally seemed to present as many problems for the Local 925 leadership as they did for Rounder management. Local 925 was part of the Service Employees International Union (SEIU).

They worked to get benefits such as formal recognition of two fifteen-minute breaks (previously, people just took breaks when they felt like it and there had never seemed to us to be any significant problem, but they wanted the clarity of a structure). We had a warehouse manager by this time, Duncan Browne, a former comic book and record shop owner who had been a good friend of George Thorogood before we knew George.

There was a fair amount of rhetoric tossed around, often to try to beat us down. After the union formed, any time there would be a contract negotiation, they would trot out our old, original statement of purpose wherein we had once proclaimed our goal to be an anti-profit collective.[54] We understood why: they wanted to hold us up as hypocrites who preached one thing and practiced another. Of course, we hadn't preached the one thing for six or seven years. And not one among the union membership ever expressed the slightest interest in becoming part of a living and working collective. That time seemed well past, with over twenty-five employees and so many people having arrived at Rounder with a variety of other personal goals in mind – some of them as simple as holding a good job.

It was a young group, those who applied to work at a record company. We were ourselves between thirty and thirty-five years old. Few of these employees had ever worked in the real world. Things that Rounder had implemented even before unionization – 100% health plan coverage, automatic cost of living increases, the twelve "no questions" floating personal days throughout the year in addition to two weeks' vacation, and an extra two weeks of pay as a Christmas bonus – seemed like a starting-off place for them. Many real-world workers would have been stunned to be offered benefits like this (forty-one-and-half days of paid time off) – and still would.

Negotiations were often protracted, and – given the small workforce – it was easy to see that Clause A benefited one employee only while Clause B benefited only one other. Further complicating matters, the contract was structured such that almost every individual worker had their own separate job title, bringing about inevitable conflicts as the work shifted and people were asked to move from one job to another. This had started as us trying to make people feel better about their work by letting people more or less make up whatever job titles they wanted; it came back to bite us since the contract called for pay increases when moving from one position to another. Almost any movement, even when we were trying to promote from within, kicked off a whole round of individually oriented discussions and negotiations. A couple of times, the union reps privately expressed frustration to us; this was a small local in their much larger portfolio.

We actually did get work done

We kept on putting out records through all of this.

In 1980, we put out forty-five albums – all on 33 rpm. January saw Béla Fleck's first album, *Crossing the Tracks*. Béla was twenty years old at the time of recording. We were pleased in 2008 to welcome Béla back to the label where he'd put out his first six albums. The same month in 1980 we released a calypso album by the Growling Tiger, thanks to the dedicated efforts of Steve Shapiro. A later attempt to record Roaring Lion (we liked the idea of both

Cover of *Crossing the Tracks* by Béla Fleck (Rounder 0121; Janaury 1980)

Lion and Tiger on Rounder) fell apart after we'd flown Lion to New York from Trinidad, only to find him renege on almost every aspect of the agreement. We had to cancel that session.

And we released a guitar album from Mark O'Connor. Not only was he a prize-winning fiddle player, but he had won the National Flatpicking Contest at Winfield, Kansas for many years. Only in 2016 did we learn from Mark, after he had re-signed with Rounder, that our request that he do a guitar album for us – and our helping to bring in Tony Rice and David Grisman (David wrote the liner notes, too) – was instrumental in alleviating a considerable depression that had haunted Mark while his mother was slowly dying from cancer.

Dry Branch's 1981 album *Antiques and Inventions* was processed with an inventive flair by someone at our cassette manufacturer, who misprinted the title on the label as *Antiques and Inventories*. Years later, Katy Moffatt titled her album *The Greatest Show on Earth*. Ringling Brothers and Barnum & Bailey objected and threatened a civil suit. The album quickly became *Evangeline Hotel*. Something of a design flaw truncated Jeff White's name into "Jett" White on a later album, as well. From a few years earlier, another collector's item was the first album by J.D. Crowe & the New South, which showed J.D. flipping off the photographer. We replaced that cover photo with another one. The album was reissued with its original front jacket as LP only, on Record Store Day in 2016.

From France, we put out a couple more Pierre Bensusan albums. Bensusan is a brilliant French guitarist, a friend of Bill Keith's. We had licensed the first album, *Près de Paris*, from Cézame and released it in March 1978. From Nashville, there was Vernon Oxford, one of the more soulful of the pure and underappreciated straight-ahead country singers. It was almost twenty years later, but we were pleased when *Music Row*'s Bob Oermann once wrote of Rounder's work, "Sometimes it takes an 'outsider' to show us The Way . . . By clinging to tradition [Boston's Rounder Records] has wound up sounding more revolutionary than anybody on Music Row these days." He was writing in 1997 about a month in which we released albums by Claire Lynch, Paul Williams, Jody Stecher, Kate Brislin, and a few more.

From the Boston area itself, we put out the first Preacher Jack album. This mad, skinny preacher who played piano was a favorite of the Destroyers – so much so that Jeff and Billy played drums and bass on the record, with Sleepy LaBeef playing guitar. Talk about talent: playing both Jerry Lee Lewis and Albert Ammons. And charisma – it wouldn't be unusual for Preacher to hold the Shipwreck Lounge room rapt for a full five minutes between numbers as he declaimed about the wonders of orange juice.

We put out albums by Robert Junior Lockwood, John Hammond, Jo-El Sonnier . . . the list goes on. It includes *Three on the Trail*, the first of an even dozen albums by Riders in the Sky. This cowboy trio consisting of Woody Paul, Too Slim, and Ranger Doug ("the idol of American youth") was first brought to our attention by Dr. Charles Wolfe. Charles simply told us we had to sign them. There is no substitute for word-of-mouth recommendations by good friends whose musical taste we came to trust. We weren't disappointed, not in the least. This was a group that did everything the cowboy way. Ranger Doug was Doug Green, a folklorist in his spare time. Years later, in 1996, we released four albums that Doug edited, a retrospective of seventy years of recorded cowboy music. "Cowboy Crooners Get Their Due" was the headline of Daniel Buckley's feature piece in the *Tucson Citizen*.

Tony Rice veered off in another direction with a jazz album, recording a Miles Davis track and seven of his own compositions on *Mar West* as the Tony Rice Unit, with Richard Greene and Todd Phillips, with Sam Bush and Mike Marshall on several of the tracks. Another company might not have wanted to follow Tony on his musical explorations, but we were game.

In October came the third Thorogood LP, *More*.

Heartbeat Records (and also our first Grammy)

In addition to the 50/50 tour with the Destroyers, 1981 also saw us start another label and launch a reggae line, Heartbeat Records. We had decided to elaborate our offerings under different label names and Heartbeat was the first such imprint. The reasons were twofold: one, it was a reggae label, and, two, it had slightly different ownership. It was Duncan Browne's idea. He'd come to know a promoter named Mike Cacia, who knew there was a market for reggae. The 1972 film *The Harder They Come* had grown on U.S. audiences over the years, and there was a viable touring market for the better acts from Jamaica. We set up a company with Duncan, Mike, and the three Rounders all as co-owners.

We pretty much chose the first three records all at once – licensing Linton Kwesi Johnson's *Dread Beat An' Blood* from Virgin (we'd seen that film, too), and albums from both Mikey Dread and Big Youth. LKJ's record was issued in December 1981, and the other two followed in January 1982.

Duncan and I had already taken our first trip to Jamaica, landing on July 30, 1981. We didn't really know the lay of the land. On arriving, we found there were no rental cars to be had, since Independence Day in Jamaica was on August 6, and already people were flocking home from abroad. That it was also Duncan's birthday had nothing to do with the crowds. The tourist desk booked a room in a guest house on Mountain View Road, the Beverly Cliff House, and we took JOS city buses from the airport to get there. It was right across from the National Stadium. We had a beer at a bar named National Hideout and some chicken at Jerkland. We visited briefly with Mikey Dread to try to make arrangements for his album, but Big Youth was out of town at first. We took a train to Port Antonio just to look around, riding on top of the train cars for a good part of the way. After we got back to Kingston, the bus

Duncan Browne

passed two or three men with automatic rifles standing over a dead body in the road. We nevertheless decided – against all warnings from the people at the guest house – to catch the bus to Spanish Town where I-Roy had a sound system going that night at 2 Prince Avenue. Somehow we managed to get the last bus back, stopping once for four police vehicles which blocked the road with twenty or more guys bearing machine guns and automatic rifles. We decided to give ourselves Jamaican nicknames; Duncan adopted the name "Prince Sky Juice" for himself, and I picked "Dr. Ginger Beer."

Then we made our way to Montego Bay and took in Sunsplash, meeting Mutabaruka, the Mighty Diamonds, and finding Mike Cacia easily enough. This was an early Sunsplash, not as crowded as it quickly became in subsequent years.

Three days after I got back to Cambridge, I was off to New Zealand and Australia with George Thorogood & the Destroyers.

I returned to Jamaica in January, carrying $5,000 in cash, and met up with Mike Cacia for a truly unique recording venture. We had decided to record a live reggae album on January 20 at Skateland Roller Disco, an outdoor facility at Half Way Tree in Kingston, which Mike had booked for the event. During the day and early evening, it was a roller-skating rink where people skated to disco and reggae. We had posters printed up advertising the show as "A Dee-Jay Explosion" and listed numerous performers who were to "toast" as DJs over the Gemini sound system. Everything was done at the last minute.

Earlier in the day, we bought a couple of dubplates from Winston Riley, and went to the 3M facility in town to buy some 10 inch reels of tape, then traveled to Gussie Clarke's Music Works to hire him to run the tape machine at the show. We met with D&G about having Red Stripe sponsor the show, but that didn't fly. We got there around 6 pm but the action didn't really begin until after 10. The place was mobbed, and some people told us they'd had to wait in line for an hour just to get in. It was the hottest event on the island, packed out with several thousand people inside and on the streets outside. Eek-A-Mouse reported that he'd been "harassed" on the way in – meaning that security took his knife. It was, he had told us at Tuff Gong earlier, one he had "for domestic purposes." Mike had hired some security to protect Gussie's equipment (and us): a gent toting an M16.

We were operating the sound system from inside a concrete booth, which had an iron rail grating almost totally blocked up by tape recorders tied to the bars. There was one fluorescent table lamp to provide lighting and that was it, but Archie at the controls never once missed and no one ever bumped the turntables. Some rhythms ran for as long as half an hour, over and over as different DJs took their turn voicing. Numerous performers went on for a track or two each – Dillinger, Lone Ranger, Brigadier Jerry, Sister Nancy, and more. Eek-A-Mouse was one of the billed stars of the show and, just as he was about to go on, he was arrested by police – not for the knife but for an earlier incident when he'd thrown a brick through producer Junjo Lawes' BMW windshield. The sound was stopped and lights flashed on. Appeals for calm were made over the microphone. The crowd was menacing and the police finally agreed to let Eek-A do his thing after about fifteen tense minutes of haggling over the arrest. Big Youth arrived and made his first appearance at a sound system in something like six years. Ringo, Little John, Trinity, and U-Brown all got shots, as did Prince Mohammed, Welton Irie, Prince Jazzbo, Lee Van Cliff, Nigger Kojak, Principal, Michigan & Smiley, and Yellowman. More than once, the scene seemed to be devolving into total chaos, but it worked out well enough that we were ultimately released two albums from the evening's activity. Led by the man with the M16, we left around 3 am with Gussie and the recorder and made it back to the room – in time for me to get back up at 5:30 am to catch an early flight back to Boston.

A Dee-Jay Explosion Inna Dance Hall Style (Heartbeat HB-04) was released in September 1982. It remains one of the most vital live recordings ever done during this period of Jamaican music.

It wasn't just Heartbeat in 1981, not by any means. We released forty other titles, too. Notable recordings included:

- Our first with Sleepy LaBeef, with another one of our long titles: *It Ain't What You Eat It's the Way How You Chew It*. Peter Guralnick was one who shepherded this record to completion, and wrote the notes.

- *Sweet Mother*, by Nigeria's Prince Nico Mbarga, whose infectious West African hit record Dan Kahn and I had heard repeatedly while recording the Togo album in 1977. In 1980, we both traveled to Nigeria and concluded a licensing deal with Prince Rogers Okonkwo of Rogers All-Stars of Onitsha. Royalty.
- The soundtrack of the independent film *The Atomic Cafe.*
- Reissues of Flatt & Scruggs and Lefty Frizzell, and – from an even earlier era – Haywire Mac.
- Johnny Copeland's *Copeland Special*, which won the W.C. Handy Award as "Blues Album of the Year." Also featuring Dan Doyle and Ken Vangel, it was the first of several albums from this Houston bluesman. Dan later helped promote the album at MIDEM in Cannes, and had an unusual way of avoiding the need to pay for a hotel room. He had a Eurail pass so he left Cannes at night, rode the train to the Spanish border, got off, and then took the next train back, sleeping both ways on the rails.
- Our first Grammy Award-winning album, Clarence Gatemouth Brown's *Alright Again!*, produced by Jim Bateman and Scott Billington in June, in Bogalusa, and released in November.
- Second albums by Guy Van Duser and the Tony Rice Unit, and first ones from Rory Block and David Olney.

Winning a Grammy was a big deal, of course, for Rounder. It was ultimately funded by someone we came across who had represented an investor who had some money he wanted to shelter from taxes by investing in a production. There were hence three or four albums we recorded which we otherwise would have thought unaffordable. Scott Billington had bought Gate's single 'Okie Dokie Stomp' from Skippy White's Record Shop in Boston, back when he was a teenager.[55] His idea was for this record was to

> ... bring him back to the big band Texas R&B sound with which he had made his mark in the first place. Kind of extension of what T-Bone Walker had done in Texas in the Fifties, but Gatemouth made it a little more exciting. He played a little faster and he had a very distinctive guitar style using a capo in open tuning, and playing these absolutely rapid-fire blasts of notes.

Scott continued:

> I didn't quite know what I was getting myself into. If you're going to make a "little big band" record in the studio, live, you've got to have that music written out for everybody to play, particularly the horn players. We were using the recording studio as a rehearsal

Cover of *Alright Again!* by Clarence Gatemouth Brown (Rounder 2028; November 1981)

space, while the horn players were out in another room scribbling out their parts. We added other musicians in, too, like Red Tyler on tenor sax, Stanton Davis on trumpet. Finally, the rhythm section would be rehearsed, the horn chart would be written, and we'd get out into the studio and listen to Gate for whatever he had in terms of fine-tuning groove and tempo. We'd get a couple ready and then cut them live, and then go back and do the same process again. At the end of eight days of recording and mixing, we had the record done. It was an exhilarating experience, seeing everything come together like that. It was a different approach from the documentary approach that Rounder had used on many records.

It was Scott's first recording in Louisiana, made in Bogalusa.

We didn't even know the record had been nominated; no one from Rounder was a member of the Recording Academy at the time. Both Scott and I later became "governors" – in effect, on the board of local chapters. I was on the board of the Texas Chapter (that's another story), but I can truly say today I was a Texas Governor – serving contemporaneously with George W. Bush.

In later years, I have served several times on "craft committees," helping with screening entries in some of the fields such as Best Historical Album and Best Liner Notes. The finalists are then put to the vote by members of the Academy. As Scott says,

Little by little, I just kept making proposals to the founders to make more records in Louisiana. I did a record with Tuts Washington, the piano player, his debut record at the age of seventy-seven. He'd always been very suspicious of recording. And then James Booker, the great genius of American piano, who had only had one studio record in his life up to the point when we recorded his album *Classified.* He died the year after that.

Scott produced dozens of albums for Rounder, many from Louisiana, where before long Rounder became the most active record company in the state. After Rounder sold the company to Concord, and the new regime decided to move Rounder to Nashville (that's another story, too), Scott arranged things so that he could move to New Orleans and do A&R work from there.

In this period of plentiful releases, we also toyed with the idea of diversifying into books, but that was not to happen until 2004, and in the 1980s we remained focused on records.

1983: sixty albums, more than one per week

Although the 1983 average comes out at over one a week, in July that year we only released one.

The release of *Best of Studio One* (Heartbeat 07) was the brainchild of Chris Wilson, and launched an extraordinary series of reggae reissues, which

Cover of *The Best of Studio One* on Heartbeat (Heartbeat 07; July 1983)

ran uninterrupted for twenty-five years until Chris lost his position in the dramatic staff reductions of 2008. Chris had grown up in Jamaica, where his father ran a security business, only leaving the island when it was time to go to college in the Boston area. His musically formative teenage years were spent hearing the sounds of young Jamaica, which became an independent country in 1962, unleashing an unparalleled period of musical activity that has likely never been approached in any other place at any other time. Literally thousands of singles were cut by a wide variety of artists, and Clement Dodd's Studio One sound system and label were at the heart of it all. Chris revered Mr. Dodd – aka "Coxsone" – and the work he had done over the years, always knowing that, when he heard a new record he liked, the chances were it was a Studio One release.

Over the next quarter-century, Chris selected and annotated over sixty-five albums of Studio One music which appeared on Heartbeat, even at the same time that he was pulling together compilations from other Jamaican labels and producers – Treasure Isle, Matador, Clancy Eccles, Channel One, Niney the Observer, Derrick Harriott, and many more. Arguably, no single person has done as much to preserve the recent musical history of Jamaica than Chris Wilson. In another place and time, he might have been knighted for his efforts – a suggestion I made in person to Minister of Culture and Sports Olivia "Babsy" Grange at Mr. Dodd's funeral in May 2004.

Coxsone Dodd founded Studio One in 1963 and launched the careers of Bob Marley & the Wailers and countless other reggae acts. And it was Chris Wilson who helped bring Studio One's music to wider attention outside the West Indian diaspora. The Dodds had moved to Brooklyn in the late 1970s, where the family still has the Coxsone's Muzik City shop on Fulton Street. Plenty of bootleg tapes had been circulating, since Mr. Dodd had always been protective of his music and very reluctant to license it. Chris's evident reverence for the music won him over, and Mr. Dodd (I never could quite call him "Clem") and I bonded to a degree as kindred spirits, each of whom was running (or in my case helping to run) a record label dealing in music that had a specialist appeal.[56]

Chris dug into the work with love. As *Billboard* noted, "Heartbeat set a new standard for reggae reissues with the use of the original master tapes, good liner notes and rare photographs."[57] Chris himself added, "Rounder already had their standard in place. I was only trying to achieve what Ken Irwin had already done with bluegrass. Heartbeat and Rounder are both about roots music."

In addition to the Studio One œuvre, as I'll call it just for fun, we jumped into Heartbeat with both feet. We visited Lee "Scratch" Perry's house before he deliberately burned it down. He was a true character – who else would kick off an album chanting the words "Hello, spit. Hello, saliva," as he did with our 1982 release *Mystic Miracle Star* (Heartbeat HB 06)? Peter Simon (Carly's brother, who took the photos for Rounder 0002 back in 1970) took the photos of Scratch for the album.

We put out about 300 more albums of Jamaican reggae, ska, and other musics from the island.[58] One brainstorm that never eventuated was to bring a few bands into Kingston's General Penitentiary and produce an album: *Live at G.P.* After all, hadn't Johnny Cash recorded *Live at Folsom Prison* back in 1968? We had in mind bringing in dub poet Mutabaruka and two or three other bands. Mike Cacia had spent a night there for something or other – though it was neither for the totaling of a rental car nor for the unsatisfactory accounting for the cash we had advanced him, which was what led to us severing our ties with him. We visited G.P. and met with a couple of officials inside but nothing came of the idea. It's possible the authorities figured they had more to lose than to gain. For my part, I had envisioned Muta performing his track 'Set De Prisoners Free' which he had contributed to our album *Word Soun' 'Ave Power*.[59] That might not have gone over well with the prison authorities.

Brad Paul and how we wound up owning Philo Records

In 1983, we also welcomed Brad Paul to head up the promotion department, in the wake of our previous head of publicity who had been let go after we found dozens of uncashed checks stuffed in her desk drawers. She'd had other mail which she brought back from her apartment, some of it from weeks earlier but still unopened. When Brad took over as Promotions Director on August 1, the department he oversaw consisted of Brad Paul, Brad Paul, and Brad Paul. His responsibilities at the time covered radio promotion, publicity, advertising, retail promotion, tour support, liaison to distribution sales reps, and whatever else needed doing. It was another case of needing a true self-starter, but this time we'd found one who was competent. Brad came to us from Emerson College where he started *The Coffeehouse*, a very successful folk and acoustic music show on Emerson's radio station, WERS-FM. While under Brad's direction, the program was a mix of all styles of roots music and it developed into a hugely popular show. Brad played a lot of Rounder recordings, including Tony Rice, Norman Blake, Rory Block, and Buckwheat Zydeco. Airplay on *The Coffeehouse* helped to launch some of the artists that would later be signed to Rounder: Bill Morrissey, Patty Larkin, and Nanci Griffith, to name a few. So it was fitting that upon graduation from Emerson, Brad would come to work for a label that best represented the eclectic mix of music that he championed on the air via WERS.

Not only did Brad do a fine job promoting our records, he also brought us one very important artist very early on. He'd come just before we had taken over administration of financially struggling (read: bankrupt) Philo Records, and Brad was much more tapped into singer-songwriters than we ever had been. When a singer-songwriter approached us, we typically referred them to Philo or to Flying Fish, and were glad to do so. We were into more hardcore, rootsier material. But there were a lot of good writers out there, and Ken was always looking for new material for various artists. Philo was, as Ken once put it to a reporter, "artist-oriented to a fault" – the Vermont-based label led by Bill Schubart and his half-brother Michael Couture produced a lot of fine albums recorded at The Barn in North Ferrisburg. They produced around a hundred albums. Philo's better-known artists included Mary McCaslin, Jim Ringer, Jean Carignan, Dave Van Ronk, Rosalie Sorrels, Jean Redpath, the Boys of the Lough, U. Utah Phillips, the New Black Eagle Jazz Band, Bill Staines, Kilimanjaro, Patty Larkin, and Nanci Griffith.

But the company let budgets get out of control and spent much more money than they needed to on things like album design, almost always more than double what we'd spend and sometimes three times as much. (We learned this sort of thing even before taking over management of Philo because in those days the indie labels shared all sorts of information. We wondered why they were so profligate, but they seemed to be doing well. Until it caught up with them.) Brad was watching *Austin City Limits* and saw Nanci Griffith singing her song 'Once in a Very Blue Moon.' Years later, he told *The Gavin Report* (a bulletin for radio professionals), "At one point she looks into the camera, and I see that 'something' in her eyes. I immediately think, 'Here's a talented artist who's going to go a long way.' That moment is crystal clear to this day."[60]

Brad brought Nanci to our attention, and when we took over ownership of Philo in August 1984, her album *Once in a Very Blue Moon* was the one of the first we released to launch the label afresh. It came out in February 1985. We re-released two of Nanci's earlier albums as well, and another new one, 1986's *Last of the True Believers*. Then she left for greener pastures, having been offered the opportunity to work with MCA. After a dozen albums in fifteen years for MCA and Elektra, Nanci returned to Rounder with a live album in 2002, *Winter Marquee*.

Philo was indeed experiencing financial struggles and was forced to declare bankruptcy. At the time, Rounder was their largest distributor and accounted for 35% of their sales. Rounder had distributed Philo since their very first album. It only made sense for the bankruptcy trustees to approach Rounder to see if we would be willing to manage the label and then, about fifteen months later, to see if we were willing to make an offer to the creditors and assume ownership. We were. We did.

Modern New Orleans Masters

The roots of the Modern New Orleans Masters series dated back to Scott's first trip to the Crescent City in 1979, to the Jazz Festival. "There was so much music there that wasn't getting on record," he recalled. "All this incredible music. The next year I came back to record Clarence Gatemouth Brown at Studio in the Country and the record ended up winning a Grammy."

With the full support of the Rounder founders, Scott dug in and, as mentioned, in 1983 and 1984 recorded albums by pianists Tuts Washington and James Booker, and also vocalist Johnny Adams. Seeing Tuts, Scott thought,

> Gee, this guy has never made a record. And in spite of the hotel-y lounge music that he played, he also had a lot of integrity and was the repository of a certain tradition that just wasn't being played much anymore. I thought Booker – when he was at his best – was the most amazing musician I've ever heard, and one of the most *messed-up* people I've ever met, too. It's really a miracle that record ever happened. I mean, up to the last day of the session there was no record![61]

We had developed a marketing sense by this time and so began to bill the New Orleans recordings as a series starting in the summer of 1986 with a second album by "the tan canary" (Johnny Adams) and first albums by Irma Thomas, the Dirty Dozen Brass Band, and Alvin ("Red") Tyler. As a producer, Scott later won a second Grammy in 2006 with an Irma Thomas recording, *After the Rain*.

1984: a brave new world, grappling with business realities

The crisis of 1984 was the first time when we really worried that Rounder might not make it. It was the year that we experienced that what goes up can also come down. It was as though we'd been living a charmed life as a label up to this point. Most things went well, despite our business naivety. Sales kept increasing. Almost every record we put out at least broke even and some had done quite well.

We had grown rapidly in the preceding years, with the success of George Thorogood culminating in the 1982 signing to EMI America. This led to a classic mistake, and one we even talked about at the time but did not watch carefully enough: we saw a sharp decline in billing after the Thorogood sales income tailed off. But we didn't cut overhead in tandem.

Rather than renting, we also bought our own building – at 1 Camp Street, in North Cambridge – and it didn't really cost us all that much: $190,000.

We found ourselves hemorrhaging cash in the early part of 1984. We were losing money at a very rapid pace: a thousand dollars a day. That was *really* scary. We weren't *that* big a company at the time. We were doing something like $4–5 million of business a year. We had twenty-four employees. We were looking at a loss of maybe $350,000–400,000 for the year – i.e. $1,000 a day. It was a very discouraging feeling to wake up in the morning and realize that, by the time you went back to sleep that night, you'd have lost another

One Camp Street

$1,000. Given the penny-pinchers we always were, a thousand dollars was a huge sum. It still seems that way. There was no reason to think this was a temporary problem, either.

What I did was to go have a few meetings with SCORE – the Service Corps of Retired Executives – a group of business people who counseled businesses in need, under the auspices of the SBA (Small Business Association). There were two men in particular I met with, and they basically just told me (after looking at our books) that we had to cut staff. The prescription was to cut staff by one-third: in other words, eight of the twenty-four.

We had never laid off anyone. We had never fired anyone (well, except for the promotions woman who kept all those checks in her desk, who we "let go" – she left of her own accord after her incompetence was exposed). People had come and gone, of course, and we suspect there were some people who left knowing they weren't really doing the job, but we had never terminated anyone nor had we truly edged anyone out. It was something we realized we had to do, but we weren't looking forward to it.

We called a full warehouse meeting (meaning all twenty-four people, plus us) and explained the situation, then asked for volunteers. We asked people to think about it and let us know if they might not mind being laid off. A lot of people were musicians, relatively young people without families (we can't recall much of anyone who was even married at that time). It was possible that they could get laid off, and be (in effect) paid not to work for six to eight months, or whatever Unemployment Assistance paid at the time.

Eight people volunteered. No more, no less. So it worked out almost magically, and with no pain whatsoever. We laid off those eight people, and everyone was more or less content with the process. The feeling we had at the time was that everyone understood the crisis as a grave one, and thought very carefully about it. Most of the time, people know when they're doing a good job and when they are not. Perhaps these eight realized that their hearts weren't in it as much, and so they were willing to come forward?

Anyway, it worked. We righted the ship and weathered the crisis. Those who remained were able to handle the workload. We all felt better about everything. And we stopped losing a thousand dollars a day.

It's never just one thing that saves the day, however. That May we released the double album of Solomon Burke (2042/2043) and it took off later in the year, selling exceptionally well (in the tens of thousands), so that really helped as well. There were also other albums that did well for us: Béla Fleck (0181), Johnny Adams (2044), Tony Rice (0183), Buckwheat (2045), and a number of others. We'd invested a lot in production, and it began to pay off with releases in mid to late 1984.

It was another ten-plus years before we reached the next "life-threatening" crisis (1995–96). We got through that one, too. But little did we know that the entire twenty-first century was going to seem like a never-ending death-defying struggle for survival.

9 The Middle 1980s

In 1985, we celebrated our fifteenth anniversary with a couple of events that proved propitious: a special fifteenth-anniversary showcase stage at the Telluride Bluegrass Festival which also presented workshops with Béla Fleck, Tony Rice, Darol Anger, and Mike Marshall, among others and gave form to the emerging "New Acoustic Music" movement which was picking up steam, and which we promoted through a special sampler and poster. In the fall, there was a fifteenth-anniversary concert at Harvard's Sanders Theater, promoted by our friend Kari Estrin's Black Sheep Productions. The show featured Tony Rice and Norman Blake, Nanci Griffith, and the Nashville Bluegrass Band, which released its first album that month. The after-show party crowd was wowed by some picking by Tony and Norman, which led to the two Blake & Rice CDs which we released in later years.

Perhaps related to the employees' demand for more clear-cut roles was the lack of strategic planning for the company as a business per se. We were always overwhelmed with work to be done, and would have been impatient if asked to sit down and try to plot a future for the company. At least twice, people from Harvard Business School came to visit to do a case study of the company or to offer their services gratis. It was like oil and water; they couldn't wrap their heads around the idea that we were just flying by the seat of our pants, and we were too restless to sit in a room and talk with them when there was so much work to be done.

Others picked up on this. When I visited Australia in 1985, journalist Judy Jones asked me the sort of question one wouldn't really expect to be posed to a leader of a company in its fifteenth year: "Do you make plans for the future?" My response, in part, was:

> We don't, really. We've always pretty much just done what strikes us as a good album. We'll hear of a group, we'll see a group, somebody will tell us of a group – it's all pretty much word of mouth how we

get to find groups to record. And we've pretty much always done whatever struck us at the time. We don't really get into marketing surveys or great research strategies as to what's selling. We need to know what's selling and we need to pay some attention to that, but that certainly hasn't been our motivation. We've been economically successful nonetheless but it's not because we've been following the dollars – enough of them have happened to come in, I guess, in the process. Really what we will do is more of the same, and that's all any of us hope to do. We'll just try to do it better so that more of these bands can support themselves and get the chance to tour more widely and not give up out of frustration.[62]

The dialogue was more about the A&R process, but it applied to other areas of the business as well. There simply wasn't much in the way of planning. That didn't mean that the company didn't run in a businesslike fashion. When "The Shaggy Accountant" first arrived on the scene, he found the books in good order, even though the Rounders didn't know the terminology. By 1985, *Mix* magazine wrote a story about the company's computerization – for mailing lists and simplification (through word processing) of artist contracts. Hard as it might be to believe in this day and age, the fact that Rounder was computerizing was considered novel enough to merit a two-page article in *Mix*: "Rounder Records Goes Online."

Annual sales in 1984 had passed one million albums for the first time. The decision to computerize had been taken, with Eric Weinberger leading the way, in mid-1982. Those interested in the subject may find it interesting that Rounder's computer of choice was a CompuPro System 816/C, bought in April 1983. One of the first goals was to computerize the calculation of royalties. At the time, Rounder already had over four thousand compositions that we had to account for, and I had done royalty statements entirely by hand. A simple dBase II program was written, and it was able to deal with even such matters as rate difference for foreign sales, artist sales, and the like. I told *Mix*, "Using the computer I save approximately a month out of each year of my own time." It's quaint to read my explaining to *Mix* how using a word processor could change the particulars in a contract with a few keystrokes – changing a name, a rate, and so forth – without recomposing and retyping each contract. So modern!

It's worth remembering that these were still the days before fax machines and other modern extravagances became commonplace in the workplace. It's not that Rounder was ahead of the pack technologically; it's just an illustration of how basic much of the business was in our first decade-and-a-half. At the time of the interview, we'd just finished entering our inventory (over ten thousand stock keeping units [SKUs] – though they weren't called that at the time) and our 300-plus-page catalog into the computer.

It wasn't as though everything was easy, clear sailing. By the time we'd reached this point, in the fifteen years they'd been in business, we had seen fifteen distributors bite the dust. Marian admitted that the company had had to become much more businesslike around this time. In an interview for the university magazine *Clark Now*, she said that the unexpected sales of the second Destroyers album had changed things.

> We no longer had the luxury of thinking of ourselves as an artistic, specialized, sensitive little business. We were transformed into a company that had to take the business matters more seriously, because with the kind of volume we were doing with George's record, you have to watch the money more carefully or you can start losing it fast and compromise the existence of the company. I don't think we've taken any different directions because of the prominence that album brought us, but it did force us to get a handle on our business procedures a bit sooner than we might have otherwise.[63]

It remained true at the time, though, that the hundreds of lesser-known albums that sold steadily, a few copies here and a few copies there, were the bread and butter of the company, in contrast to the major labels which shipped records out in huge lots, often took back large returns, and then dumped the returns in cutout bins. They hoped to score big on one out of every ten releases. Rounder hoped to show at least a modest profit on every album – and pretty much did so for the first fifteen years. We were seeking, Marian explained, to cultivate a wider audience "by educating people who are hungry for something they don't get from top-40 radio or major record labels, but who don't know what else is out there." Rounder tried to provide an alternative to pablum and pop, the music that succeeds on lowest-common-denominator appeal.

It was already true that a portion of Rounder's audience was aging, just as we Rounders ourselves were approaching forty. Our goal was to reach the forgotten and alienated audiences who liked what Marian liked:

> The elements I appreciate are soulfulness, emotionality, good playing. I like hard-hitting music with drive – the antithesis of background music. We need to find those people – many of them around our age – who were once enthusiastic about music, but who have since become involved in professions and families and whose interest in music has become part of their past rather than part of their daily lives. For many of those people, I think life would seem more satisfying and whole if they made music a part of their daily lives again.[64]

It was also in 1985 that Marian moved farther afield, to Newburyport. And I got to know one of our artists better. That was the goal I'd set for myself at the start of the year, something like a New Year's resolution. It took a direction I had never anticipated. Spending so much time working on the contracts, on royalties, working with Duncan on employee issues and union negotiations, I was in the background most of the time, not going out to as many shows or spending much time in the studio. The times I did get out of the office were often to go farther afield – like out of the country, to help build up foreign distribution. It was by choice, of course, but these were things that I felt needed to be done.

I met Mimi Fariña when she came through Cambridge early that year, and there were certainly signs of mutual attraction. A month or two later, I was off to China to a trade show, but on the way back I stopped in to see her in Mill Valley and stayed for a few days. For our second date, we met at the Las Vegas Airport and took a plane to the Grand Canyon, for Mimi's fortieth birthday. We hiked down to Phantom Ranch on the canyon floor, stayed overnight, then took two days to hike back up to the South Rim and stay at the El Tovar. This cemented a true bicoastal relationship that lasted for a full year, during which time we managed to spend about a third of the time together, and which included trips to the Newport Folk Festival, a show at San Quentin, a clothing-optional resort on St. Maarten, and to the Hotel Oloffson in Port-au-Prince, Haiti, for New Year's. There we stayed in the "Chambre Mick Jagger."

In November 1985, Mimi's album *Solo* came out on Philo, recorded and mixed in Cambridge by John Nagy who also played guitar and mandocello on the sessions. The show we'd been to at San Quentin reflected Mimi's other lifelong work as the founder of Bread and Roses in 1974, a nonprofit which as of 2020 still provides entertainment to people in convalescent homes and senior day centers, drug and alcohol rehabilitation centers, special needs schools and centers for the developmentally disabled, mental health facilities, detention facilities, hospitals, and homeless shelters. Performers like Neil Young, Carlos Santana, Robin Williams, and Mimi's older sister Joan Baez have helped bring some joy to people who couldn't get out to concerts and shows.

The romance lasted about a year and then faded. Mimi died way too young, of cancer, in 2001, at the age of fifty-six.

It wasn't the first time that one of the Rounders found themselves in a personal relationship with someone in the business. Ken had a longtime friendship with bluegrass singer and guitarist Hazel Dickens; Marian lived with mandolin player Jack Tottle for some time, and later married bluesman Ron Levy in March of 1987, in New Orleans. She was the first of the Rounder founders to tie the knot and also the first to have a child. Their son, A.J. Levy, was born on November 18, 1988.

Best man at the wedding had been Hammond Scott of Black Top Records in New Orleans. Black Top was a very tasteful label, primarily blues, born from the love for the music by Hammond (an assistant district attorney in New Orleans at the time) and his older brother Nauman. Rounder handled national distribution for Black Top. With Scott Billington's frequent forays into Louisiana, recording blues, jazz, and zydeco, and our continued work with Cajun music, before too long we joined Hammond in buying a house in the Garden District. Rounder kept an apartment on the second floor, until after the time of Hurricane Katrina in 2005, and there was frequent travel to the area. The address of the house was also a Camp Street address. There was 1 Camp Street in Cambridge and 5342 1/2 Camp Street in New Orleans! Hurricane Katrina did a number on the Camp Street apartment; it literally blew the roof off.[65]

In 1985, Ken was a key player in the formation and development of IBMA, the International Bluegrass Music Association. He served on the board of directors for a number of years, and then chose to rotate off. He was later similarly involved in the founding of Folk Alliance. In 2015, Marian was elected to the board of IBMA. She had previously served on the board of the Blues Foundation and the advisory board of the R&B Foundation, and for a term on the board of the International Bluegrass Music Museum.

Years later, Brad Paul was among the founders of the Americana Music Association. In the early 1990s, as previously mentioned, I served a couple of terms as a Governor of the Texas Chapter of NARAS, the National Academy of Recording Arts and Sciences – the organization best known for the annual Grammy Awards. For about a decade, I was on the board of Passim, the old Club 47.

Ken and I later both got married, too, Ken's being the one that endured. I married Yleana Martinez in her hometown of Laredo, Texas, in February 1989. We honeymooned in India, visiting the Taj Mahal. Our son Emmet Raul Nowlin was born on July 19, 1991. I had been introduced to Yleana by Rosemarie Straijer (later Rosemarie Straijer-Amador) of the group Flor de Caña. Yleana was working in Connecticut as a reporter for the *New London Day*, and it was a 111-mile commute back and forth between Cambridge and New London. She'd lived in Austin, while a student at the University of Texas. Had we decided otherwise, Emmet might have been Ted Williams Nowlin, or even named "Che" but we settled for another revolutionary, Robert Emmet of Ireland. The name's origin was the Hebrew word for "truth." Who knew the name would be that of a main character years later in *The Lego Movie*? Really, we just liked the name.

Emmet got to see live zydeco music at Richard's Club in Lawtell, Louisiana when he was about two. He got to see Charley Pride, Brad Paisley, and Alison Krauss play for the Obamas in the East Room at the White House in July 2009, and he got to see Bobby Rush (and Bobby's dancers) play at the Bull Run in Sudbury, Massachusetts in 2016. Bobby's given first name is Emmit. For a while, one of Emmet's favorite groups was Delta Spirit, who recorded for Rounder back in 2008 and 2009. He's more into video games, though. And

Yleana Martinez at the Guadalupe Cultural Arts Center booth at the Tejano Conjunto Festival, Rosedale Park, San Antonio

movies. I still drag him out to see shows when I can – the Jim Kweskin Jug Band at Club Passim in 2015, and the Earls of Leicester when they came to Boston and played the City Winery in August 2018.

Ken met Donna Wilson in Toronto when Folk Alliance held their annual conference there in 1997. Donna was the producer for Toronto's First Night festivities. They kept in touch, eventually got married, and live north of Boston.

Before the various Rounders got married, we had often talked of the records we released as Rounder's children being born. Their offspring. It's not that strange, is it?

Back to 1985 for a moment. That was also the year that Rounder released the first album of the Whitstein Brothers, *Rose of My Heart* (known to some as Rounder 0206.) Released in January, it kicked off the year. The title song was by contemporary writer Hugh Moffatt (naturally, we did an album with him, too). Ken first heard them when Jesse McReynolds sat in his car and played a cassette of their music. They sounded so much like the Louvin Brothers that

Emmet Nowlin

Ken pulled over to the side of road – astonished that a group like this could be unknown. He called and got Charles Whitstein's wife Ida on the phone, who knew nothing about Rounder. He had to sell them on the idea of recording for Rounder, and drove all the way to Alexandria, Louisiana to do so. At the first recording session, Charles was so nervous he lost his voice so Ida sang guide harmony parts so other players would know what was going on.

Ken introduced them to 'Rose of My Heart.' It's one of the things Ken has always enjoyed most, finding a song and bringing it to someone for whom it clicked. He's said that "bringing in songs to the repertoire and our bringing women into bluegrass are probably our two major contributions."[66]

Building national distribution

Rounder Distribution was the best distributor we had, and it was the biggest distributor for many of the labels we represented. We'll need to return to this in a bit, but first let us look at the new format that transformed the business, before the succeeding format that threatened to ruin it. When music was first made available digitally, it was on compact disc.

Compact discs

Don Rose from Rykodisc approached us in late 1984, telling us that he had started this CD-only label, importing compact discs from JVC in Japan. The company was based north of Boston. Rounder didn't have any CDs out; it was a brand-new configuration. Don talked about perhaps a partnership of some kind between our two labels, and the idea intrigued us. We talked about Rounder releasing an initial set of three or four CDs, funding the manufacture ourselves. We discussed a couple of variations, but in the end agreed that we would license three anthologies of Rounder music to Rykodisc for a two-year term. Rykodisc offered to use their good offices to process Rounder orders for other CDs of our own through their system. We signed the agreement in a document dated January 1, 1985.

September 1985 saw the release of two compact disc compilations from Rykodisc which were drawn from the Rounder catalog: *New Acoustic Music* (with more than an hour of performances from sixteen different artists, such as Béla Fleck, David Grisman, Andy Statman, Tony Rice, Norman Blake, and Rob Wasserman) and *Out of the Blue*, with seventeen blues tracks by John Hammond, J.B. Hutto, Clarence Gatemouth Brown, Johnny Copeland, Solomon Burke, the Nighthawks, and – of course – George Thorogood & the Destroyers. The two CDs accompanied parallel LP and cassette releases on Rounder, and first introduced Rounder to the new medium. Don Rose, and his partners Rob Simonds and Arthur Mann, were clearly onto something. The initial response was so strong that a *Heartbeat Reggae* compilation was pulled together, and *Rounder Folk*, a folk sampler including Mimi Fariña, Mary McCaslin, and John Fahey.

Rounder's New Acoustic Music campaign was launched with the CD on Rykodisc. It became a highly successful initiative. As Brad Paul told *Digital Audio* in 1988, the campaign to market some of our music that way was

> wildly successful. Copies of the sampler sold like hotcakes, and the artists' records began selling very well. The next thing we knew, a lot of these musicians were getting signed to major labels. MCA Masterworks was established, Windham Hill got Darol Anger and Mike Marshall, CBS Masterworks got Pierre Bensusan and so on.

The matter of Ryko helping us get CDs was very important, because they weren't easy to acquire at this time. Ryko was able to do so because of their connection with Doug Lexa, whose Sound Trading firm was deemed a Japanese company and thus able to get preference in dealing with the Japanese plants. By this time, Rykodisc was working with a manufacturer named CTA. We placed an order for our first five Rounder CDs in October: the two first George Thorogood albums, Tony Rice's *Cold on the Shoulder*, John McCutcheon's *Winter Solstice*, and Alan Stivell's *Renaissance of the Celtic Harp*, the latter three because we thought they would appeal best to the early semi-audiophile audience interested in the new medium. There was much more demand than there was manufacturing capacity. Our total order was for 37,000 units. We were told we could get 10,000, then another 10,000 in January. The plant told us they had a backlog of hundreds of thousands of orders, and any reorder would be about a three-month wait. There were no alternatives. It took a long time to truly get under way, but by June 15, 1986 we'd hit a dozen titles of our own on compact disc.

When Nippon Columbia (Denon) began to manufacture CDs, Ryko moved there from CTA. CDs were costing us about $5.00 each with print and shipping to the U.S. Distributor price was in the $9.20–$9.75 range. Of course, there were royalties and all the other costs to be covered out of the markup. Despite the correspondingly higher price to the final consumer, we still couldn't get enough of them. The year of 1986 saw a great deal of detailed correspondence going back and forth as we all learned how to prepare masters, as we waited for orders to be processed, and a myriad of other issues.

Finally, over a year later, a plant opened in the U.S., and not too far from us: Paul and Tony Gelardi's Shape Optimedia in Biddeford, Maine. We were invited up for a tour and had to go through an elaborate process of putting on hazmat-type clothing, even covering shoes and hair, before entering an airlock to enter the "clean room" where the manufacturing was done. It was good for the mystique, if nothing else.

Rykodisc had started to talk of an "environments" series, beginning with four recordings to be done on Cape Cod. That seemed like a great idea to me; I thought there might be an audience for travel-based discs: Sounds of the Sahara, Mount Everest base camp, Bathing in the Ganges, the Sounds of Victoria Falls.

We tried to make deals with the majors to license Flatt & Scruggs recordings from Columbia to go on CD, and Cajun recordings from smaller independents like Swallow. Almost none of this activity came to fruition. But we did jump into compact discs with both feet, gaining a head start over most of the other independent labels. All three Rounders gave up our salaries in 1987 in order to invest the cash saved into building up the CD side of the operation. Ken and Marian at first thought I was nuts betting so much on CDs, but they gave me leeway and it paid off. Rounder issued the first bluegrass CD, the first blues CD (the *Out of the Blue* compilation), the first Cajun CD, and firsts in a few other genres.

When retailers received the first CDs, they realized they didn't have an adequate way to display them. All of a sudden, after the CDs were first shipped out, we were told they had to be placed in hard plastic blister packs so that the package containing the five-inch CD would stand eleven or twelve inches tall in existing retail bins. The first blister packs were so hard they were extremely difficult to open – even with a pair of scissors. Manufacturers began to offer a light cardboard longbox to hold the CD, with a window to display the front and back of the disc. Those weren't that easy to open, either, and presented a lot of packaging material to be thrown away after opening. All the plastic or cardboard packaging was just to hold the CD and present it to conform to existing store fixtures, which had been created to hold LPs. Two longboxes fit side-by-side in the same fixture that had held LPs. It was convenient for music retailers not to have to reconfigure their stores to accommodate a different-sized package – but it was far from ecologically responsible.

Ever-prescient and visionary that I was, with all the attention being paid to CDs, I wrote an editorial for *Billboard* magazine in 1986 declaring "Don't write off LPs or cassettes yet."[67] Not that anyone was about to. But CDs cost twice as much as the other formats, and both retailers and customers had only limited budgets. I was worried that if the industry lurched too far in the direction of CDs, we'd lose ourselves some of the traditional customers that had brought us all to where we were. Still playing cassettes? By the end of 2019, I couldn't recall the last time I played one. Ten years previously? More? And yet you never know. In January 2018, *Digital Music News* published an article saying that cassette sales had increased more than 136% in the previous year.[68]

I wrote another "op-ed" for *Billboard*' in 1988, which they published under the headline "6-by-12 Package Inflates CD Prices."[69] A movement began to build within indie ranks, and in February 1989 NAIRD announced its opposition to the wasteful and costly longbox. Early in 1990, Rob Simonds of Rykodisc organized the Ban the Box Coalition. In her October 1990 review of the controversy, *Billboard*'s Moira McCormick noted that the coalition

The Rounder warehouse, showing CDs in longboxes

had "gathered steam with the support of indie labels (including Rhino and Rounder) and various artists (Grateful Dead, R.E.M., Sting, U2)."[70] In early 1992, Rounder took a bold step, incorporating a message onto the longbox itself. A portion of the back of the box was designed to look like a postcard to be sent to Members of Congress, and the text read:

> This postcard is printed on a piece of unnecessary packaging, a compact disc longbox. Rounder Records, despite its commitment to a cleaner environment, sells it [the CD] in this packaging, only because the U.S. record industry dictates that [CDs] are to be sold in this format. *These longboxes are used nowhere else in the world.*

The card concluded with an appeal for action to eliminate this packaging. The overall campaign worked. Within a short period of time, CDs were routinely manufactured in just the jewel box without the excess packaging.

Packaging issues aside, CDs came on fast, and LP sales suffered. Around 1990, our pressing plant in Phoenix, Wakefield Manufacturing, went out of business. Dick Wakefield told Ken in a December 1, 1989 phone call that someone had broken into the plant that summer and stole a bunch of metal parts. He felt it was an "inside job as not many people would know the worth of the nickel or where to sell it." He told us he was insured, but in a March 27, 1990 letter wrote that their insurance company took the position that "the metal that was stolen last summer actually belonged to our clients and [was] not our own property." Then there were jackets. Correspondence from the time indicates that several times Wakefield told us they had run out of jackets for particular albums, so we printed more and shipped them to Wakefield – only to be told later that they found they already did have plenty from before. Things seemed to be falling apart there.

We shifted a bunch of our LP manufacturing to another plant, RTI, but it was a sad time. We'd kind of grown with Wakefield, they'd treated us really well, especially when George Thorogood first broke big, and they were something akin to a distant family.

Even though we had quickly moved to make our own CDs, rather than licensing to Rykodisc, we remained friendly. Rounder Distribution was a major distributor for Rykodisc, right from the start. At a certain point, we talked about joining forces once more. If you can't wait to find out what that was about, jump ahead to 1992.

10 Alison Krauss: 1986 and for Decades to Come

Ken was listening to tapes on the roof of the Willow Avenue garage and popped a cassette into the tape player to give it a listen. Not being able to skip through tracks in those pre-CD days, he listened to each song from start to finish until reaching track four, when he hit the "pause" button as a new voice sounded.

"That was the first time I heard Alison," he says.

At the time, thirteen-year-old Alison Krauss was a fiddle player in a bluegrass band that mailed us an unsolicited demo cassette. Ken explained how it unfolded, in *Acoustic Musician*'s September 1995 issue:

> She was playing with a group called Classical Grass and, for the first three tracks, basically played fiddle and sang harmony. Then, on the fourth track, she sang lead. I was real impressed and followed through and finally, through a friend, got her home number and called her up and asked for some more material, and about a week later a tape came with five songs on it. I spoke to my partners and said, "I really want to do this," and they said, "Go ahead." They could've said, "A 13-year old fiddle player who sings, and she's a woman, trying to make it in bluegrass?" But they were real supportive.

Alison's mother Louise had often accompanied her on guitar, just the two of them at fiddlers' contests. Louise provided Dave Samuelson's name as a reference and Dave had said, "She can be anything she wants. She can be Joe Venuti or Stéphane Grappelli."[71] No one imagined she would enjoy the extraordinary career she has. Ken recalls thinking that, if he liked her, someone else would, too.

It was on May 10, 1986 that we signed our first contract with Alison Krauss (born July 23, 1971: she was indeed only fourteen at the time.) The contract was also signed by both of her parents, since she was a minor.

She wasn't the first very young musician we'd signed, and she wouldn't be the last. Mark O'Connor's mother Marty co-signed our first contracts with Mark, who had been younger than Alison when he signed. As noted, Béla Fleck was a teenager, too, when we first started with him. And a woman trying to make it in bluegrass? This was still rare, but we had some experience there, too, with the pioneering Hazel & Alice recordings way back in 1973.

The budget wasn't a large one, but it was healthy by our standards at the time. The first album was Rounder 0235, *Too Late to Cry* (released in July 1987). The recording expenses totaled $7,940.50 and we pressed 3,029 records to start with. Alison was active selling records at shows; she started with 500 of those 3,029. At the September 30 close of that first royalty period, we had 879 records remaining in inventory. We'd sold 1,650 copies: 1,400 domestic sales and 250 to foreign distributors. Sales built slowly but gradually: the March 31, 1988 statement reflected 546 more domestic sales, overshadowed by 738 more foreign sales. In the U.S., we sold 2,188 in the third period, but then things leveled out for a while until the 3/31/91 statement, which jumped to 4,060 sales. Given the budget, we were doing well – but there was a lot more in Alison Krauss's future, in stature, respect, and sales. In May 1989, we released the follow-up: *Two Highways* (Rounder 0265). *I've Got That Old Feeling* (Rounder 0275) came out in June 1990. August 1992 saw her fourth album emerge: *Every Time You Say Goodbye* (Rounder 0285).

The first music video Rounder produced was to promote *Every Time You Say Goodbye*. We had had a video on CMT (essentially Country Music Television) before that – Nanci Griffith's 'Once in a Very Blue Moon' – but, Ken recalls,

> it was simply a clip from an episode of *Austin City Limits* that we obtained permission to use for promotional purposes. The impetus for considering the video came from a discussion that I had with Art Menius when I was staying at his house at the time of the Denton Bluegrass Festival. Art expressed that Traci Todd from CMT has said they would play a bluegrass video if they only had a professionally done one and suggested that we do one for Alison."[72]

We did, and it was one of the ingredients that helped that album achieve new levels of success.

The Alison Krauss album that really rocketed to prominence was Rounder 0325, *Now That I've Found You*, in 1995. That one went platinum. And beyond. A gold record is 500,000 sales; a platinum record is 1,000,000. It was the year Rounder turned twenty-five, about which bluegrass artist Holly Tashian noted: "I think it's great that on Rounder's twenty-fifth anniversary, Alison Krauss's record is selling a million copies. I think it's a nice recognition for Ken, who's worked really hard to give women, especially, a chance in music and in bluegrass."

Cover of *Now That I've Found You* by Alison Krauss (Rounder 0325; 1995)

Why did Alison stay with Rounder for thirty years? Speaking only of the first seven or eight years, Ken told *Acoustic Musician* back then:

> I think she knows that the three of us have been here for 25 years and aren't going anywhere, that we know where she's coming from, musically. We're fans who learned the business side of things, rather than the other way around. Also, I think there's something about having success on your own terms. Alison knows that with us and the rest of her team, there hasn't been outlandish hype or anything that could be construed as lack of tact. Everything's been done because of her music and the music of the people in her band. There are a lot of people you heard of being successful because of an amazing amount of money being spent, and sort of forced down consumers' ears, and then two years later, or three years later, you never hear of them. Alison has done it on her own with a really good, loyal, hard-working team.

She loved bluegrass music, too, and – like George Thorogood with the blues – was really pleased with the work Rounder had done with others in the genre, and actively continued to do with the music. We were a comfortable place to be. And there's something to be said for being a bigger fish in a smaller pond, as long as the smaller pond is competent and caring.

It's wonderfully affirming when quality music can reach out to a large audience. It's nice when a really good person making really good music can succeed while forging her own path and controlling her own destiny.

Alison went on to reach wider audiences. She has won more Grammy Awards than any other woman, surpassing Aretha Franklin. And when Ken, Marian, and I were all inducted into the International Bluegrass Music Hall of Fame at Raleigh in October 2016, it was only fitting that the two who presented the award on stage were John Virant ("the fourth Rounder"; see Chapter 13) and Alison Krauss.

You win some, you don't win some

We thought we'd signed Mary Chapin Carpenter, too. In September 1986 we sent Tom Carrico copies of the contract, and understood that the parts for her first LP were already in place at Wakefield. At the very last minute, though, something else came through for Chapin and *Hometown Girl* came out of Columbia in 1987. We had to wait a full twenty years before we released an album of her music, when we put *The Calling* on Zoë Records in 2007, followed in 2008 with *Come Darkness, Come Light: Twelve Songs of Christmas* and later albums such as 2014's *Songs from the Movie*. What could we say? We couldn't begrudge her the shot at success via the major-label route, and we can't say it didn't work out for her, either.

We touched on Iris DeMent earlier, in passing. We released her album *Infamous Angel* in January 1992, on Philo. She attracted interest from the majors, too, from Warner Brothers in particular, and they really wanted our album, not just to sign her for the future. We'd sold more than 22,000 copies. Warners made us an offer we could refuse – but chose not to. Iris really wanted the chance to grab the brass ring, and we didn't want to be ones to deny her it. Maybe nothing would ever come of it, but she'd never know if she didn't give it a try. We didn't want that sort of bad karma on our consciences. Warners paid us well, and went on to sell over 230,000 albums, so it was a win for everyone.

The money wasn't the only thing Warners gave us, though. As part of the deal, we asked them for something unusual: the opportunity to earn them money. We asked for the right to license five albums from them, albums that were out of print in their back catalog and which had never been on CD. Among them was John Hartford's *Aereo-Plain*, featuring John with Norman Blake, Tut Taylor, Vassar Clements, and Randy Scruggs. We put the albums out on CD, they sold well, and we paid Warners royalties. It was another win–win.

Sales didn't always go up when an artist transitioned to a major. The grass may have seemed greener, but things didn't always work out that way. Tish Hinojosa's album *Culture Swing* (October 1992) sold over 60,000 copies for us. She went to Warner's, too, but her first album for them sold 41,000 and the one after that 26,000.

In May 1986 we launched the Sixty Plus Series of compact discs. These didn't feature just an extra cut or two, but were an attempt to use the CD format to its fullest by ensuring that every CD in the series contained more than one full hour of music. Our July 1 new release sheet listed the first six CDs in the series: Tuts Washington, *The Bluegrass Compact Disc*, *The Norman & Nancy Blake Compact Disc*, and collections from Johnny Copeland, Mark O'Connor, and Tony Trischka.

That same month, Mason Daring, Carol Fubini (our local attorney and Mason's significant other at the time), and I traveled to Tortola and recorded a couple of albums for the Daring Records In the Absence of Man series. In one case, we drove a rented boat into a bay on a small uninhabited island, set up a tape recorder to record 120 minutes' worth of music and then left. Later, Mason took the middle sixty minutes and issued a CD of it. It was a brilliant concept, borrowed from Rykodisc. Some people thought it was putting out an album of nothing.[73] On the Daring series, you can hear the sounds of the island, without the human species around – birds, a fly checking out the microphone, and so forth. Some years later, I came up with the idea of putting out a CD of pure silence and calling it *Music of the Taliban.* We never did. We should have. The idea's still out there for an adventurous label.

This was the same Mason Daring who worked on the scores for many of the movies of esteemed film producer John Sayles. In October 1987, Mason invited me to Bush Stadium, Indianapolis, where John was shooting the film *Eight Men Out.* I only stayed for a couple of days, but got myself a 1919-style haircut and the appropriate clothing from the wardrobe department and enjoyed being an extra – and then watched John work intently viewing the dailies while eating dinner with Maggie Renzi and Mason.

Earlier that very same year, I was coincidentally also an extra in a film starring Brian Dennehy and Brooke Adams, *The Lion in Africa*, filmed in Nairobi. I had been in South Africa. First, I dropped off some small camera equipment I had "smuggled" into South Africa for the African National Congress people in Boston. In Johannesburg, I left it at *The New Nation* with Gabu Tugwana. Then I set to working on what became a few albums of South African music. My primary contact was Lloyd Ross of Shifty Records, whose house I stayed at. After an afternoon braai on December 28, I borrowed his car and went to visit Dr. Veit Erlmann to make arrangements for an album of early South African records he compiled, entitled *Mbube Roots: Zulu Choral Music from South Africa 1930s–1960s* (Rounder 5025, released May 1987).

Working with Shifty, we released three albums: *Forces Favourites: Eleven Songs by South Africans Supporting the End Conscription Campaign* (Rounder 4023), *South African Trade Union Worker Choirs* (Rounder 5020), and Mzwakhe Mbuli's *Change Is Pain* (Rounder 4024). The latter album had been banned in South Africa.

I took off on my own for a few days in Namibia, and after climbing atop a 300-meter sand dune, returned to find my rental car had settled into the desert sand such that I was stuck until I was rescued by a ranger who towed me out. I spent the night at nearby Maltahöhe, then returned to Windhoek where I bizarrely spent New Year's Eve in a movie house watching Rodney Dangerfield's *Back to School*, and then had a cheeseburger and a Pepsi at a drive-in named Granma's Road House, replete with trays for the food that hooked on the window. I flew from Windhoek to Capetown, then Kimberley, and finally drove back to Johannesburg where Lloyd and I went to see the group Winston's Jive Mix-Up at the Hotel Oxford. On Monday 5, I stopped by Gallo South Africa and met with the publishing folks and listened to some of the music from the Hugh Tracey Collection. That night I had monkey gland burger with South African composer, producer, and engineer Ian Osrin. The next day I met with EMI South Africa and later visited Rob Allingham for the evening.

On the way home from South Africa, I stopped in Kenya to visit Douglas Paterson, who lived in Machakos. He was putting together a compilation for Rounder we named *The Nairobi Beat: Kenyan Pop Music Today* (Rounder 5030). Doug met me at the airport in Nairobi around midnight on January 7, where, despite only seven or eight people being on the plane, it still took an hour to get my bag. We stayed at the New Swanga Hotel, but got up early to work as an extra on the film *Lion of Africa* with Brian Dennehy. The two of us donned blue work coats and blue hard hats and were meant to be "European miners" (mining supervisors) at an African mine. Carrying clipboards, we walked back and forth on a set which was a lane in an African village with goats, oxen, street vendors, and all. There were a couple of explosions in the pit and rocks (made of cardboard) rained down on our heads. We're actually in the film for about five seconds. We got paid 300 shillings each (about $18.00). I'm betting the three hundred or so African extras got paid a fraction of that. We spent the night in Machakos, where the college Doug was at was guarded by security men carrying bows and arrows. The next day we went to see a few bands, and ultimately the record resulted.

The other two films for which I worked as an extra were both baseball movies: *Field of Dreams* and *Fever Pitch*. Both were filmed at Boston's Fenway Park. Only in the *Lion of Africa* did I ever actually show up on the silver screen. I did get to sit two rows behind James Earl Jones and Kevin Costner in *Field of Dreams*, though, and maybe my knees show in one of the scenes. And I sat at the same table with John Cusack having a meal with the crew on the *Eight Men Out* set.

Back to 1986, though. John McCutcheon, his then wife Parthy Monagan, and I traveled to Nicaragua for the seventh anniversary of the Sandinista Revolution and a couple of albums resulted. One was a double album of music we recorded from various contemporary musicians; the other was the presentation of a documentary album named *Guitarra Armada.* At the time of the revolution, 1979, more than half the Nicaraguan population was unable to read or write, so the revolutionaries composed songs as a teaching tool to help spread the word about how to disassemble and clean an M1 rifle, etc. This was music with a purpose and would likely have otherwise been lost to history. We released it as Rounder 4022 in August 1987.

We later released an album recorded by Parthy's brother, Michael Monagan: *The Kids of Widney High*. It was an album of songs composed and performed by students at a school where he taught, a public school in LA serving severely handicapped children. Smokey Robinson and James Garner both wrote blurbs for the back of the album. Our kids series was always a little eclectic (which should come as no surprise).

With all this flying, I had accrued enough miles for a free airline ticket; and, in those early days of frequent traveler programs, miles expired if you didn't use them by a certain date. With a "hot ticket" due to expire at the end of the year, I asked myself, "Where shall I go?" For some reason, and with a couple of suggestions from Arhoolie's Chris Strachwitz, I decided to go to San Antonio and seek out some Tex-Mex music. I returned again in May 1987, for the San Antonio Tejano Conjunto Festival, allowing me to see, among many others, two acts whose pre-recorded albums we had just agreed to release: Brave Combo and Joe King Carrasco.

It was kind of amusing when I first planned to meet them at the festival. "Will I be able to get backstage?" I wondered. The Rounders have never been much for expecting red carpets to be rolled out, or to assert any status we may have had. Yes, it was easy to meet both bands. It was like any bluegrass festival. After the artists performed, they just sat down at picnic tables in the public park like everyone else.

Meeting Carl Finch of Brave Combo led not only to a long relationship with the group but also to a successful series of reissues of conjunto music produced by small independent labels from the border and San Antonio.

My Tex-Mex trip came early on in my relationship with Yleana. When we married in Laredo, music for the wedding was provided by Brave Combo, Flaco Jimenez, and also a mariachi band hired by Yleana's parents. Around the time Rounder started, my father had once told me that I'd probably lose interest in bluegrass music within a year or two. Clearly, he called that one wrong. Other musics had lasting appeal, too. On one visit to Laredo, Yleana and I went out one evening to see Tony De La Rosa at the Casa Blanca Ballroom. Her parents were a little surprised that we would go to a place like that. Did her parents see this as kind of "lowbrow" or maybe a form of rebellious behavior?

Three sorts of partnerships. Or not.

In July 1987, we formed a new joint company with reggae producer Gary Himelfarb called The Real Authentic Sound. We had been distributing the reggae label RAS Records since the 1970s. Gary said his goal was to benefit more from our distribution and business direction. Not having to worry about taking care of some of the drudgery – like calculating and reporting royalties – would free him up to focus more on the music.

On January 1, 1988, we raised our list price to $9.98 (for vinyl LPs), the first time we'd reached that threshold. Our pricing was pretty much always in line with other labels.

We won another Grammy in early '88. Professor Longhair's 1987 album *Houseparty New Orleans Style* earned a five-star review in *DownBeat* and won a Grammy. This may have helped spark *Newsweek*'s interest that summer. On July 18, they ran a story headlined "Rounder's Real Deal" with a photograph of Scott, Marian, and Ron Levy. The article described our Modern New Orleans Masters series as "the best possible introduction to the deep, rich world of pop music made in New Orleans." By the time of the *Newsweek* recognition, there were thirteen albums in the series. Ron enthused about the fertile music scene, "It's everywhere. You got the Cajuns over here, the zydecos over there, the Indians, the brass bands – 20 different styles of great music that people just grow up with." He stressed that Rounder wasn't going to include just anything in the series, though: "It's gotta be *good* more than just *there*." We'd just put out our second album by Walter "Wolfman" Washington (and bought him a set of dentures, to boot), another Irma Thomas LP, an album by the Golden Eagles Mardi Gras Indians – the first album of a New Orleans "Indian tribe" to be recorded without studio sweetening – and one by Earl Turbinton and his brother Willie Tee. The article ended with Ron talking about the fast-food restaurants one finds on any road leading into any town today; he said: "Some of these kids have never had a real Italian dinner. Never had real spaghetti and meatballs. We're like a little mom-and-pop restaurant. That's us. The real deal."

Irma Thomas turned up in both *Cosmopolitan* and *Vogue*, in part the result of a publicist hired to promote the series.

Both the Dirty Dozen and Buckwheat Zydeco gravitated to major labels. We soldiered on, eventually releasing well over a hundred albums of Louisiana music. Even as far back as 1991, Ben Sandmel wrote in *Offbeat*, "Rounder has been the only record company to show consistent, extensive interest in Louisiana music." In the nearly twenty years since that time, we've maintained that interest, if not at the same level as during the late Eighties and early Nineties. Irma Thomas was a Grammy finalist as recently as the fifty-first annual Grammys in early 2009. Just two years earlier, her album *After the Rain* won the Grammy for Best Contemporary Blues Album. After fifty years in the business, it was her first Grammy.

We were running out of space fast, so we bought not one, but two more buildings. One was a few blocks away, on Harvey Street, next to a lumberyard. We just used that for dead storage. Not all that long after we had bought that, the building next door to us came up for sale. So, in 1989, for $1,370,000, we bought the 23,000-square-foot building at 2419 Massachusetts Avenue that had been home to the New England Food Coop. That gave us plenty of room to grow into.

Irma Thomas at Rounder's fortieth anniversary

11 1990: Rounder Turns Twenty

There was a time in 1990 when we reflected on how many artists had started with Rounder, or been with Rounder at a certain stage in their career, and then moved on to a major label. It was an impressive list, and we wondered if there might be a better way we could serve as a production company – as we had with George Thorogood & the Destroyers – to help stay involved with artists if they developed major-label interest. The list included a number of artists who later came back to Rounder, or the world of independent labels: Darol Anger, Pierre Bensusan, Rory Block, Buckwheat Zydeco, Burning Spear, the Dirty Dozen Brass Band, Do'a, Jerry Douglas, the Dynatones, Béla Fleck, Nanci Griffith, David Grisman, Flaco Jimenez, Mike Marshall, the Neville Brothers, NRBQ, Mark O'Connor, Maura O'Connell, Lee "Scratch" Perry, Zachary Richard, Riders in the Sky, Ricky Skaggs, Jo-El Sonnier, Sun Ra, Loudon Wainwright III, Rob Wasserman, and Keith Whitley.

We also listed artists with whom we'd been deep in discussions and thought we had a good chance of signing, and further believed that we could well have signed had we had major-label backing. Among them: the already-mentioned Mary Chapin Carpenter, but also Tracy Chapman, Shawn Colvin, Robert Cray, the Fabulous Thunderbirds, Steve Forbert, Michelle Shocked, Pam Tillis, Stevie Ray Vaughan, and Suzanne Vega.

The EMI America deal hadn't worked out but perhaps we should keep trying, even if there was something of a leadership "musical chairs" going on at a number of the majors. Gerry Margolis, our attorney, broached the topic of a production alliance with some of the larger labels: Elektra ("fast pass"), RCA ("dicking around . . . then Bob Buziak got fired"), and Geffen ("Gary very much into it but can't get Ed to pay much attention").

We got a call offering us the opportunity to buy the Modern and Specialty labels, but didn't think we could take that on at the time, without some better form of partnership. It was just another one of those opportunities that passed us by – like the time we could have purchased Trojan Records for a song. Passing that up – at a time shortly before compact discs let labels print money by selling back catalog all over again – wins one of our retrospective missed opportunities awards. But there was a reason we didn't explore that one too deeply – karma. Trojan had a really bad reputation among reggae artists, and we didn't really want to get tarred with that. As it turned out, the people who bought it simply made new deals with artists and handled it fairly well. That could have been us.

We had our eyes on some other artists we would have liked to have recorded at the time if we could set up a joint venture label with one of the majors: Booker T & the MGs, Pops Staples, Morphine, and reunions of Stax artists and those from Hi. There were discussions with Steve Berkowitz and David Kahn of Columbia which went on throughout the end of 1991 and into early 1992. They began to move more in the direction of a logo deal, whereby Rounder would become brought into Columbia, than a joint venture. We had a sense that the main artist they were after was Alison Krauss, but Steve himself had always been a passionate fan of all the musics we were talking about so we had more trust in the possibilities with Columbia than with some other labels. People higher up, however, had other thoughts. In mid-January, Gerry Margolis advised us against the logo deal, saying that they didn't seem to be sensitive enough to the idea we were an ongoing business who didn't really want to have our work cherry-picked. He felt we should not rush into anything, but take a more conservative stance, and that Rounder was building well as a label on our own. What they were seeking, Gerry characterized as a "glorified production deal" and we would have to see sales at least quadruple to come out even on the deal compared to what we could make on our own. Without such a deal, there would still be artists we couldn't sign, but with those artists we already had or were in a position to sign, we'd likely be better off just as we were: achieving that massive leap in sales was nothing we could count on. By February it had become clear this was a direction we'd no longer be pursuing. Meanwhile, we had things to celebrate.

The twentieth anniversary – where we were at

In September 1989, we had helped orchestrate the first Smithsonian Folkways releases. Rounder Distribution was stocking some 20,000 different titles on close to 500 labels, according to a July issue of the *Boston Business Journal*. The distribution side of the business accounted for about two-thirds of annual revenues. The company was operating out of three adjacent buildings on two North Cambridge side streets, occupying around a half-acre of space. There was a sales office in New York City, and part-time salespeople in New Orleans, Nashville, Chicago, and Albany. The *Boston Globe*'s Nathan Cobb wrote a feature for the Sunday magazine and portrayed a company that for all its success was pretty home-grown.

Lest you think that Rounder has donned a silk shirt since 1970, however, consider the hand-scribbled sign that greets entrants to its accounting department: "This door is about to fall off its hinges. Please open and close it slowly and carefully." Nowlin describes Rounder's current quarters "a little unkempt," which is like calling the Atlantic Ocean a little damp. All the trappings of the record business – cassettes, compact discs, posters, trade magazines, publicity stills, a gold record, a snoozing dog named Boise the Promo Puppy – seem to have been deposited in the cluttered rooms by a high wind. The lackluster architecture is straight from the industrial warehouse school of design, and only a single hand-painted word above the front door – ROUNDER – suggests that the interior houses anything other than, say, a sheet metal shop. But at least this place has bathrooms.

That was Cobb's reference to the earlier Winchester Street warehouse where employees and visitors alike needing to use the facilities were directed to a nearby gas station around the corner. And as it happened, the first acquired of the three Rounder buildings in Cambridge had been a metal shop in its previous incarnation.

The larger two of the three buildings were connected through a clever but (apparently) legal ruse. Zoned differently, the two buildings were not meant to be connected, and we never got a city permit to do so. What we did was punch out two extra "emergency exit" doors on opposite but facing sides of the two buildings, and then built a sort of covered bridge to enclose the passage thereby created between then. The "exits" were always open, and hand trucks and people passed back and forth all the time.

Cobb further characterized Rounder by noting that only a dozen or so of Rounder's releases had sold more than 25,000 in sales. He quoted former Rounder Bruce Kaplan as saying the success of George Thorogood was "somewhere between a mistake and an anomaly." With a break-even point on most releases that hovered between 4,000 and 5,000 units sold, Cobb said that "such numbers are to a major record label what a sawbuck is to Donald Trump." That Rounder had the one gold record was nice, but he observed that the Recording Industry Association of America had awarded 1,300 gold records during the 1980s. With one such prize, Rounder "is not exactly a major industry player." Further, Michael Jackson's *Thriller* album, released in 1983, had already sold 35 million copies, roughly six times the number of all of Rounder's 850 albums taken together. We got the point. Not that we didn't know it already. Duncan Browne told Cobb, "In terms of the music we record, and the numbers we sell, and the labor intensity of it all, 99 percent of the record industry thinks we're crazy." Bruce Kaplan said he was taken by the way Rounder hadn't let the Thorogood success turn their heads. "I admire the way they've stuck to doing roots stuff when they could have become another

A&M. That just doesn't happen very often in this business." Ken admitted to a sense of relief after the deal with EMI America meant we didn't have to deal as directly with all the types who were attracted to the Thorogood bandwagon. "Everyone we ran into was money-oriented. In that type of situation, you stop hearing very much talk about the music."

One of the real low-water marks had been when the Rounders brought George Thorogood to Las Vegas for a NARM convention. That would be the National Association of Record Merchandisers, the big boys who talked "tonnage" instead of music. Looking back on it, what were we thinking? That these people would forgo the cocktails, the pool, and the casino to actually sit and listen to this band that was having such success? Only one real executive did turn up, but Barrie Bergman of The Record Bar (a major chain in the Southeast) sat in the front row and stayed for the whole show. He was different, and wrote us a note in 2009, saying:

> I've always loved Rounder, and I still buy your stuff regularly. You were the perfect complement to our stores. Music that was different in style, but obviously chosen with great care by someone who loved the artist. From the Riders to George Thorogood to Alison, we all loved the label. I can still hear Woody Paul doing his imitation of Marian.

This was something we may have missed. We'll have to see if the Riders in the Sky fiddle player can conjure up that impersonation next time we see him.

Ken explained one thing that was different about this anniversary:

> The twentieth anniversary was the first time that we decided to make the label the focus of a publicity campaign. Until then, we had always promoted a recording or artist, but had not promoted the label.

We later learned the buzzword was "branding."

> For the twentieth, we hired an independent publicist who had previously worked with Bonnie Raitt, among others. Part of our rationale was that we were told that the higher profile the label had, the more respect the artist would feel and the higher profile we would have at retail.
>
> She decided that in order to best promote Rounder, we should focus on three artists who would be representative of the label. For this we chose Charles Brown, Marcia Ball, and Alison Krauss. While we got some coverage on Charles and Marcia, the real benefactor of the publicity push was Alison.

There were several events planned. Among the highlights:

- Rounder Twentieth Anniversary night at the Strawberry Festival in Yosemite Park, California. Rounder artists included Alison Krauss & Union Station, David Grisman, Béla Fleck, Norman Blake, and Rory Block. We also had a Rounder retail section in their merch tent.
- Rounder Twentieth Anniversary New York live broadcast on WFUV; two nights of Rounder music from Tramps featuring Alison Krauss & Union Station, Charles Brown, Marcia Ball, Rebirth Brass Band, David Bromberg, and Brave Combo.
- Telluride Bluegrass Festival Rounder Twentieth Anniversary mainstage night with Alison Krauss & Union Station, David Grisman, Nanci Griffith, Tony Trischka, Jerry Douglas, etc. . .
- PBS television series *The Lonesome Pine Special* hosted a Rounder Twentieth Anniversary tribute with Rebirth Brass Band, Brave Combo, Marcia Ball, Flaco Jimenez, and an all-star bluegrass band featuring Tony Rice, David Grisman, and Alison Krauss.

In was in this year that Ken was a key player in the formation and development of the Folk Alliance. And it was also the year in which we launched the Bullseye Blues imprint: a deliberate attempt to market a more targeted product. We'd been envious of labels like Bruce Iglauer's Alligator, founded and built by Bruce on his passion for the music. (I'd first met Bruce at the 1971 Ann Arbor Blues Festival; he had just recorded, but not yet released, his first album, by Hound Dog Taylor.) His was a "genre-specific" label that had a clear and focused direction, and that seemed to give it a sales edge, too.[74] There was a slight suspicion that the Rounder label was perhaps too broad in its scope to get a handle on. Brad Paul provided an insight:

> Rounder is doing so many different things. That's one of its strengths but it can be a problem in terms of marketing. If people buy an Alligator record or a Black Top record, they have a pretty good idea of what it is about. But if you buy a Rounder record, you don't know what the hell you're getting.

That was blunt enough. In contrast, he said, "With Bullseye Blues, you'll know you're going to be getting some very strong, contemporary blues." At the same time, he acknowledged that Rounder did have an established name, noting a recent time when Bonnie Raitt had mentioned that Charles Brown had a new album coming out on Rounder (Charles's *All My Life* was the first release on the Bullseye Blues label), and got a murmur from the crowd. Had she said he was going to be on Bullseye, no one would have known what she meant. It would take a while to establish an identity.

Charles Brown (with A.J. Levy)

In 1991, Alison Krauss won the Grammy Award for Best Bluegrass Album for her 1990 album *I've Got That Old Feeling*. No one knew then that she'd also win Grammys in the same category in 1992, 1997, 2001, and 2003 – not to mention more than twenty other Grammys for this and that, including Album of the Year and Record of the Year in 2008.

We released the complete Jimmie Rodgers on eight CDs under license from RCA, and prepared to release nine CDs comprising the complete Carter Family in 1994. They'd still be in print today, except for the vagaries of major labels. They sold so well that RCA declined to renew the license, then put out their own "best of," but allowed that to go out of print after a few years. Marian was quoted in *Rolling Stone*: "People always say, 'Those Rounders, it's like they're on a mission.' Well, we are."

During this year, we took over distribution from The House Distributors. A story in the July 27, 1991 *Billboard* reported our ongoing negotiations, intended to result in a September 1 takeover of the "financially insolvent" Olathe, Kansas-based distributor. House had done a really good job for us in earlier years – right from the start. Back in 1972, Hal Brody had been one of those distributors who joined us in Chicago to help found NAIRD. But they were no longer successful.

While those discussions dragged on, we started thinking of just going ahead and opening our own Midwest outlet. Duncan said:

> It's like two trains traveling on parallel tracks. These negotiations are going to take a while. As more time goes by, the less viable the distribution entity becomes ... Why go another sixty days losing market share in the area? We perceive there to be a need for effective distribution dealing with non-hit independent product.

We developed a strategy to have three distribution centers, one in Cambridge, one near Kansas City, and one on the West Coast. We had in mind buying up Bayside, run by Robin Wise and funded in part by Robin's old friend (and our former partner) Bruce Kaplan. That would give us a third distribution center, in the San Francisco area.

By mid-September, *Billboard* reported that we'd opened up our own Midwest branch – in the warehouse that had been used by The House, even as the negotiations with Hal Brody continued. Hal had previously owned the Pennylane chain of retail stores, before selling to Schoolkids in 1989. He also owned *Pitch*, an alternative arts newsweekly in the Kansas City area.

Hal had called us in August the previous year. There were steps being taken by others to build up a strong independent national distributor known as INDI, starting off by buying up California Record Distributors (CRDI.) The word was that INDI was moving to take over Schwartz Brothers in the DC area, with rumors that Cleveland-based Action Music might join the fold, and maybe MS out of Chicago. With a strong distribution base, the investment group doing all the buying might even attempt to set up a seventh major label (there were six at the time). One financier called up Gary Himelfarb and inquired about buying Gary's RAS. They told Gary they'd be interested in talking to Rounder. Mel Kline, the front man, said he wanted to see that the Thorogoods of the world don't leave the Rounders for the EMIs. Wary wouldn't be a strong enough word for the way we felt.

Hal in particular said he was feeling squeezed on the distribution side, and he began to think about a possible Bayside–House–Rounder combination of some sort. He was open to some form of networking, merger, whatever. Bayside was our distributor in Northern California, in itself a successor to Tom Diamant's Rhythm Research.

For our part, we moved ahead talking with House and Bayside both, and finally just decided to open our own facility in Kansas City. I noted in announcing our unusual entry into the Midwest, "This has nothing to do, per se, with House Distributors, while oddly enough we are renting the same building." We'd signed a rental agreement starting on September 3, just in time for the busy fall season that led into the holidays. We also placed on payroll eight or nine employees who had been working for The House, including warehouse manager Charlene Deaver and ace salesman Bill Brownlee. The accounting and buying would be based in Cambridge. The phone number stayed the same, but now employees were answering the phone: "Rounder Distribution."

If that doesn't sound confusing enough, as far back as May, Hal had held a public meeting with all of The House's creditors who were attending the annual NAIRD meeting and told them he'd worked out a deal to be acquired by MTS Inc., the parent company of Tower Records. It would have been a nice deal for Tower, to buy up a distributorship and acquire records for their extensive and growing chain of retail stores at the price accorded to wholesalers (in effect, cutting out the middleman). The creditors shot down that approach, among them labels such as Fantasy, Sugar Hill, and Antone's. The House owed Rounder about $250,000 and we opposed the Tower takeover, too. It was at that point, after the Tower plan was rejected, that Rounder had finally stepped in – encouraged by some of those same labels. No doubt a few of them saw Rounder as the lesser of two evils; it still galled some of them that Rounder was a competitor label, which also ran a distributorship. It wasn't our intent to build an empire. We wanted to assure we had good distribution for our label and to protect ourselves against a crippling loss. "We hadn't planned to expand," I told *Billboard*, "but this situation kind of fell into our laps."

Tower, however, was incredibly important to all the independent labels as a retailer. They were a chain, yes, but one that hired knowledgeable people who really cared for the music they were selling, and knew it well. At one point, Tower was selling 25% of the records that Rounder were issuing. This was a little too much concentration; we had 25% of our eggs all in one basket. But they were great retailers and their success forced us, and all the other indie labels, to become more reliant on them.

1992: more wheeling and dealing, and some disillusionment

As I hinted above, in May 1992 Rounder partnered with Salem-based Rykodisc to form a new distributorship, as yet unnamed. Two "brother" distributors – Schwartz Brothers and Richman Brothers – went out of business in 1992. Schwarz filing for Chapter 11 in March helped to precipitate Ryko's interest in the deal. The House had gone out. It felt like a shaky time. Rounder had expanded into Kansas, and opened our warehouse there. And we'd gotten deep into talks to buy Bayside. Indeed, Duncan and I had even gone to the Bayside warehouse and taken inventory as part of the plan to open the third warehouse in our national distribution network. All of a sudden, and out of the blue, when it was the eleventh hour and the fiftieth minute, we got word that Tower Records had swept in and bought Bayside, armed with promises to Robin Wise that they would make him a key executive. But within what I remember to be fifteen months, Robin was gone.

The INDI group was reportedly closer to buying up Big State Distributors, from Texas. When the NAIRD convention convened in Austin from May 6–10, all this consolidation and the thoughts of national distribution was the topic of the day. Many of us might have preferred the original system of strong, viable regional distributors, but the ones that had remained seemed to be less and less viable. Labels were getting stiffed. Maybe national distributorship should not be seen as such a bugbear. Action Music's Clay Pasternack reminded people that there were already six national distributors: "We call them the majors."

For the Ryko troika (Rob Simonds, Arthur Mann, and Don Rose), independent distribution was a means to an end: more attention devoted to their label, while controlling their own destiny to a greater extent than if they had been dependent on the vicissitudes of distributorships run by others, several of whom had proved they weren't making good business decisions. That same goal had, of course, prompted our original entry into the world of distribution, but, having done it for so many years, we really had distribution in our blood, too, now. In some years, we made more money on the label side; in fallow years, the distribution business carried the label. Distribution wasn't just a means to an end for us. We believed in it as a business, believed in representing the various indie labels and getting them into stores.

From Rounder's perspective, the founders and distribution manager Duncan Browne realized how important a label Rykodisc had become – the label had managed to secure the digital rights to a number of albums by key artists who were not yet poised to control their own catalogs: David Bowie, Jimi Hendrix, and Frank Zappa among them. We were trying to license old Flatt & Scruggs recordings; they were going after some of the biggest names in music. Rounder worried about losing Rykodisc, which had become a very important cornerstone of the Rounder distribution company. What could be better than to create a true national distributorship anchored by two of the larger independent labels: Rounder and Rykodisc? We did just that.

That's just the way Rob phrased it to *Billboard*: "Having our labels be the anchors for our company gives us an edge in the market. We won't lose our two biggest labels, which gives us the stability that a lot of other distributors, new ventures, and networks don't have."[75] He told the *Boston Herald*:

> We both have large catalogs that really provide the basis for our year-to-year operations. We're not driven by hit records, which most major labels are. We would probably get lost in any major label distribution system because of that and because we don't have any kind of clout with them because we don't deliver hit records.

Hey, it all made sense to us, and it made intuitive sense to folks throughout the music biz.

With the sale of Bayside to Tower's parent company, and the evident desire for a West Coast presence, eyes had turned to Seattle's Precision Sound, which repped Eastside Digital – the Twin Cities-based operation run by Rykodisc's Rob Simonds. Ryko suggested to Rounder that the two labels jointly buy Precision, and Rob and I visited the company in Seattle. Precision's owner Frank Klammer came to a pretty quick agreement, since he was ready to retire and we were prepared to pay book value for his company. The sale was effected on November 18, 1992. We then ran Precision as a separate company in tandem with Rykodisc before we formalized the agreement between Rounder and Ryko.

We decided to name the Rounder/Ryko company REP, letters that stood for Rounder, Eastside, and Precision. The goal was to merge the three distribution companies along with what was left of The House that hadn't already been snapped up by Rounder. It was in effect a plan to combine four regional distributors into one effective national distributor.

There was one fly in the ointment. Bayside wouldn't let us leave. We had been distributed by Bayside since the day they began. Now owned by Tower, Bayside (read: Tower) insisted that we continue to sell them Rounder at wholesale price, even though there was no question in anyone's mind that Bayside was simply a front for Tower to buy records at wholesale prices for the Tower chain. Basically, Tower's stance was akin to blackmail. In no uncertain terms, Tower told us that, if we didn't sell to Bayside, Tower wouldn't carry our records in any of their stores. And, as noted, Tower represented about 25% of our sales. We thought we could probably win some kind of antitrust suit, if we pursued it, but we had no appetite for a lawsuit and in any event it would likely be a pyrrhic victory: Tower had far more resources than we did, and we'd likely have nothing left by the time the legal battle was resolved.

As for other indie labels agreeing to sell to REP, several were understandably reluctant to put all their eggs in one basket, since it wasn't their basket – but at least Rounder and Rykodisc were stable healthy companies coming together out of strength and not out of weakness.

Setting up REP truly did make intuitive sense, but there were some potential structural and philosophical weaknesses to be addressed.

As it happens, Ryko and Rounder had different ideas about how to run a distributorship. Rounder would have been all-inclusive, taking on almost all comers, as had been the Rounder approach since the beginning – though steering fairly clear of classical and jazz labels, two realms where we had no expertise. Rykodisc really wanted to feature their own label more and not have it swallowed up among hundreds of other imprints. Their goal was to create more of a boutique distributorship and focus on a core group of key labels – maybe twenty to thirty at most.

The decision to go the boutique route was as envisioned by the Ryko owners, and the Rounders decided to acquiesce. We felt a sense of responsibility, both to the many labels that wouldn't make the cut and to our employees, and so decided to keep the "rest of the business" intact and run that ourselves as a separate distributorship. The idea of focusing more on the Rounder label through REP had a strong appeal, and we thought we might be able to have the best of both worlds, in some regards.

With REP being owned 50/50, the Rykos anticipated a time that there might be disagreement as to direction and demanded the casting vote in any such decisions. Rob Simonds became CEO. The Rounders – in the spirit of true partnership – bought into the boutique concept and also agreed to grant our new partners their requested "upper hand."

To some extent, we were tired with trying to do as much as we had, and it felt something of a relief to let someone else take the lead. We'd had such a successful partnership among the three of us for so many years at that point that we were perhaps naive about how things like this could shake out. The concept made so much sense, and we so much wanted it to work out, that we were perhaps blinded.

There were some good things that happened that year. In 1992, two new people joined Rounder. John Virant came on as an intern, soon to become president (more on that later), and we hired Susan Piver as director of marketing in October. She had run Antone's Records in Austin and impressed us with her professionalism.

And – a longer tangent is required here – an "investment" in an artist we had believed in paid off. Ken recalled:

> In Keith Whitley, J.D. Crowe found a kindred spirit, someone who loved both bluegrass and traditional country. Both loved George Jones, Hank Williams, and Lefty Frizzell among others. In their first album working together, J.D. produced an album that blended bluegrass and country in a seamless manner. The resulting *My Home Ain't in the Hall of Fame* (Rounder 0103, released January 1980) is a classic album which blurs the borders between bluegrass and country, reminding us that bluegrass was and is a part of country music. For their next studio album, J.D. decided to produce an album on Keith. J.D. and Ken spent several days going around to publishing companies listening to and collecting songs which J.D. felt would be good for Keith to sing. A studio was booked and J.D. contacted the studio musicians. Keith learned all the songs, but it wasn't until he arrived at the studio that he learned that this was going to be a traditional country album. His eyes lit up and his smile rarely left during the sessions.

Afterwards, Keith approached Ken about signing with Rounder, but was told that we wouldn't sign him while he was still with J.D., as J.D. was a priority artist for us and that we wouldn't do anything to jeopardize our relationship with him. We added, however, that if at some point he left J.D., we would be willing to discuss the possibility of a solo project. Months later, Keith called to tell us that he had left J.D. and wanted to resume the discussion.

Ken and Marian strongly believed that Keith had major-label potential and came to a production agreement with him in November 1982 for one album plus two options. We agreed to something we'd never done before: Rounder provided Keith with an advance and then living expenses for a fixed period of time. Ken contacted record producer Don Gant and asked him to produce four tracks as demo recordings, writing Gant in March, "Our intention is to attempt to place Keith with a major label."

The demos were cut, and within a year Keith had signed with RCA. We had hoped to become Keith's label manager as we had with George Thorogood, but Don Light made it clear that RCA had no interest in our being involved and that, were we to insist, it would be a dealbreaker. Similarly, RCA did not want Don Gant involved. Keith and Gant had developed a close friendship which was based on their mutual love of the music (and fishing). Keith was disappointed. Gant was distraught; he died a short while later following an unusual accident.

RCA released a mini-LP first and we were concerned that they would try to deem that an album under the terms of the contract, limiting the income they might ultimately owe us. Our original deal with Keith also called for us to publish his original compositions. We worried that RCA was trying to edge us aside, but our attorney Gerry Margolis was able to work with Keith's attorney to achieve a satisfactory outcome.

After Keith died of acute alcohol poisoning in May 1989, RCA offered us a small sum as a buyout of our rights. By this time, we knew that Keith had enjoyed three consecutive #1 country singles. In an internal memo, I wrote that I saw no advantage in accepting their offer. By August 1990, we knew that Keith's first two albums had gone gold. Throughout that year, Keith's widow Lorrie Morgan was entangled in court proceedings trying to get RCA to pay money due his estate.

In the end, we received a fair amount of money, but most of that would have been lost had Ken's concern that we be properly accounted to not prevailed over my initial willingness to accept the out-of-pocket reimbursement.

In December of '92, we were shocked to learn that former Rounder Bruce Kaplan had died (wholly unexpectedly – he was only forty-seven) of bacterial meningitis. He'd been complaining of intense headaches, but only two days before his death had been on the phone with me and said he suddenly felt a lot better. Then he was gone. Jim Netter had been Bruce's right-hand man and he continued to lead Flying Fish. Bruce's widow Sandra struggled to cope (she and Bruce had just adopted Anna, a young girl from Romania), but after a couple of years Sandra knew she wasn't cut from the same entrepreneurial cloth as Bruce and decided she didn't want to have to look after Flying Fish. So she decided to sell the company. In August 1995, Rounder signed a letter of intent to purchase the label that had, in one sense, grown out of the early Rounder Records. The Fish catalog remains part of Rounder.

Helping Smithsonian Folkways enter the age of digital sound

It was between our 1993 and 1994 catalogs that we lost some key labels to competition from Koch (a new entrant jockeying for national distribution), among them Smithsonian Folkways and Sugar Hill. Both were bitter pills to swallow, since we'd been friendly with Barry Poss even before he first sought our advice when he was thinking of starting Sugar Hill. He had, after all, been a Rounder artist on the seventh album we had released: *The Fuzzy Mountain String Band* (Rounder 0010, May 1972). And he'd worked with Dave Freeman of County, then launched Sugar Hill, the first album being with Boone Creek, the follow-up album to Rounder's *Boone Creek*. For many years, we only signed artists to one-album deals, so – fair enough: he was free to sign them. He was also free to change distribution networks.

In the case of Smithsonian Folkways, though, we did feel some disappointment. We were key to restarting the label and we had sweated through several days of unloading four massive tractor trailers which had dropped off all of Folkways' inventory of 170,000 vinyl LPs at Rounder's warehouse. We cleared a large space taking up more than half of the warehouse floor and stacked the boxes in rough numerical order, organizing them all, and eventually finding shelving for them. Appreciating our efforts, Tony Seeger of the Smithsonian Institution said, "Nothing seems to faze them in terms of hard work." Tony had been placed in charge of Folkways. He was talking to the *Boston Business Journal* in July 1990, after an unfortunate first misstep in which the Smithsonian placed Folkways with another company that wasn't really in the distribution business – the Birch Tree Group, a music publisher – and was far from maximizing the label's potential. Smithsonian archivist Jeff Place said that the Birch Tree Group had set prices way too high, in part because they "never thought Folkways was viable for store sales." The move to Rounder, he told the *Globe*'s Scott Alarik,[76] was because "we wanted to work with somebody who was not just looking at the bottom line, but genuinely excited about exploring all the possibilities. Not that they're not good business people, they obviously are. But you feel they all grew up listening to folk music, that Folkways Records is important to them."

It was. Rounder had been working with Folkways for over fifteen years, before the Smithsonian had stepped in and taken the distribution off in this other direction. Now, Seeger felt, in coming back to Rounder, they'd worked out an agreement that was "pretty much a perfect fit." Alarik agreed, editorializing that "the Smithsonian could not have found a better ally" and quoting me as saying how Rounder had consciously patterned itself after Folkways, holding to "an ideological as well as a cultural commitment to bring minority and marginal cultures to as mainstream an audience as possible."

It's not as though the industry was going to be set on its ears. *Tower Pulse*'s J.B. Griffith wryly suggested that the announcement of the agreement "will likely elicit a yawn or two from scribes covering the showbiz beat . . . Shows you where their heads are at . . . It's good to see Folkways back in good hands."

We wanted to really help develop Folkways, and toward that end worked closely with Tony to begin to produce the first Folkways compact discs. For his part, Tony was having each Folkways album reappraised as to quality, and in many cases having the accompanying booklet notes brought up to a higher standard. We got the first three Folkways CDs out in September 1989, five more in October, and seven in November. We brought in someone from the outside to work for Rounder as our coordinator of all things Folkways. These were still the days before we looked at resumes before hiring someone; Matt Walters was working as a house painter in Austin, but really loved the music. Never let it be said that we didn't give some people some wonderful opportunities.

We had things pretty well under way with Folkways, but wanted to go over and above and really offer them something more, so we hired Matt to look after Folkways as his main order of business. It was the responsibility of the Smithsonian to keep every one of Folkways' reported 2,165 albums available to the public, and they quickly began to develop an on-demand cassette operation to be able to handle orders in the likely case that it was not feasible to market every title on CD.

170,000 Folkways LPs at the Rounder warehouse

We worked to add another twenty titles in 1990. At the same time, we were selling off all the thousands upon thousands of LPs – the four tractor-trailers full. We'd hit new highs with our own releases, with seventy-one albums in 1986 and then, after a dip to fifty-five in 1987, a new high of an even eighty in '88. Because of the work on the Folkways CDs, we "only" released sixty-five albums of our own in 1989, but it added up to eighty in all. It was our nature to see the Folkways releases as "our" releases, not "their" releases. Including Folkways, we released ninety-six albums in all in our twentieth-anniversary year of 1990.

Matt left working for us in Cambridge and moved to Washington to work directly for Folkways at the Smithsonian. Not that long afterward, there arose a dispute suggesting that Rounder was, in effect, double-dipping. The way national distribution worked is that the Rounder label marketed our records, and any NDLs (nationally distributed labels), through our distribution network. We took a percentage of each sale, say 15%. On a record that we wholesaled to distributors for, say, $5.00, we would thus take 75¢ as our commission. (We were fronting all the costs of manufacturing, too.) The wholesaler might then sell the record to retailers for $6.00, and make the 20% markup for themselves. There was no problem if we, say, sold the records for $5.00 each to Bayside. We kept the 75¢ and Folkways got the remainder, $4.25, once we recovered the invoiced costs of manufacture.

We sold to Bayside, to CRDI, and so on, and we also sold to Rounder Distribution. They argued that, since we owned Rounder Distribution, we shouldn't take an "extra" cut. If Rounder Distribution bought a record from a non-NDL, say County Records, Rounder Distribution would pay County the $5.00 and sell it to a retailer for $6.00. But Folkways now advanced the argument that Rounder should not assess them the 75¢-per-unit commission on those sales via Rounder Distribution. Instead of paying them a net of $4.25 for each record, we should pay them an extra 75¢ for those we sold via Rounder Distribution. We shouldn't be taking a commission for handling national distribution and then make a profit equivalent to all the other distributors.

Naturally, Rounder Distribution had overhead costs. It paid the warehousing and shipping, and it paid its salespeople a commission. They were fine with that, but they felt that the Rounder label side should, essentially, give them a break and not take the commission on sales via Rounder Distribution. In other words, they expected the Rounder label to do all the work of preparing the records, fronting the cost of manufacture, and selling it to the network that we had set up, but not get paid for that aspect of the service – for that portion of the records that the Rounder Distribution sales staff sold and shipped.

If all Folkways had said was they were ready to go on their own, and didn't feel they needed us anymore, that would have been fine. They were under no obligation to stay with us any longer that they wanted to. Smithsonian Folkways has done wonderful work, admirably building on Moe Asch's legacy. At the time, we were sad to lose our working relationship with them.

This was a difficult stretch. Much of Rounder's growth had been pretty magical to this point. We really could be characterized as The Little Record Company That Could. But changing business conditions brought more and more headaches. We had to adapt. We had a lot of responsibilities – to our artists, to those who worked for us, and to our families, and to what we had built. Fun? Not so much as in our first couple of decades. But we were still releasing good music, still building a legacy.

REP

In 1993, REP expansion discussions were well under way, with the Ryko partners pressing to centralize warehousing in Minneapolis, and shuttering the other facilities. We started bargaining with our in-house union in Cambridge regarding a good portion of the jobs leaving to go to Minneapolis. REP opened an Atlanta sales office early in the year. Rounder as a label picked up three more nationally distributed labels that summer, in American Clave, Corason, and World Circuit, all to be handled by REP.

The decision to consolidate in Minneapolis was taken in the early fall. This would result in closing the Precision Sound warehouse in the Seattle area, and the operation in Kansas in early 1994, to time with the expiration of the lease on March 1. We would have loved to have some of the better managers involved, but "No amount of money could make me leave Kansas City," said warehouse operations manager Charlene Deaver. Duncan Browne declined the opportunity to move to Minneapolis as well, as did Bob Carlton who had been a key figure at Precision.

The plan to consolidate REP's operations left the Rounders briefly uncertain as to what to do with the rest of our business, a sizeable distribution company that did a chunk of business with another 425 or so labels that weren't among the select group of labels to be handled by REP. We felt there could be a separate and viable business drawing from sales of the many labels not moving to REP.

Duncan and I met with Barney Cohen of Valley earlier in the year, at a diner in Connecticut, and talked about setting up another, different national distributorship, the better to service these several hundred labels. At the time, Valley was the largest one-stop on the West Coast (a source for records from the majors as well as the indies) – perhaps the largest in the country – and a perennial winner of the One-Stop of the Year Award from NARM. They really had it together in terms of warehousing and efficiency. They were anxious to get into distribution, too, and saw that each company's interests (Valley and Rounder) meshed with the other's. By partnering with us, they could get into distribution right away, rather than taking several years to start up a service. For Rounder, the benefits were evident. We'd have a much-improved home for all this existing business and would be able to let others worry about most of the details – though we'd be on the board, and Duncan Browne would be GM. Barney suggested that Valley hold a 20% share in the combined operation.

We never anticipated the way the next year-and-a-half would unfold.

We did keep putting out records, same as always, even while all these machinations were going on. And distribution was still essential to getting our records around.

1994: Valley

Rounder had started working with Valley to merge our distribution and to form Distribution North America (DNA), and the two companies came to agreement in May. The plan was to have all the warehousing done in Valley's large complex in Woodland, California. Pip Smith, from REP, became VP of Sales. John Ruch, from Rounder, became Director of Vendor Relations. The Valley partnership truly helped on the West Coast, and throughout the industry because of the stature Valley held as one of the largest and most-respected one-stops. They were a $100 million company at this point, though operating on such slim margins that they sometimes made less than $1 million a year. Even though they were many times Rounder's size, there were years we made more money than they did.

All began well. As noted, Duncan was the GM, operating out of Cambridge. In all, Rounder brought to the table those 425 labels (the printed catalog was almost an inch thick), a twenty-person marketing, promotion, and sales staff, and all the usual goodwill and expertise. Valley brought more modern and highly developed fulfillment and system capabilities.

We had two buyers (Steve Burton and Tom Lawrence) and an import product manager (Rick Lawler), and four phone salespeople. Representing DNA were a far-flung regional sales staff:

- Clem Billingsly – Northern California
- Alan Blumberg – New York
- Bill Brownlee – Kansas City, St. Louis, Midwest
- Darrell Burnitt – Texas
- Scott Cameron – Chicago, Midwest
- Sylvia Giannitripani – Tennessee, Alabama, Mississippi
- Michael Goldberg – Los Angeles
- Jeff Hannusch – New Orleans
- Sam Melada – Seattle, Northwest
- Harry Nixon - Florida
- Gordon Soutar – DC, Virginia
- Terri Weaver – Hawaii

Our goal was to offer national distribution to labels that wanted it, but also to be willing to work regionally for labels such as Alligator. Alligator would definitely have made the cut as a REP label, but preferred not to make the move to national distribution.

At home in Cambridge, Paul Knutson became GM of Rounder in 1994 when Duncan took on the same role at DNA. Paul had started at Rounder in the fall of 1987 after graduating from college. Music had always been a big part of his life and he was naturally drawn to Rounder. He started in accounting but quickly took on a more operational role, helping to oversee things generally.

In December of 1996, after seeing things with both REP and DNA fall apart (neither of which was his responsibility), Paul left Rounder to attend Harvard Business School. Upon graduation in 1998, he was one of the first people to join Exchange.com, which was acquired by Amazon.com in the summer of 1999. Exchange.com developed several collectibles sites with deep selection (music, books, sports, etc.), which were integrated into Amazon.com's platform. After working at Amazon for a couple years, Paul left and began looking for a small company to buy and develop; he now runs a niche producer of high-end furniture with a friend from Harvard.

Hmm . . . an Amazon connection. Right in our neighborhood, almost just on the other end of Cameron Avenue, Pierre Omidyar graduated in 1988 from Ken's and my alma mater, Tufts University. He founded Auction Web and then eBay in 1995. Down the street about a mile the other way was Harvard Square where one Mark Zuckerberg – who grew up in Dobbs Ferry, New York, less than eight miles from where Ken grew up – started Facebook in 2004. One can easily imagine a grand Rounder–Amazon–eBay–Facebook conglomerate, right?

Back in the real world, things with DNA fell apart. The logic of the business combinations didn't supersede ambitions and self-serving. At least that's the way we saw it.

In July 1994, Rounder sold its interest in REP to Rykodisc. What had happened? It was a forced sale. Essentially, the Rykodisc owners had moved to force Rounder out. Up to this point, the distribution effort had been a true disaster. Rob Simonds had a conception of what a modern distribution warehouse should be like, foregoing alphanumeric shelving of inventory in favor of a computerized system that would always have the titles most in demand closer to the packing and shipping area. That way, orders could be picked more efficiently since the people picking the orders would have fewer steps most of the time. It was indeed the modern way to go – if you had a computer system that worked. The fly in the ointment was that Rob insisted on implementing the system without any alphanumeric backup plan. And the computer system did not work. It didn't take long to learn that the man he'd hired to develop the system was just someone he had met on an airplane, someone who talked a good game but who was – like Rob, in this respect

– over his head, and unable to produce. He was a sole practitioner, not part of any established business, and therefore had no support staff. He was, in the parlance of the day, a "trunk slammer" – someone who worked out of the trunk of his car. The entire fate of the company rested on this one guy, and he didn't come through.

Before even testing out the system, Rob had brought all the inventory from all four regional warehouses into the multi-story Minneapolis building. With the inventory control system not functioning properly, but with orders coming in daily, the Minneapolis warehouse staff simply couldn't find certain Antone's records (and Heartbeat records, and those of all the other labels). After all, they were filed in random bin locations, not alphanumerically. When the staff couldn't find stock on given titles, they assumed it had sold out – the system didn't interface to match up sales to stock, so there was no way to check this assumption – and so they ordered more. Sticking with the Antone's example, when REP placed large new orders, Antone's was naturally thrilled and shipped more stock to REP, meanwhile going to their plant and having more stock pressed up to replenish their own inventory. It was only after at least a month that REP employees began finding – *oops* – here are 750 copies of this album that we just reordered last week from Antone's. And here are another 500. Every REP label was hurt badly.

Fills were typically terrible, because the pickers couldn't find the albums being ordered, purchase orders were going out for more copies of those albums, the labels were incurring unwarranted pressing and shipping costs – and then it turned out that the albums REP thought they'd sold hadn't sold at all. The labels thus had more stock on hand than they'd begun with, there was no income from sales, and now they owed larger sums to the pressing plant. All because of the stubborn decision to forgo alphanumeric inventory until the computerized system had been tested.

Why were the losses quite so large before the problem was discovered? Something else was going on at the very same time, something in the marketplace beyond the control of all the principals: retail was starting to contract. There had been a vast over-expansion of retail with all the big-box stores (Best Buy, for instance, who began to sell sound recordings and set up large record departments); Tower was expanding; and other retail stores were trying to offer more depth by stuffing their own stores to the gills. There were so many new outlets that the Tower percentage declined from around 25% of our sales to closer to 10%. That would seem good on paper. But, really, there was no large expansion in the number of actual customers – the expansion was just in retailers wanting to stock deeper catalog in order to compete for market share.

And there were a lot more records being released. We were told that in 1998 alone some 30,000 different albums were released. Many of them were quirky, many of them self-released. But that was still a lot of "product" – and there just weren't *that* many more sales to be had. Returns started flooding in from all sides. It was worse at REP than other distributors, because at least the other distributors had a system in place to deal with returns. With REP's inability to maintain inventory control, it was receiving returns from retail while ordering fresh copies of the same records from the labels who had entrusted their distribution to REP.

The Rounders were maybe a little too vocal in complaining about the way our many years of distribution experience had been ignored and overridden, and the Rykos apparently just decided to force us out, invoking a right to buy out our share that they had inserted in the agreement. The Rounders, steeped as we were in twenty-four years of our own partnership, naively had never anticipated that partners would act this way. We were later told by more than one employee within Rykodisc that the plan from the beginning had been to take over the distribution company and ditch Rounder. It felt like a divorce. Many of the employees had believed in the greater picture, too. Unfortunately, the process killed off more than one independent label, Antone's perhaps being the leading example. There had never been any need for the haste to consolidate; Rounder, for instance, had plenty of floor space. Shipments could have been processed out of Cambridge until the Minneapolis system was up and running. Rounder suffered over a million dollars in losses. Rykodisc had to be hurt badly, too. Both Rounder and Rykodisc survived as labels. R.I.P. Antone's. They weren't the only one.

At some point in 1994, Rykodisc also purchased the entire Frank Zappa catalog from Frank's widow Gail. It took a few years for the weight of the debt incurred to sink the label but that was the move that ultimately nearly bankrupted them, resulting in a sale of Rykodisc to Chris Blackwell in 1998.

At the time, it wasn't immediately clear what Rounder would do with its own label – keep it with REP, despite the sour taste and the company's disorganization, or move it to the planned Distribution North America. As late as mid-August, Rob Simonds was telling *Billboard* that "nobody has a lot of confidence it can be brought in [to DNA] by January 1 . . . I think it's very possible they'll never leave . . . It wouldn't surprise me if they remained a REP label." As if it were that easy to forget the actions of a purported partner who proved unfaithful to the concept of partnership.

September was a very busy month. We had talked with Barney Cohen and the others at Valley about the opportunity to buy into children's music distribution but they weren't interested. There was an opportunity that had cropped up, and it seemed like too good a deal to pass up, so we did it on our own. Rounder purchased the children's music distribution unit from Music for Little People on September 12, 1994 and from it founded Rounder Kids, keeping the MFLP staff based in Vermont but doing the shipping and accounting out of Cambridge. Rounder had our own active series of kids' music recordings, but this added a real boost to that focus.

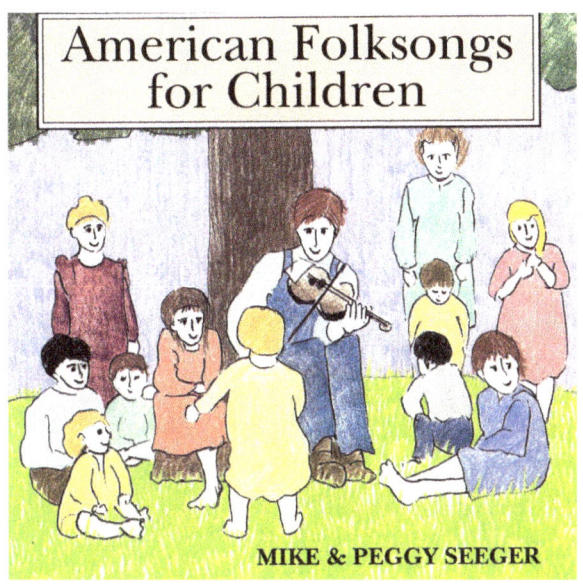

Cover of *American Folksongs for Children* by Mike & Peggy Seeger (Rounder 8001/2/3; January 1978)

Two years later, in 1996, the leading children's music artist in North America – Raffi – became free of major-label commitments when his deal with MCA expired at the end of July. He had retained ownership of his own catalog, licensing it first to A&M and later to MCA. Now, all twelve albums of his were becoming free and clear, and John Virant and Marian both stepped in and forged a long-lasting tie with Raffi that was renewed once again in 2009, with Raffi's most recent new release *Dog on the Floor* coming out on Rounder in 2018.

At the time he signed on to Rounder, Raffi said:

> My musical roots are folk, so with Rounder, in a sense, I've come full circle, Since I'm not a dinosaur or a marketable cartoon character, I thought Rounder would fit what I am. They've had stunning success with Alison Krauss, of whom I'm a big fan. I felt they could handle the sort of sales I hope to achieve.[77]

Raffi's sales increased, rather than declined, with the move from MCA to Rounder. There aren't too many artists with as evergreen an appeal as Raffi. For years, it would be have been difficult to find a week when Raffi's albums didn't hold five of the top ten chart positions on the Children's Catalog chart. *Singable Songs for the Very Young* seemed to have a lock as the #2 album and *Baby Beluga* the same with #3.

Though our original talks with Barney Cohen envisaged Valley primarily doing fulfillment, we moved over the summertime toward a joint venture agreement with Valley. Barney was the one who initially suggested Valley take a 20% share. Now he was looking for 50% ownership of the joint venture, which startled us initially, but we got there. We kept thinking that through partnership we could "bake a bigger pie" and our slice of the larger enterprise would be larger than what we currently had.

Barney and his associates always seem to have seen DNA through Valley lenses, though. How can DNA help Valley? We should have seen one red flag right away: the original draft agreement set a five-year term for the joint venture. Was Valley seeing this as just a marriage of convenience, after which they'd fly on their own? After all, they'd have all the inventory and all the relationships, and – if nothing else – they very much believed in themselves. Rounder was contributing the 400 labels we represented as well as our expertise and experience in distribution sales. Valley was contributing its "expertise in operations, including inventory management" – which was both considerable and a burden of responsibility we wanted to shed. But one could argue that the contributions were a bit one-sided, in that Barney Cohen refused throughout to offer any personal guarantees to the banks or any financial institutions. Valley would provide a guarantee, but Barney himself would not. On the other hand, the agreement drafted by Valley's attorneys had the "Rounder Principals" offering personal guarantees. That should have been another red flag – a very big one.

We felt better in that Duncan was the managing officer, John Ruch the sales manager, and our CFO John Chase was to be the CFO of DNA as well, on a part-time basis. Valley's Rob Cain was to be the part-time operations manager, but the systems were meant to be handled fairly routinely within Valley's ongoing workflow. We also felt better because the agreement provided that, in the event of dissolution, Rounder would have the right to buy out Valley's share at fair market value.

Unlike the REP experience, the inventory management and operations did work well – but at an unexpected cost to DNA. Valley charged DNA – heavily – for such things as the use of their AS/400 computer system. We hadn't anticipated that, nor did we ever think of charging DNA similar fees for what we contributed (the sales expertise, etc.). Valley was loading DNA down with ongoing costs, and Rounder was contributing our ongoing work gratis. Imbalance was the word.

When we'd merged into DNA with Valley, we had expected to simply shift all our inventory to the new company. That was one of the goals in our mind – to have the new distributorship take over everything that hadn't already been placed with REP. What happened instead – and we still don't know how we let them get away with this – was that Valley picked and chose what it wanted to bring to DNA, leaving us with the dregs to the tune of a couple of hundred thousands of dollars of pretty dead inventory. We let it happen, in the interest of being good partners. We managed to sell off some of it over time, but most of it we were simply stuck with.

Sometimes we just tried too hard to be good partners with people who hadn't shared the same spirit.

Ultimately, though, the story of Rounder is one of triumphing over challenges. In the beginning, it seemed like everything went so easily. Over the years, there were times it was really an uphill struggle. I like to think that our dedication to the music and our sense of mission helped us see our way through the rougher patches.

A "second wave" of traditional music recording

At some point in 1994, Ken ran into fiddler J.P. Fraley (twenty years earlier – way back in March 1974 – we'd put out *Wild Rose of the Mountain* by J.P. and Annadeene Fraley, as Rounder 0037). Ken asked if he'd be interested in doing another record. J.P. asked if Mark Wilson would be able to do the recording. Mark hadn't done any records for ten years or so, but he had recently moved to Columbus to take a position at Ohio State. It was feasible to get down to Denton, Kentucky to record them. He agreed to do it, and became freshly conscious of the fact that . . .

> a lot of old fiddle music was still extant but about to disappear unrecorded (or recorded inadequately). This motivated me to assemble a gang of regional collaborators and for about twelve years we tried to capture as much of this older traditional music as we could (we recorded a lot more stuff in this period than we had done previously).

The gang included Lou Curtiss from San Diego, John Harrod from Frankfort (Kentucky), Ozarkian Gordon McCann, and Morgan MacQuarrie, who helped make arrangements for another round of Cape Breton recordings.

Mark recalls:

> Since you folks were comparatively flush at the time, we could depend upon expense reimbursements and extend small advances to the artists, both of which made the work a lot easier. As I've stressed to you many times, this is one of the few cases where a commercial record company funded a preservation project of substantial magnitude (the main analogs were Lomax's efforts in the '50s). And the North American Traditions [NAT] series was certainly the main set of records that adhered to your original range of interests without much change (including supplying the very long research notes that the PDF files permitted).

He added in a note to me, one that was strongly opinionated as Mark often was:

> You and I dreamed up the NAT tag because we felt that collectors like Lomax or John Cohen sometimes garnered better name recognition than the artists themselves, but we didn't want to introduce that same self-promoting slant into our projects. So we hoped that an identifiable "label" might collect a greater degree of collective recognition for our sustained efforts in preservational work than they had typically received heretofore on a record-by-record basis. In point of fact, I don't think this ploy worked very well, partially because your publicity people never lifted a finger on our behalf (insofar as I was aware). You were lionized in the press for your records of other types of music (loosely characterized as "folk"), but rarely for the completely traditional stuff we did. Looking back on it all, I don't really care now, but back then I hoped to bring a greater degree of recognition (and $$$) to the truly remarkable people we managed to record. But that never happened either, except for a few cases like Dwight Lamb.[78]

One hopes and believes that the artists recorded at least felt good that their music had been recorded, preserved, and made available. They may not have received much in the way of $$$, but seeing one's self on a CD cover that contained one's music had to feel good. And they did receive the compensation due them for what meager sales we achieved.

Generally, the practice of the NAT group was to assemble as many components of a project as they could outside of Rounder. Mark never met John Virant or any of our other key people, and would mail me the results as in-house supervisor. This sometimes created tensions because Mark was always concerned about delays in light of the advanced age of many of his artists, but my attention was often diverted by business affairs of a greater practical import. Because of the manner in which these projects gradually came in, I didn't appreciate the sheer magnitude of the research that we had sponsored over the years until Mark and I compiled a listing of them in 2018. In dealing with an Alan Lomax, the extent of the collection was evident from the beginning, but this one sort of sneaked up on us.

Mark Wilson's NAT productions

LPs

1. Asa Martin & the Cumberland Rangers, *Dr. Ginger Blue* (with Gus Meade). Rounder 0034, November 1974.

2. J.P. & Annadeene Fraley, *Wild Rose of the Mountain* (with Gus Meade). Rounder 0037, March 1974 (reissued on extended CD).
3. Buddy Thomas, *Kitty Puss* (with Gus Meade). Rounder 0032, March 1976 (reissued on CD).
4. Ed Haley, *Parkersburg Landing* (with Gus Meade; home recordings). Rounder 1010, December 1975.
5. Wilson Douglas, *The Right Hand Fork of Rush's Creek* (with Gus Meade). Rounder 0047, December 1975 (reissued on extended CD).
6. Fields Ward, *Bury Me Not on the Prairie*. Rounder 0036, May 1975.
7. Nimrod Workman, *Mother Jones' Will*. Rounder 0076, April 1978.
8. Various, *Just Something My Uncle Told Me* (with Lou Curtiss). Rounder 0141, March 1981.
9. Art Galbraith, *Simple Pleasures*. Rounder 0157, September 1982.
10. Almeda Riddle, *Ballads and Hymns from the Ozarks* Rounder 0017, August 1972 (reissued on extended CD).
11. Almeda Riddle, *More Ballads and Hymns from the Ozarks*. Rounder 0083, July 1978.
12. Sarah Gunning, *The Silver Dagger*. Rounder 0151, June 1976.
13. Glenn Ohrlin, *The Wild Buckaroo* (with Lou Curtiss). Rounder 0158, May 1983.
14. Van Holyoak, *Tioga Jim: Ranchhouse Songs and Recitations* (with Lou Curtiss). Rounder 0108, December 1981.
15. Sam Chatmon, *Sam Chatmon's Advice* (with Lou Curtiss). Rounder 2018, August 1979.
16. Joe Cormier, *Scottish Violin Music from Cape Breton Island*. Rounder 7001, November 1974.
17. Joe Cormier, *The Dances Down Home*. Rounder 7004, August 1977 (reissued on extended CD).
18. Winnie Chafe, *Highland Melodies of Cape Breton*. Rounder 7012, September 1979.
19. Jerry Holland, *Jerry Holland*. Rounder 7008, May 1977.
20. Doug MacPhee, *Cape Breton Piano*. Rounder 7009, January 1978.
21. Theresa & Marie MacLellan, *A Trip to Mabou Ridge: Scottish Music From Cape Breton Island*. Rounder 7006, September 1979.
22. John Campbell, *Cape Breton Violin Music*. Rounder 7002, March 1977 (reissued on extended CD).
23. Carl MacKenzie, *Welcome to Your Feet Again*. Rounder 7005, October 1977.

24. The Beatons of Mabou, *Marches, Jigs, Strathspeys, and Reels of the Highland Scot*. Rounder 7011, March 1978.
25. Graham Townsend, *Classics of Irish, Scottish, and French-Canadian Fiddling*. Rounder 7007, February 1979 (reissued on CD).
26. Various, *Traditional Music on Rounder: A Sampler*. Rounder 0145, May 1981.
27. Harry McClintock, *Hallelujah, I'm a Bum* (reissue). Rounder 1009, March 1981.
28. *Ernest V. Stoneman & the Blue Ridge Corn Shuckers* (reissue). Rounder 1008, December 1975.
29. Fiddlin' John Carson, *The Old Hen Cackled and the Rooster's Gonna Crow* (reissue). Rounder 1003, May 1973.
30. Blind Alfred Reed, *How Can a Poor Man Stand Such Times and Live?* (reissue). Rounder 1001, July 1972.
31. Dick Burnett & Leonard Rutherford, *A Ramblin' Reckless Hobo* (reissue). Rounder 1004, September 1975.
32. Gid Tanner & the Skillet Lickers, *Hear These New Fiddle and Guitar Records!* (reissue). Rounder 1005, March 1973.
33. Gid Tanner & the Skillet Lickers, *The Kickapoo Medicine Show* (reissue). Rounder 1023, June 1977.
34. Frank Hutchison, *The Train that Carried My Girl from Town* (reissue). Rounder 1007, November 1974.
35. Various, *Poor Man, Rich Man: American Country Songs of Protest* (reissue). Rounder 1026, December 1980.
36. E.C. & Orna Ball, *Fathers Have a Home Sweet Home*. Rounder 0072, July 1976.

CDs

37. Joe Cormier, *Old Time Wedding Reels and Other Favorite Scottish Fiddle Tunes*. Rounder 7013, April 1992.
38. Joe Cormier, *Informal Sessions*. Rounder 7017, June 1998.
39. Joe MacLean, *Old Time Scottish Fiddle Music from Cape Breton Island*. Rounder 7024, February 1998.
40. Theresa Morrison, *Laments and Merry Melodies from Cape Breton Island*. Rounder 7026, April 1999.
41. Bob Holt, *Got a Little Home to Go To* (with Gordon McCann). Rounder 0432, October 1998.
42. Various, *Traditional Fiddle Music of the Ozarks. Vol. 1: Along the Eastern Crescent* (with Gordon McCann). Rounder 0435, August 1999.

43. Various, *Traditional Fiddle Music of the Ozarks. Vol 2: On the Springfield Plain* (with Gordon McCann). Rounder 0436, October 2000.
44. Various, *Traditional Fiddle Music of the Ozarks. Vol. 3: Down in the Border Counties* (with Gordon McCann). Rounder 0437, October 2000.
45. J.P. & Annadeene Fraley, *Maysville*. Rounder 0351, October 1995.
46. Owen "Snake" Chapman, *Up in Chapman's Hollow* (with John Harrod). Rounder 0378, May 1996.
47. Owen "Snake" Chapman, *Walnut Gap*. Rounder 0418, August 1999.
48. Roger Cooper, *Going Back to Old Kentucky* (with John Harrod). Rounder 0522, January 1996.
49. Lonnie Robertson, *Lonnie's Breakdown: Classic Fiddle Music from Missouri* (with Gordon McCann; home recordings). Rounder 0375, October 1996.
50. Fred Stoneking, *Saddle Old Spike: Fiddle Music from Missouri* (with Gordon McCann). Rounder 0381, October 1996.
51. Gerry & Bobby Robichaud, *The Slippery Stick: Traditional Fiddling from New Brunswick* (with Frank Ferrel). Rounder 7016, October 1996.
52. Various, *Traditional Fiddle Music of Kentucky. Vol. 1: Up the Ohio and Licking Rivers* (with John Harrod). Rounder 0397, January 1997.
53. Various, *Traditional Fiddle Music of Kentucky. Vol. 2: Along the Kentucky River* (with John Harrod). Rounder 0398, January 1997.
54. Glenn Ohrlin, *A Cowboy's Life*. Rounder 0420, February 1998.
55. Various, *Kentucky Old-Time Banjo* (with John Harrod). Rounder 0394, March 1999.
56. Paul Smith & Friends, *Devil Eat the Groundhog*. Rounder 0409, February 1999.
57. Dwight Lamb, *Joseph Won a Coated Fiddle: And Other Fiddle and Accordion Tunes from the Great Plains*. Rounder 0429, August 1999.
58. Various, *The Land of Yahoe: Children's Entertainments from the Days before Television*. Rounder 8041, May 1996.
59. Willie Kennedy, *Cape Breton Violin* (with Morgan MacQuarrie). Rounder 7043, June 2002.
60. Donald MacLellan, *The Dusky Meadow*. Rounder 7044, March 2003.
61. Joe Peter MacLean, *Back of Boisdale*. Rounder 7060, November 2005.
62. Morgan MacQuarrie, *Over the Cabot Trail*. Rounder 7041, August 2007.

63. Theresa Morrison, *Lake Bras d'Or: Scottish Violin Music from Cape Breton Island.* Rounder 7053, May 2005.
64. John L. MacDonald, *Formerly of Foot Cape Road: Scottish Fiddle Music in the Classic Inverness County Style.* Rounder 7051, May 2005.
65. Buddy MacMaster, *Cape Breton Tradition* (with Burt Feintuch). Rounder 7052, March 2003.
66. Alex Francis MacKay, *Gaelic in the Bow.* Rounder 7059, 2005 (month uncertain).
67. Jerry Holland, *Parlor Music.* Rounder 7057, 2005 (month uncertain).
68. Various, *Traditional Fiddle Music of Cape Breton. Vol. 1: Mabou Coal Mines* (with Morgan MacQuarrie). Rounder 7037, September 2002.
69. Various, *Traditional Fiddle Music of Cape Breton. Vol. 2: The Rover's Return* (with Morgan MacQuarrie). Rounder 7038, September 2002.
70. Various, *Traditional Fiddle Music of Cape Breton. Vol. 3: Bras d'Or House* (with Morgan MacQuarrie). Rounder 7039, 2008 (month uncertain).
71. Various, *Traditional Fiddle Music of Cape Breton. Vol. 4: MacKinnon's Brook* (with Morgan MacQuarrie). Rounder 7040, 2008 (month uncertain).
72. Roger Cooper, *Essence of Old Kentucky.* Rounder 0533, January 2006.
73. Dwight Lamb, *Hell Agin the Barn Door: More Fiddle and Accordion Tunes from the Great Plains.* Rounder 0529, January(?) 2005.

Cover of *The Art of Traditional Fiddle* (Rounder 11592; 2001)

74. Philip Kazee, *A Family Tradition* (with Loyal Jones). Rounder 0619, 2009 (month uncertain)
75. Various, *Along the Ohio's Shores. Vol. 1: Fiddle Music Along a Great River* (with John Harrod). Rounder 0544, January 2005.
76. Various, *The Art of Traditional Fiddle.* Rounder 11592, February 2001.

A new direction for Roundup

At the same time, we took a new direction regarding Roundup, our mail-order company, which had always offered customers the opportunity to draw from all the 450 or so labels we represented. After all, we had the records on our shelves so why not offer them at retail prices – so as not to undercut stores – and everybody will be happy. When all the records went out to California, suddenly the records weren't there for us to pick any more. Asking Valley to process individual mail orders was going to become a much more complicated and costly matter. We just decided, "Oh, forget it. We'll just do mail order for own records and not worry about all the other companies." It had been several years since we believed the distribution had been making much money for us. It certainly always took a lot of time and care that perhaps could be better spent thinking of our label's artists, and them alone. There were undeniably at least a few years when we had in effect been subsidizing other labels. In some of the early years, there's no question that the distribution made money for us when the label did not. Our label seemed stronger now, and it was distribution that seemed more iffy. So we took the decision to focus more on our own products. This was what Roundup became as well: a way to offer our recordings directly to interested customers. We'd always tried to be even-handed in the past, not featuring Rounder acts over those on other labels. Now we were taking a different approach. Every issue of the *Record Roundup* would feature a Rounder Group artist on the cover, and we wouldn't feel compelled to give equal time to non-Rounder artists.

Rounder Distribution would be the name under which we'd operate Rounder Kids. We had tried to talk Valley into working in the kids' music field, too, but they didn't want to. On 9/9, Rounder Distribution was formally incorporated.

A new structure in Europe

Further reconfiguring our distribution set-up, we created Continental Record Services in November 1994. Bert Pijpers from Munich Records agreed to head up the operation and rented space directly adjacent to Munich at an office/warehouse complex in Wageningen in eastern Holland (despite its name, Munich Records was located in The Netherlands, nowhere near Bavaria).[79]

CRS was our own operation, building on the work we'd done the prior five or six years since helping start "The Network" in 1988 or 1989. I haven't mentioned The Network before. The Network had grown out of communication, which we helped facilitate, between several nationally based independent record labels in Europe. Munich in The Netherlands was the key one, in a way, both a distributor and a label, and always the best distributor at selling Rounder on a per capita basis – though, to be fair, that's in large part because (as far as those born after the Second World War are concerned) virtually every Dutch citizen speaks English and the country has always shown an openness to American music.

The Network was a confederation formed to help release certain Rounder albums (and occasional ones from other labels). Participating in The Network were Munich, Topic Records from England, Zensor from Berlin, and Amalthea from Sweden. Amalthea went through a couple of growth stages and name changes and grew into a Scandinavia-wide distributorship later known as Playground. Burkhardt Seiler from Zensor had an active label going for a while, but burnt out. The Network began to issue selected albums such as Bobby King & Terry Evans, Flaco Jimenez, and a Chicago-based band named Big Shoulders.

We had several meetings consisting of Tony Engle from Topic, Torgny Sjöö from Amalthea, Ben Mattijssen and Bert Pijpers from Munich, Burkhardt from Zensor, and myself from Rounder, meeting in one or another of the countries, at MIDEM, or even in Paris, the better to meet Media 7, an affiliated distributor based in France. After several years, and seeing various distributors go belly-up in one European country or another, Rounder began to think more and more about owning our company in Europe. We broached the idea to Bert and Ben, and Munich's owner Job Zomer, and they liked the idea of a Rounder–Munich partnership. As they gave it more thought, however, they decided a separate company was a better idea, and Bert volunteered to be the one to run it. Working hand in hand with Ben and the Munich staff, he set up literally next door. The fluid availability of inventory to Munich without them having to import and invest in stock was a true benefit to them.

CRS was a real success, when the record business was still a healthy one. The staff grew, and Bert worked hard to bring groups over, help them tour, and establish strong sales and marketing ties with all the various distributors across Europe. Having Bert do all this work also freed up folks back at Rounder to work on other things. For the distributors themselves, it was a boon. Once the records were in the CRS warehouse, shipping time to any place in Europe was a matter of a few days, not the longer process that would involve each distributor importing records from across the Atlantic, which inevitably meant waiting to gather up enough orders so the shipping costs were more affordable on a per-unit basis. Now, if they just needed five more of this album and ten of that one, a quick call to The Netherlands got them the records quickly. There were no customs clearances or duties to worry about as long as the shipments were within the European Community – and all the publishing was prepaid, to STEMRA in The Netherlands. It was a real service that made life much easier for European distributors; hence, the name Continental Record Service.

To help with overhead, CRS also offered a degree of similar service to other American labels such as Alligator. Contrary to the U.S. case where Rounder's distribution had always worked hard not to favor Rounder over other labels, things were structured otherwise with CRS. There, Rounder was to get favored treatment. CRS would warehouse and ship for other labels, for a 25 "dollar cents" fee, but did not offer marketing, sales, or promotion assistance.

After a few years, we decided to make the Rounder connection even more explicit and began trading under the name Rounder Europe. Bert began to press more and more records in Europe, always excepting Studio One, which preferred to play things closer to the chest for the many collections on Heartbeat (which they let us press in the U.S., but only there), rather than have Studio One albums being manufactured at yet another facility, and one further afield.

Over time, as the European market contracted, thanks to many of the same pressures facing the U.S. market, it became harder to sustain the operation. Several distributors were on shaky ground, others started to cut back, and at the same time Rounder found that licensing certain key albums to Universal really paid off. Universal simply had more market power and could ring up bigger numbers, on a limited number of more popular releases. This was tempting, but we didn't want to lose sales on all the rest of the catalog just because of a few bestsellers. It worked for a couple of years, licensing a Madeleine Peyroux album or an Alison Krauss to Universal for Europe. In some cases, the Universal tie was a benefit in signing an artist; we wouldn't have been able to secure European rights unless we put the album through Universal.

It came to the point when a few things intersected and led to our selling off the European operation. Digital downloads – almost always pure piracy at first – had become a plague. We were subsidizing Rounder Europe, at least through cash flow, with it taking nine or more months to collect revenue from Europe. It looked like we were actually losing money, too. Bert had some ideas, but, from the U.S. vantage point, we could envision the business shrinking, with more and more downloads, more and more retailers closing up shop. There was a potential – even a likely – downside, and there just didn't seem to be a foreseeable upside.

Universal, for its part, was scrounging for sales, too, more interested in digging deeper into our catalog, and now it was ready to take on albums that might only sell 500 or 1,000 copies instead of what were once much higher thresholds. Sheri Sands, our head of sales, worked out the framework of a deal that would give Universal worldwide rights to Rounder – not only in Europe – and carry many hundreds of our titles, not just the very top sellers.

Fortunately, we were able to work out an arrangement with Bert so he could take over CRS and keep it running on its own, inheriting the company into which he had put so much work, and still try to help sell the more specialized titles on Rounder. As of early 2021, Bert and Continental are both still active. That gives us a good feeling. This was an effort, unlike REP and DNA, where things worked out satisfactorily all the way around.

Some of the distributors Bert worked with over the years included: A&N, Amigo, Bebop, Classic, CM, Crosscut, Dargil, Direct, Disctrade, EFA, Fenn, Gael-Linn, Geppard, Goodfellas, Good Stuff, Greensleeves, Harmonia Mundi, Hoanzl, in-akustik, Interdisc, IRD, Ixthuluh, Jetstar, Karonte, Libra, MNW, Media Sept, Munich, Musisoft, Next Music, Nocturne, Night & Day, Nuba, Odeon, Playground, Proper, RMG, Statera, Trainwreck, Why Not, and Zensor.

12 1995: A Quarter of a Century In, and Still Scuffling

As mentioned, Paul Knutson became the general manager after Duncan took the position with DNA. Paul put in over nine years earning our respect for his hard work and trust in his approach, but the future didn't look all that bright for the record business. It was no great surprise when he left the company at the very end of 1996 to enroll at Harvard Business School. He had had no difficulty, though, adapting to the Rounder system; we perhaps could say lack of system, but that wouldn't reflect the reality of it. We did have a system. It just wasn't as well defined or as clear-cut as most business systems are.

We were an adult company by 1991, twenty-one years old! We really did have departments and even department heads. But the lines were by no means rigid. Yes, there were employees under each department head, but we owners had no compunction about talking directly to anyone in the company. We realized that some employees would rather have a more defined structure where they only had one person to report to, and were absolutely clear with him or her as to what sort of work was expected from them. We also knew that some more old-style department heads might feel slighted that we would not go through them to talk to one of their charges. We always saw the company as more organic than rigidly hierarchical, and believed that hierarchy and compartmentalization would inhibit the sharing of information and inspiration between departments. This wasn't any military organization and we were all hopefully aiming for the same goal. To some extent, though, we also knew we were still flying a bit by the seat of our pants.

When Lara Pellegrinelli conducted a series of interviews with us in 1995, as part of her studies at Harvard, she asked me about Rounder's organizational chart. Part of my response, paraphrasing here to be more concise, was:

> It's an unorthodox situation here in that now, with a hundred people or so, it's rather a large enterprise but it does work and works reasonably efficiently. There's no org chart and the flow of

lines of reporting wouldn't look like something you would expect to see at any business school. Some people really get into job titles, but we couldn't care less. People can make up their own titles as far as we were concerned. We're getting more specialized but we know that one of our areas of weakness is training. Typically, we'll hire someone and just tell them, "Go!"

When we asked Leland Stein to take over the export area, whatever training he got came from the guy who preceded him. That used to be my area, and I'm still the one who would make any final call regarding exports, but Lee's been working on export for four or five months now and we've never yet sat down and talked about it. He asked about something a couple of times at the beginning, but I was too busy to sit down with him. He didn't follow up and I didn't follow up either. We'll both be going over to Europe for the MIDEM convention in January and that will probably be the first time that we sit and talk seriously about stuff – with him maybe six months into the job. And I don't suppose at that point I'm going to have much to tell him because he'll know more than I will about the specifics of the existing accounts. Probably he'll pick up some historical information, like why we don't have a distributor in South Africa. We'll talk about some things we tried that didn't work out. Probably he'll learn more about the philosophical approach I take to the various distributors. We've got a lot of feedback from people in the company that we should really try harder at training.

Lara, who became a regular contributor to NPR and WNYC as Dr. Lara Pellegrinelli (ethnomusicology, Harvard), perceptively inquired if it could be the case that people without as much training might come to think a lot more independently. That hadn't been our goal, but, yes, it could well be true. I answered:

> You certainly can have too much training. I think that there's something to be said for our approach, but it's like sink or swim in a way except that people don't necessarily sink. Sometimes they just wind up doing mediocre jobs. We always tell people that you've got to be a self-starter around here. No one's going to hold your hand. We just don't have time for it. Some people have thrived at Rounder, but even some of those who have say they wished they'd had more training. I think people wish things were more clear-cut than they are sometimes, but it's not necessarily reassuring to tell them that things often aren't clear-cut.
>
> Maybe they want more direction. They wish they could get more radio stations to play these records and maybe there's some magical

The three Rounder founders (left to right Marian Leighton Levy, Ken Irwin, and the author) in the back of someone's pickup truck in front of the Camp Street building

structure that would achieve that. Or they wish that we could sell more records of a given album. Maybe we can and maybe we can't, but some people believe that if somebody would just show them how to do it better, it could be done better.

A lot of people think about taking a course to become a better manager. I've read several books on how to set up small business systems and I never get much of anything out of them, but maybe if I were a better manager, I'd get more out of those "how to" books. I can't say I've ever gotten even one insight from any of those books; they just seem to offer what you would assume is common sense.

The best insight I got was the unexpected one from Carol Evans [head of Rounder's accounting department], when she imparted some thoughts as she left the company. She thought the single biggest problem was that Ken, Marian and I didn't distance ourselves enough from the other employees and she thought that it confused people because we looked too much like them and we acted too much like them, and that caused some confusion in terms of responsibility and authority. We expected her to say we should be working more closely with people, right in there, side by side. Instead, we heard the opposite.

The growth of DNA leapt exponentially when the Rounder label unexpectedly moved to DNA effective 1/1/1995. We'd let the sales staff know a month or so earlier. Rounder was bringing almost $20 million worth of billing into DNA. The originally unanticipated addition gave the fledgling partnership a major boost. The Rounders didn't ask for any further consideration for bringing this huge block of business in; we were just trying to be good partners.

Duncan told *Hits* magazine (October 30, 1995):

> When we started DNA, we had no expectation that we were going to distribute Rounder. Our plans were for a distribution company that did not include Rounder Records as part of its offering, and so the addition of Rounder in January of 1995 was wonderfully unexpected. What Rounder offers as a label is, to some degree, a mirror of what Distribution North America wants to offer as a distributor. Which is a diverse and eclectic roster of quality music from many different genres. Rounder gave DNA more credibility than we already had in the marketplace. The label and Alison opened doors for us that would have probably been a little more difficult to open without them.

We held the first DNA sales conference in Woodland, California on January 19–21, 1995. (Duncan called it the first annual DNA Love Fest.) We'd begun to talk about courting some of the disaffected REP labels and perhaps even building a bifurcated sales force within DNA which would, in effect, offer some labels "elite status" – the kind of boutique treatment that REP had promised them.

And Rounder 0325 came out almost immediately – on February 7: Alison's fifth album, *Now That I've Found You*. Our CD and production plants acted like true members of a team, anticipating our needs and even manufacturing product before we ordered it so it would have stock available to ship out really fast. Other indies faced with a true hit were at times unable to keep up with demand, unable to keep the pipeline filled with product at critical times. In contrast with the REP experience, where they couldn't even find records in their own warehouse, the entire Rounder label was integrated seamlessly into the DNA system. It probably helped that Rob Cain had a supermarket chain background. It was so uneventful an integration that notes taken during the pre-Love Fest board meeting summed it up in just five words: "didn't even notice the addition."

In January 1995, the major label BNA released a single of 'When You Say Nothing At All' by Alison Krauss, from a tribute album to Keith Whitley.

Rounder, in particular Brad Paul, worked closely with BNA to get the single off to as strong a start as possible. The single had already been getting airplay as a track on *Now That I've Found You*, a compilation which ultimately went double platinum in the U.S., in good part thanks to the single. It was the company's first platinum album, but it went way past double platinum, and has sold well over three million copies worldwide. Two other Alison titles have since gone platinum.

We weren't going to let all this success throw us off-stride if we could help it. In talking with *The Gavin Report*, Brad Paul said, "To quote an old Flatt and Scruggs song, 'Never get above your raisin.'"

Just because we had a double platinum album, we weren't going to blow that money frivolously. It did give us some more room, though, to try a little more advertising, add a few more staff, try to work a few more areas. Commercial radio was particularly frustrating, though. Tightly programmed stations provided little room for new sounds, or music that wandered off the path even a little. And Brad heard all the excuses. He admitted to *Gavin* that he was disappointed with the evolution of the radio industry . . .

> as far as how much more difficult and how much more money it costs to get a record happening there. Obviously, I haven't given up. I'm conscious that Rounder is many things. What drives me crazy is the comment about Rounder being "that folk label." When Atlantic Records started out, you could have said almost the same thing: "Oh, that R&B [or jazz] label."

Back in the early 1990s, Brad had helped to create the genre now called Americana. Working with Rob Bleetstein and Jon Grimson, the three convinced *The Gavin Report* to create the first Americana radio chart back in the early Nineties. It was a relatively easy sell: Gavin was very open to the idea. Gavin had been the first to start Triple-A (adult album alternative) radio, too, some years earlier. Brad was a regular at their annual conferences in San Francisco and the Triple-A one in Boulder.

> I went back to Gavin and said, "Let's do a separate Americana conference. I've got just the place for it – this beautiful summer camp up on Squam Lake in New Hampshire, the lake where they filmed *On Golden Pond*." The camp was Rockywold Deephaven. It's a historic camp, over a hundred years old. Beautiful.
>
> My argument was: let's do an event where there's no distractions. Everybody's going to be together and the bands that showcase, everybody will see them. To their credit, they said, "Sounds like an interesting idea."
>
> Rob did a great job convincing artists to come. There was Emmylou Harris. There was Buddy & Julie Miller. Ricky Skaggs.

Doug Sahm. Quite an illustrious line-up of core artists for the format. Marian [Leighton Levy] came to that one.

It was at that event that we all said wouldn't it be great to include this to be more than radio? Radio but also retail and club buyers and festival presenters and publicists and magazines. Grow it to be an all-encompassing industry event, not just radio. A few years later, that eventually led to a group of us getting together – initially, a smaller group at South by Southwest – Jon Grimson, Al Moss, Jesse Scott, and a few other people. We thought we should form a trade association that was committed to advancing the genre overall. It wasn't like we were coming up with a wholly original idea; it was like: let's do what the Country Music Association has done for country music and what the IBMA has done for bluegrass music. That led to a group of about twenty people gathering in Nashville a couple of months later in 1999. We brought in a facilitator, Liz Allen Fey, who got us through that and many subsequent annual meetings. We hashed out the framework for what would become the Americana Music Association. I was on the board of directors and over time served as president a couple of times.[80]

The Americana format embraced a wide variety of roots-based music. Begun as a way of circumventing the narrowly programmed formats of country and rock radio, the Americana Music Association (AMA) provides networking support for existing Americana stations and helps expand the format into new markets. Some twenty years later, the AMA now hosts an annual American Music Festival and Conference and an annual awards show, while still publishing a weekly chart.[81]

In March 1995, Rounder pulled out all the stops at South by Southwest in Austin and threw a party at the Driskill Hotel indoors, as well as a street party outdoors on 6th and Brazos, with the streets blocked off and about three thousand people enjoying Rebirth Brass Band, Johnny Adams, Irma Thomas, and Beau Jocque & the Zydeco Hi-Rollers.

This was when Austin was still legitimately weird. Yleana and I had a second house in Oak Hill, southwest of Austin, and commuted back and forth from time to time. We were doing a lot of Texas music at the time. On July 23, 1999, the music club Liberty Lunch held its last show on West 2nd Street. It had been there for twenty-four years, but the City of Austin had decided to lease the property to Computer Sciences Corp. (could there have been a more symbolic change in the culture of Austin?) and the venue was closing. What did they do for the club's final twenty-four hours? Musicians from all over Austin came and played 'Gloria' for twenty-four hours straight! Round the clock: "G-L-O-R-I-A, Gloria." We didn't stay the whole time. We had eight-year-old Emmet with us, and – besides – that was a little much for anyone. But Joe Ely played, Joe King Carrasco played, and so did Jimmy

Cover of *Feel Like Funkin' It Up* by Rebirth Brass Band (Rounder 2093; 1989)

LaFave, David Garza, Beto y Los Fairlanes, and many more. Van Morrison himself even phoned in from England and the phone call was plugged into the sound system.[82]

Writer Jeff Wagenheim wrote around this time:

> Roots are what Rounder is all about . . . These are sounds concocted in Louisiana barrooms rather than L.A. boardrooms, full of regional flavors seldom tasted by those with a musical diet homogenized by commercial radio and MTV. Such organic music neither follows trends nor sets them. Unlike the exotic feel of world music – that other popular roots genre – these roots are something American listeners feel in our bones, familiar on first listen. Yet this music is art, not anthropology.

We actually had a film made about Rounder in 1995, timed with the twenty-fifth anniversary. It was Bob Mugge's film *True Believers: The Musical Family of Rounder Records*, which included segments on Marcia Ball (filmed in Austin), the Johnson Mountain Boys, Little Jimmy King (filmed in Memphis), Steve Riley & the Mamou Playboys, Beau Jocque (shot in Lake Charles, Louisiana), Bruce Daigrepont, Irma Thomas, Bill Morrissey (from a Philadelphia folk venue), Tish Hinojosa, and Alison Krauss. The film was, according to Stephen Holden in the *New York Times*, "a testament to Rounder's clarity of vision and consistency of taste." The film shows the Rounder offices and warehouse, with people at work, as well as numerous performances.[83]

A series of shows was staged once more, with one in September at the Kentucky Theater in Lexington featuring J.D. Crowe & the New South, the Del McCoury Band, and Laurie Lewis.

And Ken organized the Longview sessions, bringing together bluegrass vocalists Dudley Connell, James King, and Don Rigsby. The three had performed together at a festival for a short Rounder segment and Ken knew he *had* to get it down on tape. Longview was a residential recording studio in Massachusetts. The artists could stay there; the staff prepared meals. All the singers and musicians share the same love and passion for traditional bluegrass. Ken said it was like a twenty-fifth anniversary gift to himself. And everyone else.

We have always been gratified to see comments like those of David McLaughlin to *Acoustic Musician* (September 1995): "Rounder is one of those companies that, because they put out so much, people feel that they might have a chance with some unusual music. But Rounder is very selective, very high quality in what they choose. That's why I feel so lucky to be a part of it." McLaughlin played with the Johnson Mountain Boys and then as part of Crowe & McLaughlin.

Ken Irwin added, "Rounder receives about 1,500 demo tapes a year now, but, really, there's no typical way an artist comes to us." Ken has always been diligent about trying to listen to every demo that comes in – a task Marian and I abhor – and it's paid off a few times. Rory Block recounted the first feedback she got from Rounder:

> They told me a tape I had sent was "too commercial," and that they didn't need a single, they just wanted a record that I considered beautiful. I was stunned. This was too good to be true. So my old pal John Sebastian and I made a straight-ahead blues album, and suddenly I had a career. Since that day, I have been doggedly insisting that if I can make a living at it, it must be commercial.

Ken defined the criteria for taking on a new artist. "There are three things we look at when we're signing artists. One, do we like the music and do we feel that it will hold up over time? Two, do we like the people and their representation? Three, do we think we can make some money from it? They are all of equal importance to us." The sequence that Ken expressed is the sequence we follow. If it doesn't pass the first threshold, the second and third questions don't get raised, Marian explained. "We had to learn business realities. We have to run Rounder as a viable business, and we do, but we don't even get to financial consideration unless we're agreed that we really like the artist's music, that everybody will get along well, and that we have mutual goals and expectations."

There's little worse than an artist who expects more from a record company than can reasonably be delivered. We always tried to be wary of the artist who will feel bitter because their expectations were unrealistically high. Many of those artists weed themselves out, though, when they come in looking for $100,000 tour support for a European tour and grandiose plans of that nature.

By 1995, Rounder was consistently releasing over a hundred albums a year (an average of more than two per week represented by the 123 releases on Rounder and affiliated or nationally distributed labels in 1993). We represented nineteen other labels for national distribution, and had over a hundred employees working out of three adjacent warehouses in North Cambridge, with a fourth warehouse a few blocks away for storage of less active items.

After purchasing Flying Fish in the fall, we added their 500-odd titles (and some of them *were* odd, recorded with a somewhat different aesthetic) to our own holdings. Following Bruce Kaplan's untimely death in December 1992, the initial plan had been to keep Fish going from its offices in Chicago, with all nine employees kept on board, but it was probably inevitable that the office was closed and everything brought to the Boston area. We assumed ownership of Flying Fish on November 22, 1995. We had begun to put out albums on Fish, including several new ones from Fish artists, but, after a year or two, there simply stopped being new Fish to fry.

We knew that paperwork had never been Bruce's strong point, but we were still a little surprised to find contracts lacking on more than half the albums. Fortunately, almost all the artists had held Bruce in very high regard and it wasn't difficult to work with the ones without contracts to determine the proper royalty rates – those who were in touch.

One amusing quirk of Bruce's was in his use of carbon paper. He bought double-sided carbon paper, so he wouldn't make the mistake of putting it in upside down. (Why anyone even made double-sided carbon paper is a good question.) But this meant that every letter he wrote, and for which he kept a carbon, had a reverse image of what had been typed or written on the other side of it. (These were the days before one could send emails or write letters in a word processor, simply keeping a copy in your computer.)

We released a nine-CD set to help celebrate Rounder's twenty-fifth anniversary called *The Real Music Box*. It was set at a very low price, and sold surprisingly well. Recognizing that it was "25 years of a record company's history squashed into a little box," *Fusion* dubbed it "a drop in the ocean." For all the artists that might break through into national consciousness, like Alison Krauss, the company's mission has always been "to nurture many other artists who will never sell millions, but through sheer musical talent, deserve to make records and be given a voice."[84]

The Real Music Box slipcase contained four two-CD sets, available separately as well, packaged with a ninth CD of oddities; the sets were: *Hills of Home*, gathering twenty-five years of folk music; *Hand Picked*, featuring Rounder bluegrass; *Deep Blues*, delving deep into that genre; and *Louisiana Spice* (I'm confident that most readers can venture a guess as to what those discs covered). The bonus ninth CD led with a holler from Leonard Emmanuel, music from the Klezmer Conservatory Band and the Holy Modal Rounders, Jonathan Richman and Joseph Spence, Tabu Ley Rochereau and Alhaji Bai Konte, and sixteen other eclectic tracks ranging from Sleepy LaBeef to the Blue Sky Boys.

Said Marian in 1995:

> The whole Rounder experience has been like taking a walk in a strange and wonderful city. Before you know it, you're hearing Tex-Mex conjuntos or you stand on another corner and you're hearing brass bands from New Orleans. It's a fascinating experience to see where things are going to go next.[85]

We released the world's first CD-ROM record catalog in April 1995, a complete catalog of the label in digital format, with all tracks and personnel, cover art, and twenty- to thirty-second sound bites of each album. Of course, the full catalog was available online as well. Five years later, we stopped issuing print catalogs. The 2000 catalog was the last one printed on paper.

By 1995, Bullseye Blues was up and running, and was beginning to focus a fair amount on Memphis musicians. Little Jimmy King was one of the first, but Ron and Marian brought in albums by Ann Peebles and Preston Shannon as well. Smokin' Joe Kubek was discovered playing at Huey's, and signed to the label, though he was really a Texas artist. Memphis might have become another New Orleans for Rounder, with an ongoing cluster of albums, but it didn't work out that way.

Down in the Valley

We had joined with Valley but it wasn't as smooth a relationship as we had hoped. John Chase's note on April 9, 1995 commented on the many fees Valley continually assessed to DNA: "distribution fee, returns fee, IS fee, general operation fees which include rent, depreciation, taxes and insurance, accounting fee, human resource fee, general service allocation fee." It seemed like Valley was imposing on DNA every fee they could dream up, while Rounder was supplying DNA on consignment, not charging for John Chase's services as part-time CFO (given that it was part of our contribution), etc. What we hadn't sufficiently realized at the time was that Barney was negotiating with Rykodisc about doing fulfillment for REP for a flat 5%. But Valley was assessing the joint venture – his actual partners – 6.79% of billing.

At the same time, Valley was leaning on Duncan and John Ruch to stimulate business by offering customers extra discounts – not only a 2% prompt pay discount, but also a "5% off the bat discount," and a 7% new release discount. It was the one-stop mentality, probably unnecessary for a distributorship that was a national distributor, and it shaved margins dramatically. Valley was used to running a $100 million business while returning less than 1% to the bottom line. It wasn't a healthy way to set out to run a business, however, and it became clear that Valley was trying to pass on many of its costs to DNA. And meanwhile they were pressing us to lower the price that Rounder charged DNA, from $8.00 per CD to $7.75.

We talked about this, anxious as we were to be good partners. Ken suggested possibly working it as a rebate, where Rounder took less but then the Rounder partners would recover it from later profits on a preferential basis. John Chase kept advising us to be wary, to be "cautious and suppress our desire to help out too much."

By May 1995, there were signs that things could start falling apart – and this despite all the large bump in business which *Now That I've Found You* offered DNA. The fees Valley was charging DNA were high enough so that DNA looked to be losing money. The information services fee alone was $471,000 in the 1996–97 budget, an astonishing figure for a relatively simple operation. DNA was supposed to benefit by taking advantage of Valley's systems, not end up being taken advantage of in order to subsidize Valley's systems. After all, the systems it brought to the table were part of what Valley was supposed to be contributing. Rounder had brought in the 400 labels, and when we added Rounder itself, we had added another $20 million or so of billing.

1996: at the height of our distribution activity

This was the year we peaked in terms of the number of labels we distributed nationally. A listing generated in January of that year shows the following roster of nationally distributed labels (NDLs): Accurate; American Clave; Atomic Theory (and Mouthpiece); Black Top; Bohemia Beat; Claddagh (and Phaeton); Clean Cuts; Corason; Daring; Dead Reckoning; Greenhays; Globestyle U.S.; In & Out; Lucky Seven; Messidor; Omnium; Rooster Blues (and Okratone); Temple; Tone-Cool; Traditional Crossroads; Upstart; Vestapol; World Circuit. They represented an eclectic mix of blues, jazz, world music, and more, most of them being U.S. labels but some based in Ireland, Mexico, the Bahamas, Germany, Scotland, and England.

We'd renamed Rounder Distribution as DNA (Distribution North America) late in 1993. The following list of labels (which includes NDLs) is drawn from the 1993 Rounder Distribution catalog and the 1994 DNA catalog. For those who might be interested, see the endnote for the list of labels we carried.[86] How many can you recall?

If we'd ever tried to carry classical music, the list would have been much longer. For some readers, there will be a number of label names that will evoke memories of one sort or another. There was a lot of music being released, much of it quite good. I knew them all at the time, but, twenty years later, I have to admit that some of these names don't raise a single memory. I'd wager that some of those you never heard of had ten or more albums on the label. How few of them made it into the twenty-first century? It would be a lot shorter list.

Over twenty of the labels listed in note 86 had only one album at the time (denoted by an asterisk against their name in the note). Contrary to what it might appear, we didn't just take on any label that approached us – but we were a lot more open to taking on a fledgling label than a number of other distributors. After all, you've gotta start some place, and we never forgot our own desire to secure distribution when we began. Among the labels we worked with from their very first album (some left us after they became larger, and struck other deals, and some of them ended up as part of the Rounder Label Group) are: Alligator, Philo, Redwood, Rhino, Rykodisc, Shanachie, Smithsonian Folkways, Sugar Hill, and Windham Hill.

It was wonderful to start from scratch with these labels and others like them. Every one of the above labels that we'd help nurture (we were almost always, by far, their best distributor) eventually left us for greener pastures.

At one point, three of our employees came to us and wanted to form a label for more contemporary music. They decided to call it Upstart Sounds. It was very well received, and they had some modest hits early on. In the end, Tor Hansen and Glenn Dicker left Rounder and moved to North Carolina where they began Redeye Distribution and Yep Roc Records.

Passim

As the fall arrived, it had become clear that Passim, the Cambridge folk music club that had been the successor to the Club 47, was in serious financial difficulty. Bob and Rae Anne Donlin, who owned the club, were over $125,000 in debt to Harvard Real Estate, the club's landlord. The Donlins were in deep over their heads, and unable to come to grips with the situation. At the very last moment, a few concerned folk music lovers pulled together a small group of four or five people to try to save the club and brought me in from Rounder. All three Rounders agreed to provide the club enough money to stay afloat, half to go to Harvard and half toward keeping things running as part of an effort to convert Passim back to the nonprofit status it had held as Club 47 before the Donlins had taken over ownership about twenty-five years earlier. The half that went to Harvard Real Estate was sufficient to assure them of the sincerity of the effort to save Passim, and various people at Harvard in the ensuing years have demonstrated care for the survival of the folk music center. In 2020, Passim is still going strong, a vital music club, often an incubator for new talent, and still a nonprofit.

The end of DNA

By February 1996, there were frictions regarding DNA. We suggested it was a little unreasonable to expect any company to show a profit in its very first year. Barney started leaning on Duncan as well, calling him "way too nice a guy" and saying that he "gets distracted too easily . . . doesn't have good delegating skills." He was watching over Duncan's shoulder the whole time, understandably nervous about a downturn in record retail (the first contraction from the period of over-retailing), and perhaps worried most of all about Valley being able to maintain its own financing. We urged him to put more capital into the company – a few hundred thousand dollars – but this was completely off the table as far as Barney was concerned. He was, however, thinking about starting a label of his own, believing now that that was where the real money was.

By 1996, we were talking about whether Rounder was going to buy out Valley or Valley was going to buy out Rounder. Boston's Fleet Bank was uncomfortable with continuing to finance the operation, particularly with the evident uncertainty regarding the partnership.

There were discussions internally, but there was really no way we were going to be able to buy Valley out – and there was no desire to do so. This meant that we would have to jump back into distribution with both feet, so to speak, and basically be spending more of our time trying to help other labels get distribution.

There had now been two attempts – first with Rykodisc and then with Valley – to create a solid national distributorship. Both times we'd unfortunately partnered with people who left us disappointed. We finally came to the point where we'd had enough of looking after the distribution of other labels' records, and decided it was time to just do what was best for the Rounder label. It was, in effect, back to our original mission. Distribution had originally been a means to an end, and, at times, had been very helpful in getting the records on the Rounder label to a wider audience. We had also felt good about helping other labels. Now it seemed the work of distributing was routinely getting in the way. Before 1996 was done, we let Valley take over DNA.

On November 20, 2001 Valley Media filed for bankruptcy. Fortunately for Rounder, we were long gone.

13 John Virant: "The Fourth Rounder"

In 1997, John Virant was named President and CEO of Rounder Records. He served in that capacity for the next twenty-one years and truly became "the fourth Rounder." He started as an intern; from intern to president – it's a good Rounder story. When John first arrived, he says, we had one marketing person and one promotion person, but by 2000 we had thirty-five in the combined departments.

John told his story in an interview in 2011:

John Virant with Alison Krauss at IBMA, 2012

I was born on September 6, 1966. St. Louis, Missouri. I am the oldest of five children. I have one sister, who is after me in the pecking order and then three younger brothers. Obviously, being the oldest that's why I am the responsible one! I had many, many chores growing up and was always looking after them. For the first six years of my life, we lived in more of a regular suburb of St. Louis – Creve Coeur. It is sort of an unremarkable suburb.

"When I was six, my parents moved way out. They had always wanted more land, and horses, and a bit of the farming thing. Things were much less expensive back then. They bought out there. It was country. Very rural. It was called Chesterfield at the time. Now it's called Wildwood. My parents built this house, which they still have. I don't quite remember how many acres they started with but over the years they added it. It sits on sixty acres now. They built a barn and we had horses and all sorts of other animals.

We all had a lot of chores but there were other people who came in [to take care of some of the farm work]. Obviously, in terms of playing with the five siblings and us being farther out, we ended up playing more with each other. There were a few kids around. A lot of outdoor play. There was a creek down in this valley – didn't always have water in it, a dry creek. Then when it rained . . . We did a lot of playing in there, with forts, and building dams.

There are many private schools in St. Louis for whatever reason and many of them are Catholic. One of them was an all-boys school called St. Louis Priory. It was founded and run by Benedictine monks who came over in 1955 from Ampleforth Abbey in Yorkshire, England. It was relatively new. For grades 7 through 12, that's where I went.

My dad has always been a passionate music fan. Growing up, him and his buddies would go over to the east side [East St. Louis, Illinois] and they would often see Ike and Tina. I think they were living there. There were all these small clubs in East St. Louis. So growing up . . . music was on all the time. He had all these records. It was all of the greats – Buddy Holly, Muddy Waters, Howlin' Wolf, Chuck Berry . . . it goes on and on. Once you get into the Seventies, he got into some other things, too. Bob Seger, the Eagles, Fleetwood Mac – those two big records they had in the late Seventies. Gordon Lightfoot.

My mom loved music, too, but I think my dad was the real driver behind all of that.

I don't remember which came first but in the Seventies, across the river at the Edwardsville Campus of the University of Illinois, they had an outdoor summer festival where you could sit on a hillside and watch the bands play. The Mississippi River Festival.

We used to go over there a fair amount. Either Gordon Lightfoot or Willie Nelson was my first concert. We saw them both the same summer within a relatively short period of time. I was ten or eleven.

I got very interested in music just by osmosis or whatever. I was just very interested in music. One Christmas I asked for a stereo of my own. I got one of those one-piece Sony contraptions – 33s, 45s, and it also had a cassette component to it.

I think it was that same Christmas I got . . . *Elton John's Greatest Hits* – that first one with 'Crocodile Rock' on it, and *John Denver's Greatest Hits*, and an Olivia Newton-John's greatest hits. I think my mom picked out those three records. My room was downstairs and . . . I don't think the FM worked that well in terms of getting reception. We got AM radio and I did listen to things like Three Dog Night, Neil Diamond.

At one point . . . my parents belonged to a country club in St. Louis where they played golf. I was like on the swim team there. There were these casual friends of ours and the kids were all running around. These relatively casual friends of ours, one of the daughters was three or four years older than me. She'd just had her birthday and somebody had given her a Kiss record: *Destroyer*, their big breakout record. She didn't want it. I remember her asking me, "Oh, do you like Kiss? Do you want this record?" I held it, and if you've ever seen the cover of this thing. When you're like ten, this was the most amazing thing I'd ever seen in my life. I had never heard of them. Didn't know anything about it. I said, "Yeah! I love Kiss." So she gave me this record, just gave it to me. That was definitely the end of the Olivia Newton-John record!

Streetside Records was a big one. There was a Camelot at the mall. Streetside, there's a lot of fond memories there. Peaches was the closest store, a Southern chain with the crates. The first record I bought on my own, with money I made, was at Peaches. I got the one Kiss record and then . . . my dad . . . even to this day, it was one of the neatest things he's done for me. Kiss was coming to St. Louis. I was ten – '76 or '77. It was December and it was cold and it was snowing. We had a steep driveway and our cars were at the top of the hill. You couldn't even go down the driveway. I had wanted to go see Kiss but it wasn't happening. We didn't have tickets. After dinner, we were just sitting there. And all of a sudden, my dad was, "Get your coat. We're going." I remember making it up the hill, going all the way downtown to the Checker Dome, the arena at the time. We didn't have tickets, but I vividly remember him in the parking lot. There were people selling tickets, scalping tickets and he got us floor tickets somehow. You didn't have to worry about counterfeits at the time. Twentieth row on the floor maybe. And we went to the show. I'm sure he hated it. It was just Kiss – larger than life. I remember, at one point, he took me up to move forward toward the stage and being in front of Ace Frehley, the guitarist, it was awe-inspiring. It was such as great memory. Christmas was coming and I got *Kiss Alive* and *Kiss Alive II*. Then their next album came out – *Love Gun* – that was maybe the first album I bought at the store.

Partly it's just the time you grow up in. I was in the Midwest and in the Seventies and getting into the Eighties, it was the arena rock. You grew up discovering Rush, REO Speedwagon, Styx . . . all of this stuff which maybe hasn't quite stood the test of the time, the way some of what he [my father] was listening to, but that was a thing for a long time. I laugh now how I went down that road, and then – having worked in the business and now being the age I'm at, you come back around and go, "Oh, he really did have great taste in music."

The radio station that somehow I found was KSHE, KSHE 95. That was like the heritage rock station in St. Louis. They would play the Allmans and Stones and Led Zeppelin and things like that. It wasn't like the NPR station."

Once you started to get into the later Seventies, there was the New York scene, and Talking Heads and U2. I never really was into the overtly pop second wave from Britain, like Duran Duran. That was never my musical center.

I always did keep exploring and then, particularly when I went to college at NYU, there was a lot of exposure there because it's so eclectic. In New York, there was some more folk-based stuff. I had roommates, but it was really my family. At NYU, it was only when I started to intern. Then I was around like-minded people who were like all music, all the time.[87]

John hadn't known he wanted to pursue any form of career in the music business, or even go to law school. NYU (New York University) had just started a music business program and, when he later met fellow NYU alumnus – and long-term Concord Records executive – Glen Barros (they were both at NYU at the same time, though they didn't know each other), he learned that Glen had taken that program. John had pursued a liberal arts education, majoring in Philosophy with a minor in Economics.

His interest in music influenced his decision to go to NYU. He could have stayed in St. Louis: he'd been accepted to the University of Chicago and to Columbia, the latter seeming to him somewhat like a prep school.

Of all the schools, NYU – even Washington Square Park – that was the place that was sort of the most "foreign" from where I was coming from. There were just all these people that looked different, seemed different. There was all that music in the Village: the Bottom Line was there and the jazz clubs and everything else. It was just so different. I was terrified, but I pushed myself. Before I decided to go there, that might have been maybe the third or fourth choice on paper, but after visiting and spending time there, it became the place. I still say that in terms of the school, that really was the best – the most rewarding educationally. It was the perfect place for me, not at all like a traditional college. There was no quad – even Columbia had that – there were no fraternities or things like that. Even the sports team, they were the Violets. That was perfect for being in the Village.

But the music business is what I wanted to do.

Glen [Barros] did a number of internships, like in a publishing company, and that was good. He got a range of experience. Because I was just kind of doing it on my own (not part of that program), I just kind of thought about labels. Rush was with Mercury. That was part of PolyGram, that conglomerate. They were at 810 Seventh Avenue. I just knocked on their door. It was kind of the same as coming to Rounder. It's so different now with these internships. Either you're paid or you have to get school credit. It all has to be kind of official, whereas back then you could just kind of be around or whatever. So I did.

At PolyGram, Jim Urie was head of the sales department while I was there. I think I did some photocopying for him. Things like that. He definitely was one of the people I would ask about how to get a job, or what was a good way to go. He was one of the people who encouraged me to think about law school as a good path. I didn't realize this at the time, but obviously a lot of people in the business ... look at Scott Pascucci, Clive Davis – it goes on and on. Not that it has to be, but having that legal background can be a good way to go even if you're only on the business side.

That's when I started. It was during the course of the PolyGram years that people started mentioning law school. That's when I started thinking about it. I was there maybe three days a week. It was a lot of time. I would take the R train from in the Village and you got off at 49th Street. There was like Sales, and Production ... it's funny, given that I ended up going to law school, I never did anything with Business Affairs. There was Production and Creative Services. These two women – Traci Werbel and Libby Fried – they really took me under their wings. I worked a lot with them, helping out with all kinds of errands. Gofer-type stuff. There was always a ton going on. At one point, I think I could have moved to another department, but those two wanted to hold onto me so I just stayed there. The label had a lot of . . kind of like that hard-rock glam stuff – they had Scorpions, Def Leppard, Deep Purple, the Reunion stuff. Bon Jovi and Cinderella. Bon Jovi was already big, but then they had that huge record, *Slippery When Wet*, with 'Livin' on a Prayer' on it. That thing sold like ten million. That came out while I was there. I remember those guys coming into the office. And Cinderella, if you remember them, they had a bluesy sort of feel to them but it was also that kind of glam rock. Tom Keifer. They used to come in all the time. That's mainly what Mercury was doing.

There was sort of a UK-based signing off of maybe Phonogram, Swing Out Sister, with kind of a smooth jazzy thing. But the one thing they had, and that the staff just adored, was maybe kind of the most Rounder-related, was Robert Cray. *Strong Persuader*. I was an intern when *Strong Persuader* broke out. That was a big deal. Otherwise, it was a lot of like of the harder rock kind of stuff, which was never really my . . . Rush was sort of the exception. The rest of all that was fine and everything, but wasn't really like my inspiration or whatever. You'd go see some of those shows, and I don't remember why. They weren't on Mercury but I remember going over to the Meadowlands complex in New Jersey to see Mötley Crüe one time. We all went and saw Ratt at Madison Square Garden. Maybe a Mercury band was opening. I was never really passionate about all those bands, but I would definitely go see a lot of the folk stuff. Suzanne Vega was coming on the scene. Things were going on in the Village at night.

That was when the big Tower Records was right there on West 4th Street in the Village. I feel like I lived in that store. Tuesdays were release days but I was in there if not seven days a week, at least five. Just looking around and getting things. That was also back when CDs were just getting under way. Island Records was right there, before they got merged. It was quite a ride.

John graduated NYU in 1989, and ended up going to Harvard Law School, graduating in 1992. One year before him, in the class of 1991, was one Barack Obama. Michelle Obama had graduated Harvard Law in 1988.

John wasn't able to pin down just when he first approached Rounder and – as with PolyGram – simply just asked for an internship. Law school was pretty intense, he said.

> It might have been in my second year. I think I sent a letter at first, and Jake Guralnick responded. I think I just wrote to you all, but Jake . . . it was all pre-email . . . Jake was the one who reached out. Probably because I was in law school and he was the one helping out with the business affairs stuff and the publishing. I think there

had been somebody else who had maybe come in at one point and maybe that didn't work. I remember coming up there and it was Jake who I met with. I think I was overdressed to begin with. I probably wore a suit.

Even before I got up there to law school, I knew about Rounder. I knew that you all were in Cambridge. That was always a thought, that it would be neat to connect. I think that . . . whenever I reached out, that was the earliest possibility for me to do so . . . I definitely was not getting paid. It was just casual. I did like what I did at PolyGram. I just kind of showed up and never left. We organized all the files. There was always stuff going on. There was a Harry Fox audit. All these different things.

While interviewing him, I said to John:

My memory is there was a time . . . maybe you had already been there for a while. My memory is that you were trying to talk us into you becoming an intern and I was resistant: "You're over-qualified. We don't need a lawyer or somebody from law school. I do the contracts and all."

John replied:

I do remember that but I think that might have been after I had already been an intern there for some time and me trying to talk you into hiring me. I had graduated and that's what I wanted to do. I remember you being "What would you do? We just don't have the need." That was in the context of getting hired. [John had already been a Rounder intern for most of two years.]

I worked with Jake on the publishing. Everything was filed by record number. I remember going through all of those files, just in terms of organizing them and figuring out which ones had contracts and which ones didn't. Some of them, if you had contracts that covered more than one record, indicating which record numbers those were. We had to get up to date with mechanical licenses.

Business affairs – that was kind of your department. You had Jake run the publishing and I was working with him. Later, I was helping you with contracts, after I got hired.

John was married at the time, to classmate Katie Willard. Katie's brother Marty later came to work for Rounder and, as 2021 begins, is still on staff at Concord as an attorney.

Katie and I met in January of the first year at a Super Bowl party just as the second semester got started. We chatted because football wasn't really that much of an interest. We dated all through law school. We got married when we graduated, at the end of May there.

John became an employee in mid-July 1992, not long after graduation from law school. Katie and John had a daughter, Zoë, in 1997.

In 1998, after six years of making himself pretty invaluable, John was offered an opportunity to work in Business Affairs for Jive Records in New York City. They made him an offer through a lawyer there who he knew. He asked the three of us – Ken, Marian, and myself – to come into the upstairs conference at 1 Camp Street, where he told us the news.

I didn't think he was angling for anything: he was just telling us that he was going to take the position. I looked at Ken and Marian, and then asked John if he could give us five minutes. The three of us quickly huddled and said, "We don't want to lose John. What can we do?" Very quickly – within those five minutes – we came up with the double idea of offering John the job of president but also the opportunity to create a separate imprint where he could work with some other kinds of music that sometimes interested him personally – an imprint on which he could release music of his own choosing. Zoë Records was the result. It released 150 albums, beginning with Juliana Hatfield's *Bed* in August 1998, and including six albums (most in multiple configurations) of Rush. The DVD of *Rush in Rio* sold over 200,000 copies within about a year of its October 2003 release.[88]

Maybe more importantly than the imprint, we told him that, if he accepted the position as president of Rounder, he would be empowered to make the final call on decisions. We wanted to stress we weren't offering him a mere title for a figurehead position. Yes, the three of us would still be around but we recognized that it could be an impossible task to report to three owners – founders, no less – who might squabble and second-guess or overrule him at any time. We told him he'd have the final word. Ultimately, we could fire him, but we weren't offering him the position to fire him. We were all ready to step back and let him be the one to make the final call. We had progressively been relying on him anyhow. That's why we wanted to hold onto him.

Intern to president! Audacious, but John believed us, and it worked out. He talked with Katie and accepted the position. Fifteen years later, when we sold Rounder, and the second closing was consummated, John remained head of Rounder after we went off payroll.

At the time John took over, the company had about 140 employees. Some had been there for many years, longer than the six years or so that John had put in. We had released somewhere around three thousand albums.

It doesn't take much to imagine how having three owners – the entrepreneurs who founded the company and built it up – could present leadership

John Virant with Rush in 2015: (left to right) Ray Danniels (SRO Management), Alex Lifeson, John Virant, Neil Peart, Geddy Lee, Pegi Cecconi (SRO Management). Photograph by Matt Butler.

challenges to John. Looking back on it in October 2018, John acknowledged there had been frustrations but they were more with some of the senior management team, others who had been working for us. "They kind of squabbled a bunch," he said. "I don't know that that's manuscript-worthy." And it probably is just as well not to get into that. There were no hard landings that we were aware of.

The process of passing leadership on to another generation so the company was no longer led by its founders is probably a good transition to make, and it worked out very nicely from our perspective. John truly did become "the fourth Rounder."

The company had grown quite a bit since John first came on board as an intern in 1992. For the fiscal year ending March 31, 1992, Rounder reported assets of $9,307,346. We changed to align fiscal year and calendar year. At the end of the year 2000, when John had been president for a full year-and-a-half, the company reported nearly double that amount: $16,784,053. Total revenues had climbed from more or less $20 million per year to $30 million. The company had weathered the partnerships that hadn't worked out, and continued to grow. We hadn't yet borne the full brunt of the challenges beginning to be posed by the shrinking of retail and the whole phenomenon of free downloading of music.

1997 and the launch of the Alan Lomax Collection

When we finally released *The Alan Lomax Collection Sampler* on April 22, 1997, it represented the end of one long road and the start of another. In our earliest days at the Library of Congress, no name came up more often than that of Alan Lomax. Before we were three years old (Rounder, that is), we'd already worked with some of the people Alan recorded – such as Almeda Riddle (her first Rounder album came out in 1972) and Estil C. Ball (his first album for us came out the month we turned three), and we'd already organized the first reissue of some of Lomax's recordings with the Aunt Molly Jackson album. It was one of the very first agreements we signed: with Molly's siblings Sarah Ogan Gunning and Jim Garland – on March 29, 1971, just five months after our first release.

As Rounder founders, we'd started as record collectors and fans of folk music, and, as mentioned right at the beginning of this book, it wasn't long before we made that first pilgrimage to the Archive of Folk Song at the Library of Congress. Alan's father John A. Lomax had a relationship with the Library dating back to June 1933, when he and his eighteen-year-old son traveled across Texas recording American music in small towns and cities, work farms and prisons in various parts of the state. John was named the "Honorary Consultant and Curator of the Archive of American Folk Song." Alan's professional employment with the Archive began in 1937 and continued until 1942. Both on field trips with his father and in work of his own, Alan recorded a great legacy of American and other musics ranging across the American South, to Haiti, and even embracing documentation in Washington DC itself, such as the extensive recordings he made of Jelly Roll Morton in 1938 in the Coolidge Auditorium.

We knew of Alan through his recordings of Woody Guthrie, Lead Belly, Aunt Molly Jackson, E.C. Ball, and numerous others. As mentioned, one of the reasons we chose the name "Rounder" was because the word was often used in folksong referring to someone who rambled 'round the country. We had romantic visions of ourselves traveling around making recordings of singers and musicians who might otherwise never be recorded. We were very aware of those who came before us, and in whose footsteps we could only hope to follow. We also wanted to honor their work, and help in any way we could to release some of the many field recordings by Alan and others that had never been available in the general marketplace.

So we reached out to Alan, very early on, and began to talk of possibilities. When we first met him, it was at his combination apartment/office in New York City. He was his usual self, flush with ideas and wanting to play one track and then another – and then another – for us. He was warm and welcoming, and took us out for a meal. He was passionate and enthusiastic about everything he was recording.

He related one of his dream projects, what he then called the Recorded Treasury of Black Music in America, a projected twelve-album set drawing on the field recordings he had made over the previous fifty years. (This was the series that later unfolded on Rounder – a quarter-century later – as part of the Alan Lomax Collection under the title "Deep River of Song"). We loved the idea, and indeed would have welcomed any kind of working relationship with this legendary figure.

He suggested that we start out with an album by Texas Gladden and her brother Hobart Smith, one side for each of the two Saltville, Virginia artists. We thought it a fine idea and Ken visited relatives to obtain permissions. Alan signed a contract with us in September 1972 and Chris Gladden and Brookie Smith signed for the Gladden and Smith families. Alan was in touch with other family members as well, wanting to make sure that all were in agreement with Rounder releasing the album. They were. Alan was to edit the tapes and send Rounder interview material for the album notes. We had the Library prepare masters and had copies sent to Alan as well so he could refresh his memory about the work he'd done so many years before; we spent a couple of hundred dollars on the 10 inch reel audio masters – a fairly significant investment for us at the time. These were perhaps the first 10 inch reels we'd encountered, having typically worked with the cheaper 7 inch reels that were designed for home use.

We were very excited to be working with Alan Lomax and releasing some of this important music. Little did we know it was going to be twenty-nine years before the music saw light of day – and then in a format none of us could have conceived of back then: the compact disc. Rather than one side apiece, Texas Gladden and Hobart Smith each had a full CD devoted to their music – both released in 2001.

Back to the 1970s, though. After we sent Alan the copies, much time elapsed. After a reminder or two from us, Alan wrote in October 1974 that he would be getting to the tapes soon. The following June, he wrote again with another update. We kept writing each other, but the project never progressed. We understood that Alan had a lot more pressing matters on his mind, but it was particularly frustrating because we had hoped that this first collaboration would lead to an expanded one where we would work together on releasing plenty more recordings over the years. We just wanted to get started.

It was always hard to actually do business with Alan, because he wanted to play snatches of music for us, sharing this piece and that. He was "selling us on it" – not that he needed to – but never consummating the sale. His mind was firing in many directions at once, and sitting down to do business was perhaps less inspiring for him.

Maybe if we'd offered a big advance, it would have opened things up. Alan's situation meant outside funding was necessary but back then Rounder couldn't offer anything more substantial than after-the-fact royalties. Even though the royalties were pegged at a level higher than industry standard, the number of sales was necessarily uncertain and any income would inevitably only arrive around a year after final release of the albums. No government funding for Alan's work was forthcoming; at the time, those in a position to help didn't adequately appreciate the treasure they had in Alan Lomax, with his vision, drive, and energy – and his talent for eliciting strong folk performances. Few private institutions or foundations supplied funding, and even then only on a sporadic basis. Alan needed to devote a disproportionate amount of his time to trying to raise money rather than actually doing the work we all revere today. Would that it had been otherwise. He could easily have doubled, and doubled again, the vast body of work that enriches us all today.

I wrote him once a year about the Gladden–Smith recordings, but finally stopped after the tenth year. We never forgot about the Recorded Treasury, though, and finally got to the point where we could offer as much as $6,000 or $7,000 per album by way of an advance – in the $75,000 range for the whole series – but he always seemed more consumed with present work and less interested in seeing releases of things he'd recorded in the past.

I thought it was mostly economic – that we were too small potatoes for him. That's why we made the larger offer; but it still didn't grab his attention. He always seemed to have a lot of hopeful irons in the fire, but it appeared that what he really longed for were colleagues with whom he could work on preparing a series like the Treasury, to help shepherd things along. We were based in Boston and Alan was in New York and we didn't really feel we could take the time to move to the City and work with him on his schedule. We reached out to several people whose work we respected and who we believed Alan would respect as well, and we tried to steer a couple of potential collaborators (or assistants) his way – people like Ken Bilby – but none of those matches ever took, for one reason or another. Nothing came of it; perhaps he was a somewhat intimidating presence.

In the meantime, we pursued other projects that connected to, or drew on, Alan's work. Years had passed, but in 1987 we started working with some Woody Guthrie material. The Bonneville Power Administration was celebrating its fiftieth anniversary and, in February that year, Rounder was invited to bid on a project to release an album of Woody Guthrie's 1941 recordings for the BPA. We moved very quickly and came to agreement with Harold Leventhal of Woody Guthrie Publications and the other rights holders, such as Folkways Records and the publishers, and by August 1987 we had the Woody Guthrie *Columbia River Collection* (Rounder 1036) in the marketplace.

Harold and Rounder talked about getting some other Woody material out, and we wasted no time in re-releasing the classic *Dust Bowl Ballads* that had been out on RCA decades earlier. It came out a year later, in August 1988.

We also came to an agreement to release a three-LP set of Woody's Library of Congress recordings which Alan had made in March 1940. Naturally, we asked Alan if he would collaborate with us on this, and write fresh notes telling the story of the recordings and placing them in contemporary context. After all, he'd been the one who recorded Woody, yet the earlier edition of the Library of Congress sessions on Elektra contained little from Alan himself.

He said he was interested, but, despite writing him several times, he never got around to it. We finally decided we didn't want to hold it up any longer and sent him a deadline, telling him that we'd love to have his notes but would feel compelled to go ahead without him if the deadline passed. We knew he'd been an employee of the Library at the time of the recordings, and had no real claim of ownership – but it would have been wonderful to get his fresh first-person account of the sessions. We worried that we'd be burning a bridge, but that didn't prove to be the case. The three-LP set was released several years later, in October 1988.

We went through the same process again with the six albums of Lead Belly's Library of Congress recordings which we released beginning in 1991. Larry Cohn had written some excellent notes for the Elektra edition, but, again, we wanted to involve Alan in telling the story in the first person. Once again, the invitation, pushing back the release numerous times, but still no notes. So, again, we released the set without no contribution from Alan. There were good notes, though, provided by Kip Lornell, drawing from the biography of Lead Belly that Kip had written with Charles Wolfe. Charles was, throughout his too-short life, a friend and a dedicated advocate of the sorts of musics that we at Rounder all enjoyed.

And we went through the same process once more when we first released the Library's Jelly Roll Morton music. Rounder Records' 1994 release of four CDs (CD 1091–1094) contains essentially all the Morton music recorded at the Library of Congress by Alan Lomax. The original recordings contain an extensive amount of conversation as well: mostly Morton talking, with Lomax prompting – one of the earliest and most successful attempts at oral history. Lomax published Morton's account in the book *Mister Jelly Roll*.

We had first talked to staff at the Library of Congress at least a decade (and maybe two) earlier. There was concern at the Library – appropriately so – that Morton's heirs be contacted, their permission secured, and any royalties be paid to them. Others had tried before us and not gotten anywhere, we were told, so we never really pursued it. Some years passed before we determined that we should make the effort anyhow, however unlikely the result. I took the bull by the horns, asking for the names they had on file as the proper heirs of Mr. Morton. I succeeded in contacting them and, to our surprise, it was quite easy to reach agreement. All set to proceed, I reached out to Alan once more and requested his participation, but he was preoccupied with other efforts at the time. I asked around and was soon given the name of Prof. James Dapogny, who fortunately agreed to take on the task of editing the material. As Jim worked with the masters, it was clear to him that some of the masters were originally recorded at the wrong speed and that all of the earlier releases drawing on the material had failed to correct it! So Jim worked with Library engineers to restore the recordings to the way they sounded as Morton played the music, not the way the faulty equipment had recorded it. The story is told in more detail in the notes to those four albums.

What we wound up with was a set of digital masters embracing nine hours of sound and music. We had originally planned to release the full body of work, which would have amounted to something like eight or nine CDs, not the four we actually did release. There are two reasons for our selectiveness, one practical and the other political. From the beginning of this round of conversations with the Library, Alan Jabbour of the American Folklife Center had the idea of convening a symposium at the Library and inviting various scholars to present papers on Morton, which would then be gathered into a booklet and issued along with the complete set of recordings. For one reason or another, the symposium never eventuated. The Center at this time was also going through a tortuous process of self-preservation, where every two years, if I recall correctly, funding for the Center had to be re-approved by Congress. There was always this sword of Damocles hanging over the Center: the potential loss of its funding. Some connected with the Center worried that the release of the full set of Morton recordings could jeopardize Congressional funding. If too big a splash was made by the release, and members of Congress actually listened to the language Morton used and some of the things he said, it wouldn't be too much of a stretch to envision someone grandstanding: "Why is the Library of Congress releasing these dirty, vile, filthy lyrics?" The repercussions could be significant.

To put out individual albums, rather than the entire set as a package, was perhaps preferable. But that prompted another concern: how would the albums appear to the public? More than half the actual recording time was comprised of Morton's colorful monologues. As a series of several individual CDs – rather than one big multiple-CD set – some would therefore contain only a small amount of music. To release the work faithfully, presenting the sequence of Morton's talk and performance – the only way that really made sense in treating the full body of work – would result in one of the albums only having two musical performances on it and another just three. I worried that a customer picking up a CD in a store and seeing it had just two tracks on it would simply not buy it. I came to the conclusion that perhaps the best way to go was to take the digital masters we already had and simply extract the music from them, leaving the spoken word material for later release. This idea was well received at the Library as a way of testing the waters at Congress.

Ultimately, the lack of negative feedback (as it happens, there never was any reaction from Members of Congress, either positive or negative), and the fact that the Center received permanent funding, opened the door for a release of the complete recordings at a later stage. The final package came out in 2005, complete with additional material and a copy of the book *Mr. Jelly Roll*.

Some other projects took a comparably long time to mature. In 1996, I started working with Alan Jabbour on a set of Moroccan music drawn from Paul Bowles' 1959 recordings for the Library. The set was finally released twenty years later, in 2016, and was one of five Grammy nominees for Best Historical Album.[89] Alan Jabbour died in January 2017, but not before learning of the nomination.

Getting back in touch with Alan Lomax

After a few years of almost no contact, I wrote Lomax again and the letter might have arrived at just the right time. He'd been involved with his retrospective book *The Land Where Blues Began*, and he was aware that Moe Asch had made arrangements for the Folkways label to be sold to the Smithsonian Institution. He may have been thinking more about his own legacy – what would become of all this wonderful music when he wasn't around? By early 1994, we had begun to talk about a truly ambitious project well beyond just the twelve volumes of the Treasury: releasing all of Alan's life work, in a collection embracing several series of recordings that would total over a hundred albums in all. Marian and I visited Alan in New York on March 14, 1994 to discuss the idea further, though he got caught up in playing several of his Spanish recordings for us and enthusing about the "Global Jukebox" on which he'd been working. He referred us to an attorney, however, with whom we started communications, but then that got bogged down, too. When Alan switched attorneys and started working with Jeff Greenberg, the deal moved toward a conclusion – though the terms shifted in the process. A final contract was signed on August 30, 1995. It wasn't as good a deal as we'd originally struck, but we were entranced with the idea of such an extensive collaboration (how many record companies would commit to releasing over a hundred albums of field recordings by one collector?) and we conceded on two key points regarding publishing and ownership.

The answer to that rhetorical question is, of course: not many. Nor would they have paid a non-recoupable $100,000 for the privilege. In fact, maybe no other company would have agreed, as we did, to release anything and everything he presented for release, and to pay additional advances for each album.

Before we got properly under way, Alan suffered a serious and debilitating stroke in 1996. (He survived for several years but died on July 19, 2002.) Alan's daughter, ethnomusicologist Anna Lomax Chairetakis (now Wood), assumed the responsibility for his care, his life's work, and the Association for Cultural Equity which he had established. We worked closely with Anna in developing the collection and its various series: Southern Journey, Caribbean Voyage, Deep River of Song, Folk Songs of England, Ireland, Scotland & Wales, Italian Treasury, The Spanish Recordings, World Library of Folk and Primitive Music, the Concert & Radio Series, the Portrait Series, and a number of individual albums that were outside the purview of a particular series. The first release was the sampler, Rounder 1501, released in 1997.

Over the next ten years, Rounder released ninety-four albums in the Alan Lomax Collection before the series was effectively suspended. We were ready to keep going. We had already assigned numbers in sequence for another fifty-five albums, and we knew there were numerous further candidates. Two things prevented the series from doubling its initially intended size: in other words, two hundred (or more) albums rather than one hundred. And – no surprise – they were both about economics.

As we have learned, the full Jelly Roll Morton package came out in 2005. *Jelly Roll Morton: The Library of Congress Recordings* was an eight-CD set complete with a lavish large-format eighty-page booklet and a reprint of the *Mr. Jelly Roll* book in a 344-page edition from the University of California Press. All the elements were presented in very elaborate – dare I say, elegant – packaging, and the 7,500-copy limited edition quickly sold out. Disc eight contained twenty selections from interviews that Alan had done with various New Orleans jazz musicians, as well as a PDF document offering expanded liner notes, a complete transcription of all dialogue and lyrics contained on the other seven discs, Alan's research notes, other interview material, and archival Morton correspondence.

It was a beautiful package in the shape of a piano, with a die-cut piano lid and all – so beautiful that maybe some might have purchased it for the packaging alone, notwithstanding the fact that inside were the violently misogynist lyrics that the Library had feared would somehow come back to haunt them. We decided to use the sticker to comply with industry standards usually applied to gangsta rap records: the parental advisory warning (though we didn't imagine any little kids buying an eight-CD set). When it sold through so quickly, and people like Walter Cronkite were calling trying to buy copies as holiday gifts, Anna wanted us to make up more of them. The packaging alone was extremely expensive, and it had been planned all along as a limited-edition package. Had we felt confident we could sell another 7,500 copies, we would have done so, but we weren't sure we could count on selling more than a couple of thousand. Anna told us that the Library of Congress wanted to buy fifty copies. She said she wanted to buy some more, too.

If all we sold were a couple of thousand more we stood to lose some tens of thousands of dollars. It made more sense to combine all the same material, but into a more streamlined standard package. We agreed to an additional run of 5,000 of the original elaborate package, which would have cost us $142,950 at a unit cost of $28.59 apiece (not even counting the cost of the discs or the assembly), as long as we had a genuine commitment to just 1,000 sales – but that was more than the Lomax side wanted to guarantee. It all left a bad taste in Anna's mouth. I think she sincerely believed that this was a masterpiece (it was), in some demand, and that considerations about money shouldn't enter the process. Of course, it was our money and not hers.

The Jelly Roll Morton Library of Congress collection

The second issue was about the ongoing series of recordings: the Spanish Recordings and the Italian Treasury, for example. With the collapse of record retail, most clearly evidenced in the 2006 closure of the Tower Records chain, there were fewer and fewer outlets for these records. We were shipping only a few hundred of some of the recordings, not nearly enough to break even.

The compromise we suggested was that we stop printing the elaborate thirty-two (or more)-page booklets, but move instead to offering the text and photography as a PDF file embedded in the disc itself – just as we had done in the Jelly Roll Morton package. That way, anyone with a computer could easily access all the annotation (without the limit to the number of pages or photographs posed by a CD jewel box, and they could all be in full color). Anna's concern was twofold and we agreed with both points: first, printed books are indeed much nicer to have and to hold than a file on a computer; and, secondly, there were still a lot of people who didn't have computers, particularly in rural communities, for example in Spain, where some of Alan's original informants still lived. Bringing the music back to those communities was a wonderful thing to do, but embedded PDFs were not going to reach as many people, even if they might have access to computers in libraries and local community centers.

Although we appreciated her points, we were starting to lose several thousand dollars on each release, so we had to stand firm. There was no question that making music accessible via computers would be more the mode of the future (and our Spanish distributor had only been getting a couple of hundred copies into Spain as a whole, even with the printed booklets), but neither side budged and further progress of the Collection was suspended through inertia.

We take pride in having made those nearly one hundred albums available. Partly because of their accessibility through our series, Lomax recordings were used in two feature films: *O Brother, Where Art Thou?* by the Coen Brothers and Martin Scorsese's *Gangs of New York*. We were never able to come to an agreement to revive the series and make the remaining fifty or sixty planned albums available. But the Lomax folks have been working ever since to make more material available online. In March 2004, the Lomax Collection was acquired by the Library of Congress.

O Brother, of course, was a huge success as a film and the soundtrack album (released in 2000) has sold more than 8,200,000 copies through mid-2020, and helped sell many other albums in the bluegrass field. Notably, Union Station's Dan Tyminski was the singing voice of George Clooney, who played the lead singer in the Soggy Bottom Boys.

April Fools press releases

We did have a little fun, too. A new release sheet we issued on April 1, 1999 announced the availability of the Alan Congress "It's a Small World After All" Collection. Our blurb:

> Ethnovideocartographer Alan Congress's ground- (and back-) breaking collected works. If it happened, he was there. If he was there, he recorded it. If he recorded it, we collected it. If we collected it, we're for damn sure going to issue it. Over 3½ years total playing time on 6473 conveniently packaged compact discs. Subscribe to the whole series and keep the forklift as our gift – free!

There was a tradition of unusual new Rounder release announcements on April 1, and no one was spared, ranging from *Raffi Sings Whaling Songs for Kids* to the series we purportedly released in 1992, featuring *Alison Krauss Karaoke*. Munich Records got the joke. They sent us a purchase order after our announcement of the April 1, 1992 release, ordering 2,900 pieces of each of the five karaoke albums but only if they were delivered on the 1st, and only if we included a Joseph Spence karaoke album and a karaoke album from the "In the Absence of Man" series. They also informed of their plans for video karaoke and their release of *Casablanca* as the first title, without Humphrey Bogart. *You* could be Bogey as Rick Blaine.

There was an occasional tradition of press releases on other dates – though perhaps the first fake release had been on June 23, 1977 (what prompted it I can no longer recall). In it, Rounder announced its commitment to record an historically significant British group by entering into a ten-year deal to record the Beatles. "We know we're taking a chance here," Marian was quoted as saying, "but we feel that the addition of the Beatles will help boost our British Isles folk imports and help us round out our own catalog as well." Rounder's commitment was to release a minimum of two albums in the ten years. "We have to protect ourselves," I was quoted as saying. "If sales merit additional recording, we will certainly consider issuing a third or fourth LP." All sales were to be done in the basement Mixing Lab of Newton, Massachusetts under the direction of Beatles Executive Producer Ken Irwin, with the first session set for late summer 1978.

Other announcements included the *Complete Jelly Roll Morton Library of Congress Recordings: Deluxe Edition*, specially packaged inside an actual full-size upright piano. And, acknowledging how far afield Alan Lomax had traveled, there was his album *Atlantis: Tradition and Ritual in the Undersea City* released in April 2002. "We figured, here is a society untarnished by the prying hands of air-breathing colonialists, carpetbaggers, imperialists, and documentarians," Lomax purportedly said. In 1999, two of our artists were said to have collaborated on *The Best of Skaggs & Shaggs*. And two years before that, Rounder followed up our *Hollerin'* album with *Whisperin'.*

Dramatic changes at retail

We released the first volumes of "Southern Journey," the first series in the Alan Lomax Collection, in January 1997, and that was also the year that Rounder took a new direction in distributing our recordings. Late 1995 and 1996 were times of unparalleled attrition in record retail, as the big-box retailers such as Best Buy began offering CDs at rock-bottom (almost certainly loss leader) prices, and doing so nationally on such a scale that hundreds of independent record stores were driven out of business, while deep-catalog chain retailers like Tower Records were gravely impacted, too, and ultimately done in. Returns were coming back at triple the usual pace – or worse – as retail contracted. As noted earlier, quite a few established indie labels did not survive.

Rounder largely left the distribution business which had helped keep us vital for some twenty-five years. We developed a new bifurcated distribution strategy for our recordings that we hoped could help us have the best of both worlds. Beginning in August 1997, we worked with Mercury Records to be distributed by PolyGram in an agreement with complexities we need not go into here; by and large, the goal was to get better distribution through one of the majors. At the same time, we reserved the right to sell our deeper catalog to a large number of specialized indie distributors with whom we had worked with over the years and whom we did not want to spurn. We figured PolyGram (which a little later morphed into Universal) would really only be interested in our better sellers, and we didn't want to burden them with records unlikely to sell more than, say, five thousand copies. At the same time, we remained committed to continuing to release, as best we could, the same array of traditional music recordings that we always had – ranging from Cape Breton fiddle to folkloric albums from Trinidad and old-time country music.

Trends set in motion around 1995 continued for more than a decade, though with twists. Only ten years later, very few of our "top ten" accounts were the same as they were just a decade ago, while newcomers such as Amazon and iTunes not on the radar (or not even conceived) edged their way into the upper ranks. The adaptations we had to make over the ensuing ten to twenty years were dramatic and far-reaching.

One such adaptation was in the actual presentation of traditional music CDs. As it became increasingly difficult to get exposure in regular retail stores, we hoped for better sales through outlets like Amazon, iTunes, and Spotify, as well as relying on money coming in via Sound Exchange, which collected money from new sources such as satellite radio. Terrestrial radio is still exempt from paying artists and producers, a disadvantage in America. Throughout the rest of the world, radio pays the creators.

We've also had to figure out ways to save money in manufacture, but fortunately technology has anticipated this need (it's not unique to Rounder) and it has become much more feasible to produce lower-quantity runs of CDs – even "press-on-demand" CDs, just as publishers in the book trade (or individuals) now can offer "print-on-demand" books.

We also used the proposed Lomax solution for recordings with extensive documentation, and offered a whole range for which the booklet is a PDF file embedded in the CD. These PDF files were made available for free download from Rounder's website. The hope was that some people might become intrigued by what they read in the free booklet download and then move to purchase the recording – either by downloading it from iTunes or one of the other services, or by buying a hard copy of the disc. We'd win, by keeping costs down and being able to continue to release albums of traditional music. The consumer would win, too, not only through access to the music and the documentation but (in some cases) because we could offer much more extensive documentation this way. The annotator would win as well, because she or he is not forced to delete material in order to fit the constraints of the printed booklet. With the passage of the time and the proliferation of digital media, there are numerous ways that information can be conveyed.

Sadly, most record labels are not taking advantage of such opportunities. The kind of information that helped us learn so much about the sources of the music we loved, and helped us track down connections – the reason we put so much emphasis on album notes from our very first albums – is just not being made available any more. Perhaps one can track down this information through the internet, but having it all made available as part of each album's presentation is not happening much any more. It's a loss.

Sales of CDs plummeted in the two decades from 1997, as consumers turned away from physical carriers of music to online music sources. It's a rapidly changing world and the Music Modernization Act, along with two other pieces of legislation that were signed into law in October 2018, brings about some changes that are expected to facilitate payments of money from music streaming to songwriters and producers. But in 1997 and 1998, we were only seeing the beginning of trends that would transform the music business.

1998: major distribution

1998 was the year that marked the start of our relationship with Universal, a three-year deal signed with Mercury's Danny Goldberg. We began talking in 1997 and completed the agreement in time to effect the transition on August 6. At the time, the company was known as PolyGram; it only picked up the Universal name a merger or two down the line.

We'd been approached by Seymour Stein of Sire Records who wanted to propose a partnership of sorts. That got us thinking. The business was a mess on the indie side of things with the largest distributor (Alliance) in bankruptcy, and we were still smarting from the way the DNA deal had shaken out. Attorney Jonathan Horn made some inquiries to see who, aside from Seymour, might be interested and, through Jonathan's partner at the time, Elliot Groffman, we met Danny. We also suffered through an ill-fated meeting at Sony with about fifteen people seated in a conference room with perhaps fifty feet between us and the Sony participants on the other side of the room. Distant was the feeling we got throughout. With Danny, it was a whole other feeling.

He was gung-ho to go, but Jim Caparro on PolyGram's distribution side was concerned about the large number of slower-moving titles in the Rounder catalog. At the time, Paul Foley was the head of catalog sales for PGD (PolyGram Group Distribution). Paul was also from the Boston area and in years past had built his own small chain of record retail stores. Jim asked Paul to make a visit to Cambridge in March to meet with John Virant and the

Rounder founders, to assess the question of the deeper catalog, to answer any questions about PolyGram, and to become a liaison.

In the end, we worked out a split distribution system, an agreement between Mercury and Rounder characterized as a P&D (pressing and distribution) deal, with about 1,000 of Rounder's 2,500 releases going through major distribution. In terms of volume, that 40% represented about 90% of Rounder's $24 million in sales. DNA and Bayside (the blackmailers from Tower) would handle the rest. Goldberg said of Rounder, "By a wide margin, they are the premier label for folk music and blues in the world . . . so unique and excellent in their field, it was worth creating a deal that would accommodate them." Rounder was one of the "tiffany businesses" in the music industry, he said. All of the NDLs, with the exception of Tone-Cool, were to stay with Rounder rather than go through PolyGram.

There was another aspect to the deal, an A&R angle, which was intended to identify and jointly sign mutually agreed-upon artists. Typically, these would be artists who were likely to require signing fees or needs that were beyond Rounder's comfortable grasp. If Mercury saw sufficient potential in artists we recommended, we would jointly sign them and work out an appropriate sharing of any profits. There was even a middle road, where Mercury would get involved in the promotion and marketing of a particular artist's release for a percentage of the gross. All three were, in different respects, ways that artists who valued things about Rounder (a closer connection with key people at the company, the continuity of ownership, being a bigger fish in a smaller pond) could also have some of the benefits that come from working with major distribution, and in some cases promotion.

Promotion was always a challenge, with us always working with necessarily limited budgets and needing to make decisions what albums to put more promotional money behind than others. An amusing story cropped up in the 2018 book *Bitten by the Blues*, quoting Wendell Holmes of the Holmes Brothers, a band who had four albums on Rounder between 1990 and 1996. They were well received and did well enough, but not as well as the group itself would have liked. When they made a move to Alligator around 2000, they told Bruce Iglauer that they had been in Rounder's "artist protection program" – i.e. not seen or heard.[90]

Manufacturing of Rounder CDs would henceforth be done by PolyGram. We assumed that the majority of our releases would still be niche recordings that would continue to go through independent distribution.

Needless to say, moving to major label distribution was a major change in our business. We were worried that we might get lost and ignored inside the world of PolyGram with its big building in downtown Manhattan and executives who saw the business through a different prism than us. Danny Goldberg was reassuring, but would he still be around in years to come? (It was a legitimate concern: he wasn't, and was actually gone rather quickly.)

Paul Foley worked with John, Duncan, and Steve Netsky to assimilate Rounder into PolyGram until August of 1998. Duncan himself was looking around. He was perhaps feeling increasingly marginalized. The Rykodisc partners in REP had treated him poorly, and he was frustrated that the Valley partners had similarly disparaged his talents during his time with DNA. Meanwhile, after John Virant had taken over as President of Rounder, Duncan may also have felt he was more consigned to the back seat at Rounder itself. One day in August 1998, he surprised us by announcing that he was going to Newbury Comics. It worked out well for him; more than twenty years later he is Newbury's COO.

When Duncan decided to leave Rounder, John reached out to Paul Foley for a recommendation for someone to fill Duncan's position at Rounder. Paul answered, "Yes, me!" That started the discussion on bringing Paul back to Boston, to Rounder. He was hired as Vice President of Sales and Marketing, beginning on September 7, 1998. Duncan had been the general manager at Rounder, and it wasn't long before Paul added that title.

Sheri Sands was still at PolyGram and running the West Coast office when we began selling Rounder through PolyGram, but she left the company that November and began working as an independent consultant. She met John and me at MIDEM in January of 1999 and, on June 29, John hired her to run both independent sales and look after our Canadian business.

Paul was quite a change from Duncan. He came from the major-label milieu in New York and ran what must have seemed to many a tighter ship in perhaps a more focused fashion. Not having worked side by side with employees packing boxes and shipping orders, he likely came across as more distant. We valued him for his contacts within PolyGram; that was more important to us than any friendships with those he supervised.

This was a major passing of the torch, with John as president and Paul as GM. As described earlier, the three Rounder founders will readily admit that our own management style lacked clarity. Duncan himself was sometimes stuck in the middle, unable to act as decisively as he might have done had he felt he had more leeway. But he was close to us as owners and we were still actively involved. He looked to us for direction, perhaps unsure how much autonomy he truly had. He knew we were right there and with an eye on how things were going, and with our own opinions.

With John, we'd quite consciously agreed to be more hands-off, to allow him freedom without our looking over his shoulder quite as much. When Paul came in, this further solidified the transition in management style. Rounder began to take on a more typical company structure. One could argue that it was becoming a more "rational" structure, and less a personal and idiosyncratic one. There are strengths in this, but also weaknesses. There's no question but that it required a period of adjustment, and some employees chafed under new ways of doing things.

Rounder was a bustling, vibrant enterprise, always in something of a hurry. The union did accomplish certain things that helped Rounder. It provided a structure where none had previously existed for managing employer–employee relations in a growing company. It offered a framework for the resolution of disputes – though I suspected there wouldn't have been nearly as many disputes had there not been a union in the first place, I'll take it on faith that that's only because employees were formerly more hesitant in raising issues. All the same, as is probably often the case in such situations, some employees – and they told us this directly – were reluctant to raise certain matters with the union because the local stewards would come down on them. All in all, my sense is that the union provided a stronger sense of job security for its membership but at the cost of suppressing wages. It was convenient that the union also policed its own members, though at times this may have dampened the initiative of some who might have risen higher had they not been so worried about peer pressure from their fellow workers.

There had been times – both before and after the union was in place – when we needed to discharge an employee for cause, though it happened very rarely over the years. Two employees were discharged for theft and one for embezzlement. Given the several hundred people who have worked for Rounder over nearly fifty years, that was pretty minimal. The first time we were ripped off, it wasn't by an employee but by a "friend" staying at the Willow Avenue house. He wrote a check to himself, forged one of our names, and cashed it. We saved for posterity a photograph from the bank's video camera showing him at the counter cashing the check.

One person claimed a work-related injury when some record boxes fell on him in the warehouse shelves; that one went nowhere when a fellow employee spoke up and said he'd seen the guy stage the accident. We let go a less-than-competent information services manager around 1993, who then filed a claim with us alleging age discrimination. At a hearing before the appropriate state agency, we pointed out that he was younger than us, and younger than a couple of others at the company. That claim went nowhere, too.

I mentioned above how, in 1983, we let our head of promotion and publicity resign after finding her desk stuffed with unanswered mail dating back months. It wasn't as though she took money. The unanswered mail contained a lot of checks she hadn't processed and orders she hadn't fulfilled. She tried to explain to us that she hadn't known what to do with the checks or the other mail. There was no provision in the union agreement for termination on account of being a doofus, but she didn't contest the mutual decision to part company.

In early 1986, I discovered that one of our bookkeepers had pocketed $10,350.94 in cash receipts, rather than depositing it. A couple of years later, we got a call out of the blue from another record company in another part of the country. They told us they'd just caught their bookkeeper embezzling and were calling us as her prior employer. We sympathized and told them that they'd discovered a good example of why it's always good, *before* employing someone, to actually call the prospective hire's references.

The person in charge of preparing our print catalog was terminated at one point, and complained to *Billboard* that he was unjustly fired, having been only "responsible for one typographical error in the 310-page Rounder catalog." That set me off. Spending a long weekend, I typed up a 109-page report documenting such minor matters as forgetting to include the new Alison Krauss album in the bluegrass section, and omitting from the reggae section the album that had won the Grammy of the Year for Best Reggae Album! A few albums were missing entirely. There were geographical errors: Morocco was defined as being in the Middle East; Lebanon, Kurdistan, and Armenia were placed in Europe; an album described as Bolivian music was placed under "Peru." Somewhat more than just "one typographical error."

The union was in place for quite a long time, about twenty years, but times changed. There had already been at least one employee-initiated campaign to decertify the union. The first one fell short of the number of signatures needed to schedule an election, but a couple of years later another one succeeded, an election was scheduled, the issue was debated, and after months of discussion among the bargaining unit employees, the union was decertified in 2003. No reign of terror ensued.

Though these incidents were all distasteful, there have, fortunately, only been a few bad apples or regrettable hires over the years. Duncan once hired a warehouse worker whose job was to pick orders for shipping. It took almost a week to realize that he didn't understand alphanumeric ordering, yet all our records were shelved alphabetically by label and numerically within the label. Who would have thought you needed to have each employee prove they knew the alphabet?

A few years earlier, we had a warehouse manager who apparently thought standing around with a glass of water, keeping his eye on things, was the way to manage. It turned out the water was actually vodka, but that wasn't the point. This was when we were still in Medford. We only had about a dozen employees at the time. We didn't need someone to just stand around.

Much later, we discovered a CFO who had "nickeled and dimed" Rounder for years with expenses on his company American Express card – things like a morning coffee while commuting to the office – amounting to thousands of dollars.

After we let go that less-than-competent information services manager who fruitlessly sued us for age discrimination, his replacement didn't work out all that well, either – at least not for us. He'd been trained offsite for a few weeks so that he could come in and take over in what we hoped would be a seamless transition. He put in four full days, then told us on his first Friday to watch TV that night, because his wife was one of something like forty finalists for a Massachusetts State Lottery "Set for Life" promotion. I watched from home. It got down to the final two or three and she hadn't been eliminated. Then the winner's name was called out, and it wasn't his, so I thought, "Oh, well. Too bad. They got pretty close anyhow" – but then I saw our guy bounding to the stage with his wife, who had a different last name from him. They had won what I recall as $1,000 a week for the rest of their lives. It may have been more; that doesn't sound today like as much money as it did at the time.

I came in to do some work on Saturday morning (a far from uncommon experience) and there he was! He said it was a ton of money but it wasn't really going to change him. He worked until about noon, and then said he was going to take the rest of the day off (not that I'd expected him to work Saturdays, in any event). Then he called on Monday and said he and his wife were going to take a week's vacation in Antigua. We never saw him again; we never even got a postcard.

14 2000: Rounder Turns Thirty as We Enter a New Century

We put on a number of thirtieth-anniversary shows – the one in New York at Town Hall was on October 3, and featured Alison Krauss & Union Station, Jimmie Dale Gilmore, and Balfa Toujours. The *New York Times* review characterized Rounder as "America's most prominent independent roots-oriented label" and said the company "has succeeded by subtly stretching the genres it promotes."[91] At the end of the month, we launched our Heritage Series.

At the Bostonian Hotel, John Virant accepted a proclamation from Mayor Thomas Menino wishing Rounder continued success. In the Boston area, we arranged for Rounder artists to appear at over a dozen concert and club dates in a five- or six-week span. Featured artists, in addition to those at the Town Hall show, included: the Blazers, Slaid Cleaves, Chris Duarte, Joe Ely, Ray Wylie Hubbard, Candye Kane, Klezmer Conservatory Band, Natalie MacMaster, Bill Morrissey, NRBQ, Riders in the Sky, Roomful of Blues, Jules Shear, Tarbox Ramblers, Irma Thomas, Tony Trischka, and Rhonda Vincent.

We had 110 employees at that time.

As part of the thirtieth-anniversary celebrations, there was a special issue of *Billboard* devoted to Rounder (we will note that such "special issues" were commonplace and not an altruistic tribute by the magazine; they were funded by advertising pulled together by, say, our pressing plant and distributors – it was, in effect, a tribute to ourselves financed by putting a gentle squeeze on vendors and suppliers). Nonetheless, respected writers such as Jim Bessman and Richard Henderson wrote the editorial material and interviewed the owners at some length. A number of comments made at the time give an insight into what proved to be a watershed era, given the collapse of record retail that began to escalate right at the turn of the century.

John Virant talked about the decision to start his Zoë imprint at this juncture. As we will recall, the three Rounders had encouraged John to do so, in part as a means of keeping him on board. The new label, John explained, was created

... to some extent out of necessity. Though Rounder's name is synonymous with a certain quality of music, it also brings to mind different types of music: folk, bluegrass, or zydeco. We made the decision to try to start working with some acts who could go beyond certain niche markets with greater sales. We felt it was important to create a fresh sales identity so that a buyer wouldn't stereotype a release.

Juliana Hatfield, the Nields, and Sarah Harmer were among the first records released. Marian chimed in:

Ken, Bill, and I all have our own preferences that we've been pursuing for thirty years. I don't think we'd be doing some of the things that we're doing now – certainly not on Zoë – without John's sensibility and energy and the kinds of people that he has brought to the label to work for us, as well as the artists. He's definitely a member of the Rounder family, and he's bringing his own outlook and intelligence to what we're doing.

In 2000, *Billboard*'s Larry LeBlanc wrote a nearly full-page feature on Rounder's increasing forays into recording Canadian music. He noted the Cape Breton fiddle recordings Mark Wilson had begun as far back as the 1970s, and was continuing to do. What he focused on was the fact that Rounder had begun to work with Universal Canada, a relationship that evolved out of both outfits signing a deal with Canadian singer-songwriter Sarah Harmer, whose album *You Were Here* was released by Zoë in the U.S. with Universal handling distribution of her label in Canada.[92] Rounder had already been working with Raffi for about three years, and LeBlanc quoted North America's pre-eminent children's artist: "Before signing, I looked at Rounder's roster. Rounder is held in high regard by the artists that they represent and distribute. That's quite remarkable ... Rounder understands what I'm for and knows how to bang the drum for that."

John said, appreciatively, "Raffi is an icon and his catalog is evergreen. It was evident to us that he was falling through the cracks at MCA." Rounder also added Canadian acts such as Natalie MacMaster, April Verch, the Cash Brothers, and – later – both Bruce Cockburn, Cowboy Junkies, and future Rock-and-Roll-Hall-of-Famers Rush.

Sometimes Rounder caught people almost completely off-guard. Back in 1977, we worried that releasing George Thorogood & the Destroyers' first album might cost us support from fans of our growing bluegrass and folk catalog. Having released *Mountain Moving Day* in January 1973, the first album to emerge from the women's liberation movement, that ought to have already signaled that we might be a little unpredictable. In September 2002, there was another quirky release: *Buffy the Vampire Slayer*.

Buffy the Vampire Slayer was a television series that ran for seven seasons from 1997 to 2003. It became a cult phenomenon with spin-offs, comic books, and a very passionate fan base. During the sixth season, creator Joss Whedon decided to shoot a musical episode, with songs written by him and with the actual cast singing them (no ringers). Keep in mind this was well before the "resurgence" of *a capella* and musical theater on TV (*Glee*) and in the movies (*Pitch Perfect*). The resulting episode, entitled "Once More, with Feeling" (Rounder 9058 was the soundtrack of the same name), was an example of "event television" and was aired by the network without commercials.

John Virant and his wife Katie had been fans of the series since the beginning, and watched the episode live (with popcorn). John clearly remembers thinking as "The End" appeared on screen and the credits began to scroll, "this was astounding – one of the most moving shows I've ever seen ... there must be a soundtrack album." He reached out to a contact at Fox (the television studio) the very next day and was basically told, "Oh, we tried, but too many clearances are needed and it's just not feasible." One might find home video rights discussed in a standard television contract but certainly something like a music album would not normally be included. That meant arrangements would have to be worked out with every actor and key participant. And this wasn't a one-person show ...

John was not deterred. After some back and forth, Fox essentially said, "OK, we'll enter into a joint venture with you, and if you can clear all the necessary rights, you can release an album." Fortunately, Joss loved the idea of a soundtrack album and, with his enthusiasm and tireless support (and that of his lieutenant Chris Buchanan), we were ultimately able to navigate the obstacle course, jump all the hurdles, and make it happen. The album was released on September 24, 2002, and ended up selling over 500,000 copies worldwide, roughly half of which was in the U.S., and was certified silver in the UK (for sales of 60,000 units). The success led to a number of other soundtrack releases with our partner Fox, including a second *Buffy* album, but none came close to achieving the magic (or sales) of the first. John says:

> We wondered if the good folks at Fox might have initially thought we had special marketing powers ... but in reality, all we really did was recognize the brilliance of what Joss Whedon and cast had created. One reviewer aptly summed the whole thing up: "All in all, this is by far the greatest TV musical of all time."

Though we never strayed from our roots, this was another reminder that one never knew what to expect from Rounder.

Richard Henderson had dubbed Rounder "the Mothership label of roots music," while noting the expansion into other areas. He asked if the Rounders were still "unrepentant folkies" to which I replied with a laugh, "I haven't repented yet!" Marian added that we were also "very much children of our time. Going to hear B.B. King open for the Rolling Stones was as important as going to hear Fiddlin' Steve Ledford or somebody like that. Folk was the music that we had difficulty finding on records." She cited Greil Marcus's appreciation of what he termed "old, weird America." Of course, the true originals we met along the way weren't truly weird at all. They were different from us. No doubt some of them thought we were the ones who were weird. For his part, Ken reminisced about falling in love with old-time fiddle music, traditional blues, and folk music, and said:

> We got into the music business because of the music and the artists. When we started out, we weren't even thinking of making a living ... Our goal at the time was to make one classic record, something that would be cited in a list of the ten best bluegrass or fiddle or banjo records. An early review written by Pete Welding referred to Rounder as "a label specializing in roots music and its contemporary offshoots." This could well serve as our mission statement, one that hasn't altered appreciably in the ensuing years. It's still basically what we do.[93]

Rounder Books

From the beginning, I always thought we would publish books. We had several meetings about it and sketched out a number of ideas, It just took us a long, long time to get around to it. Even working on some of them has taken an awful long time, including this one (most of which was originally written in 2008).

In the meantime, Michael Scully began work on his dissertation at the University of Texas. We gave him free access to all our files and, beginning in June 1999, he went through dozens of file cabinets reading correspondence with artists and others, and interviewed us at some length. It took him a few years – raising a family at the same time – but in 2008 his book was published: *The Never-Ending Revival: Rounder Records and the Folk Alliance* (University of Illinois Press).

The Rounder Book of Bluegrass is still not out. We have most of the chapters, but still never quite wrapped it up. In early 2016, though, I self-published *The Rounder Book of Bluegrass Music Trivia*, and, in 2019, *The Early Days of Bluegrass*, working with the Bluegrass Country Foundation.

In the meantime, Rounder started publishing, ranging from a raft of books on the Red Sox to drummer Neil Peart of Rush and his book *Roadshow*, telling the story of the band's thirtieth-anniversary tour, and his travels to their fifty-seven shows by motorcycle. Neil's book and my *Mr. Red Sox: The Johnny Pesky Story* are the only two that made any appreciable profit. The Pesky book was the first. I had written a few books for other publishers, but decided to bring it all in house and write for nothing (being already on salary);

even going without royalties didn't help achieve predictable profitability. The margins are maybe a bit worse in the book trade, in that the distribution fees are perhaps a little higher, and the returns are definitely higher.

What is it about the Red Sox that has appealed to me to write more than two dozen books about them – and Fenway Park – for a half-dozen publishers in about one dozen years?

Wasn't writing about baseball a bit of a stretch for someone at a record company? It's never felt that way. I'm far from the only person who grew up in New England and felt bound to the Red Sox. Baseball has always been stronger in New England than in most parts of the country and it truly feels as though rooting for the Red Sox is in the blood of people born and raised in the region. In no way does that exclude those who have come to the area, perhaps to go to college or for work. One of the quickest ways to assimilate comes courtesy of Red Sox baseball. "How 'bout them Sox?" I don't know when I went to my first game, and my father wasn't able to help answer the question, though he did tell me that his father – the one I never met, because of my grandmother's Catholic intolerance – had been a big Red Sox fan.

Genetic or not, I'd always been impressed and proud that my father had sold hot dogs for Harry M. Stevens at Fenway Park for two seasons in the late 1930s, to raise money to go to the New York World's Fair. Neither of my parents did a thing to discourage me from traveling all by myself from

The author at age eight or nine

our quiet suburb into the Big City as early as the age of twelve to take in Red Sox games from the bleachers. That the Red Sox never won the World Series and hadn't since 1918 didn't trouble me. I don't recall ever fixating on it. I was there in those first few years to see the team play and to see Ted Williams hit. Win or lose, I always enjoyed the game – and it was more losing than winning most of my formative years, but that made the wins all the more special. After the sixth inning, the usher manning the gate that used to separate the bleachers from the higher-priced seats left his post and we were able to explore the rest of the park, trying out this seat or that seat – as long as we didn't venture into the lower box seats. There simply weren't that many patrons at most games – one of the reasons I was one of only 1,247 fans who saw Dave Morehead throw his no-hitter in September 1965.

Exploring the park became a passion, and something I dug into more deeply with a Fenway trilogy: *Fenway Saved*, *The Fenway Project*, and *Fenway Lives*. Later, there was *Fenway Park at 100* and *Fenway Park Trivia*. *Fenway Lives* told the stories of the people who work in and around Fenway Park – most of them just on day of game – from the ushers to the organist to the night cleaning crew. One night after a game, author Rob Neyer and I roamed the ballpark until 7 am the following morning, just to see what it was like. I'd previously interviewed the head of the night cleaners and told him I wanted to do some more research. I turned that experience into a story for *Boston* magazine. It made an impression; more than ten years later, I still get the occasional person ask me about it.

Today's hot dog vendors aren't all that different from my father's generation in the 1930s. One of the 200 interviews I did for the book was with my father and he told me of the "Depression lunch" he'd have from time to time. Vendors signed out a certain number of hot dogs, sold them, and then reported back with the money. But, because buns sometimes split when serving a dog, the control was only on the number of hot dogs and not on the buns. So when he got a little hungry, Bill Sr. would spread some mustard on a bun and scarf it down. "Oh yeah, I've done that," vendor Rob Moynihan told me in 1999.

Maybe the Red Sox gene is one of those that skips a generation. Perhaps my grandfather was into them more than my father. My son Emmet never got the bug, though it hasn't been for want of my trying. When he was six weeks old, Yleana and I took him to his first game. That was a momentous occasion in Fenway Park history, though appreciated by few. When it was time to change him, we took him to the first aid station that's under Section 12 and asked if they had a place we could do the deed. The nurse pointed to a diaper changing station affixed to the wall and told us it had just been installed earlier that day. I've been tempted ever since, though not sure he'd welcome it, to have made up a special metal plaque and, perhaps when no one was looking, affix it with adhesive to the wall alongside, reading, "This changing station was inaugurated by Emmet Nowlin on September 4, 1991." The Red Sox, for the record, shut out the Angels behind the pitching of Joe Hesketh, 2–0. A solo home run by Wade Boggs in the bottom of the fifth was the winning hit.

It means a lot to me that Fenway Park fit the pattern of all the history I grew up with. Built in 1912, it is the oldest park in the major leagues. Almost all the great legends of twentieth- and twenty-first-century ball have played there – be it those who began with the Red Sox like Babe Ruth and Ted and Yaz, or opponents like Ty Cobb and Mickey Mantle.[94]

It's no exaggeration that I've been quoted a few times as saying I've traveled to more than a hundred countries but there's no place like Fenway Park. It does feel like home. I can still remember the thrill I so often felt when I'd run up a ramp and get the first view of the green field deep in the middle of downtown Boston. And the good guys wore the whitest of white.

Writing about the Red Sox was easier for me than writing about musicians ever could be. I had myself experienced what it meant to shade toward second base. Ballplayers and musicians are both entertainers with certain skills. I just had a better feel for one than the other. I knew deep inside what it felt like to connect with a ball and drive it, in a way that I had never experienced with striking the right musical note in just the right way at the precise best moment. I experienced the sweet spot in baseball more than I had in music. Ballplayers were public figures whose skills I admired and could get to know. It may have even helped that most of them had careers that ended by the time they hit forty, if not before. This offered intrinsic interest in researching older ballplayers. What did they do with their lives after baseball? Unless a musician suffered an unusual and debilitating injury, he or she might play music throughout their lives. At the end of the first decade of the twenty-first century, many of the most successful touring bands are ones that began in the 1960s or '70s. Since a baseball player's career tends to be done halfway through his life, it is possible to talk with him about a career in wholly retrospective, and reflective, terms. That's different than talking about the continuing career of a singer or musician.

Even the most obscure ballplayers have more written about them than most musicians. Game stories and box scores offer a way of following daily progress for ballplayers; newspapers don't print set lists or chronicle the differences in music performance from one day to the next. When working on the *Early Days of Bluegrass* boxed set, I could never find the Hamm Brothers or anyone who knew them, though they assuredly left behind a couple of recordings of their music. What about Eusebio Gonzalez of the Red Sox? I decided I wanted to write about him for the book *When Boston Still Had the Babe*. He intrigued me because of his obscurity: born in Cuba in 1892, died in Cuba in 1976, and in 1918 he appeared in three baseball games for the Red Sox. That was about all anyone knew about him in 2007 before the book came out. That and the fact that he had two hits in five at-bats, one of them a triple, had walked once and struck out once, and had never made an error (in the total of three chances he had in the field). What more could I learn? Quite a bit. Determined digging and some field research in Troy, Scranton, Miami, New York, and Toronto turned up all sorts of details – even without a return visit to Havana's Biblioteca Nacional where I had once researched a Red Sox spring training visit to Cuba.

Much has been written about how Ted Williams feuded with Boston sportswriters. Gonzalez was on the receiving end – he was once shot by Havana sportswriter Pepe Conte. One of the reasons he was on the 1918 Red Sox was because he was a Cuban national and not subject to First World War conscription. I still know almost nothing about his life after he left baseball in San Antonio in 1928. So there are almost fifty years unaccounted for prior to his death on my birthday in 1976. But, from what I was able to unearth, I wrote a biography that runs some 16,000 words. There really is a lot more information about a guy who played three days in the major leagues compared to, say, the bass player in a bluegrass band that may have played for three years in the 1950s. Or the Hamm Brothers.

One of my favorite baseball books is *The SABR Book of Umpires and Umpiring*. After finishing up a book on baseball scouts (*Can He Play? A Look at Baseball Scouts and Their Profession*), I was thinking about some other kind of book looking at baseball, and in 2013 came up with the idea of a book on umpires. After getting down some of the historical stuff, I started interviewing current big-league umpires about their work. They're in a world of their own, traveling on their own, not fraternizing with ballplayers but deeply concerned with getting the calls right – to the point of losing sleep in the days before replay, if they thought they might have gotten one wrong. And there were the personalities. In talking with Ted Barrett over the course of a few interviews in 2015, I learned that he – like me – had a PhD. (He's not the only ump with a doctorate; Dan Bellino has one, too.) Ted's was in theology and he's actually an ordained minister. He jokes that the umps in his crew call him Rev. Dr. Crew Chief Barrett. I also learned that he had been a sparring partner for professional boxers, and has indeed sparred with seven world champions: George Foreman, Evander Holyfield, Greg Page, Razor Ruddick, Obed Sullivan, Tony Tucker, and Mike Tyson. You can meet some very interesting folks when you start asking questions.[95]

SABR is the Society for American Baseball Research. I've been on the Board of Directors since 2004 and active in research, writing, and editing – and encouraging others to do the same. Filling much of the time spent in "retirement," I've written over a thousand articles – mostly brief biographies and game accounts – for SABR, and the number of books I've written or edited (almost all on music or baseball) has now surpassed a hundred.

I did have an instinct for the game. In music, though, if I sang five or six notes in a row that were on key, it would be a minor miracle, or a coincidence like the monkeys who – given enough time – would by happenstance type the Gettysburg Address. I couldn't tell if my banjo, guitar, or bass was in tune or not.[96] If I'd studied it mathematically and been able to block out the rest of my thoughts to focus on the notes in question, maybe I could have pulled it off. I always feel like my mind is firing on so many cylinders at once that I can't concentrate on the music or let myself develop the discipline to even get my instrument in tune. Besides which, the music excites me so much that it's too easy to let myself be transported by where I know a familiar song or tune is going that I don't seem to be able to synch myself up to go along with it as a participant. I can enjoy the music, but can't slow down enough to really take part in it, much less try to create my own. I'd be satisfied to just faithfully render an old-time tune on a banjo, or play bass with a reggae band, or drum to Stones songs. Maybe when I get older – though time seems to fly by even faster the older I get. It remains one of the disappointments in life that I can't take part in something I love so much. So I play records instead and go to see the Po' Ramblin' Boys at the Lincoln Theater in Raleigh.

In 2008, I finally started writing more on music, helping work on the booklet of notes in Woody Guthrie's *My Dusty Road* and expanding the booklet material for our *Early Days of Bluegrass* boxed set. Not to mention working on this history of Rounder. It seemed to be clear at that point that no one else was going to write the book about Rounder, so . . . dive in. Aiming at Rounder's fiftieth anniversary, for a while I gave it a working title named for a country song that seemed to reflect how Rounder began as a company: *20–20 Vision (and Walking 'Round Blind).*

And I did help edit or prepare several music books for Rounder Books. There was *Waiting for a Train: Jimmie Rodgers' America*, *Bob Marley and the Wailers: The Definitive Discography*, *Beethoven's Wig*, Raffi's *Everything Grows*, and one book that spanned music and baseball: *Love That Dirty Water: The Standells and the Improbable Red Sox Victory Anthem.*

Working on *The Early Days of Bluegrass*

In our earlier days, we offered longer liner notes than in most of our more recent releases. We researched and wrote the life of Blind Alfred Reed and the many short bios for the booklets that accompanied the albums in the Early Days of Bluegrass series. Those were all shorter pieces, though far longer than many other labels would offer as notes, save Folkways. It was a treat in 2008 and 2009 to work on the more extensive annotation for two boxed sets, *My Dusty Road* by Woody Guthrie and *The Early Days of Bluegrass* box – though the box took another ten years to see the light of day.

Ed Cray wrote all the material on Woody's songs and most of the material about Woody himself. He'd written about Woody before in the excellent *Ramblin' Man: The Life and Times of Woody Guthrie* (W.W. Norton). He told the story of how the Stinson masters had been burrowed in the basement of a Brooklyn brownstone (how's that for alliteration?) for more than half a century and how astonishing it was to be able to hear Woody better than ever before when digitized masters were worked up from the original parts. No longer would listeners have to suffer through the sub-par sound that the Stinson LPs had offered. It had been quite an experience for me to travel to Brooklyn and see the large barrels in the basement in which the masters had been kept. More of the story is told in *My Dusty Road.* Ed and I were finalists for the Grammy Award the year the set came out, both for Best Historical Album and for Best Album Notes

To come up with the booklet for the *Early Days* box, I wanted to fill out the details we'd offered in the early Seventies. Brad San Martin scanned the texts for each of the original ten albums, and I strung them together. The result was an uneven 57,275 words, in that Volume 9, for example, had only 1,471 words while Volume 5 had 15,414. We were able to interview Rich-R-Tone's Jim Stanton at length, as well as some of the artists talking about him, and so could tell a more complete story on *The Rich-R-Tone Story*, which we released as Volume 5. We identified with him as the founder of a small label and found his story a compelling one. I wanted to accomplish three things in expanded notes to the CD set: to even out the notes a bit, let readers know what has transpired with these music makers in the thirty-five or more years since the original LPs, and to see if I could take another shot at locating some information about some of the groups we hadn't been able to locate before. I came across some fascinating new information and, in the end, the word count almost exactly doubled.

It wasn't that difficult to expand the stories of Bill Clifton and the Lilly Brothers. Everett Lilly was still living and his son Everett Alan helped a lot, too. And Bill Clifton agreed to a more complete interview by telephone, before he took off to visit a daughter practicing medicine in Gabon. We still don't know much of anything more about the Hamm Brothers, despite locating the guy who bought the Bullet Records masters. We still don't even know, for certain, their first names. Every attempt to reach out to a musician named Hamm has proven fruitless.

Another group about which we knew very little was the Colwell Brothers. Here we came upon a wealth of information. The wonder that is the internet was key. I always thought that, if I lost my eyesight, I'd be OK because I had such a good record collection I could enjoy. With so much information available on the internet, I now value more than ever what the eye helps me learn. (If I did lose my sight, though, maybe I could finally learn to play music.) Browsing the Web helped me find the Colwells – rather easily – and to connect with Steve Colwell. I could have written a whole book on them alone – and someone did: *A Song for the World* by Frank McGee (Many Roads Publishing, 2007). This early bluegrass group metamorphosed into the musical leadership for the group Up With People and, before they retired, they brought their music to over sixty countries, traveling the world as musical ambassadors and playing before world leaders such as Tom Mboya of Kenya to U Nu and U Thant of Burma, Prime Minister Kishi of Japan and

President Magsaysay of The Philippines, Vinoba Bhave of India, and Chief Albert Luthuli of the African National Congress. Seeing photographs of them in Western wear, with their bluegrass instruments, in the Congo and elsewhere showed how far some bluegrass has carried. The internet struck out when it came to the Hamms, though.

The final book for the expanded boxed set of *The Early Days of Bluegrass* grew from the 57,275 words to, at last count, 123,996. I financed the re-release of the package, to benefit the Bluegrass Country Foundation.

Travel: a tangent

As long as I'm exploring tangents, that's another thing. Over one hundred countries. As of this writing, something like 130. It all depends on how you define a country and how you define a visit. Touching down at an airport doesn't do it for me, so I don't include Senegal or Liberia or Saudi Arabia even though I've landed in all three places. My two rules of thumb are that I have to have spent twenty-four hours there, and have a good story to tell about my time there. There are a very few exceptions – The Vatican, San Marino, and Kuwait – though I did spend twenty-three hours and fifty-five minutes in Kuwait and have two or three stories to tell. Is East Germany a different country than West Germany? Yes, it was the couple of times I visited before reunification. There were most definitely customs and passport formalities to be observed – to say the least – and the Ostmark was its own currency.

What is it about travel that appeals to me? Aside from counting countries, which reflects my old preoccupation of creating lists of this and that, there's a romance to it that I enjoy. I think there are two facets to this – partly egocentric and partly voyeuristic, if that isn't too strong or misleading a word. As I write these very words, I'm on a bench on the Roc del Patapou above Andorra La Vella looking down on the city during the stay of a couple of days in Andorra before I head to Barcelona. "Hey, it's me, and I'm in Andorra!" It's fun impressing myself, with how I manage to find myself literally ducking flying fish on a dory ride from Punta Gorda, Belize to Livingston, Guatemala or hitching across the Sahara for five days with Yleana the year after we got married. We were also among the first hundred or so Americans not of Albanian ancestry to visit Albania after that country opened up to the beginnings of U. S. tourism in the same year. Holding the small airplane door shut with my elbow hooked out the window while flying from Ciudad Bolívar to Canaima.

There's also the vicarious sense of being in another time and place. I naturally like the old quarters the best, the parts of a city that seem to be from another time. Visiting Prague for the first time, even as late as 1974, was like traveling back in time to the early 1920s. There were streets only two or three removed from Wenceslas Square which had an old tram from those

The author with wife Yleana in the Sahara Desert

days creak by in the night fog and then disappear into darkness; there were no motor vehicles, just the dimly lit entrance to a beer cellar perhaps around the next corner.

In Albania in 1990, it was like going even further back in time. Tirana's main square is Skanderbeg Square. We stayed just off the square in a hotel which the Greek travel agency had booked for us. But one could walk back and forth across the square as we did many times without having to look either left or right for traffic. There wasn't any. There was also nothing else competing for attention – no music blaring out of shops, and hardly any shouts or conversation from people, even the children. The mood was still pretty somber – though we greatly enjoyed being unexpectedly invited (total strangers that we were) into a wedding party the next day just because we happened to be walking by on the street. (Gary Himelfarb and I had the same experience in Samarkand, Uzbekistan a few years later.) Every once in a while, a car belonging to some official would whiz through Skanderbeg Square, but among the general silence it was easy to know when a car or occasional tram was approaching. Other than that, all we heard was the slapping of leather against stone as hundreds of Albanians made their way from one place to another. Nothing but footsteps, and this was midday in the Times Square of a European country. I still consider myself extremely fortunate to have experienced it. It was like watching a movie from 1910, but being inside the movie at the same time.

A similar "time capsule experience" was visiting the Democratic People's Republic of Korea – North Korea – in 2008. Communist regimes are very good at isolating themselves from modernity – paradoxically for a philosophy proclaiming itself progressive. None has done a better job than Albania through the Hoxha years and North Korea under the leadership of Kim Il-sung (the "Great Leader") and his son, Kim Jong-il (the "Dear Leader"). If it weren't for the misfortunes of the citizens under these regimes, unable to leave to seek lives elsewhere if they wished, one could more fully enjoy a visit and even wish they'd be preserved as timepieces. Americans visiting Cuba and seeing all the U.S. automobiles from the 1950s still on the streets can see something similar. Those of us on our Koryo Tours visit to North Korea, who arrived on the sixtieth anniversary of the founding of the country, felt ourselves really fortunate to have visited before times changed, before the country became "spoiled" (one could say with sardonic irony). In some ways, a country like North Korea had some of the characteristics of an amusement park writ large, though it was hardly amusing to those in the North Korean gulag who had run afoul of official policy. We were under no illusions as to why the Americans were housed in a hotel situated on an island in the Taedong River, and why we were instructed not to leave the grounds of the hotel.

I was fortunate to visit Yemen in 2010, when it was still relatively safe, though in two cities I was assigned (not given a choice in the matter) a guy with an AK-47 to accompany me everywhere. Zanzibar was magical. So was Khartoum, seeing real whirling dervishes as one of maybe five or six non-dervishes at a ceremony on the other side of the Nile, in Omdurman. Turkmenistan and Tajikistan were special trips, too, as was two days of horseback riding in Mongolia in minus 23 degrees Celsius temperatures.[97] And, of course, how could I not forge out on my own to Ukraine and Moldova, and a day visit to Chernobyl, in 2017?

In the earliest days of Rounder, the romantic image of a bucolic banjo player on the back porch held a compelling appeal. I'd still rather see the Johnson Mountain Boys play at Suzie's Bar in Sikesville than on the stage of the Kennedy Center. I'd still rather remember Beau Jocque at Richard's in Opelousas than to see him convert New Englanders to zydeco at a folk festival in the Northeast. Context means a lot, but there's an element of romance as well. (That you will never see better dancers than those at clubs like Richard's only fills out the picture further.)

That people could create good music despite such difficult circumstances gives them almost an heroic aura, if one is so included as to view things that way. Many musicians worked toward success in the marketplace in hopes of alleviating or escaping lives that would otherwise be more difficult. In no way did this do anything to diminish the notion of an idealized past which one could construct as a way of more thoroughly enjoying their music – and country musicians themselves were not immune from the temptation: witness the innumerable paeans to "the old home place." Even the very name "Rounder" embodied the many currents of romance: in no way did we expect to be hoboes, drifters, or bums. The original Rounder man in the woods with his phonograph, and the dandy in the barroom on the early LP labels, fit the playful image as well.

Sales tanking: the start of a new century (2000–2008)

From 2000 through 2008, sales of CDs declined by 48.9% according to Nielsen Soundscan. In just four years, 2005 through early 2009, a reported 2,680 record stores were shuttered, including the entire Tower Records chain and the 567 stores within Circuit City, which closed due to bankruptcy. Some of the larger big-box retailers such as Best Buy and Wal-Mart cut display space for CDs, then cut it again, and then cut it further.

It was the reverse of the process that chains like Tower had kicked off earlier. There had always been a good number of free-standing but generally small independent record stores (often they were a record department in a music store that sold instruments and sheet music), and then there were the mall stores, which were limited to a very circumscribed number of albums, bought by a central buyer and with little or no freedom for regional responsiveness. Many of these stores just carried the top 200 records and a smattering of others. Tower really popularized the deep-catalog store. As the chain expanded, when a Tower store came, that's where music fans would gravitate because they had such a wide selection – and often had pretty knowledgeable salespeople as well. In 1991, Tower's owner Russ Solomon instructed his store managers: "Tower cannot have a competitor who has a better selection. Don't let your catalog down."[98] So many other retailers began to emulate Tower's strategy that it wasn't that unique after a while, but the others hardly ever did it as well as Tower.

It really was a golden era, though deceptively so and short-lived. There were other forces at play in the market. When the big-box stores like Best Buy and Circuit City started stocking much deeper inventory, and pricing their records well below Tower's, labels were glad for the additional business – but rather shortly it became evident that the additional business was illusory and really just cannibalized sales from other stores that cared more for the music itself.

Best Buy and Circuit City weren't record stores. First and foremost, they were electronics stores, and what they really wanted to sell were televisions, telephones, fax machines, and other gear. Compact discs were typically sold as loss leaders – if not strictly below actual cost, then almost always below cost taking shipping and overhead into account. The goal was to build traffic into the stores, in the hope that the people buying a record would also buy some new stereo components, a boom box, or a TV. The independent record stores found it increasingly hard to compete and started going out of business.

With the maturation of Soundscan and the more sophisticated use of computerized inventory analysis, another trend that began hopefully came back to bite the people it had seemed to reward. There had been a shared conviction in the music industry, for instance, that country music didn't sell. Once more and more retailers began using optical scanners at the checkout counters, and the results transmitted to Soundscan for objective tabulation, this notion was upended. Country music had a much deeper and broader sales base than had fully been appreciated. All of a sudden, the album charts started reflecting strong sales of country music albums, records that had previously been consigned to the ghetto of the country album charts. Other kinds of music seemed to sell, too, and this helped feed both a burgeoning floor space devoted to records and the depth and diversity of selection that stores would stock.

Around the time we were expanding our national distribution, sales were truly picking up. That was one thing. But stores quickly started tightening up, too. There had been too much of an expansion all at once – too many retailers selling records, and too many of those retailers carrying deeper inventory. The number of consumers wasn't growing at anywhere near the same pace as retail was expanding. Like a rubber band that had been stretched, it all had to snap back sometime, and it did with a vengeance.

This was nowhere more evident in the short run than in the kids' area. David Schlessinger had started a chain of bookstores, Encore Books. In 1991, he founded Zany Brainy, a retail chain devoted to children's products of a more educational nature. The company did very well at first, as did rival retailer Noodle Kidoodle. After Zany Brainy bought up Noodle Kidoodle in 2000, it went bankrupt within a year. Rounder Kids lost its best customer. No other chain stepped in to fill the void. From a time when sales were booming, the bottom fell out of the market and never recovered.

It wasn't just in kids' retail, though. There was an "over-retailing" in general. It seemed easier to find investors willing to fund the placing of big-box stores in malls all over the country, but there really was no corresponding quantum increase in the number of customers interested in buying recorded music.

Faced with inventory that wasn't turning as quickly as projected, retailers turned to Soundscan again and began to trim (in some cases, slash) their inventories to the predictable hits, the records topping Soundscan. Stores took fewer chances, and the first thing that "gave" was the commitment to deep catalog. For a while, we'd been able to make the argument to store owners that they needed our records in the stores – even if they didn't sell! It was like window-dressing; they needed to offer a wide variety of music so they could build and maintain the reputation of a store that "had everything" – even though that could never truly be the case. As the margins thinned, due to competitive downward pressure from the loss-leader big-box stores, indie record stores had to become more conscious of what was selling through and what was not.

Record stores took a double hit, one blow right after the other. First, the mega-chains and over-retailing, and then something altogether different: the availability of digital downloads – at first, mostly for free (if illegal).

Record stores felt forced to narrow catalog, and focus more on hits. There was a market for deep-catalog stores, but if every store offered deep catalog there was not enough differentiation between them. There was a greater rationalization of buying, with the advent of Soundscan and more widespread use of computerized inventory.

Once Napster brought music right into your house, through the personal computer, record stores were no longer – in the age of the download – a destination business. Many people under a certain age have never purchased a compact disc, and many fewer a cassette. Many under a certain age have never visited a record store and, in some places, teenagers might have little idea what a "record store" actually is. Even fairly large record departments in, say, a Wal-Mart around the beginning of the twenty-first century – which might offer consumers a seemingly large selection of some 5,000 different titles – were dwarfed in the past by Tower Records, which often offered 60,000 different titles. And, in the second decade of the twenty-first century, Wal-Mart was cutting back much more sharply.

In an interesting aside, Napster actually sued Rounder in January 2009 for "costs incurred to copyright infringement lawsuits brought by the owners of musical compositions provided by Rounder" when Rounder had granted Napster a license back in 2001 and 2006. Rounder moved to dismiss the suit and the Honorable Paul A. Crotty did so in United States District Court in January 2011.[99]

Shelf space in all retail environments was itself becoming more of a commodity – supermarket style, where manufactures have to buy shelf space. For a while, listening stations were the rage, and labels would be charged to have their music available on the listening stations, or for "positioning" in the store. Retailers wanted to maximize their real estate. This all led to fewer choices for consumers. Labels that couldn't afford to pay to have their records featured in retail programs, positioned near the registers, or featured in weekly circulars, were simply shut out. The days when Rounder could put out a record and make money selling 1,500 or 2,000 copies were in the rear-view mirror. The commitment to marketing made it increasingly difficult to take a chance on records that didn't seem certain to sell 5,000 units. A lot of good music just wasn't going to get released.

Bookstores, of course, have suffered a very similar fate. The ease and pricing benefits of buying from an online retailer such as Amazon undercuts the independent bookstore. Regardless of the pleasures of browsing and the serendipity it fosters – walking out of a store with a book in hand you never knew existed until you saw it there on display – there are real benefits in the ability to buy the book you *did* know you wanted, for 20% off, and having it delivered to you. With the development of the Kindle and other electronic devices, the actual printing of books may – like the duplication of recorded sound carriers – become threatened as well over the next generation or two.

Radio, too, became increasingly concentrated in the hands of a few – one business alone, Clear Channel, reportedly came to own over a thousand radio stations. Increasingly, as well, there have been two other trends: more and more stations work with tighter formats, often restricting the variety of musics that can be played, and even college and university stations (previously a bastion of idiosyncratic, even experimental, broadcasting) have quite often elected to ape commercial broadcast facilities as the notion of college radio as a career apprenticeship has spread. That is to say, college stations try to sound commercial so students who run the stations will be better prepared for the business of broadcasting.

There is some hope offered by the advent of satellite radio and the varieties of music available over the internet (instead of having to make your way to Mamou, you can sit home on a Saturday morning and listen to the music from Fred's Lounge over KVPI).[100] A serious devotee of bluegrass can listen to *Bluegrass Junction* and a wide variety of other shows over Sirius XM radio. It's great to be able to hear this music wherever you might be, and the music itself is probably being exposed to millions of people who would otherwise never hear it. But there is something lacking, as Michael Scully points out in *The Never-Ending Revival*: "Such stations provide diverse music and knowledgeable disc jockeys, but they cannot tell you which unknown folkie is playing in your town next week, and they are unlikely to spotlight your local club."[101]

It is what it is, of course, and even though narrowcast programming on digital radio does not promote community other than in general terms, it is still much better than nothing. It will be a challenge in years to come to try to make access to Rounder's 3,000-plus recordings more widely available, and also to try to reach people of similar tastes and find ways to create as much a sense of community as we can in the process. That should involve live music as well as just recorded, downloadable music. Streaming is growing, and there are revenue streams to be had; fortunately, at the same time there are still live musics that are prospering due to musicians' love of jamming and audiences' desire to come out to see shows – the bluegrass festival scene still seems strong, with regional organizations helping keep the music growing.

Business adjustments

There were moves that we made, of course. We sold all four buildings in Cambridge and moved to a warehouse we bought in Burlington, Massachusetts, northwest of Boston. It was a very nice facility, on two floors, and it served us well. It was a good crew we had working with us.

Cover of *Raising Sand* by Robert Plant and Alison Krauss (Rounder 9075; 2007)

The Burlington building was located on a street named Commonwealth Executive Drive. Sounded kind of spiffy as an address – but, considering our building was the only one on the street, I thought it would be fun to petition the town's Board of Selectmen for a name change. For years, we'd always talked about "the Rounder way," and so, we thought, what better name for the street than . . . Rounder Way? I went to a town meeting, made my pitch, the name change was approved, and our address became 1 Rounder Way.[102]

We continued to have successes with certain albums. In 2008, Folk Alliance honored us with their Lifetime Achievement Award. And in 2007 we came as close as we will probably ever come to having a #1 record album. The album was *Raising Sand*, a collaboration between Alison Krauss and Robert Plant. The two had met in Cleveland at the annual Rock and Roll Hall of Fame American Music Masters Tribute to Lead Belly on November 7, 2004. They'd hit it off and started talking about doing something together. That blossomed into a full album, produced by T-Bone Burnett. The album was released on October 23, 2007 and it debuted on the Billboard chart at #2. It never quite made it to #1. But, in February 2009, at the Grammy Awards in Los Angeles, it won five Grammys – including both Album of the Year and Record of the Year. It also won Grammys for Best Contemporary Folk/Americana Album, for Best Pop Collaboration with Vocals, and for Best Country Collaboration with Vocals.

It's pretty hard to do better than win *both* Album of the Year and Record of the Year. Only one other independent label had ever accomplished that – Concord Records, in 2005 with the Ray Charles album *Genius Loves Company*.

There were a few more honors that followed. In 2010, the Boston Bluegrass Union presented Rounder Records with its Heritage Award. In 2015, SERFA (the Southeast Regional Folk Alliance) presented its Founding President's Award to the Rounder Founders. Much earlier, back in 1986, the Blues Foundation had named Rounder the Blues Label of the Year.

And, as previously mentioned, the Rounder founders were inducted by IBMA into the International Bluegrass Music Hall of Fame, along with New Englander Clarence White, in October 2016.

Honors aside, though, actually running a record company heading into the second decade of the twenty-first century was a major challenge.

15 Selling the Company: The Next Iteration – The Concord Connection (2010)

You get really good at doing something and then the whole paradigm shifts. We had very good staff. They were doing a good job promoting and selling records. And then the marketplace changed. Here in 2020 (as I write), you ask someone, "Where's the nearest record store?" and, if they're under thirty, there's a good chance they've never even been in one. Some of them may not know what you mean.

The goals are the same today, but now you're selling music and not selling records. That's really what it was all along, of course. But Rounder Records was not called Rounder Music. It was all about selling records, because the Rounders grew up in one of the generations that saw music embodied, stored, and accessed in physical objects. Rounder itself began with vinyl LPs, but within fifteen years had already offered 8-track tapes, cassettes, and compact discs as well. They were all physical objects; they had to be manufactured, stored in physical warehouses, transported to retailers, and were carried home by customers and stored on "record shelves."

There were advantages and disadvantages. One shortcoming of records is that they can warp, get scratched, and have their jackets damaged by water. There was once a flood at the Rounder warehouse at 1 Camp Street. I was the one the alarm company called when there was a problem and there had been a few false alarms. Not this time. The water triggered an alarm and, at about 4.15 am, I found myself working to find and then shut off the water valves to the building, and then doing what I could to salvage things. Fortunately, very little damage was done because we had most of the records on shelves, with the bottom shelf about three inches above the ground.

The advantages? Album covers were often pieces of art, the 12" × 12" canvas offering a designer a lot more to work with than a 5" × 5" CD. An album can also offer plenty of information right there on the back jacket, more if it has an enclosed booklet; the text that comes with a CD is generally less accessible, and its small booklet is usually limited to thirty-two pages without resorting to additional packaging.

But even the CD offered far more than a digital download or stream. There is no reason why digital offerings need to be limited. They could offer far more but companies choose to save their money, perhaps correctly assuming that not enough consumers would care. There is no reason at all why anyone downloading a single song could not be offered – for free, or even at an additional cost – a 400-page ebook presenting biographies of the musicians involved, their thoughts on making the music, videos of them working on the recording, etc. etc. But most people downloading music today don't know any more than the name of the performer and the name of the track. They rarely know who the songwriter was, who produced the music, who the accompanying musicians are, and so forth. Those who grew up in the decades from the 1950s through the end of the twentieth century were much more able to learn about the roots of the music, to notice that – say – Jim Keltner was the drummer on this record, and on that record. You listen to the average downloaded track today, and you may be truly impressed by the drumming – but you have no idea of knowing who that drummer might be unless you go to the extra trouble of hunting on YouTube and trying to work the internet from there. And if you hear a song you like, you don't know if the singer was also the writer, or got the song from someone else. If you don't know that, you can't seek out other songs by that writer. If there are no credits and no notes, how can you know that when the Rolling Stones perform 'I Gotta Go' it came from Little Walter? You may never discover Little Walter and all the rest of his music. It's a dumbing-down.

Anyhow, that sermon aside, the Rounders faced the same pressures every other record company faced – not to mention book, magazine, and newspaper publishers. The "data" that was all in digital form could now be transmitted anywhere, by computer. If you didn't care about holding a tangible object – a record, or a book, say – you didn't have to. You didn't need record shelves, or book shelves.

There are good and bad sides to this. It is certainly more convenient not to have to store objects, and there is more portability as well. Plus, if you are halfway adept at a computer keyboard, a lot of what you once had to pay for (unless you were shoplifting), you could now "shoplift" digitally, downloading it without paying. This meant the musicians didn't get paid, the songwriters didn't get paid, and the record companies saw revenue decline, too. One could imagine a world in which much less music was being made, since there were fewer opportunities to make money from it (or even recover the investment made in recording).

On the positive side, many people don't live near a record store, fewer still near a *good* record store. There had never been much chance that Rounder Records were going to turn up almost anywhere in Africa, for instance. But through computers, the music that Rounder had recorded could show up anywhere there was a computer. That should be a good thing, on a number of levels.

"Monetizing" music in the digital age is another matter entirely. This isn't the place to launch into a full-fledged look at the economics of iTunes, or of subscription services such as Spotify, but it became very clear, very quickly, that the economics of the music business going forward were going to be challenging, and probably very difficult in the short run. Napster, the Digital Millennium Copyright Act, Pandora, iTunes, Apple Music, Spotify, Sound Exchange – there was a whole raft of new models and attempts to rationalize them. One record label head calculated that, if someone streamed one of his tracks on Spotify 233 times, his label would receive 70¢. That's slightly better than nothing, but clearly not enough to sustain a business.

We believed it would all work out in the long run, but we weren't sure we had the wherewithal, and perhaps the energy, to see the company through another reinvention all by ourselves. That might take a decade, or more. We weren't getting any younger. We felt, as before when we sought out a partnership with Rykodisc, that there could be benefits to allying with another enterprise that was strong enough to see the company through the challenges of adapting to this new digital world.

We started talking about whether it was a good time to sell the company – to sell Rounder. We figured we had a strong enough catalog and a solid enough standing in the music world that we could probably fetch a price good enough to take care of the three of us for the rest of our lives. We'd never gotten in it for the money in the first place, and our tastes weren't such that we felt the need to live in luxury in our latter years.

There were three concerns that governed our conversations. We wanted to do as well as we could for the employees with whom we had worked for so many years. We'd been in the trenches, so to speak, with Scott Billington for thirty-five years, with John Virant for over fifteen, and a number of others – Steve Netsky, for instance – for many years as well. We wanted to stay active ourselves. Golf held no interest for any of us three, nor did sitting by a pool or on a beach. It really was the music that mattered, and that combined two elements – the musicians with whom we'd worked (in some cases for a decade, or two, or three) and the music itself, the body of work that we'd built up – the legacy. We had over three thousand albums, each one representing a lot of talent, thought, care, and effort. They were our "offspring" – even if there were a lot of them.

We cared a great deal about what we'd built. We didn't want to just trade it in for a bunch of dollar bills.

So, what to do? Just as when we went around with George Thorogood looking for a new home for the Destroyers, we were looking for the "right home." We were looking for a company we could believe in, which we thought was large enough and strong enough to make its way through the years to come, but which was also run by people who appeared to care for the music – as music, not just as a commodity – and would respect the Rounder legacy. Hopefully, these might even be people who would let us keep adding to it, instead of just buying the catalog, letting 90% of it go out of print in the first year or so, and putting us out to pasture.

We believed we found the right place in the Concord Music Group. They'd started from the ground up, as a jazz label in Concord, California. We used to distribute Concord. And they had grown, in large part through acquisitions. They had, for instance, bought Fantasy Records. We talked to a couple of friends who worked at Fantasy and got good reports.

We never put Rounder up for auction. In fact, most of the firms in the music field never knew we were contemplating a sale. We might have been able to realize 50% more had our goal been to maximize the money we took in. But most of all we were looking for a good home. We had Rounder professionally appraised, and John Virant (working with our attorney, the late Mark Fischer) discussed the possibilities with Glen Barros at Concord and he agreed to the valuation. At the time – not long after the financial crisis of 2008, and while undergoing a recapitalization of their company – Concord didn't have enough money to buy the company outright, but we worked on a deal that more or less allowed both Concord and Rounder to get to know each other over a period of thirty-six months. They gave us 10% down with the rest to be paid at the end of the three-year period. They could have backed out if they had been unable to raise the additional capital (or perhaps thought they had grievously overpaid) and we would have kept the down payment and retained 100% ownership of the company. But, by this point, that's not what we were looking for.

We were ready for the transition, just hoping we could stay on and most of our key people would be kept on, so that we could continue to run what had been a profitable enterprise and one that was respected for its musical taste. Somehow the "little folk label from Cambridge" had become one of the most active and sizeable independent record labels in America. Rounder had a brand, and that was a big part of what they were paying for. We moved to combine "back office" functions – the billing and accounting, royalties, etc. – for the beneficial savings in those areas, but Rounder kept A&R going, signing the artists that made sense, the sorts of artists who had built the label from the beginning.

The sale was announced to the public on April 14, 2010. The press release was headlined thus: CONCORD MUSIC GROUP ACQUIRES CELEBRATED AMERICAN ROOTS LABEL ROUNDER RECORDS, with the subhead: *Acquisition Firmly Establishes the Combined Entity as the World's Preeminent Independent Music Company.*

The full text of the press release may be of note. It was, of course, a collaborative effort:

The Concord Music Group today announced the acquisition of storied Massachusetts-based independent music label Rounder Records. Rounder, celebrating its 40th year as the world's leading American roots music label, is a major force in a broad range of musical genres including bluegrass, Americana, singer-songwriter, Cajun & Zydeco and children's music. Rounder possesses an extraordinary recorded catalog and current artist roster including bluegrass superstar Alison Krauss, singer-songwriter Mary Chapin Carpenter, banjo virtuoso Béla Fleck, actor/musician Steve Martin, jazz singer Madeleine Peyroux, the iconic Robert Plant, notable children's artist/activist Raffi and country legend Willie Nelson, to name just a few. The acquisition of Rounder and its essential collection of over 3,000 masters combined with Concord Music Group's rich catalog of more than 10,000 master recordings strengthens Concord's status as one of the world's most significant independent record companies, with a leadership position in multiple genres.

Rounder's creative and marketing functions will continue to be based in Boston and its owners and founders Ken Irwin, Bill Nowlin, and Marian Leighton Levy will remain active with the company in a creative and advisory capacity. The company's senior management will also remain in place: John Virant will continue as the President of Rounder; Sheri Sands will stay on as General Manager. Operating synergies will be achieved by combining the sales, administrative and support functions of the two companies.

Rounder, founded in 1970 by Cambridge folkies, Irwin, Nowlin, and Leighton Levy, has been at the center of nearly all of the American roots revivals that have reshaped the music world in the last 40 years. The self-titled 1975 record by J.D. Crowe and the New South (featuring future stars Ricky Skaggs, Tony Rice and Jerry Douglas) revitalized bluegrass and inspired such modern superstars as Rounder's own Alison Krauss, who is the most decorated female artist in the history of the Grammy® Awards and has also sold over eight million albums and DVDs. Her collaboration with Led Zeppelin front-man Robert Plant on the album *Raising Sand* emerged as one of 2007's major critical and word-of-mouth sales success stories. The album was RIAA certified platinum in early 2008 and won five Grammy® Awards including Album and Record of the Year in 2009. An unequaled leader in the preservation and re-release of precious historic recordings, Rounder has brought the music of Jelly Roll Morton, Woody Guthrie, Lead Belly, the Carter Family, Jimmie Rodgers and Mississippi John Hurt back to vibrant life. In addition, their dazzling work on the epic anthologies from the Library of Congress and the Alan Lomax Collection has been universally respected and admired.

Glen Barros, President and CEO of the Concord Music Group, said, "The combination of Concord and Rounder makes so much sense on a creative, strategic and cultural level. With the addition of Rounder, Concord is gaining a magnificent catalog of recordings, the opportunity to work with more of the world's most amazing artists and a company filled with some great people. Plus, Rounder's uncompromising commitment to authenticity and intense independent spirit is perfectly in line with everything that Concord is about."

Norman Lear, Concord Music Group Chairman and co-owner added, "We couldn't be more honored to join together with Rounder in our collective mission to deliver great, timeless music."

Marian Leighton Levy, co-Rounder Founder, concurs and adds, "For us, it's always been about the music. We have long been aware of Concord's commitment to great catalogue labels within a vibrant and contemporary independent context, and feel the Concord Records Group provides not only a great home for our music and artists, but also a stronger and more secure position going forward."

John Virant, President of Rounder, said "We've always been the little label that could, and our new affiliation with Concord – another fiercely independent organization that shares our core values – ensures that we can remain true to our central calling: discovering and nurturing quality musical talent."

About Concord Music Group:

Concord Music Group is one of the largest independent record and music publishing companies in the world and is owner of a rich and historically significant catalog of recordings. Concord Music Group's legendary family of labels include Concord Records, Concord Jazz, Fantasy, Stax, Milestone, Riverside, Specialty, Telarc, Peak, Heads Up, Prestige and several others. They include titles from some of the most admired and enduring names in music, including Ray Charles, John Coltrane, Creedence Clearwater Revival, Miles Davis, Ella Fitzgerald, Isaac Hayes, Little Richard, Thelonious Monk, Oscar Peterson, Rosemary Clooney, George Shearing and Mel Tormé. The group's current roster of world-class artists includes George Benson, Chick Corea, Kurt Elling, Will Downing, Kenny G, Ladysmith Black Mambazo, Sergio Mendes, Esperanza Spalding, Macy Gray, Angie Stone and many more. In 2007, Concord partnered with Starbucks Entertainment to form Hear Music, an innovative record label rooted in quality, authenticity and passion. Hear Music works directly with artists, both emerging and established, to bring quality music to the widest possible audience, in both Starbucks locations and music retailers worldwide. Hear Music releases include records from Paul McCartney, Joni Mitchell, James Taylor, John Mellencamp, Elvis Costello and Playing For Change.

John Virant, Glen Barros, and the sale to Concord

How did the sale come to pass? In late 2018, I asked both John Virant and Glen Barros – the two principals who did most of the negotiating – to recount how it transpired. We trusted John to look into the sale, fully believing that he would keep our personal best interests – including those of Rounder – at heart. Let's learn a little more about Glen Barros.

Glen graduated from NYU in January 1998 with a Bachelor of Science degree *summa cum laude* in Music and Business. It was a new major at the time, one of very few in the country. In between his sophomore and junior years he called Chappell Music and talked them into letting him become an unpaid intern there, and interned there for the rest of his time in college, learning the business of music publishing. Chappell was purchased by Warner, however, and the company wanted Glen to move to Los Angeles. The offer was not sufficiently attractive for him to make the move so he sought out and secured a position with publisher SBK, which was expanding. He worked there for a year and then moved on to a record distribution company called Sound Solutions. Through a series of moves, the American arm of European-based Sound Solutions was purchased by the expanding distributor Alliance Entertainment, which also added Bassin Distributors in Florida and Encore Distribution out of Denver.

Glen went to work for Alliance and chairman Joe Bianco at the company's corporate office in New York. Alliance was vertically integrating and building an empire. "They were just on the verge of buying CD One Stop," Glen explained. They were buying a number of one-stops and eventually bought INDI – a network comprised of three former regional distributors (including California Record Distributors [CRDI] which had distributed Rounder for many years). Alliance then added Passport to its growing portfolio. Bianco then told Glen, "You have a good knack for translating music speak into finance speak, and vice versa. That's what I need, and I want you to find me some labels. Now I want record labels. You know a good number of them out there and you can do this. But I'm not interested in competing with any of the majors." They were our main suppliers on the one-stop side of things. "Find me things on the periphery that make sense and are good deals."[103]

Glen continued:

So I started looking around and I came across Concord. I had heard that it was for sale. I always knew what Concord was, and I admired it, so I called Carl Jefferson up and I talked to him about it. He said, "Come on out." So I went out and I learned that he had gone through about twenty different suitors – including Sony and Al Shulman, who had been sitting in his office with a checkbook and he had thrown him out. "I'm not selling to you." Hearing this, I didn't know what I was in for but I went out and met him.

This was around January 1994.

Carl Jefferson was an independent label head – an entrepreneur who had built a label, Concord Jazz, from the ground up. He was, quite naturally, concerned about seeing his company acquired by another enterprise, and concerned about what might happen if it were swallowed up by another company: what would happen to the artists, the company employees, and its legacy. Jefferson also wanted to continue with the company. Glen recalled, "In that first meeting, I didn't know if I was buying a company or asking for his daughter's hand. He literally said to me at that dinner when we first met, 'State your intentions.'"

This was Alliance's first acquisition of a record company, but Glen was already clear that they wanted to buy a successful company and build on its strengths. He told Jefferson:

> You're the first one we're talking to. We'd love to build around you. We certainly want to honor your artists. We're building off this platform and your people for the same reason. We have the intention to buy some other labels and handle them the same way. We want you to keep running it and doing what you're doing with it. We'd like to add some capital. We'd like to add some distribution power and make things better, but essentially the core of your business is the artistic side and that's what we'd like you to run.

Glen says that he and "Jeff" – as Carl Jefferson was known – worked on the deal and became good friends over the course of the negotiations. The deal closed in December 1994, with Carl paid $6 million. Concord at the time was doing about $4 million of annual business.

Two months later, Carl called Glen and said he'd been diagnosed with terminal liver cancer and wanted to talk about arrangements for after he died. Glen asked him who was the person who would be running things. "Well, *you* are," Carl replied. "Do you really want to be in the corporate ranks here. Wouldn't you rather be out to sea than to be a fleet admiral?" "It was like a lightning bolt," Glen recalled. "He was right. He could see that." Glen spoke to his wife about moving to Northern California and he spoke with Joe Bianco. Joe was in the hospital visiting his mother, who had just suffered a stroke. Joe said, "What, are you crazy? We've got big plans for you, kid. Why would you want to do that? Run a little division?" Glen said, "We don't have to keep it a little division. We can make it a big one. But it's really what I want to do."

Carl Jefferson didn't have the time the doctors had anticipated. He died on March 29, 1995. "That was it," Glen said. "I found myself the head of a label and flying back and forth between New York and Northern California for four months." He made the move and took over as head of Concord, essentially running a modestly sized $4 million company. The division he had been running at Alliance was doing much more business but this is what Glen wanted to do. Bianco told him, "Go ahead, kid. Go do it."

Glen ran Concord Jazz and kept it healthy. Alliance, however, maybe grew too quickly at a bad time in the record business and a couple of years later found itself facing bankruptcy. Glen was getting offers from a number of other players in the music business, but running Concord had become something very personal to him.

In 1997, Alliance filed for bankruptcy. They sold off parts of the company – Red Ant – reorganized the one-stops, shut down their distribution business. The process of reorganization within bankruptcy was enervating, but Concord was a small part of the overall picture and it was doing well so Glen and the label were left alone. Finally, in 1999, Alliance (and the eleven banks that now owned it) accepted an offer from Hal Gaba and Norman Lear. Concord was ready to operate on its own again.

> We took a little time to just get things stabilized and in 2002 we moved it from Northern California, from Concord, to where we are now, to LA, to Beverly Hills, which is where Hal and Norman were. There were two key strategies. One was to grow by strategic acquisition. Labels that we felt fit with who we were and where we were going. The second part of it was to find alternative retail. We always believed that our music was not going to be searched out by all but the aficionado. The more casual fan was never going to find what we were doing, and so we wanted to find them.

Concord began working with Starbucks, providing music to the chain's customers.

In November 2004, Concord bought Fantasy Records, a strategic acquisition and one that Glen had had in mind for years. Just one year later, in November 2005, Concord bought Telarc, a jazz and classical label that was very compatible with what Concord had been doing. There were other deals they explored, but backed away from for one reason or another. The next label they acquired was Rounder.

There was a four-year gap between the Telarc acquisition and the initiation of serious talks with Rounder. Glen had talked with John Virant once or twice in the intervening years, 2006 or 2007. In 2008, of course, the financial crisis hit – after Hal and Norman had purchased half of the Australian film company Village Roadshow Pictures. Banks weren't financing films. It was a difficult time.

It was a year later that John called Glen and said the Rounder founders might be interesting in exploring a deal. Glen says he recalls replying, "Well, John, I'm as enthused and motivated as I've ever been. But right now, we've got a problem. I can't do the deal as a straight acquisition, because we're in the middle of a major recapitalization for the entire business. But maybe there's another way."

John agreed. There was. That was the two-stage closing noted above – initially in 2010, with a thirty-six-month period for Concord to raise the rest of the money.

John had explored some other possibilities beforehand, at least in passing. We'd talked to Giles McNamee in the Boston area; his brother Roger was a big private equity guy who was partners in a private equity firm with Bono of U2. Nothing came of that. Never met Bono. But it's nice that Giles has remained very much involved with the Boston Bluegrass Union's annual Joe Val Festival.

We might have thought about the Welk Group back then, but there were no discussions.

We were being distributed by Universal at this point – which was very important, since Tower Records had closed up shop entirely in December 2006. Had we still been selling to Tower directly, through Rounder Distribution, we would have been left holding the bag for a big chunk of change. Naturally, John mentioned a possible sale to the executives at Universal. "They were interested," John recalls, "but that was really more like a courtesy. We didn't really pursue that. Their interest would have been for the catalog and we all wanted to continue – if possible – as a going concern. That just wasn't going to be their model."[104]

John continued:

> On the finance side, sure, we had some kind of modest line of credit with the bank but there were no investors. You guys did not have separate retirement plans . . . *everything* you had was in the company. That gets riskier and riskier over time. You had no diversification. It was all just about Rounder. Given where the business was at, at the time, that was kind of a big weight on all of you. I think that kind of goes to the decision about kind of combining or selling.

I'll pause for just a moment here to reflect on some good luck regarding our timing during three different crises. In 1984 there had been a significant crisis, but we still had good cash flow from George Thorogood & the Destroyers sales and other projects we'd started on around that time. That may be one of the years that having the distribution company helped us get through some of the problems on the label side, but we had some very strong albums that year, such as *Soul Alive!* by Solomon Burke, *Cold on the Shoulder* by Tony Rice, and *Winter Solstice* by John McCutcheon. With one-third of the staff volunteering to take lay-offs, we got costs back under control. We had another set of crises in the middle 1990s, with the unfortunate REP experience and the unfortunate DNA experience with Valley, two attempts at partnerships that could have been much worse for us financially, except that 1995 was the year that we had a platinum album with Alison Krauss's *Now That I've Found You.* Those sales certainly helped us through those times. And then when the nationwide financial crisis of 2008 hit, we were particularly fortunate because we had released *Raising Sand* by Robert Plant and Alison Krauss just the year before, and it sold steadily throughout 2008. So while we truly weren't diversified (everything we had but our homes was in Rounder), we definitely did benefit from some good timing.

I told John during our December 2018 discussion:

> We were very fortunate. If we liked something, we could put it out. That was the driving force. As time went by, we talked more about whether we could break even, or if we could make money, but, really, when it came right down to it we put out a lot of pretty obscure stuff that had no right to succeed, and sometimes it did and sometimes it didn't.

John said:

> Right. That's what was so special about it. It was very different. People can give lip service to not having a profit motive, but that really was never it with you guys. It was never like, "We've got to have X percent return on our investment each year." Like you always said, if everyone got paid and there was a little bit of money in the bank, you guys were happy – because you were doing what you wanted to do.
>
> It wasn't Rounder itself – it was the industry that got torpedoed. We were part of that.[105]

When it came time to think about selling Rounder, John agrees.

> The only idea we really explored was working with Concord. There wasn't that sort of major label disconnect where what we did wasn't really understood, or was just very different. Glen really "got" us. He had run Concord through Alliance and so a lot of the same travails with consolidation on the distribution side . . . he knew all that. He knew that world.

> Concord was a jazz label and they were doing smaller records. It was very analogous to what we were doing on the bluegrass and other music. It was very similar in that way.

Naturally, it didn't all work out as originally anticipated. Probably no one ever really thought it would. In fact, within three years, Concord itself was sold. Concord was actually already owned by another entity, Village Roadshow Entertainment Group. Their main interest had always been in motion pictures.

On March 25, 2013, Village Roadshow sold Concord (and the rights to Rounder) to the New Haven-based Wood Creek Capital Management LLC. We were happy to learn that Wood Creek CEO Brett D. Hellerman was a banjo player.

The three Rounder founders had meanwhile begun to know the folks at Concord. The principal contact was with Glen Barros, but we got to know others throughout the company and, as the thirty-six months wore on, it still seemed a reasonably comfortable fit. That despite an unfortunate couple of words Glen uttered during a meeting at Rounder when he referred (not with any indication of self-consciousness) to records as "entertainment products." He did know "corporate speak" and how to converse with people in the field of finance, but it caused us a little trepidation.

And the purchase of Rounder was perfected. The deal in 2010 had given Concord three years to raise the money and complete the purchase. It all worked out on time.

Within a few months, the new Board determined to close down the operation in Massachusetts and relocate the company to Nashville. We didn't want to see it go, and we thought it a mistake. We felt from the start that one of the things that kept Rounder from becoming like most other record companies that it kept its distance from the music centers: New York, Los Angeles, Nashville. We know that a number of our artists – even those who lived in Nashville – felt the same way. A little distance can be a good thing.

It was a big disappointment to all of us, including "the fourth Rounder," John. We felt we had a vibrant, active company operating out of 1 Rounder Way, and with Concord continuing to handle all the "back room" support functions through its shared services effort, we could continue to thrive. We started to lose a few artists, for one reason or another. We did understand, though, that it was no longer our company and that there were likely strategic benefits for the larger company that was Concord which we were not able to fully appreciate from our perspective. Indeed, as it happened, Concord moved many of its own functions from California to Nashville and established a strong presence there.

Be that as it may, once the sale was 100% consummated, the decision was entirely theirs. The *Boston Globe* ran a story on October 16: "Rounder Records Moving to Music City."[106] It was on the front page of the Business

A Rock and Roll Hall event at the Waldorf Astoria in 1999: (left to right) the author, Yleana Martinez, Wilson Pickett with companion Gail, Lady Judy Martin, Sir George Martin

section. Writer Geoff Himes was quoted: "It's a double-edged sword. Rounder flourished for many years based in Boston; there's something to be said about not being part of the herd."[107]

Much to our surprise, New England's largest newspaper, the *Boston Globe*, published an editorial that lamented the company's departure:

> Rounder Records quietly made the Boston area a hub of the roots music universe. Founded in the folk haven of Cambridge in 1970 by Ken Irwin, Marian Leighton Levy, and Bill Nowlin, the label grew to promote music ranging from bluegrass to South African township jive, cowboy classics to New Orleans crooners, prison songs to Celtic strings. Many of its artists became well-known in their genres, such as Béla Fleck, Buckwheat Zydeco, Irma Thomas, Mary Chapin Carpenter, and George Thorogood and the Destroyers. Some, like Alison Krauss and Robert Plant, won Grammy Awards. Pianist and singer Allen Toussaint is enshrined in the Rock and Roll Hall of Fame. All that history is being packed up from Rounder's headquarters in Burlington by its parent Concord Music Group and trucked to the country music capital of Nashville.
>
> The move places Rounder closer to the artists and producers of the label's core Southern sounds. But it's a familiar corporate effort to consolidate quarters. What may be lost is the spirit of Rounder's eccentric beginnings, in which a trio of Northern college students

with no industry experience lent a fresh ear to sounds around the globe. Such innovation was characteristic of Massachusetts, even without a music scene like Nashville's.[108]

Concord offered positions on staff for those Rounder employees who were willing to relocate. There were four who took them up on the offer: Mike Annis, Eliza Levy, Matt Miller, and our longest-tenured employee Scott Billington. John Virant was to remain president and the Concord plan was that he would move to Nashville, too. He helped find new quarters for the company, which no longer needed a warehouse as all those functions would be handled by distributor Universal Music. Concord came to quite fair severance agreements with all who did not move, and ensured that health plan coverage would continue in the interim, even outside of COBRA requirements. One employee, Amy Loews, was pregnant and Concord made special arrangements for her. Concord HR head Melanie Lewis showed us that the faith we had had that Concord represented "good people" was not misplaced. The same was true for Glen Barros and, in time, CEO Scott Pascucci and others. Business was business, but business with a heart paid dividends, too. The music business is a small world, in many regards, and musicians and others in the industry learn when a company is not treating people well.

As it happens, Scott Billington never moved to Nashville. He moved to New Orleans instead, and got married, too. This didn't go over too well with the folks at Concord, who felt they had relied on Scott making the move and made special accommodations for him, but adjustments were made.

John Virant moved instead to St. Louis. His father co-owned an investment firm there, and John was best positioned as the scion to eventually take on the Virant portion of the Eidelman Virant firm. John's heart was in the music business, but with all the many acquisitions and changes, and his loyalty to the Rounder founders and their vision, the future seemed particularly uncertain. St. Louis isn't too far away from Nashville, and he commuted as necessary (increasingly, of course, a great deal of work can be done remotely – and sometimes even more efficiently).

We don't know what would have happened if the three Rounder founders had declared, "We'll move to Nashville, too!" Probably there was some relief on the Concord side that it didn't come to that. We were realistic enough to know that we might not be altogether welcome; after all, Concord had the right to hire its own staff and put its own stamp on Rounder. And we were content enough to stay in Massachusetts, where we each had homes and family and networks of friends.

We weren't just cast aside, though. John worked on a plan with Concord that provided a way to continue to involve the founders both for the goodwill involved and to offer continuity, providing an opportunity for us to continue our involvement with A&R. There have been a good number of very fine albums that followed. It seemed like something of a win–win.

With the numerous changes at Concord, it's no surprise that there was some muddling through in terms of strategic direction. Yet there were reasons behind the decision to move Rounder to Nashville. In March 2014, a small, homey office was opened in The Gulch, more or less an alley away from Nashville's Station Inn. J.D. Crowe, Carlene Carter, Ranger Doug Green, and Mayor Karl Dean were among those who came to the Open House on May 14, 2014, along with many from Music Row.[109]

On April 1 (this was no joke), 2015, Concord Bicycle purchased renowned independent record labels Vanguard and Sugar Hill from the Welk Music Group.

With Rounder newly settled in its Nashville digs, it made perfect sense for Sugar Hill to be moved there, too. So, Vanguard was merged into the Beverly Hills office – which also made sense – while Sugar Hill was moved into the Rounder office. No integration of two staffs is ever seamless, but there were good people from both labels and most people hit it off right away. Not everyone was a good fit, though, and that was most likely no surprise.

There were years, such as at the 2016 Grammy Awards, when the entire Concord Music Group had won four Grammys – and one of them came to Concord through the production agreement with the Rounder founders. That group was The Steeldrivers. Their record won the Grammy for Best Bluegrass Album at the 2016 Awards.

Actually, Concord wasn't any longer the Concord Music Group at the time. In early 2015, Concord had merged with Bicycle Music Company, a leading independent music publisher, record label and rights manager, into Concord Bicycle Music. The goal was, per internal company correspondence, to "grow Concord Bicycle Music into THE leading independent music company in the world" and in that respect it was "important to realize that we also need to expand our genre and fan base reach." Hence, other acquisitions followed such as the purchase of Mexican company Musart Music in April 2016. Musart owned catalogs of Mexican, Peruvian, and Cuban music totaling an estimated 4,000 albums and 70,000 musical compositions.

Names change. By then it was no longer Concord Bicycle but simply Concord again. And Concord had decided to move a lot of its staff from the cramped and very expensive headquarters in Beverly Hills. In 2017, the company offered employees in California and elsewhere the opportunity to move to Nashville. Through acquisitions, there were employees in New Jersey, New York, the Cleveland area, etc. What might seem a surprising number of people took advantage of the offer. The small Rounder office there was closed and everyone moved in together into a larger space a block or two away on Demonbreun Street. It was one of those glitzy new multi-story glass buildings – a fifteen-story edifice – and a far cry from the kinds of places Rounder had grown up (and, for that matter, different from the "garden level" – basement – offices of the Beverly Hills headquarters of Concord).

Among those making the move were Concord's COO Glen Barros, CFO Bob Valentine, and Chief Publishing Executive Jake Wisely. Concord leased 21,000 square feet on the sixth floor. Other tenants in the 1201 Demonbreun Street building included Sony Music Nashville and the WME Nashville offices.

On November 15, 2017, John Strohm was appointed president of Rounder, to (as the press release stated) "oversee management of Rounder's day-to-day operations in Nashville, reporting to Concord Music's Chief Label Officer, Tom Whalley." The release noted that "Former Rounder president, John Virant will remain in a senior creative role, working closely with Strohm and the Rounder staff." In fact, John Virant went off payroll, remaining as a consultant, a major disappointment to the three Rounder founders. We keep in touch.

It turns out that we had crossed paths with John Strohm over the years. As previously noted, he was a guitarist for *God Bless the Blake Babies*, a March 2001 release on Rounder's Zoë label (Zoë 1014). There were a lot of other connections, too. His familiarity with Rounder dated back to his family home in Bloomington, Indiana. His father had known Jim Rooney (and Bill Keith) while at Amherst College. In a September 2020 interview, John said:

> Rooney used to send him [my father] a lot of music that he had worked on, so we had a lot of Rounder records around for that reason. My dad was a Dylan fanatic so I grew up hearing a lot of anything that had any kind of connection with Dylan. A lot of great folk music. A lot of great blues. Country. He was not into bluegrass. He liked lyrics. Nanci Griffith was big in our house. A lot of stuff that was on Rounder.[110]

After graduating high school, John came to Boston in the fall of 1985 to study music and music engineering at Berklee College of Music. By the time he was into his second year, he had joined with others in the area and was playing in local bands – bands that developed a following. By 1988, he was working as a "grunt" at Newbury Comics in Harvard Square, where he distinctly remembers opening cartons from Rounder and redistributing the records to the chain's six stores. (As we've seen, in 1998, Rounder's GM Duncan Browne became COO of Newbury Comics.) In his spare time, with Blake Babies, he was hanging around a lot at Fort Apache, the recording studio that was housed for many years in the Rounder Records building at 1 Camp Street. He was picking up some practical experience in engineering, too. John would often run into people from Rounder.

In 1989 and 1990, he played guitar on two Mammoth Records albums by Blake Babies. He'd been playing with them since 1986, and in 1989 began ten years of active touring, first with Blake Babies and then with three other bands: Velo-Deluxe, the Lemonheads, and Antenna.

He moved back to Bloomington in 1991 and made that his home base during the heavier touring years, working as an audio engineer in a studio co-owned by John Mellencamp's guitarist Mike Wanchick. When he came off the road at the end of the decade, he was in his early thirties and he followed a girlfriend – Heather – to Birmingham, Alabama. She had a good job there and, John says, "This is what slacker musicians do when they come off the road – they go where their girlfriend is if she has a good job." Once there, he decided to go to law school.

> I didn't become a lawyer because I wanted to become a lawyer. I wanted to become a lawyer because I wanted to work with artists, to work in artist development. I had been a musician and I wanted to come up with a way that I could have a professional career working in music and be able to work with artists.

It worked out nicely, though for the first couple of years after graduating law school (at age thirty-seven) he worked as a pretty straight-ahead corporate lawyer. And he and Heather married.

> I was not a music lawyer. Just general practice, with a large firm that merged with another firm. After a few years I moved to another firm in Birmingham, one that was hospitable to me doing entertainment law. I had started practicing in 2004. It was in 2007 that I made that move. That's when I really started building a clientele. I moved to Nashville and Loeb & Loeb in 2011.
> I worked at Loeb & Loeb for just over six years. During that time, I built a more substantial, mostly artist-centric clientele.[111]

He became Senior Counsel in their music industry practice.

In his work with Loeb & Loeb, he got to know many people in the business. He recalls having a number of conversations with Marty Willard of Rounder. He represented old bandmate Juliana Hatfield and also talked with Marty about a couple of artists who ultimately signed elsewhere – the Civil Wars and Amanda Shires. He also got to know Tom Whalley, who had been chairman and CEO at Warner Brothers Records. Tom started a new label, Loma Vista, which as of 2020 is one of the front-line labels in Concord. He had, however, left Loma Vista in the first part of 2017 and taken on a broader role at Concord which included overseeing Rounder.

Tom and John had never done a deal together, but kept in touch over the years and, when Tom was looking for someone to take over the combined Rounder Sugar Hill operation, he asked John about it over a meal in September 2017. The two shortly met with the Rounder founders in Boston – mostly to get our blessing – and by November John Strohm was named president.

By the end of 2018, the Concord staff in Nashville totaled just over ninety. Glitzy though the digs may be, once inside the Concord office, one found a comfortable working environment of the sort familiar to music business folks. But as 2020 began, the company prepared to move to other quarters more downtown, at 10 Lea Avenue. Same landlord, but a larger and more suitable space for the growing presence.

In July 2018, through further acquisition, the company added leading independent Latin label Fania Records, and its publishing, bringing in another 19,000 master recordings and 8,000 compositions.

Following in something of the tradition of Rounder becoming involved in industry associations, John Strohm was elected to the board of the Americana Music Association in December 2018. As 2018 merged into 2019, the label seemed to be taking more of an Americana direction and had less of a roots music bent, save for some of the Rounder founder projects. A personal favorite of mine was the Po' Ramblin' Boys. Traditional bluegrass always gets me. Times change, of course. John says, however, that "in our A&R and in building the label's roster, we look for precedent and try to keep the spirit of the label intact. Every A&R conversation looks back at Rounder's history while looking ahead to Rounder's future."

John has helped keep the label alive in increasingly competitive times (and during the COVID-19 pandemic that chewed up most of the year 2020) and brought in a number of interesting artists which have helped keep the Rounder label vibrant, and valued within Concord.

There were to have been a number of events celebrating Rounder's fiftieth birthday – in October 2020 – but, due to the worldwide pandemic, those events were put on hold. As this manuscript is being wrapped up just a few weeks before Rounder's October 22 "birthday," the pandemic is still ravaging the globe. There are matters, of course, which are far more important than a milestone which can be celebrated at a later time.

In June 2017, Concord Music acquired publishing giant Imagem for nearly $600 million. The Imagen catalog included both the Rodgers & Hammerstein and Boosey & Hawkes catalogs, and added another 250,000 copyrights to Concord's holdings. *Billboard* estimated that the deal leapfrogged Concord into becoming the sixth-largest publisher in the world. Scott Pascucci was quoted as saying the addition balanced Concord's revenues at about 50/50 between recorded music and publishing.[112] And it has continued to grow. Just as Rounder itself had once found a certain stability between its record label business and its distribution business, Concord saw similar benefits here. Concord had become a billion-dollar business.

That said, Rounder Records – the little folk label from Cambridge – seemed to remain very much respected by the powers-that-be at Concord. Whatever else we did, we seem to have built a legacy out of love for the music, one that endured and spoke to something in the hearts of people in the business.

Culture truly is more than dollars and cents, and respect and appreciation of the culture is . . . well, I wouldn't say "priceless" but I would say important.

Time will tell where it all goes from here.

The Rounder founders in 2005: (left to right) Ken Irwin, Marian Leighton Levy, and the author.
Photo by Peter Feldmann.

16 Rounder's Sense of Mission

We each approached Rounder from different directions, but I think it's fair to say that we have always seen our work as embracing a sense of mission – though, again, we each see that in a somewhat different way.

That's understandable: we wouldn't expect it to be otherwise. Our personal backgrounds all tie into this – Ken's interest in early childhood education, myself as an historic guide in Lexington for so many years, Marian as a young Baptist believer. We all had a strong desire to "spread the word" and to teach, in one way or another. At first, we all saw ourselves as working in education. This explains the major emphasis on liner notes from the outset, as already discussed, and we also knew this would set us apart from most of the other labels. It was education, presented with a sense of mission.

That was just the packaging, of course. We also got great satisfaction out of our mission to record music from artists who might not otherwise get heard, or not heard as widely if we hadn't helped.

Romanticizing the folk?

From my experience of traveling in Europe, things didn't seem so terrible behind the Iron Curtain, and I began to question some of my understandings about America. You'd think I'd be kind of sophisticated being in graduate school and all that, but there were things that we were taught in the Fifties which I bought into and I hadn't really shaken. Getting out into the world and seeing that there are other ways of living took me till I was twenty-two. Some things are different in other cultures – maybe better, maybe not, but they're still valid. The people who live there smile, laugh, and have a sense of humor, even if you don't know the language or fully appreciate their life circumstances.

In the late 1960s, people were always asking me about racism in the United States and the United States' role in Vietnam. It was embarrassing. I was having to talk about these things but I also realized that other people had their own cultural blind spots, too. Turkey was kind of a crossroads with people of various colors and backgrounds; there they asked me in a very mystified fashion about why skin color makes a difference. There might have been some naivety in these questions; there is some racism in most every single society on earth. Maybe it is a natural phenomenon of some kind?

When Ken and Marian and I started Rounder we had each in our own way become more sensitized to what we might call minority musics. We always knew we were kind of odd. Folk music was popular for a little while, but then it became almost a small cult again. Even when it was big, many of the major artists were white and middle-class, performing to white middle-class audiences. We definitely belonged in that spectrum, but – speaking only for myself – I was more intrigued by people who came from different backgrounds: Appalachian banjo players who played on their back porch and didn't have any electricity and had to stop playing or put the candle on; blues musicians from the Delta; Cajun culture. That type of thing. Maybe I found it more interesting because, to me, it was different, and a little exotic.

We may have been romanticizing the folk, but we often saw this music as purer: coming from people who learned from an oral tradition, as opposed to the way that we learned – from records and radio and so forth. We knew that there wouldn't be many such people around much longer. We started Rounder at the tail end of a fragile time, with homogenization already spreading well over the horizon. We had an interest in documenting things that were different, "endangered," in the process of becoming lost. Maybe we could help focus attention on, or encourage a better appreciation of, certain subcultures. That appealed to us, and it tied into the political ethos of the time and even the "hippie movement" in general.

Whatever the impetus, we were doing what we thought was good work. Scott Billington described one way Rounder was different:

> There are a lot of forgotten and alienated audiences in this country. With all the demographic research the major labels do, some people just get left out – they don't have the potential to buy a half-million copies of "the latest thing," so the majors ignore them. That's where we come in.[113]

Marian gave voice to the matter in an interview for the Winter 1985 issue of *Clark Now*, the magazine of Clark University, harking back to Rounder's earliest days:

> By the early Seventies, the major company labels that had done some good folk music had pretty much abandoned it, except for some of the more urban, revivalist folk. Once they decided folk was no longer commercially successful in the mass markets, the

big labels dropped it. We thought this was appalling. We still do. We may have been naive about business, but we were not naive about the way culture functions. Now even fewer folk and minority cultures and traditions are being preserved than when we started out.

She added, with a nod to our own countercultural roots, "The way we saw it, this was our radical project. Helping to preserve the music of minority cultures was our political statement, our social contribution."

Marian also suggested to author Michael Scully that romanticizing the folk should not always be seen pejoratively, but it can help create a linkage, and – if the interest is sincere – it can be empowering to the people being romanticized.[114]

Whatever our motivations were, I believe we did a pretty good job at recording a lot of music that otherwise might well not have been, and presenting it in a way that exposed different ways of looking at things. From the first Women's Liberation Rock Band(s) record to *Hollerin'*, to *Radio Freedom*, we often put out records that were "different" but were also quite serious in their intent.

In writing earlier about the 1979 and 1980 period, I promised "more on that below" regarding traveling to Zambia with Dan Kahn for a "recording venture tied into the struggle against apartheid in South Africa." Grant me one final tangent to make good on that promise. On January 3, 1985, we arrived in Lusaka, the capital of Zambia which also served as home for the African National Congress (ANC) in exile. Bob Denton had been a friend of Ken and Marian's in Worcester in the days before Rounder. Some years later, he moved to South Africa to teach photography there. At one point, he mailed us a cassette he labeled "Beatles Songs." That was to throw off the South African inspectors; the tape actually contained some Radio Freedom broadcasts that Bob had taped off the air – broadcast into South Africa from Lusaka and elsewhere. Nelson Mandela was in prison. Even being caught listening to Radio Freedom in South Africa could get you five years in prison. But the fight against apartheid went on.

With my political science background, I had a particular interest, and I met with some ANC representatives in Boston, and then at the ANC Mission to the United Nations. I carried on a lengthy correspondence with Thabo Mbeki, Director of the ANC Department of Information and Publicity, who was in Lusaka. Their offices were a potential target for attack; in 1983, a South African commando team had raided and destroyed Radio Freedom's facility in Madagascar.

Radio Freedom programming served as a counterbalance to the state-controlled South African Broadcast Company. It broadcast in all the major South African languages: English, Afrikaans, Zulu, Xhosa, Sotho, etc., and offered poetry readings, dramatic performances, news broadcasts, interviews, speeches, commentary, and music. If you dared tune in to Radio Freedom, you could hear 'Blackman Redemption' by Bob Marley and Jimmy Cliff's 'Struggling Man.' We heard both, and even 'The Wall' by Pink Floyd. You could hear music from Dollar Brand (Abdullah Ibrahim), Dudu Pukwana, Miriam Makeba, Hugh Masekela, and more. Possession of a Miriam Makeba album in South Africa could also net you five years.

We stayed at the YWCA in Lusaka. Yes, "W." The "radio unit" was located several miles outside of the capital in a remote and undistinguished old farmhouse, with mango trees in the yard. This was where the broadcasts were assembled and edited onto tape, later to be driven to the modern facilities of Radio Zambia, which the government of Kenneth Kaunda had loaned the ANC.

We watched them work, listened to the broadcasts they put together, and made notes toward assembling an album. Thanks to Tom, Victor, Golden, Richmond, and Cassius – names we did not dare include when we first released the LP. We listened to days of tapes and made selections and transferred material to bring back to Rounder. We didn't include any of the commercial recordings (such as Makeba) but did our best to provide a representative sample of the broadcasts in twenty-four selections released on Rounder in March 1986. Operating on a shoestring, as they were, the militants often reused the recording tape they had, recording new broadcasts over old, so much of the material broadcast was lost forever. One wonders how much survives today – but the Rounder album does: *Radio Freedom: Voice of the African National Congress and the People's Army Umkhonto We Sizwe* (Rounder 4019).

A few years later, following that year's MIDEM conference in Cannes, Yleana and I were hitch-hiking across the Sahara Desert from Algeria to Niger. Picked up by some Frenchmen driving automobiles south to sell them in Niger, we were listening to the radio on the night of February 2, 1990, and heard the news broadcast that, elsewhere in Africa, the de Klerk government in South Africa announced it had rescinded the ban on the ANC and that Nelson Mandela would be freed from prison. It was a bizarre place to be when we got the news, but it was exciting news.

Mandela was actually freed on February 11 and spoke from the balcony of the Cape Town City Hall. Soon afterward, I got an invitation from some music business friends in South Africa, inviting me to come for a big event planned – the "welcome home Mandela" concert to be held in Johannesburg at Ellis Park. That wasn't something I wanted to miss! Yleana and I made the trip. It was billed as the Human Rainbow Concert and took place on March 17, 1990. Among the artists who performed were Brenda Fassie, Ray Phiri with Stimela, Mahlathini & the Mahotella Queens, Jennifer Ferguson, Mzwakhe Mbuli (we had released his Shifty album *Change is Pain* in 1988), P.J. Powers, Mango Groove, Johnny Clegg, and Thomas Mapfumo. The highlight, of course, was when Mandela appeared on stage.[115]

Thabo Mbeki served as President of South Africa from 1999 to 2008.

In 2009, Stephen R. Davis wrote a thesis on Radio Freedom, which helped earn him a master's degree from the University of Florida.[116]

Records such as *Radio Freedom*, different as they were, all seemed part of the continuum in ways that – to us – made sense. They all fit within the mission we saw for Rounder, just as recording Snuffy Jenkins and Pappy Sherrill did.

I'm writing this approaching Rounder's fiftieth anniversary. One sometimes looks back and considers what life has been all about, whether we were fortunate enough to have found some value in what we might have accomplished. As I was wrapping up my first draft of this book in late 2018, I came across an article Barry Mazor wrote for the *Wall Street Journal* at time of our fortieth anniversary. He quoted Michael Scully, from an interview he had done with Michael:

> They went on to raise that roots-music flag high. The sheer quantity – over 3,500 records by now – and the quality of their releases demanded attention for it. They made it plain that roots music was not just "old stuff," or even old-sounding stuff, but could be vibrant and beautifully recorded, and they put out records by working musicians who were ready to tour in professional shows, rather than just reviving older recordings. Unlike most post-folk-revival roots labels, they were never a one-genre label; they were more like a 50-genre label, and they showed that "roots music" could be cool stuff. When you do all that, and reach as many people as they have, you start changing the concept of what roots or folk music is in the modern world.

The Rounder founders taken on the last day before Rounder moved from Massachusetts to Nashville in 2013. Left to right Marian Leighton Levy, Ken Irwin, and the author.
Photograph by Liza Levy.

That made me feel good.

So did something Alison Krauss told Mr. Mazor:

> Rounder is about tending to the whole career of a musician. I was a kid when I started there; I thought I was going to be a choir director. They seem to enjoy the process of someone's whole musical adventure, good and bad. For me, that's meant not just the ability to record, but being left alone, musically, to play with the band and become who I was going to become. Everybody in the music business wants a successful record, and so do the people at Rounder, but they have that love for music, and for traditional music, for what it is. I love that, and I love being on the same label as a hog-calling album. That's my speed![117]

Even when we were in our first decade, people would ask what the future might hold. I always said it was my goal to see Rounder turn fifty – half a century old. We made it.

Afterword

My earliest memory of music dates to when I was four years old, and on a family vacation in Old Orchard Beach, Maine. My mother Betty was visited by her two sisters Jane and Neva, and their husbands and kids. Jane's husband Paul Gourlay worked for the public school system in Denver, and I can remember him playing 'Goodnight Irene' on his harmonica every night when it was time for me to go to bed. He had a few other tunes he played, too, but the only other one I remember was 'She'll Be Coming 'Round the Mountain.' That was the summer of 1949.

I don't remember another thing about music until another family gathering, this time at Quonochontaug, Rhode Island, in the late summer of 1956. All the grown-ups, and some of my older cousins, were talking about Elvis Presley and his new record 'Hound Dog.' This is also one of my first memories of social controversy. There was something about Elvis shaking his hips – "Elvis the Pelvis" – that got everyone talking. I didn't get the sense that anyone in my family particularly disapproved, but it was clear that there was some controversy in the broader society about Elvis. The only earlier controversy that I remember, and it is much dimmer, related to the Army/McCarthy hearings of a few years earlier, but I had no idea at the time what that was about.

It wasn't long after that summer that I bought my first record, a 45 that I bought at Peter's Music in Lexington, Massachusetts, where I grew up. I was born in Jamaica Plain, in the City of Boston, but when I turned five and started first grade (a year early), my parents apparently didn't like what they saw in the Boston public schools and took a big financial risk, moving to Lexington, a suburb known for its excellent schools. I finished up first grade in Lexington, and graduated in 1962 from L.H.S.

My father Bill (Senior) was a salesman. He sold labels for Allen-Bradley, two-way radios for RCA, and electronic components for a Cambridge company named Cambridge Thermionic (Cambion). He developed colitis working for RCA, since he was selling a product he believed inferior to Motorola's as he worked to try to keep the family afloat financially. He did bring home quite a few RCA Victor record albums, though. With Cambion, he worked his way up to become president of the company. One choice the company made that had an impression on me: they did not sell their products to the military.

My mother Betty (Binkley) was from Denver; her Hoosier father worked for Armour, the meat packing firm, as an auditor, and was transferred to Boston. He brought home some really thick steaks. My grandparents on my mother's side of the family lived with us until I was eight. I never met my grandparents on my father's side; his mother had wanted him to become a Catholic priest and instead he married a non-Catholic, a non-Christian even (Unitarian). They never spoke to him again, even though we lived just five miles apart. My mother had worked as a secretary for a while but, after I was born, she worked as a homemaker and took care of me and my younger sisters Joyce and Lisa. I remember seeing paternal grandfather William's name in the Boston phone book, but never met him. I saw my grandmother once, and only once, when she came for dinner the night after his funeral.

That taught me something about tolerance. So did an experience driving south to visit Washington DC back when I was a young teenager in the very late 1950s. There were few interstate highways back then, so it was slow-going on relatively small roads. It was a very hot day and all five of us were packed into the family car. There was, of course, no air conditioning back then. We were hungry and very thirsty, and driving through Maryland. After about forty-five minutes to an hour, seeing no place to stop, finally, way up ahead on the left, was a café. We let out a cheer. My father pulled into the lot, parked the car, and we all got out. When we got to the door, my father saw a simple sign in the window beside the door: WHITES ONLY. "Back in the car!" he said. We weren't going to eat at a place like that. We survived, of course, but he'd made an impression on me.

As a child, I always liked to count things, and to make lists of things like the longest rivers in the world. All I did was copy the lists out of books, but I guess it represented an interest in organization and ranking that probably led to my being better at business than I might otherwise have been. I was also a collector, from coins to comic books. From around the age of twelve, I would take the subway into Boston and scour the Scollay Square area for old discounted comics, books, and magazines. There were a lot of tattoo parlors and a few burlesque houses there at the time, but it's all been renovated away.

I started collecting records, too. My first 45 was a country and western single by Rusty Draper called 'The Railroad Runs through the Middle of the House'. On the other side was a rockabilly number, 'Pink Cadillac'. I had no idea that this was country music. It was just a song I liked, so I bought my first record. The second record I bought was by Elvis: 'Hound Dog' b/w 'Don't Be Cruel'.

I listened to WMEX in Boston, 1510 on the AM radio dial, where the DJ in the evenings was Arnie "Woo Woo" Ginsburg. I never did make it to his main sponsor, Adventure Car Hop, even though the jingle proclaimed it "the place to go."

> Adventure Car Hop is the place to go
> For food that's always right.
> Adventure food is always just so.
> (You'll relish every bite!)
> Out on Route One in Saugus,
> Come dressed just as you are.
> Adventure, where the service is tops,
> And you never get out of your car.

I did spend many evenings, after Arnie's show, listening to *The Jerry Williams Show* – one of the very first talk radio shows in the country. Jerry was often provocative; one frequent guest was Malcolm X. But listening to Arnie Ginsburg's *Night Train* show exposed me to all this great music. (The album *Cruisin' 1961* features "Woo Woo" Ginsburg as the host.)

I bought quite a few singles over the next two or three years – maybe fifty or so. Truth be told, I shoplifted a few as well. Sorry, Peters Music Store. If you hadn't gone out of business decades ago (not because of me, I'm sure), I'd give you some Rounder CDs to make up for it.

My parents got me a 45 rpm record changer and I would sometimes play the same record over and over again, maybe as many as ten or fifteen times in a row. 'Party Doll' by Buddy Knox, 'Tonight You Belong to Me' by Patience & Prudence, 'Rip It Up' by Little Richard, Chuck Berry's 'Sweet Little Sixteen,' and Buddy Holly's 'Peggy Sue.' My all-time record for playing the same song repeatedly was 1961's 'Hit the Road, Jack' by Ray Charles. I'd listen while I played a little made-up baseball game in my room, whacking marbles with a little wooden toy dowel into the drawers of my dresser. I pulled out each drawer further than the drawer above it; a ball hit into the bottom drawer was a single, the next door up, a double, and so forth and so on.

I took piano lessons for a couple of years, but almost nothing took. I took trumpet lessons for five days, but the first thing I wanted to do was to run down to the field behind the house and play baseball with the other kids. It was a field that Mr. Duffy let us clear and maintain as a baseball field. My mother was in the church choir and my sisters sang some there, too. I can't even sing in key.

I used to get the printed Top 40 sheet that one of the local radio stations distributed to the record stores, and each week one of the singers would be depicted in the upper right-hand corner. That was my first look at some of these singers I liked – Chuck Berry, Guy Mitchell, the Everly Brothers, the Coasters, and more. Little Richard, with all that hair, definitely looked different, but then again so did Buddy Holly with those glasses. Radio was really open in those days, willing to play pop music like Bobby Pickett's 'Monster Mash' and any number of other novelty songs. The musical comedy of Buchanan & Goodman were real favorites of mine, the way they worked pop music bits into dramatic scenarios they created.

These were all 45s. It wasn't until 1959 that I bought my first LP, *Mr. "Personality"* by Lloyd Price. My second LP was *What'd I Say* by Ray Charles, and the first concert I ever attended was a Ray Charles show in downtown Boston at the Orpheum. I was fourteen at the time. I really never went to that many shows, but that was a great one to have as my first. (Oddly enough, at a Wrigley Field baseball game in the summer of 2015 during a Society for American Baseball Research (SABR) convention, I sat next to a guy who was originally from Boston and we got to talking, and he had been to the same Ray Charles show at the Orpheum some fifty-six years earlier.)

Up to this point, most of the music I'd heard had been at home. That included sort of half-listening to the records my father brought home. Neither of my parents actually spent much time listening to music, but certainly *Belafonte at Carnegie Hall* (also released in 1959) was one of my favorites. So was a wacky song on a Christmas album that we dragged out once a year, to full family hilarity – my parents, my two younger sisters, and me. The album was *Voices of Christmas* by the Voices of Walter Schumann, and the song was 'Christmas Tree.'

The music I liked was, as far as I know, the same music that a lot of other kids liked. I had a few friends that I'd talk music with, though not a lot of them. We didn't categorize music, or know that there was music called country music, or rhythm and blues, or whatever. I think we thought it was all rock 'n' roll. I did discover folk music, though, when I was sixteen, mainly through my younger sister Joyce, who got a couple of Kingston Trio LPs. I really liked them.

Growing up in Lexington, I'd enjoyed a somewhat idyllic life in a suburb that was quiet and yet with a rich history. The church in which I was raised was the Follen Community Church, not tied to any denomination. The church's ministers came from Unitarian backgrounds. My parents were both active in the church – my mother in the choir and my father as both the MC at the annual church fair and one of the key people involved in the Christmas tree sale each December. I enjoyed both the commercial activities – working at the fair and helping sell the Christmas trees. It was an added and very meaningful bonus to me that the Follen Church was legitimately the "Christmas tree church": its founder in 1839, Charles Follen, had been the man who had introduced the Christmas tree custom to America, importing it from his native Germany. He'd reportedly had to leave Germany due to his "radical organizing" work there.[118]

Though I never enjoyed the church service itself, I loved ringing the church bell on Sunday mornings. At age eight or nine, pulling the thick rope that rang the bell took all the strength I could muster and it was a thrill to have the rope lift me off my feet as it rose back up after pulling it down. Sometimes I needed a bit of help to get it started, but then riding it up and down while I made the bell toll was both immensely satisfying and just a lot of fun.

Sunday school at the church was formative. Because it was, in effect, a Unitarian church, there was no catechism. We spent a lot of time studying nature; I think I learned more about tree leaves and the like in Sunday school than in regular school. Stan Brown's father Sandy was a great hands-on teacher who would talk about the Romans of Jesus' day, and then have us each make our own molds for Roman-style coins, liquefy metal, and pour and create our own Roman money. When we studied David and Goliath, we all wove our own slings and went out to the meadows behind the church and practiced flinging rocks. He had a cider press, too, and in the fall we'd pick apples from the trees and make our own apple cider. This truly was a childhood with idyllic aspects.

I did set the Maple Street bridge on fire once, but that's another story. So was the time the bomb squad was called out from Hanscom Field Air Force Base simply because of a couple of cardboard toilet paper rolls I had wrapped in black friction tape with some electrical wire sticking out. At the time it seemed like a more innocent prank than it would today.

When we studied theology, we studied other religions and how they worshipped. The eighth-grade class visited Congregational and Episcopal churches, but also a Buddhist temple in the area, a mosque, and a Catholic church. I literally fainted at one point during the Catholic ceremony; I really never was one for church services.

Lexington was a pretty homogeneous suburb at the time, pretty much all "white" and middle class. The Republican Party had a small office in the center of town at election times; the Democrat Party had no visible presence. At the time – this changed dramatically in the later 1960s – I was a Republican. "Democrats are dirty rats" – I have no idea where that came from, but I remember the refrain. In 1960, I reached up and touched Richard Nixon's hand reaching out from the crowd on Boston's Tremont Street as his motorcade traveled by. Why he was campaigning in Massachusetts, with John F. Kennedy as his opponent that year, I don't know, but there were crowds along both sides of the street.

Our family was the second in the neighborhood to get a television set; given that it was the early 1950s, it had a small screen and was black and white, but the kids from the neighborhood would all come over and watch *The Howdy Doody Show* in the afternoons, and *Kukla, Fran, and Ollie*. We lived in a real nuclear family in a real neighborhood, and we didn't lock the doors, even if we did have our share of odd characters such as Mrs. Tyler, who lived next door and took in boarders. One of them was a bit deficient in her perceptions and would run away every so often, sometimes only getting as far as our house – maybe seventy-five feet away – before coming to the door and ringing the bell and telling us she was lost. For a year or so, I walked

Mrs. Tyler's poodles. They were otherwise kept in her basement where they often relieved themselves. There were quiet folks like the Solbergs, who kept to themselves, and there was Ed Walsh, the bachelor, who lived across the street until one day when I was maybe in my very early teens he got married. The practical joker side of me may have come from my father. He told me that, at Mr. Walsh's wedding reception, he'd slipped something into his drink that would cause the new bridegroom to pee blue the next morning. We also had two Catholic families: the Kellys and the McCarthys, each with twelve children. It was a shock one day when Bruce Kelly just disappeared. He was about a year or two older than me. He'd last been seen walking down the railroad tracks beside his house; there were some travel brochures left behind in his room. It was more than ten years later before we learned he'd somehow gotten into the Marines at age sixteen. In 2018, I was pleasantly surprised when one of his younger brothers came up and introduced himself to me at a book reading I was doing.

Just as the Follen Church had been tied to history (Ralph Waldo Emerson preached there for a while), the town itself was situated in history. Lexington was visited by tourists from all over, wanting to visit the "Birthplace of American Liberty." Children have a natural inclination to see themselves as the center of the universe, and perhaps I was indulged by the background of the town and time in which I was raised. The United States of the 1950s and into the 1960s was the paramount power on earth, economically and militarily – yet it seemed to stand for the highest of ideals. And Boston was the cradle of democracy in the New World (as well as a center for abolition and leadership in the later fight for civil rights). I identified with the farmers and blacksmiths in Lexington who were the seventy-seven men out on the town common on the morning of April 19, 1775 when the first shots of the American Revolution were fired, and where seven of them lost their lives. I identified with the Sons of Liberty such as Sam Adams, James Otis, and John Hancock who gave voice to the high ideals of their countrymen who sought self-government and freedom from the impositions of the British Crown. And I identified with the frugality of the early Brahmins of Boston's Beacon Hill who may have been wealthy bankers and merchants but who brought their lunch to work in a brown paper bag which they then folded and took home to be used again. Today, that's called recycling.

Practicing thrift helped build Rounder, without a doubt. The pleasure of doing business at the Christmas tree sale contributed as well. Other than delivering newspapers, which I did for a year at age eight, and then again for six years through junior high and high school, my main job started when I was fourteen: I took a test to be licensed and then became an Official Historic Guide on the Lexington Battle Green. There was no national park in the area at the time. It was me out there by myself.

I felt I was an important conveyor of Lexington history, and America's history, to the many visitors who came to town during the seven summers that I worked on the Battle Green – throughout high school and college. Money was a motivator, too, and I enjoyed seeing if I could reel in $10 or so on a weekday and $20 or double that on a weekend. I worked seven days a week at it – not because I had to, since there was no supervisor, no place I signed in or reported to, and not because my parents set any quota or expectation. I only did it because I wanted to. It made me feel like I was doing good work, and I did enjoy turning the money over to my parents. I had no salary, but only worked for tips, and yet there was an inherent satisfaction I felt in teaching the history of the Battle of Lexington and its place in history. There were times when I would talk for fifteen or twenty minutes and not receive a tip. That was disappointing, but if I knew I'd done a good job connecting with the people, I felt at least partially rewarded. Many years later, looking back on my work with Rounder, I realize that much of the same motivation applied. Economic reward became more important when faced with the responsibilities of earning a living for myself and others dependent on me, but was never the sole motivation. The other rewards of the work we've done at Rounder are important ones as well.

The import of what the citizens of Lexington had done inspired me. These were, as indicated, farmers and tavern keepers – living in a small rural community – and yet they believed so strongly in self-government that they took up arms in rebellion against their own government. I loved shocking some of the tourists by underscoring to them just how courageous this was – that what we now call "patriotism" was called "treason" by the powers-that-were in 1775. It was as though, I explained, the United States Army came marching up Massachusetts Avenue and confronted a band of armed men prepared to protect their town and the gunpowder they'd stored (at the town meetinghouse, no less), and to risk being branded as traitors. The men of Lexington typified those in the communities around them. Eight were killed on the Battle Green (seven from Lexington, one from neighboring Woburn), and the British proceeded on their mission to seize ammunition supplies in Concord. A skirmish broke out there at the Old North Bridge and two men from each side were killed. By the end of that day, the British troops were driven in disarray back into the City of Boston (where they holed up under siege for the next eleven months), and seventy-three British soldiers had been killed and another 174 wounded. The die was cast.

In fact, so reads the inscription on the monument on the Battle Green where the Lexington men are buried:

> Sacred to the Liberty and the Rights of Mankind!!! The Freedom and Independence of America – sealed and defended with the blood of her sons – This Monument is erected by the inhabitants of Lexington, under the patronage and at the expense of the Commonwealth of Massachusetts, to the memory of their Fellow-citizens, Ensign Robert Monroe, Messrs. Jonas Parker, Samuel Hadley,

Jonathan Harrington, Jr., Isaac Muzzy, Caleb Harrington, and John Brown, of Lexington, and Asahel Porter, of Woburn, who fell on this Field, the first victims of the Sword of British Tyranny and Oppression, on the morning of the ever-memorable Nineteenth of April, An. Domini 1775. The Die was cast!!! The blood of these martyrs in the Cause of God and their Country was the cement of the Union of these States, then colonies, and gave the Spring to the Spirit, Firmness, and Resolution of their Fellow-citizens. They rose as one man to revenge their Brethren's blood, and at the point of the sword to assert and defend their native Rights. They nobly dared to be Free!!! The contest was long, bloody, and affecting. Righteous Heaven approved the Solemn Appeal; Victory crowned their Arms, and the Peace, Liberty, and Independence of the United States of America was their glorious reward.

I made sure to always finish my talk at the collective grave and, with my back to the monument, recited the text from memory. It was a rousing end to my talk – whether it had been a five-minute quickie or the twenty-minute version I preferred (since it offered me the chance to teach more about the battle). I usually got a dollar either way, but I was into teaching. The image of the blood of these men becoming the cement of the Union *always* inspired me. I could have recited the text in rote fashion but, just as when I became a teacher in the 1970s, I always made myself feel the words and thus could better connect more deeply with my audience.

I never felt that the later work I did with Rounder was dissociated with what came before; rather, there has been continuity. Even when plunging into writing a couple of dozen books about Red Sox baseball in later years, it's always felt as though it all ties together. From 1957 and the one-page neighborhood flyer, *The Home Run*, to 2008 and the 545 pages of *Red Sox Threads*, or *Tom Yawkey* with its over 1,500 footnotes, there is continuity as well. One way or another, it's celebrating and teaching American popular culture and history.

There is a background to my political involvement. In 1966–67, I had studied – hard – at the University of Chicago for a year living at 61st and Ellis in an apartment shared with a lovey-dovey couple who just wanted a third person to share the rent. Working through a job placement service at UC, I did some babysitting for one dollar an hour for a little extra spending money. I hit the books so effectively that I managed to win a three-year scholarship called the Graham Aldis Award, for students who had not received financial aid but had excelled in their first year. In the summer of 1967, I cashed in on an offer my father had made me: $1,000 to let me travel anywhere I wanted. These were the days when Arthur Frommer's book *Europe On 5 Dollars a Day* was still pegged to that sort of a budget. Other than New York with Ken and hitching back and forth from Chicago to Boston a couple of times (being let off in the snow at 2.30 am at a remote intersection near Jackson, Michigan threatened to be a problem, but the next ride came within fifteen or twenty minutes), I had never really left home. College was only seven miles away, so it was even feasible to go home every other weekend, to do some laundry, have a meal, maybe borrow the car.

Taking the summer of '67 off to hitchhike around Europe for ten weeks was a real adventure: landing in London and making my way up to Inverness (I devoted a full forty-five minutes to looking for the Loch Ness Monster, gave up and moved on), and then down through Wales, across France, down through Italy to Sicily and back up north through Venice and into Trieste – crossing over into Yugoslavia. This was a Communist country, where Tito was the dictator. Entering Yugoslavia was going behind the Iron Curtain.

That wasn't my first trip on my own. There was to be a re-enactment of the hundredth anniversary of the First Battle of Bull Run – which, on July 21, 1861, more or less kicked off the Civil War – and Stan Brown and I packed our bicycles on a bus from Boston to Washington DC. We were sixteen. We then rode to Manassas, Virginia – about thirty-one miles – and saw the re-enactment, which involved about 2,200 re-enactors. We planned to spend the night about twenty-two miles away at Gilbert's Corner, Virginia, which we'd seen on a map. Turns out it was only on the map because there was nothing else there! It was a gas station owned by someone named Gilbert. We went on to Leesburg. We went to the police department and asked if they knew someone who rented rooms. They referred us to some pastor, who in lieu of asking his parishioners, invited us to stay with his family. The next day we biked to Harpers Ferry, West Virginia. Our final stop was Gettysburg. We took the bus home from there. These places were all closer to each other than one might think. But, come the early days of the twenty-first century, I started riding my bike again to help raise money for charity in the Pan-Mass Challenge (PMC). Money raised benefits the Jimmy Fund, to fight cancer in children. For a few years, I rode the two-day 192-mile ride but, after I turned seventy, I did the one-day fifty-mile route instead. In 2019, PMC riders collectively raised $63,000,000 for the Jimmy Fund. That's a pretty astonishing total for one year coming from one charity bicycle ride.

The infatuation with Barry Goldwater had worn off during the 1964 Presidential campaign. I became disillusioned when "AuH$_2$O" allowed himself to be portrayed as a segregationist (despite both his personal and family history of integration of the Arizona Air National Guard and Goldwater's Department Store, as well as his own interest in Native American rights). It was the libertarian side of Goldwater that had had the most appeal – his opposition to the military draft, for instance. Goldwater wasn't a segregationist, but the Republican Party was embarked on a "Southern strategy" to try to wrest the South away from the Democrats. It worked, not for Goldwater himself, but much of the next forty years, even through the elections of Barack Obama and his successor who I will not name, still sees the South largely in

Republican hands. I still believe that, at some level, Goldwater sacrificed his own ambitions for those of the party (probably realizing he had little chance to win as LBJ was running for election, not all that long after he'd taken over for the assassinated JFK). In any event, I had slipped into an apolitical period on a personal level – though still very interested academically in political theory, interested in how people relate to power, how political socialization affects our perceptions of life and politics.

Here's how I explained it to Harvard researcher Lara Pellegrinelli:

> What interested me was political psychology as I called it or political socialization as it was usually called at the time. I think it probably still is, but I like calling it the other thing. But socialization in terms of how do kids develop their attitude about politics. The very first book was written at that time by a guy named Fred Greenstein which was called *Political Socialization* and that was a book that really excited me. How do kids develop their attitudes about the president, how do they think about the President of the United States? What do they think about their country? What do they think about the mayor of Boston or their state representatives, if they even think about them? Supposedly, according to studies and so forth, if you were to take a poll in the United States now, about 25% now could not accurately tell you the name of the President of the United States. Some would guess correctly, others might guess past presidents, but in terms of actually saying who the current president was – and that's the office with the best name recognition. From there, you go down the spectrum. Who is your state representative? Probably 15% of the people know that.
>
> I was also interested in broader issues and by graduate school, I got more interested. I was really interested in electoral politics and so things like government and how kids develop their attitudes about that; by the time I got into graduate school, I'd expanded that to things like power in general. Why do some people seek power? Why do some people respond to powerful leaders? Why does a Hitler attract attention? What need does he fulfill for people that want to be followers? You see that phenomena in the music business too in terms of celebrity. Why do people like celebrities? Almost everybody does. Almost everybody, if a famous person walked into the room, their voice would quiet down, they'd look at them, they couldn't take their eyes off them maybe if they were eating at a table in a crowded restaurant a large percentage of the heads would be eating largely like this, watching the person. And then, of course, people like to shoot them and kill them, too, it seems. So there's a kind of fascination there. It gets into all sorts of questions about racism, questions about sexism, and things

like that. Why do we develop the kind of attitudes we have about things? That very first book went into a lot of things about attitudes of the president. When President Kennedy was killed, many people, if not most of the people in the United States, cried and it was by doing some historical research that they found that the same thing had happened when Franklin D. Roosevelt died, when he was in office. And yet, all these people never met President Kennedy, hated him in fact because they were Republicans and he stood for all the things they didn't want to, but they were still emotionally moved by this because he was the father of our country in some sense; and that's what people said and people in mental institutions that were interviewed, too, said the same kinds of things. They couldn't explain it, but they were grief-stricken. It was if a very close member of their family had suddenly died. And that kind of phenomenon was what I was interested in.

I had different study habits from most other students. I used to hole myself up in the library the first four or five weeks of a semester and do all the reading for the entire semester right away. I always set myself an 11.00 limit; I wasn't going to study past 11.00 pm. So I never pulled all-nighters, and once I got all the reading done I was freer to goof off. When we graduated, I was one of the two people at Tufts who graduated *magna cum laude*, and about five or six people came up to me after the graduation ceremony and said, "I didn't know you were smart!" That was kind of funny. They'd never seen me study. It helped in test-taking that I had a very good short-term photographic memory.[119]

Back to the border post, about to enter Communist Yugoslavia. I arrived on foot. I was feeling a bit apprehensive. Would I be strip-searched (as I had been when arriving at Heathrow – longhairs were not necessarily fully welcome even in the London of Carnaby Street days)? No, not at the border crossing, it turns out. There was a plaque with a red star on it, a flag with a red star, and all that, but the border guard took my passport, stamped it, handed it back, and when I asked with gestures "What next?" he just waved his hand dismissively as to say, "Go." It would have been a different experience altogether if I'd first entered the Iron Curtain countries by way of the crossing in East Berlin.

They had youth hostels in Yugoslavia, too. $1.00 per night was the typical tariff; I did in fact pull off Europe not on five dollars a day, but on just two dollars a day for room and board, not counting the cost of the occasional train or ferry. On average, maybe two nights a week were spent sleeping in parks or on benches – once standing in a Scottish phone booth writing letters home and reading by the light in the booth. A tent on the roof of a building in downtown Athens set me back nine drachmas (about 27¢ at the time), and for four days hitching north from the then sleepy seaside town of Marmaris in southern Turkey north to Istanbul I didn't spend even one Turkish lira – it was a remarkable experience. Not one vehicle, not even a horse-drawn cart, ever passed by without giving the hitch-hiker a ride, and meals and drink were offered at every stop. My sister Joyce had been a foreign exchange student with the American Field Service and lived with the Akyoruk family in Istanbul during the summer of 1965. Her "Turkish sister" Neside came and lived with the Nowlin family in Lexington for the second half of the 1965–66 school year. So now, come the summer of '67, I headed toward Istanbul and spent a few days visiting with the Akyoruks, and seeing the city situated on the crossroads of Asia and Europe.

One evening there, living in Kadıköy on the Asian side, helped further set the stage for the new stage of politics to come in the fall of 1967. People were already asking me – quite sincerely not understanding – why it was that black people in America were not able to vote and were discriminated against. They were asking me why America had so many tens of thousands of soldiers fighting against Vietnamese halfway around the world from the United States. The answers I tried to come up weren't convincing even to me. The evening that tipped the balance for me was when the family went to a "drive-in" movie theater (there weren't any cars, and it was really just a movie screen set up in a field where we sat on logs), and recent internet research tells me that the film was *Inside Daisy Clover* with Natalie Wood. The one scene I remember featured a flashy new convertible being driven into a swimming pool and slowly sinking. Great hilarity. But I was mortified. This is what the rest of the world really thinks America is like? They weren't seeing what real life was like on the South Side of Chicago – and I knew I'd never experienced true grit, since I was a reasonably well-off college student. I was one who was frugal enough, though, returning home, after ten weeks on the Continent with $300 left over which I turned back to my father.

I crossed back into Europe, hitching up through Bulgaria. Arriving in Sofia, I went to this one hotel and was told it was for Communists only. "OK," I said, winging it. "I'm a Communist." That didn't work; it was only for certain Communists, the kind that were in countries allied with the Bulgarians. I finally found another place to stay. But it was all pretty humorous and there didn't seem to be evil torturers lurking on every corner. East Berlin was still in *really* bad shape, economically. I entered a supermarket to find that all they had in the entire store that day were hot cross buns . . . well, "Bitte," I said, pointing to the hot cross buns and holding out the single Ostmark I had. That was my food that day. That border was like a real Communist border, with the Wall and all.

Come November 1989, my wife Yleana and I were having dinner in Krakow. We had just visited Auschwitz and Buchenwald that day, when we heard that the Wall was being knocked down. We'd just left East Berlin, gone to Dresden and then to Warsaw. We changed our plans for onward travel and got back to Berlin as quickly as we could, arriving two days later. We each took a few swings with the sledgehammers – that wall was really well reinforced; it was hard to knock off more than a small chip. But it's a nice souvenir.

In 1967, leaving Bulgaria I made my way to Munich, where the Hofbräuhaus was great fun – but, after visiting Dachau the following day, I wanted nothing more than to get out of Germany as fast as I could, to get to Amsterdam. All these former Nazis (so I imagined, and many of them were indeed the right age) were driving right by me – not even stopping for a hitch-hiker – in their new Mercedes. I'm afraid I shot a few derisive Hitler salutes at rear-view mirrors.

While on Crete, I met another traveler, Bill Kornrich, and then, by pure coincidence, we met again in the covered bazaar in Istanbul. Bill had just graduated Brandeis and was going to the University of Chicago in the fall. I was about to start my second year, so we decided to room together. Bob Greenberg, another Brandeis grad, was our third roommate. They were more into leftist politics than I was. That October, even as all I'd experienced traveling around Europe was still percolating in my head, they said, "Hey, let's go to the march on the Pentagon" and I figured, "Sure, why not?"

I wasn't opposed to the war in Vietnam. It probably seems strange for someone studying politics, given that the war had been on in earnest for more than two years, but I hadn't really thought about it much before being asked some questions I couldn't answer while traveling in Europe. And I'd always been interested in what one might call political theater – for instance, when George Rockwell and the American Nazi Party had provocatively marched in downtown Boston, I went to see what that was all about. My interest in politics itself grew out of watching on TV all the balloons and goofy hats and partying by delegates at the 1956 Republican national convention. Then I collected all sorts of "I Like Ike" buttons at the town's GOP campaign office. I wore a jacket covered with maybe thirty of them. There was no such thing as an office for the Democrats in Lexington in those days.

I did walk a lot that summer in Europe. My parents gave me a pedometer and I wrote down how much I'd walked each day. Nerdy? By journey's end, it was 561½ miles, an average of over eight miles a day – more or less the distance from Boston to Cleveland.

Making our way to DC, with hundreds of others streaming in from all corners, I found that I was part of a larger community, even a tribe of sorts. I already had pretty long hair, not having cut it since sometime earlier in the year (it would actually be 1974, seven years later, before I had it cut again – by Larry Mathis, the banjo player for the Pinnacle Boys, no less).

Here were all these other kindred souls, an estimated 100,000 of us. And it didn't take long to convert to the cause, as we faced off against these Deputy Marshals on the steps of the Pentagon. There was little time to ruminate on the legitimacy of differing points of view. When the Marshals started clubbing a few people, my reaction was instinctive. I knew which side I was on. Even the usmarshals.gov website admits today that the Marshals "responded to the rioters with increasingly rough treatment," blaming it on their physical exhaustion. What it leaves out is there wasn't much of anything in the way of rioting. There were one or two small groups that tried to break into the building, but they were quickly repulsed. The rest of us were just milling around, chanting slogans and the like. Not welcome, but not really doing anything that wrong. After the happening, we went back to Chicago.

Come springtime, things were heating up and, after Martin Luther King was assassinated, the three of us had to move out of our South Side apartment for about a week, passing tanks on the streets on our way to another location. We were the only white people in about a five-block radius, living at the corner of 65th and Cottage Grove in an apartment above the Malcolm X bookstore. Needless to say, the police in Chicago had their eyes on that bookstore. We were becoming increasingly radicalized, stopped at gunpoint and searched on two occasions that winter by police. We asked, "What are you looking for?" Weapons, we were told. "Oh, we're pacifists," we said, not very convincingly. "Well, we'll look for drugs, then." "You're getting warmer," we said, though keeping things light wasn't easy.

Some of us went down to the National Guard armory, to try to block the troops from leaving there to deploy in the black areas of the city. We were wearing metal helmets – and, in my case, fortunately a fairly thick brown leather jacket. Otherwise the bayonet that did pierce me in the shoulder would have done more damage. It was really just a minor flesh wound.

It was a time when we knew the U.S. was waging war in Vietnam, killing large numbers of Vietnamese who seemed to be fighting for independence, while black Americans were still discriminated against at home. Many of us felt an obligation to put our bodies on the line, in protest marches or demonstrations, and believed that if we weren't actually in jail, it was proof positive that we weren't doing enough to fight for the right.

Martin Luther King had been leading the Poor People's Campaign since December 1967, intending to converge on Washington for a campaign meant to unite the anti-war movement with the civil rights struggle and to fight against poverty in America in alliance with the poor whites in places like Appalachia, and with other disadvantaged groups. One could well argue that part of the reason he was killed was because he was becoming too much of a threat, encompassing more than just the movement for equal rights for black Americans. Nowadays, after the election (and re-election) of Barack Obama, many aren't old enough to recall that, only three years before that time, the Civil Rights Act of 1964 had first outlawed racial discrimination in schools, public housing, and employment, followed by the Voting Rights Act of 1965 which attempted to ensure that black citizens could vote without discriminatory obstacles being placed in their way by local voting boards.

When King was shot in Memphis, the Poor People's march was put on hold as over a hundred American cities experienced real rioting. Several weeks later, with Ralph Abernathy taking up King's mantle as best he could,

Bill Kornrich and I built a plywood A-frame dwelling on the Mall as part of "Resurrection City" on May 12 and lived there for the next several weeks until the District got tired of us and the bulldozers arrived on June 24. There was some disillusionment as the leaders of the march stayed elsewhere while we were slogging around in several inches of mud, literally wearing torn deflated air mattresses for boots, strapping them over our shoes to protect against the mud. We were eating bologna sandwiches – every day, for a couple of weeks. We knew the leaders were living in hotels or with hosts. We both became bored, and a little upset at the inequities, so we published a humor newsletter (with the provocative title *Americong*) needling the leaders for not living with the people. It wasn't that well received, and the food never did improve.

After the bulldozers scraped the Mall clean, I went back home to Boston. After the summer of 1968 played out, I spent much of the following year living in New York City – moving there in the fall of 1968 to pursue a romance with Janie Julianelli.

Getting a license to drive a taxi was difficult: the NYPD vet all applicants for a hackney license and the FBI had transposed two numbers in my arrest record, showing me having been arrested in Berkeley back in May during a weekend of rioting there. They had me down for a 594 instead of a 495 (or whatever the numbers were): armed robbery of a bank instead of a simple disturbing the peace for being out on a march after the city was supposed to be locked down under curfew. I spent a night in the Santa Rita Correctional Facility before being bailed out; the father of a friend from Chicago, Louise Brotsky, was one of the top two or three "movement lawyers" in the Bay Area. After getting bailed out, smuggling out my detention center garb as a souvenir of sorts – a "Santa Rita"-stenciled pale blue denim work shirt under my regular clothes (risking rearrest on other charges) – I met up with Ken and Marian, who were at one of the crash pads in the Haight. It's difficult now to remember how we all knew where to find each other, in the days before cellphones.

I had been awaiting Janie, who was supposed to fly in to San Francisco after I'd taken a driveaway car across country – but she got cold feet, never showed, and never called. Finally, tracked down, she confessed she wasn't coming. Time for me to turn around and go back home. Nevertheless, romance called stubbornly and that's when I left to move to New York to be closer to her. Her mother was a famous shoe designer and Janie might have been a few steps too high up the social ladder for it ever to truly work.[120] I worked nights at Macy's before Christmas, restocking the toy department as part of a crew of about a dozen who had to straighten things up after the devastation wreaked by shoppers and their kids during shopping hours. The damage was sometimes made a little worse as the workers would often stage big battles with toy guns, climbing over the displays and "fighting it out" in the first hour or so on the job. Then we'd get down to work, go out for "lunch" around 3 am – this is, after all, the city that never sleeps. Driving a cab – when the FBI finally admitted to the first error in its history, and the NYPD issued me a license – that was better. Some noteworthy passengers: Martha with one of the Vandellas, and (picking them up outside court) Roger Daltrey and Peter Townshend of the Who, who had been answering charges for tussling with New York's finest on stage of the Fillmore East.[121]

It was during this time that I sought out a couple of guys who ran small indie record labels based in New York: Nick Perls of Yazoo Records and Dave Freeman of County Records. It was just curiosity, looking up these two guys who had started their own labels. Dave welcomed me in and talked a bit about what he did. Nick showed me how he worked to transfer the old 78s to make Yazoo LPs. They were both very open. This background unexpectedly helped us start Rounder a couple of years later. They provided more of a sense that it could be done. That, plus my limited experience publishing *Eritas* and *Americong*, and working on the yearbook at the University of Chicago – for the free photographic film and developing it accorded me – meshed with Ken's experience being picked up by the Davidsons and learning about the Pegram tape.[122]

I had become active reviewing records at this time. Hey, what a way to get free records! While living in Manhattan, I was in touch with Don Wilcock – who was in Vietnam. As Don told me in early 2009:

> I was an activated Army Reservist, Specialist fifth class (Spec 5) stationed at U.S. Army Headquarters in Long Binh in 1969. I wrote a weekly column called "Sounds from the World" in *The Army Reporter*, then the largest official Army newspaper in the world. (*Stars and Stripes* was much bigger, but that wasn't an "official" Army newspaper.)

Don also wrote the daily "World News Roundup" which was the only written source of daily news for the generals on down who were running the war. But it was writing about music that helped keep him sane – and he received grimy but very gratifying notes from grunts in the field.

He'd convinced the major in charge of the information office that the prior music columnist – Skitch Henderson, a popular orchestra conductor born in 1918 – was maybe representative of another demographic! The major wrote a cover letter which I copied and sent to U.S. record labels, urging them to send records for review. The review copies started flowing in – the biggest one-day haul saw just over a hundred (!) albums arrive, stacked up in entryway to my 95th Street apartment building. I selected material to send to Don.

It was during 1969 that I went to Woodstock – where I heard some of the music but never saw any. I piled into a VW bug with three others (fifty years later I can't even remember who they were) and we drove there, assuming we'd get nowhere close and have to turn back thirty-five miles away. That was the impression one got from the radio. When we stopped for gas, I looked at a map and noticed a back road that seemed to go right there. That's probably backed up even more, we figured, but decided to try it anyhow – and drove right onto the grounds. There was no one manning any fence or gate by this time. It was around 2 am and I heard Joan Baez's voice from the other side of the hill where we had pulled to a stop. That was the last song. It was cold and damp and thousands of people were tramping this way and that in the dark. Overnight, as the four of us tried to sleep in the VW seats, two of us got really bad colds. I was spared that, but agreed with everyone else that it might be wiser to leave before we all got sick – so we left. We never saw a bit of the show.

The Political Science department at the University of Chicago wasn't too impressed with my registering for a full slate of independent study courses, and then returning to New York for the year. Even though I co-authored an article with Theodore Lowi that was published in the *Western Political Quarterly*, the department let me know that I wasn't really approaching my studies in a sufficiently serious manner, and urged me to write a master's thesis and take the degree as a consolation prize, but not continue in the doctoral program. I spent much of the summer of 1969 writing the story of the Poor People's March as a political protest, comparing it to other marches on Washington such as the Bonus Expeditionary Force encampment in 1932, which brought together some 17,000 veterans of the World War seeking post-war bonuses. That was my master's thesis.

I continued writing record reviews after returning to the Boston area, and resuming graduate studies at Tufts, writing anonymously under the pen name "Willie the Weeper, the Midnight Creeper" while working as a teaching assistant. The pen name developed in part because I'd write up the reviews, then go out late in the night and slip them under the office door of the Tufts newspaper. Besides, it sounded like the name of an old bluesman. No one ever learned who the real author was, but apparently the reviews had a sufficient flair: Tufts had begun the Experimental College in 1964, an innovative approach towards academics, and the "Ex College" published an appeal in the college newspaper for the unknown author to come forward and teach a creative writing course. It was more fun remaining incognito, and Willie the Weeper's true identity is revealed here for the first time. When Don returned home safely from Vietnam, he and I split up all the records. Don got the bug; he has gone on to write something like six thousand music columns and interviews with singers and musicians.[123]

A few years later, when I was working on my doctorate and was a teaching assistant at Tufts, I ran into another music enthusiast, Joe McEwen. He said he'd met me when I was selling off some of the records I'd acquired while Don was in Vietnam. He recalls visiting the 727 Somerville Avenue apartment and helping us sell the first two Rounder titles at a bluegrass show in Cambridge. He later ended up working for Columbia Records in New York and, at one point, hiring Scott Billington to produce a Dirty Dozen Brass Band album

(Rounder had issued their *Live at Montreux* album). Joe wound up at Concord Records, hired from Verve in 2008, and in 2017 was named Vice President of A&R at Concord.[124]

As noted earlier, the global pandemic that afflicted us in 2020 – and with which our world is still struggling as this final note is added on January 1, 2021 – stole hundreds of thousands of lives. The fact that Rounder was unable to celebrate its fiftieth anniversary in October 2020 is "small potatoes."

Musicians and singers are among the millions around the globe that have been unable to live life as before. Many have had to struggle to find other work. Some offered Zoom concerts. Wearing their pandemic beards, Tony Trischka and Béla Fleck were joined by Alan Munde in a Bearded Banjo Santa Holiday Hang on December 22. Della Mae ran a weekly Facebook concert series throughout the year. IBMA even ran a very successful virtual "World of Bluegrass" weekend in September, replacing the live event that it typically hosts in Raleigh each September. An all-online bluegrass festival! It's just not the same, though it was very well done. The year presented a real challenge to creative performers, many of whom rely on financial support from touring and most of whom draw on spiritual support from their live audiences.

Those of us who love music for the joy it can bring, for the emotions it can evoke, hope for days to come when this scourge is a sad memory. There have to be better days ahead. We all look forward to the day when we can gather again in person and hear our favorites artists, and share the pleasures of music and life with one another.

The business has changed over the years: from selling vinyl LPs in record stores to streaming music – and who knows what's next?

Looking back at the past fifty years, I couldn't have asked for a better ride. There was a lot of music to hear, a lot of work to do, a lot of adventures to have. Lots of good people along the way. Challenges, for sure. Obstacles to overcome, pitfalls to avoid. We always felt we were doing work that had value and meaning. And we had fun doing it, working hard while building memories.

Endnotes

1. The United States record market went from $213 million in 1954 to $460 million in 1957, peaking at $603 million in 1959. Pekka Gronow and Ilpo Saunio (trans. from Finnish by Christopher Moseley), *An International History of the Recording Industry*. London: Cassell, 1998: 96.
2. It was forty years later when I was researching the very first home game ever played by Boston's American League baseball team (now known as the Red Sox), and found that this was the pre-game musical program performed by the Boston Cadet Band: Sousa's 'March/Hail to the Spirit of Liberty' followed (this would seem bizarre today) by a waltz, 'Welcome.' A medley of popular airs, a two-step, a selection from the 1899 vaudeville musical *The Rounders* by Austrian-born composer Ludwig Englander, a caprice named 'Cocoanut Dance,' and a march named 'Old Friends' completed the program. The game took place at the Huntington Avenue Grounds on May 8, 1901. For the record, Boston won the baseball game, beating Philadelphia 12–4.
3. "Cousin Lynn" Joiner (from Maryland) and Brian "Ol' Sinc" Sinclair (from Maine) had "a tag-team history with the show that dates back to 1960," wrote the *Harvard Gazette* in an appreciation in 2002. The two roomed together at Harvard and when they learned in the mid-1960s that the show might be going off the air, they jumped into the breach and have kept *Hillbilly at Harvard* on the air for the past fifty years. Though Sinc died in the final days of 2003, Lynn Joiner has hosted the show ever since. It's at 95.3 FM in the Boston area.
4. Email from Fred Bartenstein, January 28, 2009.
5. Michael Scully notes, interview with Bill Nowlin, June 8, 1999.
6. Ken Davidson died in Dayton on December 20, 2016, at the age of 75.
7. Jeep died of complications from diabetes in 1998. See a brief biographical sketch at https://quod.lib.umich.edu/b/bhlead/umich-bhl-2009082?view=text
8. The statute of limitations is up, but we will nonetheless leave out the name of the artist in question. For some years he's used different pseudonyms, anyhow: names like Dr. Banjo and Waldo Otto.
9. Priscilla Long later wrote several books, including *Where the Sun Never Shines: A History of America's Bloody Coal Industry*, *Minding the Muse: A Handbook for Painters, Composers, Writers, and Other Creators*, and *The Writer's Portable Mentor: A Guide to Art, Craft, and the Writing Life*.
10. I wish we could tell you what Skip went on to do after Rounder, but none of us knows; no internet searches for Skip – or Cornelius – Ferguson have revealed his whereabouts or what became of him, despite repeated attempts. I found a Skip Ferguson once, via

Facebook, who looked promising, but it was not he. If you're out there, Skip, please get in touch.

11   In 2015, Dust-to-Digital issued a deluxe version entitled *Blind Alfred Reed: Appalachian Visionary*, produced by Ted Olson, to which I contributed the photographs I had taken back in 1971.

12   Marian Leighton Levy interview with Michael Scully, June 10, 1999.

13   The book contains a chapter of philosophical reflections on the problems of recording traditional music judiciously, based on his experiences working with us: Chapter 2, "Lost Chords." This is something I only learned in the process of wrapping up this book. I find myself inadequately steeped in philosophy to sufficiently appreciate his argument.

14   Joe grew up in the Boston area, the son of Italian immigrants; his given name was Valiante, and he had a fascinating backstory. His father had, among other things, worked doing underwater construction building the Callahan Tunnel under Boston Harbor. Joe worked as a typewriter repairman by day, but fortunately had a very forgiving employer who allowed him to take occasional time off to play his music. The author's biographical article on Joe Val and Herb Applin is scheduled for publication in the 2021 *International Country Music Journal*.

15   Email from Pete Wernick, March 14, 2009.

16   Some of Joe Wilson's work may be found here: https://ncta-usa.org/the-collected-writings-of-joe-wilson

17   Richard Carlin, *Worlds of Sound: The Story of Smithsonian Folkways*. New York: Smithsonian Books/Collins, 2008: 230.

18   Murray Schumach, "Custom-Made Noise." *New York Times*, June 28, 1953: X6.

19   Sam Kaplan had very impressively worked his way up from office boy in the mailroom to become president of Zenith. He died in 1970. See his obituary in the *New York Times*: https://www.nytimes.com/1970/04/03/archives/sam-kaplan-zenith-president-and-general-manager-is-dead.html.

20   Interview with Sandra Shifrin, December 16, 2018.

21   Patrick McGilligan, "Rounder Records: Hitless Wonders of Rural Music." *Boston Globe*, April 12, 1974: 38. Two years later, Rounder had three employees and earned another *Globe* article: Steve Morse, "Sweet Sounds of Folk from Medford." *Boston Globe*, August 12, 1976: 60.

22   These are currently available as two CDs: *Louisiana Cajun Music from the Southwest Prairies*, Vols. 1 and 2 (Rounder 6001 and 6002).

23   That's not to say that there hadn't also been Louisiana field recordings of jazz from somewhat earlier. In the 1940s, Bill Russell had been recording Bunk Johnson, George Lewis, and others in dance halls and backyards in and around New Orleans for his American Music label. From the early 1950s Alden Ashforth, Jim McGarrell, and David Wyckoff made a determined effort to make documentary recordings of the dance hall scene, and this was followed soon after by Sam Charters' recordings (mainly for Folkways) of evangelists, shoe shiners, and Mardi Gras Indians. Thanks to editor Alyn Shipton for this deeper background on the jazz side.

24   A similar situation occurred in Cape Breton, with regard to Scots Gaelic. Mark Wilson believes we recorded the last native Gaelic-speaking fiddlers – Alex Francis MacKay and Joe Peter MacLean – saying, "Joe Peter was lionized by Gaelic scholars because he came from a particularly isolated part of the island." Email from Mark Wilson, December 16, 2016.

25   Neil V. Rosenberg, *Blue Grass Generation*. Urbana: University of Illinois Press, 2018.

26   *The Early Days of Bluegrass*, a six-CD set with an accompanying 204-page book, is available from the Bluegrass Country Foundation at https://bluegrasscountry.org/the-early-days-of-bluegrass.

27   Tune in at http://kvpionline.com/community-event-updates/258446

28 The *So Glad I'm Here* album was released in June 1975 as Rounder 2015.
29 Perhaps because of his folklore studies in India, Bruce originally thought of naming the company Ganesh Records, named after the elephant-headed Hindu god. It also tied into Bruce's bulk. Mark Wilson says he talked Bruce out of this, and the two of them found the image that became the basis for the Flying Fish logo – in the same book of old prints which provided the "kitty puss" image for the Buddy Thomas album cover.
30 *Only A Miner: Studies in Recorded Coal Mining Songs* (1972) was the first book in the University of Illinois' Music in American Life series.
31 Bill Nowlin, *Alexander Berkman, Anarchist: Life, Work, Ideas* (Christie Books, 2014). https://christiebooks.co.uk/product/alexander-berkman-anarchist-life-work-ideas
32 Email from Mark Wilson, December 13, 2018.
33 Steve taught himself programming and did geodata processing for Weston for about five years, then worked for a number of other tech companies, including Sun Microsystems, doing software development. Since around 2002, he has been working as a Solution Developer at TJX Companies. Email from Steve Harris, December 17, 2018.

There is a Kathleen Kete who is a professor of history at Trinity College in Hartford. She got her undergraduate degree in 1982 from Harvard Extension, and ultimately earned a PhD from Harvard. Attempts to reach her to confirm this is the same Kathy Kete were unsuccessful, though we believe it to be her.
34 For the album's fortieth anniversary edition, I interviewed all involved and wrote up a new set of notes for the album. In 2016, IBMA voters gave me the Best Liner Notes award. Marian had won the same award in 2012 for Tony Rice's *The Bill Monroe Collection* (Rounder 9128).
35 David W. Johnson, "Well Founded." *Folk Roots*, August/September 1996, 73-75.
36 *Providence Journal*, June 23, 1995.
37 David W. Johnson, "Well Founded."
38 Before the bombers were apprehended, I was confined at home with my son Emmet due to a "shelter in place" order. I was on the phone with my ex-wife Yleana, who was living about three miles away in Watertown when she suddenly said, "Gunshots! I've got to go look." It turns out that Dzhokhar Tsarnaev was captured about two blocks from her house.
39 Scully, *Never-Ending Revival*: 189.
40 Interview with Michael Scully, June 8, 1999.
41 Steve Morse, "Pushing Your Own Records." *Boston Globe*, April 12, 1979: 67.
42 A rack jobber (also known as a rack merchandiser) is a company or trader that has an agreement with a retailer to display and sell products in a store.
43 Email from Mary Weber, March 22, 2009.
44 Email exchanges with Mike Kappus, December 22, 2009, January 10, 2010, and May 16, 2016.
45 In September 2018, in Raleigh, Ken presented Walt Saunders with the International Bluegrass Music Association's Distinguished Achievement Award in ceremonies at the Duke Energy Center.
46 I don't drink much and still have a few bottles in my pantry from one of the cases Sam Adams gave us more than fifteen years ago. Now if it were Cherry Coke, it would have been gone within a couple of weeks. The video can be found at: https://www.youtube.com/watch?v=IyhJ69mD7xI where over five million people have viewed it.
47 Email from Mark Wilson, December 13, 2018.
48 Mark Wilson remembers: "I was standing in line in a xerox place with the materials for *Get your Ass in the Water* when some little Cambridge lady said, 'Well, I guess some folks like to talk like that.' To which I answered, 'Look, lady, if this is good enough for Harvard University Press, it's good enough for me.'" Mark adds, "Seriously, though,

one of the major reasons I didn't finish our Buell Kazee project was that I knew he'd be offended by some of your other records." Email from Mark Wilson, December 13, 2018.

49　Email from Mark Wilson, December 13, 2018.

50　Carl MacKenzie died in Cape Breton on December 1, 2018. Elizabeth Patterson, "Fiddler Carl MacKenzie remembered as 'great ambassador for the music.'" *Cape Breton Post*, December 4, 2018. So very many of the people we recorded are no longer with us.

51　Among the organizers of the Boston Blues Society were Scott Billington, Peter Guralnick, and Dick Waterman.

52　All Scott Billington quotations come from an interview conducted on January 16, 2016.

53　Oliver Jones, "Cruise in tune with 'Shaggs' project: Thesp options Orlean's article." *New Yorker*, December 16, 1999. http://variety.com/1999/film/news/cruise-in-tune-with-shaggs-project-1117760122. Was it an impossible mission? We're still waiting for his film about the Shaggs.

54　That original mission statement was nothing if not aspirational idealism. It understandably set us up for charges of hypocrisy. Here's how it read:

> Rounder Records is an anti-profit collective that produces records and concerts and distributes other very small record labels. It is dedicated to remaining an anti-profit service group to make available important traditions of American culture that are largely non-commercial: traditional American string band and bluegrass music, black country blues and string band music, and protest music both past and present.
>
> Our form of work organization is worker-controlled, with no bosses, and all finances in common. All money from records sold is re-used to make future records. We envision our function as that of a service organization, an alternative to commercial record companies with implications of this alternate structure to continue serving people's culture ethically and in an anti-profit mode in the new world we are all working toward.

Pretty highfalutin', right? Bordering on sanctimony, and not always strong on grammar. We did pretty much function this way for the first four years. But then we started hiring people – wage slaves. And trying to survive in the real world.

55　Skippy White closed his Boston record store in early 2020. Ken and I both paid him a visit in the final couple of weeks.

56　In Michael Garnice's *Ultimate Guide to Reggae* (Sheffield, UK: Equinox, 2016) he says: "Based on criteria known only to himself, Dodd notoriously would put good recordings on the shelf for any number of years before finally deciding to release them. Limited run singles that had been out of print for years could suddenly be re-pressed."

57　Richard Henderson, "Well-Rounded Labels." *Billboard*, February 10, 2001.

58　We put out a couple of traditional music albums, *From Kongo to Zion* (Heartbeat 17, 1983), recorded by Ken Bilby and Elliott Leib, *Churchical Chants of the Nyabingi* by Elliott (HB 20, also 1983) and even an album called *Woman Talk* (HB 25, 1986), which was a collection of dub poetry by five female dub poets produced by Mutabaruka.

59　*Word Soun' 'Ave Power* was a collection of works by seven revolutionary dub poets of Jamaica, which Muta produced for us. (Heartbeat 15, 1983). As I pulled out the LP to look at it in December 2018, I recalled that I had taken the cover photograph of a Bible that had been set on fire. "That was kind of edgy," said my son Emmet.

60　*The Gavin Report*, May 24, 1996.

61　*Wavelength*, April 1988.

62　*Cumberland County Rag*, May–July 1985.

63　*Clark Now*, Winter 1985.

64　Ibid.

65 At a certain point in the late 1990s, Black Top left Rounder and began to collaborate with Alligator Records for national distribution. Black Top was in dire straits, severely overextended, and they made a deal with yet another company, E Music, to take over the catalog, despite their written agreement with Alligator. The move soon left Alligator's Bruce Iglauer with a dilemma: "either sue a friend or to swallow hard and walk away." Bruce Iglauer and Patrick Roberts, *Bitten by the Blues: The Alligator Records Story*. University of Chicago Press, 2018: 259-91.
66 Ken Irwin interview with Michael Scully, October 13, 1999.
67 Bill Nowlin, "Don't Write Off LPs or Cassettes Yet." *Billboard*, June 21, 1986: 9.
68 Lennon Cihak, "Sales of Cassette Tapes Have Quietly Grown 136.1% in the Past Year." *Digital Music News*, January 9, 2018. https://www.digitalmusicnews.com/2018/01/09/cassette-tape-comeback. Quiet it was. And small potatoes. Under 100,000 total.
69 Bill Nowlin, "6-by-12 Package Inflates CD Prices." *Billboard*, March 19, 1988: 9.
70 Moira McCormick, "CD Packaging Debate Giving Industry a Long Look at Longbox Alternative." *Billboard*, October 20, 1990: C4.
71 Ken Irwin interview with Michael Scully, June 9, 1999.
72 Email from Ken Irwin, May 7, 2005. The video can be seen at: https://www.youtube.com/watch?v=h80lbFuhsMU.
73 Maybe we were ahead of the times; *Seinfeld* (which started in 1989) was purportedly a whole TV show about nothing.
74 See Iglauer and Roberts, *Bitten by the Blues* – a superb account of the birth and growth of an indie label. Bruce says that only eight or nine years into Alligator did he realize he was himself on "a mission to capture and preserve an endangered form of music" (page 173).
75 *Billboard*, May 9, 1992.
76 Scott Alarik, "The Bold New Ways of Old Folkways." *Boston Globe*, March 26, 1989: 33.
77 *Billboard*, July 20, 1996.
78 Email from Mark Wilson, December 16, 2018.
79 What was a company named Munich doing in Holland? It was only while researching this book that we learned the story. The original company was actually named Munnickendam Groothandel BV, started by a certain Mr. Munnickendam a couple of years after the end of the Second World War. He was a wholesaler in 78 rpm records, mainly religious music of different kinds: Jewish, Christian, gospel, hymns, choirs, etc. When he retired, he sold Munnickendam to jazz lover Job Zomer, who initially ran the company out of his garage, one I still recall from my first 1970s visit to establish European distribution for Rounder.
80 Interview with Brad Paul, December 3, 2018.
81 See the Americana Music Association site at https://www.americanamusic.org.
82 Michael Hall, "G-L-O-R-I-A." *Texas Monthly*, August 2009.
83 For more information on the film, see: http://www.robertmugge.com/true-believers/index.html
84 *Fusion*, March 1996.
85 *Acoustic Musician*, September 1995.
86 (* indicates the label had only one record out at the time.) A Touch of Magic; Accurate; Accurate Distortion*; Ace; Ace U.S.; Acoustic Disc; Action Replay; Adelphi; AF; Affinity; After Hours; AIM; Al Sur; Alacazam; Alcazar; Alligator; Ambient Sound; American Clave; American Melody; American Music; AMMP; Ansonia; Antilla; Antone's; Appaloosa; Arc*; ARC Music; Arco; Arhoolie; Ariwa; ARO; Artex; Artomax; Atomic Theory; Attack*; Attic; Audio Lab*; Audiophile; Audioquest; Authentic*; Avan Guard*; Avant; AVC; Baktabak; Band Stand; Bear Family; Bear Tracks*; Bee Bump; Beeswing*; Bert & I; Bescol; Bethlehem; BGO; BGP; Big Beat; Biograph; Black & Blue; Black Crow; Black Magic; Black Saint; Black Swan; Black Top; Black Wolf*; Blackmail; Blind Pig; Blister Pack; Blue Moon*; Blue Plate; Blue Rhythm; Blue Sting; Blue Tone;

Blues Boy; Blues Unlimited*; BOB (Best of Blues); Bog*; Bohemia Beat*; Botown; Brake Out; Bravo*; Braziloid; Brown Dog*; Bulldog*; Bullseye Blues; Burnside; C & D Productions; Capitol Steps; Carthage; Cascade; Castle; Celluloid; Celtic Music; Charly; Cherrywood Station; Chess Import; Chiarascuro; Chiswick; Circle; Clean Cuts; CMH; CMP; Code 90; Collectables; Collector's Classics; Columbia Special Products; Concert Production*; Contemporary; Copper Creek; Corason; Corinthian; Country Music Foundation; Country Routes; County; Creative World; Criss Cross; Croaker; Crosscut; Crystal Clear; CSA; DADGAD; Daffodil; Dambuster; Dargason; Daring; Db; Debut*; Decal*; Dejadisc; Delmark; Deluge; Deluxe; Demon; Demon-Transatlantic; Diablo; Dirty Linen; Disco Hit; Discovery; Discuba; DIW; Document; Double Trouble; Dr. Horse; Dreyfus*; Drop-Out*; Dunkeld; Dupree's Diamond News; Dynamite; Earwig; Eat*; Edelton* Edsel; El Diablo; Electrovert*; Ellipsis Arts; Elvis; EMI; Enemy; Erisong*; ESD; ESP; Etude; Everest; Evidence; EWM; Fantasy; Fat Possum; Fate; FFF; Flying Fish; Flyright; Fogarty's Cove; Folk Legacy; Folk Roots Magazine; Folklyric; Folkways; FOT; Fretless; Front Hall; Frontier; Fugs; Funny*; Gael Linn; Galaxy*; Gateway; Gazell; GBW; GEMA; GENES; GHB; Giants of Jazz; Global Village; Globe*; Globe Style; GM; GNP; Goldband; Goldwax; Gong Sounds; Good Time Jazz; Gospel Heritage; Gospel Jubilee; Gourd*; Grapevine*; Greatful Dead; Great Southern; Green Linnet; Greenhays; Greentrax; Halcyon; Hannibal; Harlequin; HDH; HDH Import; HDS*; Heartbeat; Hep; Heritage; Hi; Higher Octave*; Hollywood; Hollywood Soundstage; I.A.I.; Ice; IMP; India Navigation; Indigo; Instant; Intercord; Intuition; Jasmine; Jass; Jazz Band; Jazz Hour; Jazz House; Jazz Information; Jazzology; Jazz Unlimited; Jewel; Jin; JMY; JSP; Juke Box Lil; Juke Box Treasures; Junco Partner*; June Appal; K.C.; Kajun; Kaleidoscope; Keltia Musique; Kent; Kicking Mule; King; King Biscuit*; Kingsnake; Knitting Factory; Kom-A-Day; Krazy Kat; La Louisianne; Lapwing; Le Jazz; Leader; Line; Little Dog*; LL; Loom; Lucky Seven; Lyrichord; Maggie's Music; Magic; Magnetic; Magpie; Maison de Soul; Major; Making Waves; Malaco; Mango; Mardi Gras; Masters of Jazz; Matchbox; Mau Mau; Maype; MB; Medierraneo*; Memoir; Merle; Messidor; Milan*; Milestone; Millstream*; Mineral River*; Modern Blues; Moment; Monitor; Montuno; Moods; Moon; Moulin d'Or; Mountain International*; Mouthpiece; Moving Target; Mr. R&B; MTE; Mulligan; Munich; Music of the World; Music Today; Musicraft; MW*; Mythic Sound; Naked Language; Natasha; Network; New Albion; New Directions; New World; Nichols Wright; Night Light; Nighthawk; North Star; Northeastern; Norton; NRG; NYC; OBC; Off Beat*; Oh Boy; OJC; Old Bean; Old Timey; Oldie Blues*; Olivia; Omnium; Onthem; Original Cinema*; Original Music; Orleans; Outer Green; Pablo; PAN; Paradise and Thorns*; Paula; Pearl; Personal; Philo; Philology; Planet Bluegrass; PM; Powerhouse; Prestige Import; Qbadisc; Radiola; Raga; Rainbow Morning Music; RAM; RAS; Rebel; Receiver; Red; Red Lightnin'; Red Pajamas; Redwood; Relic; Reservoir; Revels; Ridgetop; Rising Son; Riverside; Rockers; ROIR; ROM; Rooster Blues; Rose Quartz*; Rosetta; Rotel; Roughage*; Rounder; Route 66; Rumba; Rykodisc; RZ; Sackville; Salsoul; Sandy Hook; Saxophonograph; Scarlet; Schoolkids; Secret; Security; Seeco; Sequel; SF*; Shiloh; Silkheart; Single Wing; Skaloid; Small Dog-A-Barkin'; Smithsonian Folkways; Solitudes; Solo Art; Sonet; Sonic Sounds; Sonic Trout; Sony Music Special Products; Soul Note; Soul Syndicate*; Sound Hills; Sounds of Nature; Southland; Special Delivery; Special Greetings; Specialty; Speedo; Spindletop*; Spruce and Maple*; Star; Star Line; Starday; Stash; Stax; Stax UK; Stockholm; Stomp Off; Stony Plain; Storyville; Stuc*; Suave; Sugar Hill; Sukay; Summertone; Sundown*; Sundown Magnum; Sunsplash; Swallow; Swamptone; Take Two; Tara; TDP; Temple; Thunderbolt; Tim Kerr Records; Tipitina's; Tone-Cool; Tonmeister; Topic; Tracer*; Tramp*; Travelin' Man; Trend; Tri Surf; Tried & True; Trojan; Trojan World*; Trout; Trumpet; Turquoise; Upstart; Urban Campfire; Varrick; Vestapol; Video Artists International; View Video; Vintage Jazz Classics; Virtue; Voice*; Volt; Water Lily Acoustics; Watermelon; Westbound; Whippersnapper; Whippet; Whiskey, Women, and...;

Wild Dog Blues; Windsong; Winner; Wolf; Workalb*; World Circuit; Wrestler; Zazou; Zu Zazz; ZYX*.

87 Interview with John Virant, October 9, 2018.
88 In March 2001, Zoë released *God Bless the Blake Babies* which featured Juliana Hatfield and Freda Love – and guitarist John Strohm, who would one day succeed John as Rounder CEO.
89 The set was not economically feasible for Rounder to release under the aegis of Concord, but the powers-that-be at Rounder readily assented that I could take it to the Atlanta-based Dust-to-Digital label, which has always specialized in putting out quirky and often lavish releases. It was released as a four-CD set in a wooden box with gold foil stamping as part of the silkscreened Moroccan artwork on the exterior, with a ninety-page leather-bound booklet inside intended to simulate Bowles' journal.
90 Iglauer and Roberts, *Bitten by the Blues*: 241.
91 Ann Powers, "Showing Their Roots, and Proud Of It." *New York Times*, October 10, 2000: E7.
92 Larry LeBlanc, "Rounder/Universal Canada Tie Pays Off." *Billboard*, August 19, 2000: 74.
93 All quotations from the special supplement to *Billboard*, February 10, 2001.
94 And there is a brick there with both my name and Emmet's name, set in the ground inside Gate B.
95 If interested in learning a whole lot more about umpires, go to Amazon or get it directly from SABR: https://sabr.org/latest/sabr-digital-library-the-sabr-book-of-umpires-and-umpiring. In 2020, Summer Game Books published my follow-up book, *Working a "Perfect Game": Conversations with Umpires*, based on interviews with over seventy umpires.
96 Turns out I'm not the only one in the music business who can't sing. Bruce Iglauer of Alligator Records has the same problem. See Iglauer and Roberts, *Bitten with the Blues*: 10. As someone in the business with no musical talent, I have always enjoyed Dean Miller's mocking song "Music Executive." You can hear it here: https://www.youtube.com/watch?v=o2usX4R89cQ.
97 I visited all three of those counties of trips with Koryo, as well. I highly recommend the company. It's rare when I have taken advantage of a tour group; most of the time I just travel on my own. Koryo is an exceptional outfit.
98 *Billboard*, November 2, 1991.
99 For the judge's opinion dismissing Napster's case, see: Activity in Case 1:09-cv-00318-PAC Napster, LLC v. Rounder Records Corp. Memorandum & Opinion. The judge politely, but firmly, suggested that Napster never had a case to bring in the first place, saying (among other things) that Napster's case "is based largely on a number of irrelevant cases" including one that "hurts its argument more than it helps." He added, "Napster has it backwards."
100 http://kvpionline.com/community-event-updates/258446 (last accessed December 9, 2020).
101 Scully, *Never-Ending Revival*: 174.
102 The City of Cambridge noted that Rounder had moved to Burlington in a resolution passed by the City Council on June 4, 2007. The resolution named the three founders and then declared, in part: "This untested trio went the distance: from humble beginnings over thirty years ago to what is now America's premier independent record label. From its early interest in rural American music (via fiddle, stringband, blues, and bluegrass recordings) to an expansive catalogue of more than 3,000 titles running the gamut from folk to world, soul to socas, jazz to juju, Cajun to Celtic, and beyond, Rounder has emerged as the preeminent source for vital, uncompromised music of all genres." The council added: "RESOLVED: That the City Council go on record

expressing sorrow at the loss of Rounder Records as they move on to another location, and wish them luck as they continue to expose new listeners to new music and sounds."
103 All of the quotations attributed to Glen Barros come from an interview with the author of November 19, 2018.
104 Author interview with John Virant, December 14, 2018. All quotes in this section come from this interview.
105 This continued discussion all comes from the same December 2018 interview.
106 Deirdre Fernandes, "Rounder Records Moving to Music City." *Boston Globe*, October 16, 2013: B7.
107 Fernandes, "Rounder Records Moving to Music City": B11.
108 "Rounder Records: A Loss for Massachusetts." *Boston Globe*, October 21, 2013.
109 A story covering the open house can be found at https://musicrow.com/2014/05/bobby-karl-works-the-rounder-records-nashville-open-house. I was chatting at the open house with this man, and asked him, "So, what do you do?" "I'm the mayor," he replied. And it turned out that Karl Dean is a Massachusetts native and a Boston Red Sox fan.
110 Interview with John Strohm, September 9, 2020.
111 Ibid.
112 "No. 83: Scott Pascucci & Steve Smith | Power 100." *Billboard*, January 25, 2018. https://www.billboard.com/articles/business/8096110/no-83-scott-pascucci-steve-smith-power-100
113 Jeff McLaughlin, "Rounder Records: A Label Grows in Cambridge." *Boston Globe*, October 28, 1984: A15.
114 Marian Leighton Levy interview with Michael Scully, June 8, 1999.
115 Concert information provided by Rob Allingham via email to author, July 30, 2018.
116 Stephen R. Davis, "The African National Congress, its Radio, its Allies and Exile." *Journal of Southern African Studies*, 35 (2009): 349-73. The article was built on Davis's master's thesis in History at the University of Florida.
117 Both the Michael Scully and Alison Krauss quotes come from Barry Mazor, "Rounder Records at 40." *Wall Street Journal*, March 3, 2010. The hog-calling album is, of course, *Hollerin'*.
118 A history of Follen Church can be found here: https://follen.org/about/history.
119 Interview with Lara Pellegrinelli, 1995–96. Lara was a Harvard graduate student working on a thesis for one of my Cambridge neighbors, Dr. Kay Shelemay. She received her PhD in music, focusing on ethnomusicology, in 2005.
120 See Jane Julianelli, *The Naked Shoe: The Artistry of Mabel Julianelli*. Woodbridge, UK: ACC Editions, 2010. Janie and I reconnected after I had seen her book and she told me it was really that her mother thought I was, essentially, too unsettled – traveling here and there, going to demonstrations and the like. I can understand that.
121 See, for instance, Jennifer Kline, "The Who's Roger Daltrey Recalls Little-Known 1969 Arrest." AOL.com, April 30, 2018. https://www.aol.com/article/entertainment/2018/04/30/the-whos-roger-daltrey-recalls-little-known-1969-arrest-we-were-on-the-run-from-the-police/23423948
122 We later distributed both County and Yazoo. Nick died of AIDS in 1987, but as of 2019 Dave Freeman is still going strong, working with his son Mark in running County and associated enterprises. Dave was a 2002 inductee into the International Bluegrass Music Museum Hall of Fame.
123 Don also wrote a book with Buddy Guy: *Damn Right I've Got the Blues*. Sussex, UK: Woodford Publishing, 1999.
124 Email from Joe McEwen, October 7, 2018.

Index

Index of names

A2IM see National Association of Independent Record Distributors
Ackerman, Dougie   103
Action   96, 100, 171, 173, 302
Adams, Johnny   142, 144, 202
Adelphi Records   33, 49, 63, 76, 96
Ahrens, Pat   46, 47
Alarik, Scott   31, 177, 302
Allen, Red   22, 40, 42
Alligator Records   34, 64, 169, 182, 195, 208, 231, 302
Allingham, Rob   161, 305
American Association of Independent Music (A2IM)   see National Association of Independent Record Distributors
Americana Music Association   201–2
Anger, Darol   90, 145, 152, 165
Annis, Mike   94, 268
Applin, Herb   11, 43, 299
ARChive of Contemporary Music   25
Ardoin Family   29
Arhoolie Records   1, 3, 18, 33, 67, 89, 162
  see also Strachwitz, Chris
Asch, Moe   21, 24, 52, 53, 54, 68, 69, 91
Ashley, Clarence   11, 23, 47
Austin City Limits   141

Baez, Joan   3, 11, 67, 148, 296
BAF   see Boston Area Friends of Bluegrass and Old-Time Country Music
Bailey, Danny and Charles (Bailey Brothers)   70, 80
Balfa, Dewey (and Balfa Brothers)   66, 67, 68, 122

Balfa Toujours   68, 236
Ball, E.C. & Orna   56, 66, 120, 219
Ball, Marcia   118, 169, 203
Ball, William J.   119
Barenberg, Russ   46
Barros, Glen   213–14, 258, 260–4, 266, 268, 270
Bartenstein, Fred   22, 298
Bastin, Bruce   91
Bateman, Jim   136
Battering Ram, the   92
Baucom, Terry   97
Bayside   171–2, 174
Bean Blossom   29
Beatles, the   8, 23, 41, 126, 228
Beaver, Loy   8, 9
Benedict, Paul B.   7
Bensusan, Pierre   132, 152, 165
Berardini, Tony   98, 99
Bergman, Barrie   168
Berkman, Alexander   78
Berkowitz, Steve   166
Berline, Byron   87
Berry, Chuck   2
Berryville   29
Bessman, Jim   236
Big Shoulders   194
Big Youth   133
Bikel, Theodore   2
Bilby, Ken   221, 301
Billboard   8, 108, 118, 122, 154, 171, 172, 173, 234, 236–7
Billington, Scott   121, 122–4, 125, 129, 136–8, 141–2, 149, 163, 257, 268, 296, 301

306   VINYL VENTURES

Biograph Records   33, 49
Birch Records   27, 28, 34
Black Top Records   148–9, 169, 302
Blackwell, Chris   184
Blake, Nancy   160
Blake, Norman   54, 58, 59, 61, 75, 77, 85, 119, 140, 145, 152, 159, 160, 169
Blake Babies   270
Blazers, the   236
Block, Rory   136, 140, 165, 169, 204
Blough, Bill   90, 100, 101
Blue Note Records   1
Blue Sky Boys   10, 206
Bluegrass Unlimited   34, 44, 45
Blues Unlimited   34
Blume, Augie   103
Boggs, Dock   9, 10
Booker, James   142
Boone Creek   97, 122, 177
Boston Area Friends of Bluegrass and Old-Time Country Music (BAF)   21, 22, 39, 40, 41
Boston Bluegrass Union   254, 264
Boston Red Sox   240–4, 287, 298
Bowles, Paul   224, 304
Boys of the Lough   141
Brave Combo   162, 169
Bray Brothers   44, 59, 61
Briggs & Briggs   11
Brislin, Kate   132
Broadside   10, 27
Brody, Hal   170–2
Bromberg, David   59, 75, 169
Brown, Charles   169, 170
Brown, Clarence "Gatemouth"   122, 136–7, 141, 152
Brown, James   8
Brown, Rev. Pearly   71, 72
Brown, Stan   21, 284, 288
Browne, Duncan   130, 133–4, 148, 167, 171, 172, 180–2, 186, 197, 200, 206, 209, 232, 270
Brownlee, Bill   171
Buckwheat Zydeco   118, 140, 144, 163, 165, 267
Buffy the Vampire Slayer   237–8
Bunkley, Jim   48, 61
Burke, John, & the Yankee Carpetbaggers   28
Burke, Solomon   118, 144, 152, 265
Burnett & Rutherford   41
Burning Spear   165
Busby, Buzz   32, 87

Bush, Sam   85, 133
Bussey, George Henry   48, 61
Busted Toe Mud Thumpers   12

Cacia, Mike   133–5, 140
Cafe Yana   10
Caffe Lena   55
California Record Distributors (CRDI)   96, 100, 104, 171
Caparro, Jim   230
Capitol Records   2
Caplin, Arnie   49
Carawan, Guy and Candie   91, 119
Carignan, Jean   141
Carlin, Richard   53, 299
Carnegie Hall   10
Carpenter, Mary Chapin   159, 165, 259, 267
Carrasco, Joe King   162, 202
Carson, Fiddlin' John   41
Carter Family   170, 259
Carter, Carlene   269
Carthy, Martin   97
Cash Brothers   237
Cash, Johnny   140
Charles River Valley Boys   11
Charles, Ray   253, 260, 282, 283
Chase, John   186, 206–7
Christgau, Robert   123
Christie, Stuart   78
Church Brothers   70
Clark University   15, 147, 275–6
Clark, Dick   6
Clark, Octa   74
Cleaves, Slaid   236
Clements, Vassar   59, 75, 159
Clifton, Bill   245
Club 47   3, 7, 9, 10, 11
   see also Club Passim
Club Passim   68, 208
Cockburn, Bruce   237
Coffey, John   41
Cohen, Barney   180, 185–6, 206
Cohen, John   2, 9, 11, 64, 68, 69, 102, 188
Collins, Charlie   85
Concord Music   138, 258–73, 304
Conforth, Bruce   93
Connell, Dudley   204
Connie & Babe   70
Continental Records Services (CRS)   193–6
Cooney, Michael   49
Copeland, Johnny   136, 152, 160

Cormier, Joe   82, 97
Cornell University   15, 39, 40, 46
Country Cooking   40, 45, 46, 47, 55, 97
Country Joe & the Fish   23
County Records   1, 3, 27, 33, 40, 44, 45, 53, 177, 295, 305
  see also Freeman, Dave
Courville, Sady, & Dennis McGee   74
Cowboy Junkies   237
Cox, Billy   14
Crary, Dan   97
Cravens, Red   44, 61
Cray, Ed   244–5
CRDI   see California Record Distributors
Crowe, J.D.   86, 87, 90, 132, 175, 204, 259, 269
CRS   see Continental Records Services
Curtis, Laurence   6
Curtiss, Lou   187

Daigrepont, Bruce   203
Dane, Barbara   27
Daring, Mason   55, 160
David, Dorothy   9
Davidson, Ken and Sherry   14, 20, 24, 295, 298
Davis, Clive   106, 214
Davis, Rev. Gary   67
Deaver, Charlene   171, 180
Deems, Deborah   50
De La Rosa, Tony   162
Della Mae   297
Delmark Records   1, 3, 33, 68
  see also Koester, Bob
Delta Spirit   149
DeMent, Iris   117, 159
Denton, Bob   276
Diamant, Tom   171
Dickens, Hazel   29, 49, 65, 66, 75, 85, 91, 148
Dickerson, Laura   129
Diddley, Bo   117
Dirty Dozen Brass Band   142, 163, 165, 296
Discount Records   25
DNA (Distribution North America)   181–7, 200, 206–7, 209, 231
Do'a   165
Dodd, Clement "Sir Coxsone"   138–9
Donahue, Irish Mike   101
Doors, the   23
Dopmeyer, Ralph   63, 64
Doubilet, David   20

Douglas, Jerry   86, 90, 97, 124, 165, 259
Doyle, Dan   136
Draper, Rusty   6, 281
Dread, Mikey   133
Drevo, Dick   65, 66
Dry Branch Fire Squad   125, 132
Duarte, Chris   236
Dylan, Bob   3, 10, 11, 23, 45, 270
Dynatones, the   165

Early Days of Bluegrass series   70, 85, 238, 242, 244–6, 299
Eek-A-Mouse   135
Eidelman Virant   268
Einstein, Damien and David   99
Elektra Records   2, 3, 23, 165, 222
Elliott, Ramblin' Jack   7, 24
Ely, Joe   202, 236
EMI America   117, 118, 142, 168
Emrich, Duncan   49
Engle, Tony   194
Erlmann, Dr. Veit   160
Ertegun, Ahmet   113
Estrin, Kari   145
Evans, Carol   199

Fahey, John   3, 36, 152
Fariña, Mimi   11, 148, 152
Fariña, Richard   11
Faurot, Charlie   20
Fenway Park   10, 240
Ferguson, Skip   36, 60, 64, 75, 94, 298
Ferrel, Frank   94, 95
Festival of American Folklife   29, 66, 67, 68, 120–1
Finch, Carl   162
Fleck, Béla   102, 131, 144, 145, 152, 157, 165, 169, 259, 267, 297
Flippen, Benton   71
Flying Fish   60, 74, 75, 76, 140, 176–7, 205, 300
Foley, Paul   230, 232
Folk Alliance   149, 169, 253–4
Folk Roots   87
Folklore Center (Cambridge)   10
Folklore Center (New York)   2, 47
Folklore Productions   7
  see also Greenhill, Manny
Folkways Records   1, 3, 8, 11, 12, 18, 21, 22, 23, 24, 33, 44, 52, 53, 54, 69, 91, 121
  see also Smithsonian Folkways
Forward, John   88, 89
Fraley, J.P. & Annadeene   49, 187

Frappier, Steve   63
Fred's Lounge   71
Frederick, Jeffrey, & the Clamtones   119
Freeman, Dave   3, 27, 40, 44, 177, 295, 305
French, Bob   43
Friends of Old Time Music   23
Fuzzy Mountain String Band   55, 56, 61, 177

Galax Fiddlers Convention   14, 56
Gant, Don   176
Garland, Jim   29, 91, 219
Gately, Connie   70
Geffen, David   117
Geils, J.   87, 111, 113–14,
Gellert, Lawrence   92, 93
Gennett Records   1
Gerrard, Alice   65, 66, 75
Gessner, Durg   20, 124
Gilmore, Harry "Tersh" (aka Lou Martin)   46
Gilmore, Jimmie Dale   236
Gladden, Texas   48, 220–1
Goldberg, Danny   230–1
Golden Eagles Mardi Gras Indians   163
Golden Echoes   59, 61
Golding, Wes   97
Goldman, Emma   78
Goldwater, Barry   6, 288–9
Gooding, Cynthia   2
Graham, Bill   113
Grammys   10, 118, 122, 136, 141, 142, 149, 159, 163, 170, 234, 244, 5, 253, 259, 267
Grateful Dead   17
Green, Archie   48, 49, 77, 92
Green, Doug   132–3, 269
Green, Rayna   49
Greenberg, Jeff   224
Greenbriar Boys   6, 7
Greene, Richard   90, 133
Greenhill, Manny   7
Griffith, Nanci   118, 140, 141, 145, 157, 165, 169, 270
Grisman, David   90, 120, 132, 152, 165, 169
Growling Tiger   131–2
Gunning, Sarah Ogan   29, 219
Guralnick, Jake   215
Guralnick, Peter   123, 124, 135, 301
Guthrie, Woody   50, 219, 221, 244–5, 259

Haley, Ed   49
Hammond, John Jr.   132, 152

Haney, Carlton   29
Hanks, Larry   49
Happy Valley Music   70
Harlan County U.S.A. (movie)   91, 92
Harmer, Sarah   237
Harris, Steve   84, 300
Harrod, John   187
Hartford, John   44, 45, 49, 58, 59, 85, 159
Harvard Coop   26, 130
Hatfield, Juliana   237, 271
Hazel & Alice   157
   see also Dickens, Hazel; Gerrard, Alice
Heartbeat Records   133–5, 138–9, 195
Henderson, Richard   236, 238
Hickerson, Joe   48, 49, 52, 69
Hickman, John   97
Hicks, Bill   55
Higashioka, Ted   100
Highwoods String Band   12, 29
Hillbilly at Harvard (radio show)   20, 298
   see also Joiner, Cousin Lynn; Sinclair, Brian
Hillbilly Ranch   22, 23
Himelfarb, Gary   163, 171, 247
Himes, Geoff   267
Hinojosa, Tish   117, 159–60, 203
Hoffman, Dustin   7
Holcomb, Roscoe   10, 11
Holland, Jeep   25, 298
Holmes Brothers   231
Holy Modal Rounders (also Unholy Modal Rounders)   10, 15, 38, 39, 84, 85, 119, 206
Holzman, Jac   23
Hooker, John Lee   89, 101
Horenstein, Henry   100
Horn, Jonathan   230
House Distributors   96, 100, 170–2, 174
House, Son   67
Hovington, Frank   90, 91
Howard, Clint   47, 61
Hubbard, Ray Wylie   236
Hurley, Michael   85, 119
Hurt, Mississippi John   259
Hutchison, Frank   82
Hutto, J.B.   152

IBMA   see International Bluegrass Music Association
Iglauer, Bruce   64, 231, 302, 304
INDI   171, 173, 261
International Bluegrass Music Association (IBMA)   149, 159, 254, 297, 300

Irwin, Jed 6
Irwin, Rita 6
Irwin, Ted 6
Ithaca Area Friends of Bluegrass and Old-Time Country Music 39, 40, 42

Jabbour, Alan 48, 49, 69, 223–4
Jack's Record Cellar 27, 96
Jackson, Aunt Molly 40, 41, 48, 50, 61, 73, 77, 219
Jackson, Bruce 120
Jackson, John 125
Jagger, Mick 8, 118, 148
Jefferson, Carl 262–3
Jenkins, Snuffy 30, 46, 47, 119
Jernigan, Doug 75
Jimenez, Flaco 162, 165, 169, 194
Jocque, Beau 202, 203, 248
John Edwards Memorial Foundation 34, 40
Johnny D's 108
Johnson Mountain Boys 116, 203, 204, 248
Johnson, Linton Kwesi 133
Joiner, Cousin Lynn 20, 298
Jones, Al, Frank Necessary & the Spruce Mountain Boys 119
Jones, Bessie 68, 69, 71, 300
Jordan Hall 7
Julianelli, Janie 294, 305

Kahn, Dan 126, 136, 276
Kanawha Records 14, 24, 34
 see also Davidson, Ken
Kane, Candye 236
Kaplan, Bruce 36, 54, 55, 56, 58, 59, 60, 61, 64, 66, 71, 74, 75, 77, 94, 167, 171, 176, 205, 300
Kappus, Mike 101, 110, 114, 300
Keith, Bill 11, 120, 132, 270
Kentucky Colonels 11, 24, 87
Kessinger, Clark 14, 30, 41, 43, 47, 61
Kete, Kathy 84, 300
Kilimanjaro 141
Kinch, Bruce 20
King, Bobby, & Terry Evans 194
King, James 204
King, Little Jimmy 203
King, Martin Luther Jr. 293–4
Kingston Trio 2, 283
Kiss 212, 213
Klezmer Conservatory Band 206, 236
Knutson, Paul 182, 197

Koerner, Ray & Glover 9
Koester, Bob 2, 64, 68
Koken, Walt 12
Konte, Alhaji Bai 52, 53, 54, 206
Kornrich, Bill 77, 78, 79, 80, 81, 94, 95, 292–4
Kosek, Kenny 46
Kottke, Leo 36
Krauss, Alison 86, 104, 118, 149, 156–9, 166, 168, 169, 170, 185, 195, 200–1, 210, 227, 253, 259, 265, 267, 279
Krauss, Louise 156
Kubek, Smokin' Joe 206
Kweskin, Jim 9, 150

LaBeef, Sleepy 132, 135, 206
Lamb, Dwight 188
Larkin, Patty 140, 141
Last Poets, the 39
Lawtell Playboys 74
Lead Belly 50, 219, 222, 253, 259
Lear, Norman 260, 263
Ledford String Band (and Fiddlin' Steve Ledford) 55, 61, 238
Lee, John 72, 73, 74
Leeds, Steve 99, 103
Leighton, Alton "Brud" 14
Leighton, Dorothy Parker 14
Leonard, Nondie 55
Levy, A.J. 148, 170
Levy, Barry 21
Levy, Eliza 268
Levy, Ron 148, 163, 206
Lewis, Laurie 204
Lewis, Melanie 268
Library of Congress 40, 41, 48, 49, 52, 61, 221–4, 260
Lieberman Enterprises 103
Light, Don 176
Lilly Brothers 11, 22, 23, 24, 25, 67, 97, 245
Lipman, Danny 105
Little Richard 2
Lockwood, Robert Jr. 29, 132
Loews, Amy 268
Logan, Tex 22, 40, 67, 84
Lomax, Alan 2, 48, 67, 93, 187–8, 219–27, 260
Lomax, John 2, 93, 219
Long, Priscilla 36, 298
Longhair, Professor see Professor Longhair
Longview 204

Lornell, Kip   222
Louvin Brothers   150
Lowell Tech (now University of Massachusetts at Lowell)   25
Lundy, Ted, & the Southern Mountain Boys   65, 119
Lynch, Claire   132

Mac & Bob   28
MacKenzie, Carl   121, 301
MacLellan, Theresa & Marie   121
MacMaster, Natalie   82, 236–7
MacPhee, Doug   121
MacQuarrie, Morgan   187
Mahal, Taj   10
Mandela, Nelson   276–7
Mann, Arthur   152, 173
Mare, Frank   40
Margolis, Gerry   117, 165, 166, 176
Marley, Bob, & the Wailers   139, 244
Marsh, Susan   124
Marshall, Mike   133, 145, 152, 165
Martin, Bogan & Armstrong   59, 61, 75
Martin, Asa   73, 81
Martin, Sir George   267
Martin, Lou   *see* Gilmore, Harry "Tersh"
Martin, Steve   259
Martinez, Yleana   149–50, 162, 202, 241, 247, 267, 277, 291, 300
Mazor, Barry   278–9
Mazza, Jim   117–18
Mbarga, Prince Nico   136
Mbuli, Mzwakhe   160, 277
McCann, Gordon   187
McCaslin, Mary   141, 152
McCoury, Del   65
McCurdy, Ed   2
McCutcheon, John   152, 161–2, 265
McEwen, Joe   296–7
McLaughlin, David   204
McReynolds, Jesse   150
Meade, Gene   43
Meade, Gus   49, 119
Melford, Mike   54, 55, 59
Menard, D.L.   67, 73, 77
Menius, Art   157
MIDEM   100, 136
Miller, John   46, 97
Miller, Matt   268
Mitchell, Charlie   36, 37
Mitchell, George   48
Mitchell, Joni   11
Moffatt, Hugh   150

Moffatt, Katy   132
Monagan, Michael   162
Monagan, Parthy   161–2
Monroe, Bill   11, 29, 46, 68
Morris, Leon   87
Morrissey, Bill   140, 203, 236
Morse, Steve   103, 129, 299, 300
Morton, Jelly Roll   50, 52, 219, 222–3, 259
Mugge, Bob   203
Muleskinner News   34
Munde, Alan   297
Munich Records   193–4, 196, 227, 302
Music for Little People   184
Mutabaruka   134, 140, 301
Nagy, John   89, 148

Napster   251, 257
Nashville Bluegrass Band   145
National Academy of Recording Arts and Sciences (NARAS)   *see* Grammys
National Association of Independent Record Distributors (NAIRD)   63, 64, 130
   see also A2IM
National Council for the Traditional Arts (NCTA)   48
National Folk Festival   48
Netsky, Steve   232, 257
Netter, Jim   176
Neville Brothers   115, 118, 165
Nevins, Rich   49
New Black Eagle Jazz Band   141
New Deal String Band   29
New Lost City Ramblers   29, 67
New Mississippi Sheiks   59, 61
Newport Folk Festival   3, 66, 67, 68, 79, 148
Nields, the   237
Nighthawks, the   62, 99, 107, 152
Northeastern University   15
Nowlin, Betty and Bill Sr.   280–6
Nowlin, Emmet   149–51, 202, 241, 300
Nowlin, Joyce (Joyce Arnason)   281, 283, 291
Nowlin, Lisa (Lisa Doran)   281
NRBQ   125, 165, 236

O'Connell, Maura   165
O'Connor, Mark   85, 86, 120, 132, 157, 160, 165
Odetta   7
Oermann, Bob   132
Old Homestead Records   37
Old Time Music (magazine)   34

Olivia Records   126
Olney, David   136
Olson, Ted   299
Osborn, Ted   40, 43, 45, 48, 55, 58
Oster, Harry   67
Oswald, Bashful Brother   54, 61

Paisley, Bob   65, 119
Paley, Tom   2
Palmater, Dave   68
Paredon Records   27
Pareles, Jon   123
Parham, Red   41
Parker, Doug   20, 30
Pascucci, Scott   214, 268, 272, 305
Passim   *see* Club Passim
Paterson, Douglas   161
Patterson, Daniel   122
Paul, Brad   140–1, 149, 169, 201–2, 302
Peebles, Ann   206
Pegram, George   2, 18, 19, 20, 24, 26, 27, 41, 42, 47, 295
Pellegrinelli, Lara   197–200, 289–90
Perdue, Chuck   49
Perry, Lee "Scratch"   139, 165
Perspective (newspaper)   15
   see also Denton, Bob
Peter, Paul & Mary   10
Petric, Faith   49
Pevar, Marc and Susan   49, 52, 53
Peyroux, Madeleine   195, 259
Phillips, Todd   90, 133
Phillips, U. Utah   29, 141
Philo Records   140, 208
Pickett, Wilson   267
Pijpers, Bert   193–6
Piver, Susan   175
Place, Jeff   177
Plant, Robert   86, 253, 259, 265, 267
Po' Ramblin' Boys   244, 272
PolyGram   214, 216, 231, 232
Poole, Charlie   10
Portnow, Neil   118
Poss, Barry   55, 177
Preacher Jack   132
Presley, Elvis   2, 6
Price, Fred   47, 61
Prince   113
Professor Longhair   28, 163
Proschan, Frank   30, 49

Quimby, Doug   71

Raffi   185, 227, 237, 244, 259
Rahn, Millie   11
Ramparts (magazine)   15
Rankins, the   82
RAS Records   163, 171
Reagon, Bernice   76
Rebirth Brass Band   169, 202–3
Redeye Distribution   208
Redpath, Jean   50, 51, 52, 141
Redwood Records   208
Reed, Blind Alfred (and other Reed family)   40, 61, 244, 299
Reed, Ola Belle   49, 66, 91
Reno, Don   87
REP   174–5, 180–4
Rhino Records   118, 155, 208
Rice, Larry   90
Rice, Tony   86, 90, 122, 132, 133, 136, 140, 144, 145, 152, 169, 259, 265, 300
Rich-R-Tone Records   1, 70, 245
Richard, Zachary   165
Richman Brothers   96, 100, 104, 172
Richman, Jonathan   206
Riddle, Almeda   61, 105, 219
Riders in the Sky   109, 132, 165, 168, 236
Riedy, Bob, Chicago Blues Band   18, 59
Rigsby, Don   204
Riley, Steve & the Mamou Playboys   203
Ringer, Jim   141
Rinzler, Ralph   49, 66, 67, 68, 120
Ritchie, Jean   2
Riverboat Enterprises   27, 36, 63, 64, 97
Robins, Butch   85
Rodgers, Jimmie   170, 244
Rolling Stones, the   3, 4, 8, 23, 89, 111, 113, 115, 116, 118, 238, 256
Roomful of Blues   236
Rooney, Jim   10, 11, 270
Rose, Don   152, 173
Rosenberg, Neil   69, 299
Rosenthal, Gene   49, 61, 76
Ross, Lloyd   160
Rossi, Neil   13
Rounder Books   239–44
Rounder Distribution   193
Rounder Europe   195–6
Rounder Kids   184, 193, 250
Rounder Records
   name   15, 16
Roundup Records   81, 193
Ruch, John   181, 186, 206
Rush   213–14, 217–18, 237, 238
Rush, Bobby   149

Rush, Elizabeth   100, 101
Rush, Tom   11
Rykodisc   152, 154–5, 172–4, 182–4, 257

SABR (Society for American Baseball Research)   243, 283
Saletan, Tony   7
Sam Goody's   8, 22
Samuelson, Dave   156
Sandmel, Ben   163
Sands, Sheri   232, 259
Saunders, Walt   44, 116, 300
Sayles, John   160
Schoenberg, Eric   90
Schubart, Bill   141
Schwartz, Tracy   66
Scott, Hammond   148–9
Scott, Nauman   149
Scruggs, Earl   46, 48
Scruggs, Randy   159
Scully, Michael   23, 79, 239, 252, 276, 278, 298–300, 302
Sebastian, John   204
Second Fret   36
Seeger, Mike   2, 9, 11, 22, 66, 122, 185
Seeger, Peggy   122, 185
Seeger, Pete   6
Seeger, Tony   177–8
SEIU (Service Employees International Union)   127–31
Shaggs, the   126, 228, 301
Shakers   91, 122
Shanachie Records   208
Shannon, Preston   206
Shear, Jules   236
Sherrill, Homer "Pappy"   30, 46, 47, 65
Shifrin, Sandra   60, 176, 299
Shines, Johnny   124
Siggins, Betsy   10
Signell, Karl   70
Silber, Irwin   27
Simon, Jeff   88, 90, 100, 101
Simon, Peter   20. 139
Simonds, Rob   152, 154, 173–5, 182–4
Sinclair, Brian "Ol' Sinc"   20, 298
Sing Out!   34, 64
Sirius XM   252
Skaggs, Ricky   86, 165, 201, 228, 259
Slone, Bobby   86
Smith, Harry   2
Smith, Hobart   48, 220–1
Smith, Pip   180
Smith, Ron "Roadblock"   88

Smithsonian Folkways   31, 177–9, 208
Smokey Valley Boys   71
Snock   *see* Hurley, Michael
Society for American Baseball Research   *see* SABR
Soileau, Floyd   67
   see also Swallow Records
Sonet Records   99
Sonnier, Jo-El   132, 165
Sorrels, Rosalie   141
Spark Gap Wonder Boys   13, 18, 19, 20, 22, 26, 27, 43
Sparks, Larry   59
Spence, Joseph   124, 206, 228
Spotify   257
Spottswood, Dick   30, 44, 49, 67, 69, 70, 71, 72, 74, 77, 91
Staines, Bill   141
Stampfel, Peter   10, 36, 84
Stanford, Ron   49, 74
Statman, Andy   152
Stecher, Jody   132
Stein, Leland   198
Stein, Seymour   230
Stellinger, Linda   26, 84
Stivell, Alan   152
Stover, Don   22, 37, 38, 40, 61
Strachwitz, Chris   3, 162
Straijer-Amador, Rosemarie   149
Strohm, John   270–2, 305
Studio One   138–9, 195
Sugar Hill Records   56, 172, 177, 208, 269, 271, 303
Sun Ra   165
Swallow Records   34, 67
Sweet Honey in the Rock   76

Takoma Records   3, 33, 36, 37, 84
Talbott, Nancy   22, 39
Tanner, Gid, & the Skillet Lickers   41, 90
Tarbox Ramblers   236
Tashian, Barry and/or Holly   157
Tasty Licks   102
Taylor, Earl   29, 40
Taylor, Tut   54, 58, 59, 61
Terry, Sonny   2
Thomas, Buddy   119, 300
Thomas, Irma   142, 163–4, 202, 203, 236
Thorogood, George, & the Destroyers   85, 87, 88, 89, 90, 91, 97, 98, 100–9, 110–18, 122, 125, 127–8, 130, 133, 134, 142, 147, 152, 155, 158, 165, 167–8, 176, 237, 257, 267

INDEX   **313**

Tidwell, Bob   40, 43
Togo   125–6
Topic Records   194
Tottle, Jack   102, 148
Toussaint, Allen   267
Tower Records   172, 174, 226, 228, 249, 251, 264
Trischka, Tony   46, 119, 160, 169, 236, 297
True Believers   118
True Believers: The Musical Family of Rounder Records (movie)   203
Tucker, George   91, 119
Tufts University   5, 7–10, 21, 23, 38, 78, 182, 290, 296
Turbinton, Earl, & Willie Tee   163
Twitty, Conway   29
Tyler, Alvin "Red"   142
Tyminski, Dan   227

Unholy Modal Rounders   *see* Holy Modal Rounders
Unicorn, the   11
Union   *see* SEIU
Union Grove   11, 12, 13, 20, 43, 47

Val, Joe   10, 11, 22, 40, 43, 90, 299
Valentine, Bob   270
Valley (retailer)   180–7, 193, 206–7, 209
Van Duser, Guy   136
Van Hoy, H.P.   11
Van Ronk, Dave   141
Vangel, Ken   136
Vanguard Records   2, 3, 23, 269
Verch, April   237
Vincent, Rhonda   236
Virant, John   159, 175, 185, 210–18, 230, 232, 236–8, 257–61, 263–70, 304
Virant, Zoë   217
Von Schmidt, Eric   7

Wainwright, Loudon III   165
Wakefield Manufacturing   34, 73, 102, 104, 155
Wakefield, Frank   22, 40, 42, 55, 61
Walker, Jimmy, & Erwin Helfer   75
Walters, Matt   178–9
Warner, Frank   2
Washington, Jackie   9, 11
Washington, Tuts   138, 142
Washington, Walter "Wolfman"   163
Wasserman, Rob   152, 165

Waters, Muddy   11, 89, 115
Watson, Doc   11, 23
Weavers, the   2
Weber, Mary   108–9, 300
Weber, Steve   10, 85
Weinberger, Eric   82, 83, 146
Wernick, Peter   46, 299
White, Clarence   87
White, Jeff   132
White, Josh   27
Whitey & Hogan   29
Whitley, Keith   165, 175, 200
Whitstein Brothers   150–1
Wilcock, Don   6, 8, 21, 295–6, 305
Wilcox, Jon   49
Wiley, Zeke & Homer (Morris Brothers)   65
Willard, Katie   216–17, 238
Willard, Marty   216, 271
Williams, Hank   6, 15, 175
Williams, Paul   132
Williams, Ted   149, 241, 243
Wilson, Chris   138–9
Wilson, Danny   80, 81, 94, 95
Wilson, Dave   27, 36, 37
   see also Broadside; Riverboat Enterprises
Wilson, Donna   150
Wilson, Joe   47, 48, 299
Wilson, Mark   40, 41, 42, 43, 47, 48, 49, 80, 81, 82, 89, 91, 94, 95, 119–21, 187–93, 237, 299–302
Windham Hill   118, 152, 208
Wise, Robin   171–2
Wisely, Jake   270
Wolfe, Dr. Charles   133, 222
Women's Liberation Rock Band (both Chicago and New Haven)   91, 92, 276
Wood, Anna Lomax   224–7
Workman, Nimrod   91, 92

Yazoo Records   34, 295, 305
Yep Roc Records   208
Young Americans for Freedom   6
Young, Izzy   2, 47
Young, Marcia   68

Zappa, Frank   126, 184
Zion Harmonizers   75
Zoë Records   159, 217, 236–7, 270, 304

Index of albums

Adams, Johnny, *From the Heart* (Rounder 2044; 1984)   144
Alan Lomax Collection Sampler, The (Rounder 1700; 1997)   219
Along the Ohio's Shores (Rounder 0544; 2005)   193
Art of Traditional Fiddle, The (Rounder 11592; 2001)   192–3
Atomic Café, The (Rounder 1034; 1981)   136

Ball, E.C., & Orna, *Fathers Have a Home Sweet Home* (Rounder 0072; 1976)   120, 190
Battering Ram, The (Rounder 4002; 1973)   92
Beaton, Donald Angus & Kinnon, *The Beatons of Mabou* (Rounder 7011; 1978)   190
Bensusan, Pierre, *Près de Paris* (Rounder 3023; 1978)   132
Best of Studio One (Heartbeat 07; 1983)   138–9
Blake, Norman, *Home in Sulphur Springs* (Rounder 0012; 1972)   58, 61
——, *Whiskey Before Breakfast* (Rounder 0063; 1976)   77, 119
—— and Nancy, *The Norman & Nancy Blake Compact Disc* (Rounder 11505; 1986)   160
Blake Babies, *God Bless the Blake Babies* (Zoë 1014; 2001)   270, 304
Bluegrass Album Band, *The Bluegrass Compact Disc* (Rounder 11502; 1986)   160
Booker, James, *Classified* (Rounder 2036; 1982)   138
Boone Creek, *Boone Creek* (Rounder 0081; 1977)   97, 122
Brown, Charles, *All My Life* (Bullseye Blues 9501; 1990)   169
Brown, Clarence "Gatemouth," *Alright Again* (Rounder 2028; 1981)   123, 136–7
Brown, Rev. Pearly, *It's A Mean Old World to Try to Live In* (Rounder 2011; 175)   71
Buckwheat Zydeco, *Waiting for My Ya-Ya* (Rounder 2045; 1984)   145
Buffy the Vampire Slayer (Rounder 9058; 2002)   237–8
Burke, Solomon, *Soul Alive!* (Rounder 2042/2043; 1984)   144, 265
Burnett & Rutherford, *Rambling Reckless Hobo* (Rounder 1004; 1975)   190
Busby, Buzz, & Leon Morris, *Honky Tonk Bluegrass* (Rounder 0031; 1974)   87
Bussey, George Henry, & Jim Bunkley, *George Henry Bussey/Jim Bunkley* (Rounder 2001, 1972)   48, 61

Campbell, John, *Cape Breton Violin Music* (Rounder 7002; March 1977)   189
Cap'n You're So Mean (Rounder 4013; 1982)   93
Carpenter, Mary Chapin, *The Calling* (Zoë 1111; 2007)   159
Carson, Fiddlin' John, *The Old Hen Cackled and the Rooster's Going to Crow* (Rounder 1003; 1973)   190
Carthy, Martin, *Crown of Horn* (Rounder 3019; 1977)   97
Chafe, Winnie, *Highland Melodies of Cape Breton* (Rounder 7012; 1979)   189
Chapman, Owen "Snake," *Up in Chapman's Hollow* (Rounder 0378; 1996)   191
——, *Walnut Gap* (Rounder 0418; 1999)   191
Chatmon, Sam, *Sam Chatmon's Advice* (Rounder 2018; 1979)   189
Chicago Women's Liberation Rock Band and New Haven Women's Liberation Rock Band, *Mountain Moving Day* (Rounder 4001; 1973)   91, 92, 237, 276 (re-released as *Papa Don't Lay That Shit on Me* [82161-4001; 2006])
Chile Vencerá! (Rounder 4009/10; 1977)   91
Churchical Chants of the Nyabingi (Heartbeat 20; 1983)   300
Clements, Vassar, *Crossing the Catskills* (Rounder 0016; 1973)   59
Come All You Coal Miners (Rounder 4005; 1973)   91, 92 (re-released as *Harlan County U.S.A.: Songs of the Coal Miners' Struggle* [11661-4026-2; 2006])
Cooper, Roger, *Essence of Old Kentucky* (Rounder 0533; 2006)   192

INDEX   **315**

——, *Going Back to Old Kentucky* (Rounder 0522; 1996)   191
Copeland, Johnny, *Copeland Special* (Rounder 2025; 1981)   136
Cormier, Joe, *Informal Sessions* (Rounder 7017; 1998)   190
——, *Old Time Wedding Reels* (Rounder 7013; 1992)   190
——, *Scottish Music from Cape Breton Island* (Rounder 7001; 1974)   82, 189
——, *The Dances Down Home* (Rounder 7004; 1977)   97, 189
Country Cooking, *Country Cooking* (Rounder 0006; 1971)   47
Crary, Dan, *Lady's Fancy* (Rounder 0099; 1977)   97
Cravens, Red, & the Bray Brothers, *419 W. Main* (Rounder 0015; 1972)   44, 61
Crowe, J.D., & the New South, *J.D. Crowe & the New South* (Rounder 0044; 1975)   86, 87
——, *My Home Ain't in the Hall of Fame* (Rounder 0103; 1980)   175

Dee-Jay Explosion Inna Dance Hall Style, A (Heartbeat 04; 1982)   134–5
DeMent, Iris, *Infamous Angel* (Philo 1138; 1992)   159
Dickens, Hazel   *see* Hazel & Alice
Dry Branch Fire Squad, *Antiques and Inventions* (Rounder 0139; 1981)   132
Douglas, Wilson, *The Right-hand Fork of Rush's Creek* (Rounder 0047; 1975)   187, 189

Early Days of Bluegrass (Bluegrass Country Foundation, 2019)   242, 244–6, 299
Early Shaker Spirituals (Rounder 0078; 1977)   91, 122

Fariña, Mimi, *Solo* (Philo 1102; 1985)   148
Fleck, Béla, *Crossing the Tracks* (Rounder 0121; 1979)   131
——, *Double Time* (Rounder 0181; 1984)   144
Forces Favorites: Eleven Songs by South Africans Supporting the End Conscription Campaign (Rounder 4023; 1987)   160
Fraley, J.P. & Annadeene, *Maysville* (Rounder 0351; 1995)   191
——, *Wild Rose of the Mountain* (Rounder 0037; 1974)   189

Frederick, Jeffrey, & the Clamtones   *see* Unholy Modal Rounders.
From Kongo to Zion (Heartbeat 17; 1983)   300
Fuzzy Mountain String Band, *Fuzzy Mountain String Band* (Rounder 0010; 1972)   55, 56, 61, 177

Galbraith, Art, *Simple Pleasures* (Rounder 0157; 1982)   189
Georgia Blues (Rounder 2008; 1972)   61
Gerrard, Alice   *see* Hazel & Alice
Get Your Ass in the Water and Swim Like Me (Rounder 2013; 1975)   120
Gladden, Texas, *Ballad Legacy* (Rounder 1800; 2001)   48, 220
Golden Echoes, the, *Heaven on My Mind* (Rounder 2002; 1972)   59, 61
Griffith, Nanci, *Last of the True Believers* (Philo 1109; 1986)   141
——, *Once in a Very Blue Moon* (Philo 1096; 1985)   141
——, *Winter Marquee* (Rounder 3220; 2002)   141
Guitarra Armada (Rounder 4022; 1987)   161–2
Gunning, Sarah, *The Silver Dagger* (Rounder 0151; 1976)   91, 189
Guthrie, Woody, *Columbia River Collection* (Rounder 1036; 1987)   221
——, *Dust Bowl Ballads* (Rounder 1040; 1988)   221
——, *My Dusty Road* (Rounder 1162; 2009)   244

Haley, Ed, *Forked Deer* (Rounder 1131/1132; 1997)   49
——, *Grey Eagle* (Rounder 1133/1134; 1997)   49
——, *Parkersburg Landing* (Rounder 1010; 1975)   49, 189
Harmer, Sarah, *You Were Here* (Zoë 1017; 2000)   237
Hartford, John, *Aereo-Plain* (Rounder 0366; 1997)   159
Hazel & Alice, *Hazel & Alice* (Rounder 0027; 1973)   65, 66, 75
Hinojosa, Tish, *Culture Swing* (Rounder 3122; 1992)   159
Holland, Jerry, *Jerry Holland* (Rounder 7008; 1977)   189
——, *Parlor Music* (Rounder 7057; 2005)   192

Hollerin' (Rounder 0071; 1976)   119–20, 206, 228, 276
Holt, Bob, *Got a Little Home to Go To* (Rounder 0432; 1998)   190
Holyoak, Van, *Tioga Jim* (Rounder 0108; 1981)   189
Hovington, Frank, *Lonesome Road Blues* (Rounder 2017; 1977)   90, 91
Howard, Clint, & Fred Price, *The Ballad of Finley Preston* (Rounder 0009; 1972)   47, 61
Hurley, Michael   *see* Unholy Modal Rounders

Jackson, Aunt Molly, *Library of Congress Recordings* (Rounder 1002; 1972)   40–1, 61, 73
Jenkins, Snuffy, & Pappy Sherrill, *33 Years of Pickin' and Pluckin'* (Rounder 0005; 1971)   47
Johnson, Linton Kwesi, *Dread Beat an' Blood* (Heartbeat 01; 1981)   133
Jones, Bessie, *So Glad I'm Here* (Rounder 2015; 1975)   71, 300
Just Something My Uncle Told Me (Rounder 0141; 1981)   189

Kazee, Philip, *A Family Tradition* (Rounder 0619; 2009)   193
Kentucky Old-Time Banjo (Rounder 0394; 1999)   191
Kessinger, Clark, *Old Time Music with Fiddle & Guitar* (Rounder 0004; 1972)   46, 47, 61
Kids of Widney High, *Special Music from Special Kids* (Rounder 8014; 1989)   162
Konte Alhaji Bai, *Alhaji Bai Konte* (Rounder 5001; 1973)   54
Krauss, Alison, *Every Time You Say Goodbye* (Rounder 0285; 1992)   157
——, *I've Got That Old Feeling* (Rounder 0275; 1990)   157, 170
——, *Now That I've Found You* (Rounder 0325; 1995)   157–8, 200–1, 207
——, *Too Late to Cry* (Rounder 0235; 1987)   157
——, *Two Highways* (Rounder 0265; 1989)   157
—— and Robert Plant, *Raising Sand* (Rounder 9075; 2007)   86, 253, 265

LaBeef, Sleepy, *It Ain't What You Eat It's the Way How You Chew It* (Rounder 3052; 1981)   135
Lamb, Dwight, *Hell Agin the Barn Door* (Rounder 0529; 2005)   192
——, *Joseph Won a Coated Fiddle* (Rounder 0429; 1999)   192
Land of Yahoe, The (Rounder 8041; 1996)   192
Ledford String Band, *Ledford String Band* (Rounder 0008; 1972)   61
Lee, John, *Down at the Depot* (Rounder 2010; 1974)   73
Lilly Brothers, *Country Songs* (Rounder SS-02; 1977)   97
Louisiana Cajun Music from the Southwest Prairies, Vols. 1 and 2 (Rounder 6001 and 6002; 1976)   299

MacDonald, John L. *Formerly of Foot Cape Road* (Rounder 7051; 2005)   192
MacKay, Alex Francis, *Gaelic in the Bow* (Rounder 7059; 2005)   192
MacKenzie, Carl, *Welcome to your Feet Again* (Rounder 7005; 1977)   189
MacLean, Joe, *Old-Time Scottish Fiddle from Cape Breton Island* (Rounder 7024; 1998)   190
MacLean, Joe Peter, *Back of Boisdale* (Rounder 7060; 2005)   191
MacLellan, Donald, *The Dusky Meadow* (Rounder 7044; 2003)   192
MacLellan, Theresa & Marie, *A Trip to Mabou Ridge* (Rounder 7006; 1979)   189
MacMaster, Buddy, *Cape Breton Tradition* (Rounder 7052; 2003)   192
MacPhee, Doug, *Cape Breton Piano* (Rounder 7009; 1978)   189
MacQuarrie, Morgan, *Over the Cabot Trail* (Rounder 7041; 2007)   191
Martin, Asa, & the Cumberland Rangers, *Dr. Ginger Blue* (Rounder 0034; 1974)   73, 81, 188
Martin, Bogan & Armstrong, *The Barnyard Dance* (Rounder 2003; 1972)   59, 61
Masters of Turkish Music (Rounder 1051; 1990)   70
Mbarga, Prince Nico, *Sweet Mother* (Rounder 5007; 1981)   136
Mbuli, Mzwakhe, *Change in Pain* (Rounder 4024; 1988)   160, 277

McClintock, Harry, *Hallelujah, I'm a Bum* (Rounder 1009; 1981)   190
McCutcheon, John, *Winter Solstice* (Rounder 0192; 1984)   152, 265
Menard, D.L., & the Louisiana Aces, *The Louisiana Aces* (Rounder 6003; 1974)   74, 77
Miller, John, *Safe Sweet Home* (Rounder 3016; 1977)   97
Moffatt, Katy, *Evangeline Hotel* (Philo 1148; 1993)   132
Morrison, Theresa, *Lake Bras d'Or* (Rounder 7053; May 2005)   192
——, *Laments and Merry Melodies* (Rounder 7026; 1999)   190
Morton, Jelly Roll, *The Complete Jelly Roll Morton Library of Congress Recordings* (Rounder 1888; 2005)   50, 222–3, 225–6
Mud Acres: Music Among Friends (Rounder 3001; 1972)   61
Music from the People's Republic of China (Rounder 4008; 1976)   91
Mutabaruka, *Word Soun' 'Ave Power* (Heartbeat 15; 1983)   300

Nairobi Beat, The: Kenyan Pop Music Today (Rounder 5030; 1989)   161
Negro Songs of Protest (Rounder 4004; 1973)   92, 93
  see also Cap'n You're So Mean
New Haven Women's Liberation Rock Band   see Chicago Women's Liberation Rock Band
New Mississippi Sheiks, *The New Mississippi Sheiks* (Rounder 2004; 1972)   59, 61
Night in Jost Van Dyke, A (Rounder 5002; 1973)   54
NRBQ, *All Hopped Up* (Rounder 3029; 1979)   125
——, *Kick Me Hard* (Rounder 3030; 1979)   125

O'Connor, Mark, *4 Time National Junior Fiddle Champion* (Rounder 0046; 1974)   85
——, *Pickin' in the Wind* (Rounder 0068; 1976)   120
Ohrlin, Glenn, *A Cowboy's Life* (Rounder 0420; 1998)   191
——, *The Wild Buckaroo* (Rounder 0158; 1983)   189

Oswald, Bashful Brother, *Bashful Brother Oswald* (Rounder 0013; 1972)   58, 61

Pegram, George, *George Pegram* (Rounder 0001; 1970)   18, 20, 21, 24–7, 41
Perry, Lee "Scratch," *Mystic Miracle Star* (Heartbeat 06; 1982)   139
Plant, Robert, & Alison Krauss, *Raising Sand* (Rounder 9075; 2007)   86, 253, 265
Poor Man, Rich Man (Rounder 1026; 1980)   190
Preacher Jack, *Rock 'n' Roll Preacher* (Rounder 3033; 1980)   132
Professor Longhair, *Houseparty New Orleans Style* (Rounder 2057; 1987)   163

Radio Freedom (Rounder 4019; 1985)   276–8
Raffi, *Baby Beluga* (Rounder 8054; 1980)   185
——, *Dog on the Floor* (Rounder 116610058; 2018)   185
——, *Singable Songs for the Very Young* (Rounder 8051; 1976)   185
Rain Dropping off the Banana Tree (Rounder 1125; 1996)   71
Real Music Box, The (Rounder AN-25; 1995)   205–6
Rebirth Brass Band, *Feel Like Funkin' It Up* (Rounder 2093; 1989)   203
Redpath, Jean, *The Songs of Robert Burns, Vol. 5* (Philo 1093; 1985)   52
Reed, Blind Alfred, *How Can a Poor Man Stand Such Times and Live?* (Rounder 1001; 1972)   40, 61, 190
Reed, Ola Belle, *Ola Belle Reed* (Rounder 0021; 1973)   66
——, *Ola Belle Reed and Family* (Rounder 0077; 1977)   91
Rice, Tony, *Cold on the Shoulder* (Rounder 0183; 1984)   144, 152, 265
——, *Tony Rice* (Rounder 0085; 1977)   90, 122
Rich-R-Tone Story, The (Early Days of Bluegrass) (Rounder 1017; 1975)   85
Riders in the Sky, *Three on the Trail* (Rounder 0102; 1980)   132–3
Riddle, Almeda, *Ballads from the Ozarks* (Rounder 0017; 1972)   61, 189
——, *More Ballads from the Ozarks* (Rounder 0083; 1978)   105, 189

Riedy, Bob, Chicago Blues Band, *Lake Michigan Ain't No River, Chicago Ain't No Hilly Town* (Rounder 2005; 1973)   18
Robertson, Lonnie, *Lonnie's Breakdown* (Rounder 0375; 1996)   191
Robichaud, Gerry, *The Slippery Stick* (Rounder 7016; 1996)   191
Rush, *Rush in Rio* (Zoë 011430409; 2003)   217

Schoenberg, Eric, *Acoustic Guitar* (Rounder 3017; 1977)   90
Seeger, Mike & Peggy, *American Folk Songs for Children* (Rounder 8001/2/3; 1978)   122, 185
Shaggs, the, *Philosophy of the World* (Rounder 3032; 1980)   126
Shines, Johnny, *Hey Ba-Ba-Re-Bop* (Rounder 2020; 1979)   124
Smith, Hobart, *Blue Ridge Legacy* (Rounder 1799; 2001)   48, 220
Smith, Paul, *Devil Eat a Groundhog* (Rounder 0409; 1999)   192
Smokey Valley Boys, *Smokey Valley Boys* (Rounder 0029; 1974)   71
South African Trade Union Worker Choirs (Rounder 5020; 1986)   160
Spark Gap Wonder Boys, *"Cluck Old Hen": Cluck six-ten, the Dow-Jones average is down again* (Rounder 0002; 1970)   18, 20, 21, 25–7, 43, 139
Stivell, Alan, *Renaissance of the Celtic Harp* (Rounder 3067; 1982)   152
Stoneking, Fred, *Saddle Old Spike* (Rounder 0381; 1996)   191
Stoneman, E.V., & Family, *Ernest V. Stoneman & the Blue Ridge Corn Shuckers* (Rounder 1008; 1975)   190
Stover, Don, *Don Stover & the White Oak Mountain Boys* (Rounder 0039; 1974)   38
——, *Things in Life* (Rounder 0014; 1972)   61

Tanner, Gid, & the Skillet Lickers, *Hear These New Southern Tunes* (Rounder 1005; 1973)   190
——, *Kickapoo Medicine Show* (Rounder 1023; 1977)   90, 190
Tasty Licks, *Tasty Licks* (Rounder 0106; 1978)   102

Taylor, Tut, *Friar Tut* (Rounder 0011; 1972)   58, 61
Thomas, Buddy, *Kitty Puss* (Rounder 0032; 1976)   119, 189
Thomas, Irma, *After the Rain* (Rounder 2186; 2006)   142, 163
Thorogood, George, & the Destroyers, *George Thorogood & the Destroyers* (Rounder 3013; 1977)   90, 97–9, 108, 152
——, *More* (Rounder 3045; 1980)   108
——, *Move It On Over* (Rounder 3024; 1978)   102–4, 108, 152
Togo (Rounder 5004; 1979)   125–6
Townsend, Graham, *Classics* (Rounder 7007; 1979)   190
Traditional Fiddle Music of Cape Breton 1 (Rounder 7037; 2002)   192
Traditional Fiddle Music of Cape Breton 2 (Rounder 7038; 2002)   192
Traditional Fiddle Music of Cape Breton 3 (Rounder 7039; 2008)   192
Traditional Fiddle Music of Cape Breton 4 (Rounder 7040; 2008)   192
Traditional Fiddle Music of Kentucky 1 (Rounder 0397; 1997)   191
Traditional Fiddle Music of Kentucky 2 (Rounder 0398; 1997)   191
Traditional Fiddle Music of the Ozarks 1 (Rounder 0435; 1999)   190
Traditional Fiddle Music of the Ozarks 2 (Rounder 0436; 2000)   191
Traditional Fiddle Music of the Ozarks 3 (Rounder 0437; 2000)   191
Traditional Music on Rounder: A Sampler (Rounder 0145; May 1981)   190
Tucker, George, *George Tucker* (Rounder 0064; 1976)   119

Unholy Modal Rounders, *Alleged in Their Time* (Rounder 3004; 1975)   85
——, Michael Hurley, Jeffrey Fredericks & the Clamtones, *Have Moicy!* (Rounder 3010; 1976)   119

Val, Joe, & the New England Bluegrass Boys, *Not a Word from Home* (Rounder 0082; 1977)   90
——, *One Morning in May* (Rounder 0003; 1971)   116

Wakefield, Frank, *Frank Wakefield* (Rounder 0007; 1971)   55, 61

Ward, Fields, *Bury Me Not on the Prairie* (Rounder 0036; 1975)   189
Whitstein Brothers, *The Rose of My Heart* (Rounder 0206; 1985)   150

Woman Talk (Heartbeat 25; 1986)   300
Workman, Nimrod, *Mother Jones' Will* (Rounder 0076; 1978)   91, 92, 189

www.ingramcontent.com/pod-product-compliance
Lightning Source LLC
Chambersburg PA
CBHW050928240426
43671CB00019B/2953